Rhetoric for Academic Reasoning

Rhetoric for Academic Reasoning

L. Bensel-Meyers

University of Tennessee

HarperCollins*Publishers*

Executive Editor: Constance A. Rajala
Project Editor: Steven Pisano
Design Supervisor: Heather A. Ziegler
Text Design: N.S.G. Design
Cover Design: Jaye Zimet Design
Director of Production: Jeanie Berke
Production Assistant: Linda Murray
Compositor: ComCom Division of Haddon Craftsmen, Inc.
Printer and Binder: R.R. Donnelley and Sons Co.
Cover Printer: The Lehigh Press, Inc.

Rhetoric for Academic Reasoning

Library of Congress Cataloging-in-Publication Data

Bensel-Meyers, L.
    Rhetoric for academic reasoning / L. Bensel Meyers.
        p.   cm.
    Includes index.
    ISBN 0-06-040627-5 (student edition)
    ISBN 0-06-500403-5 (instructor edition)
    1. English language   Rhetoric.   2. College readers.   3. Reasoning.
  I. Title.
PE1408.B4758   1991
808'.0427—dc20   91-23725
                                                                 CIP

91 92 93 94   9 8 7 6 5 4 3 2 1

———————

———————

———————

To the four men in my life,
Michael, Timothy, Joshua, and Nicholas,
and to Cindy Owenby,
for helping mother them when writing called me away.

Contents

UNIT TWO

UNIT THREE

U N I T   F O U R

UNIT FIVE

UNIT SIX

UNIT SEVEN

Preface

The more our students are asked to use writing to learn in all their courses, the more we, as the instructors of freshman composition, must concern ourselves with training these students to use written language responsibly. As English teachers, we are aware of the immense power the written word has, how one word alone can evoke ideas, arouse emotions, and pass value judgements. Confronted with deconstructionist theories, we are aware of how slippery the word can be, how it can escape the writer's control and reshape how a reader interprets the work. How then can we prepare our students, in one or two short courses, to recognize both how the written word shapes their learning and how they can master its power to communicate responsibly?

Creating a responsible citizen-orator for modern times is the goal of this book. It is predicated on how the new rhetoricians have adapted Aristotle's enthymeme as a way to lead students to see how writers make knowledge in collaboration with their readers. By leading the students through the process by which we make meaning, this book helps students identify the rhetorical situation that has shaped their thoughts and that will be ultimately affected by their words.

There are two dimensions to this book: the first addresses what is common to all rhetorical situations; the second explores what is discipline-specific about the rhetorical situations students will confront in different courses. The text begins by introducing what is common about how we use writing to reason at all stages of the learning process: reading critically; keeping a reading notebook; testing ideas in oral discussion; identifying issues, logical assumptions, and stances; writing critical responses to others' drafts; and revising to accommodate a reader's response. As the students encounter readings in specific subject areas, they are led to recognize how each step in the learning process is merely a way of becoming initiated into the types of conversations specialists have about their subjects.

At the center of this learning process is the enthymeme, introduced as a way of objectifying how specialists reason about their subject. Drawing from classical stasis theory, this text shows students how they can use the enthymeme to identify what is discipline-specific about the questions specialists ask about their subject and how these questions control the type of reasoning the specialists use to arrive at answers. However, because the enthymeme is a difficult concept for students to grasp all at once, the text is structured so that the enthymeme is not introduced until after they have discovered the rhetorical problems it can help them solve.

Each unit is divided into two parts: the first chapter devoted to discussion about the reading-writing process, the second to investigating the particular type of writing required to reason well about a specific subject. Although you may wish to use the chapters in a different sequence, the text is currently structured to carefully lead students, chapter by chapter, from fundamentals about reading and writing through progressively more complex rhetorical situations. For this reason, even a new instructor of composition, less aware of current rhetorical theories, should find it easy to use.

The selected readings have been chosen to represent both the specific issues involved in each field of study and the common issues about language and learning that echo throughout the book. There are no more than three readings per each unit, giving you the opportunity, if you wish, to supplement the readings with favorites of your own. Certainly the text could stand alone as the rhetoric/reader for the course. The material contained here is sufficient to lead a student who begins the book as a novice writer to become confident of his or her ability to argue with the specialist's best rhetoric. Ideally, students will exit the course empowered with the rhetorical skills that will lead to a unified philosophy of life, producing responsible citizen-orators for tomorrow.

ACKNOWLEDGMENTS

To give proper credit, I probably should acknowledge my debt to almost everyone I have read or worked with. However, two valuable influences on my work (their combined presence is felt in these pages almost more than mine) are John Gage and Lawrence Green. I hope my adaptations of their valuable insights have not misrepresented their intentions. I am also deeply grateful for the support and advice of my colleagues: Janet Atwill, Ann Dobyns, Michael Keene, and Don Cox come immediately to mind. Their encouragement was a constant inspiration to me. I also must thank my editors: Lucy Rosendahl, who was willing to take a chance on a different kind of text; Linda Buchanan Allen, who helped me revise this text for a broader audience; Constance Rajala, who picked up the gauntlet at a crucial time; and Steven Pisano, who guided the book through production. I am also deeply indebted to my reviewers, Chris Anson, University of Minnesota; Lester Faigley, University of Texas at Austin; Ruth Greenberg, Jefferson County Community College; Janice Hays, University of Colorado; David Lindstrom, Colorado State University; Susan Peck McDonald, University of California at San Diego; Kim Moreland, The George Washington University; Joan Mullin, University of Toledo; Christina Murphy, Texas Christian University; Mary Murray, Hobart and William Smith College; Jeff Schiff, Columbia College; Marie Secor, Penn State; John Shea, Loyola University; Dene Kay Thomas, University of Idaho; and Edward White, California State University at San Bernadino. Their insightful readings, suggestions, and encouragement inspired me to follow through with a disciplined eye.

I also must acknowledge the help of several graduate students and instructors who have taught parts of this book to their classes and offered valuable suggestions. It is due to teachers as bright, dedicated, and enthusiastic as they that this book came into being.

L. Bensel-Meyers

Rhetoric for Academic Reasoning

Unit One

CHAPTER ONE

Introduction to College Writing

When there is much desire to learn, there of necessity will be much arguing, much writing, many opinions; for opinion in good [people] is but knowledge in the making.

—*John Milton*

*W*riting is an act of conversation, either with others or just yourself. It is also an act of learning. Whenever you write, you discover more about what you think. Whenever you consider how others will read what you write, you learn how your opinion compares with theirs. You also discover how you can make a difference in what others think and say. Good writers don't know everything about their subject, but they have listened well enough to enter into conversation with others about it. And their comments can make a difference in where the discussion will go.

All of the subjects you write about in college are matters for discussion. When you read, you learn how some authors have thought about those subjects. When you write, you make sense of what you have heard and offer your own interpretations and opinions. Everyone has a right to make his or her opinions known, even when the subject is new, for there is no one on earth who has heard or read everything that has been said about a subject. A modern rhetorician, Kenneth Burke, has well described this act of entering the conversation. Let's consider what he has to say:

You come late. When you arrive, others have long preceded you, and they are engaged in a heated discussion, a discussion too heated for them to pause and tell you exactly what it is about. In fact, the discussion had already begun long before any of them got there, so that no one present is qualified to retrace for you all the steps that had gone before. You listen for a while, until you decide that you have caught the tenor of the argument; then you put in your oar. Someone answers; you answer him; another comes to your defense; another aligns himself against you, to either the embarrassment or gratification of your opponent, depending upon the quality of your ally's assistance. However, the discussion is interminable. The hour grows late, you must depart. And you do depart, with the discussion still vigorously in progress.

—*Kenneth Burke, The Philosophy of Literary Form*

The scene above may be familiar to you. If it isn't, it soon will be, for Burke describes what college writing is all about. You come late to the discussion; there is no authority to tell you what went on before you arrived; you listen until you get a sense of what the argument is about. The discussion could be about science, literature, or politics, and it has been going on as long as there have been people to listen, think, and talk. Each field of college study can be defined by the nature of its conversation. No one remembers when we began talking about the world around us, but we continue to do so. We all have "come late" and none of us has all the answers, but we still put in our oar to help move the discussion along.

In college, you put in your oar when you write essays to make sense of the textbooks you read and the classes you attend, for these are where academic discussions take place. But most importantly, you write essays to evaluate what others have said, to contribute your opinions to the discussion. College writing is rhetoric: the use of words to reason persuasively about something we are investigating, perhaps even disputing. The subjects you study in college are all founded on rhetoric. They are the result of what has gone on in the discussion before you arrived.

Consider how historians have developed what we know about World War II. Although we look to them as the experts, they, like us, have arrived after the discussion has begun of what happened and why. Even those who were in the war cannot know all the decisions that were made or what precipitated them. The knowledge they have is based on multiple, often contradictory, personal accounts and partially recovered political documents. Even if they had all the documentation they needed, they would have to do something with it, reason about it in some way. So, they develop theories—some more plausible than others—which help us interpret what went on. What we need to learn from these historians is not when the war occurred or even who fought whom; we can find this information easily on our own. What the historians can teach us is how they have reasoned about the "when" and "who" to explain "why" the war happened at all.

If we listen in on the discussions historians (or philosophers or scientists) have, we will recognize how their disputes (sometimes friendly, sometimes not) result from different ways of reasoning about incomplete evidence. Understanding the nature of their conversations—the questions asked, the examples given, the answers proposed—helps us to stay afloat in the linguistic confusion. Once we have observed the currents of their arguments, we can plunge our oar in and direct our own course to wherever we want this knowledge to take us.

WRITING AS REASONING

Rhetoric—that in the texts we read, in the classes we attend, and in the essays we write—dictates what we know. Concrete evidence, facts, accepted beliefs, mean nothing unless we can do something with them. A gap in the fossil record may mean we know nothing or it may mean a natural disaster had extinguished all life for a time; the rhetoric of scientists, geologists, and anthropologists shapes the gap's significance. Most of the knowledge we have is based on theories that fill in the gaps left by incomplete evidence—sound theories, perhaps, but speculation nonetheless. Learning a subject is not memorizing the few facts we have but learning how to speculate about them. When even the experts disagree (which somehow makes them less than "expert" and gives us more authority to arbitrate), we need to enter into the discussion. We may have no new evidence to offer, but by analyzing what we have heard them say and synthesizing their contrasting theories, we can make sense of the experts' conversation in a meaningful way.

Analysis, synthesis, and evaluation—these are the three stages of the learning process. We analyze what others are saying, we synthesize their theories with what we already know, and we arrive at our evaluation of the subject. Although you may not be aware of it, you naturally reason this way every time you read, whether you read an editorial, a scholarly argument, a novel, or a news article. Whenever and wherever words are used to communicate, the speaker or writer is advancing a particular interpretation. Novelists present us with fictional worlds that affect how we view ourselves; reporters give us their view of what happened based on the facts they have. What writers choose to say and how they choose to say it affect how we evaluate the information they give us. Their writing is their reasoning, and we reason with them when we read. When we write a response to what we have read, we take their reasoning one step further: we analyze their argument, synthesize their knowledge with our own, and propose a new evaluation. We may agree or disagree, or we may qualify and/or expand their argument. No matter how we respond, what we know and think—and ultimately write—has been shaped by what they had to say.

Discovering What Others Think

One student once told me that she thought she should not have to come to class, do the outside readings, or participate in class discussions. When I asked why, she innocently explained: "because I already know what I think and I don't need to hear others' opinions to know what to write." I was disheartened by her comment, partly because she clearly did not enjoy the class, but primarily because she had not understood why she or anyone ever writes. This student clearly perceived the act of writing as an academic exercise, as a way to put ideas—any ideas—into a neat and tidy written form. She never seemed to question what we should want to do with our writing once we have written it. When I asked her whether she ever wished to share her writing with anyone in the class, she almost angrily exclaimed: "I don't see why they would care to read it!" I sadly agreed; if she didn't care what her peers thought, then they probably wouldn't care what she had to say.

This story has a happy ending. I told the student she could present her argument to the class and they could decide whether or not she should have to continue participating in the class activities. When she did so, she discovered a whole new reason for writing: one of her friends had said something that troubled her, and that very evening she wrote an essay to make amends by justifying her position to him. This essay succeeded only because she felt a need to revise it until she was certain her friend could follow her reasoning. She immediately recognized that her first draft would not do because it merely restated what she had already said in class. Her subsequent drafts became better as she recognized that, to communicate her reasoning to her friend, she would first have to understand the reasoning he had used. Not surprisingly, the more she sought to summarize his ideas, the more she recognized the weaknesses in her own argument. Through the process of seeking to communicate through writing, she discovered why she had really felt uncomfortable in class. Her revised argument was, "I should have to participate in the discussions and do the readings only as long as others prove to me that their opinions are worthwhile"—a good contract for any course.

When that student came to class the next time, she handed her paper to her friend, saying, "Here! Read this!" Through that one experience, she had discovered several important things about why one writes and how one must go about it. The end of writing is clearly not the words on the page, but how others will respond to those words. Most importantly, those words must say something worthwhile to the reader, for if no one cares to read the essay, it is as good as one not written. Another very important thing that student learned was how to produce an essay that someone would want to read seriously. The several drafts she went through led her to recognize that she needed first to summarize what others thought and then synthesize those positions before she could effectively discover and argue her own.

To write in a way that is worthwhile to you and to others, you need to approach everything you write as a dialogue with a reader. Even when you write only for yourself, your writing is a way to control and develop an internal dialogue. This internal dialogue is a testing of your intuitive judgments against the logical criticisms your more rational side can offer. Child psychologists Jean Piaget and Lev Vygotsky called this type of writing a representation of the inner speech we use whenever we deliberate about something outside of us. It can be described as a conversation between our right and left brains, or, using terms from Freudian psychology, as the way our unconscious (the Id) negotiates with what society has taught us (the Superego) to give rise to our independent thoughts (the Ego). However we describe this process of self-deliberation, the point is that our ideas cannot develop in a vacuum, but must arise in response to a social situation. Whether we are writing for ourselves or for others, we are testing our instinctive feelings toward the subject against the many different ways others could evaluate it.

Even the most casual contact with a subject teaches us something about what others might think. Whenever we read or overhear others as they talk, we receive a sense of the different attitudes the subject under discussion inspires. The more we read and listen, the more we prepare ourselves to write. Even when we think we have developed a "new idea," when we try to create new fictions and new worlds out of our imagination, we draw from our memory experiences that arose in some social context and embody others' attitudes. When others read what we have written, what they find worthwhile are those ideas, expressions, and feelings that clearly respond to their own: they can identify with one or more of the attitudes the writer explores, and feel rewarded when the writer builds upon them in provocative new ways. When we draw our readers into the conversation, we repay them for giving us something to think about and respond to.

EXERCISE

Here is the first paragraph of a scholarly work in anthropology, *Natural Symbols* by Mary Douglas. Although you may not understand everything she says, read the paragraph carefully. When you are finished, write short answers to the questions that follow and compare your answers to those of your classmates. How are your responses alike? How do they differ? How might you account for the similarities and differences in the class's responses to the reading?

One of the gravest problems of our day is the lack of commitment to common symbols. If this were all, there would be little to say. If it were merely a matter of our fragmentation into small groups, each committed to its proper symbolic forms, the case would be simple to understand. But more mysterious is a widespread, explicit rejection of rituals as such. Ritual has become a bad word signifying empty conformity. We are witnessing a revolt against formalism, even against form. "The vast majority of my classmates just sat through four years." So wrote Newfield of what he called the ungeneration of his college year: "They didn't challenge any authority, take any risks, or ask any questions. They just memorized 'the given,' not even complaining when instructions turned them into mindless tape-recorders, demanding they recite rather than reason" (Newfield, 1966: 41). Shades of Luther! Shades of the Reformation and its complaint against meaningless rituals, mechanical religion, Latin as the language of cult, mindless recitation of litanies. We find ourselves, here and now, reliving a worldwide revolt against ritualism. To understand it, Marx and Freud have been invoked, but Durkheim also foretold it and it behooves the social anthropologist to interpret alienation. Some of the tribes we observe are more ritualist than others. Some are more discontented than others with their traditional forms. From tribal studies there is something to say about a dimension which is usually ignored—the band or area of personal relations in which an individual moves. But in trying to say it, we are handicapped by terminology.

1. As a reader, do you feel you have been included in the conversation? Why or why not?
2. What is the nature of the conversation Douglas is addressing? Are the participants in heated debate or merely speculating? What are the clues you have used to arrive at an answer?
3. What is the discussion about? Can you tell from this paragraph what Douglas' attitude might be? What is the attitude of the readers she is responding to?

The Rhetorical Situation

The social environment within which you develop new ideas and attitudes is constantly changing. A movie you see today would have a different effect on you if you saw it ten years from now. The way you reason about what the movie means depends not only on who you are but also on who you are talking to and what they think. Your attitude is always shaped by a rhetorical situation. The rhetorical situation can be identified by the following five questions:

1. Who are you talking to? (Is it a friend or the director of the film?)
2. Where and when does your conversation take place? (Is this an idle conversation right after the movie or an exchange of formal essays several months later in a movie magazine?)
3. What are you discussing? (Is it how the movie compares to another movie you have seen, or whether the movie is artistically flawed?)
4. What does your audience think?
5. How does your perspective differ?

Every time you reason, either during idle conversation or formal writing, you need to be aware of how the rhetorical situation shapes your thinking. If you are aware of the rhetorical situation that has compelled you to respond, you can more easily discover what it is you want to say—and make it worth your reader's while to read it.

THE COMPOSING PROCESS

Throughout this book, you will be asked to write in response to rhetorical situations that arise from academic conversations. The subjects themselves will shape your writing in very distinct ways, and the conversation that takes place about each discipline will dictate the kind of questions, evidence, and answers you will use. However, the composing process you use to listen and respond to these different conversations can be applied to any subject. Mastering this composing process will help you address even those rhetorical situations this book will not cover, whether they arise in an academic or a professional environment.

The composing process, the method by which you discover and express new ideas, can be divided into four stages: invention, drafting, revising, and editing. They are modern equivalents of the five canons of classical rhetoric: invention, arrangement, style, memory, and delivery. (The odd one here is memory. In classical times, orators had to memorize their arguments well if they were to deliver them effectively. The study of memory is not essential for written arguments, however, although the ability to recall what we have experienced, read, or heard enhances the composing process.) Invention is the act of discovering what to write; reading, listening, notetaking, and journal writing are all inventive acts. Drafting is the stage when the ideas are arranged into some reasonable order; it makes written sense out of what was invented. Revising (redrafting, rewriting) is the murky stage when writers analyze what has actually been said on the page and test it against what they meant to say. Revision involves a second look at the argument as the writer experiments with major stylistic changes—reordering the paragraphs, sentences, words; choosing better words, examples, transitions. After revising the argument as well as time allows, the writer edits the writing, grooms the prose, to make the expressions more precise. Editing is essential for written arguments. It delivers the ideas to the reader, using effective, clear writing to achieve the effect of the gestures, facial expressions, and voice inflections of oral presentation.

Rather than being separate and distinct steps, the four stages of the composing process are merely indications of what preoccupies the writer at any particular time. In fact, they are not equal in importance. The expression "your essay is only as good as your ideas," although oversimplified, has some truth to it: for good writers, invention—the generation and development of ideas—is always at work. When you choose one word over another, you are inventing the precise meaning you want to convey; when you add a comma or modifier (like "most" or "some"), you are inventing a more precise thought. You cannot just turn off your thinking process as you shift your attention to polishing your prose. In fact, those writers who frustratedly claim, "There's so much more I wanted to say, if I only had the time!" are merely fooling themselves. More time would only bring more ideas. These writers are merely experiencing the law of diminishing confidence: "the more you know, the less you know"—and the less time you have to express it.

Invention is so vital to the composing process that Aristotle defined the complete process, the art of rhetoric, as an inventive act: "Rhetoric is the faculty of finding the available means of persuasion." We find "the available means" to persuade ourselves as we listen to others, as we read, as we draft our responses, as we revise our ideas. We find the means to persuade our readers as we feel more confident in what we are writing, shifting our attention from the discovery of ideas to considering how well we have expressed those ideas. In this way, the composing process can be defined as a deliberative act. We discover our ideas as we deliberate to ourselves about what we have heard and experienced, and we express those ideas as we begin to deliberate with the potential readers in our minds. The deliberation changes as we shift our sense of audience, as we transform our primarily writer-based explorations into reader-based arguments. Following is a diagram that illustrates the various shifts in a writer's focus while composing:

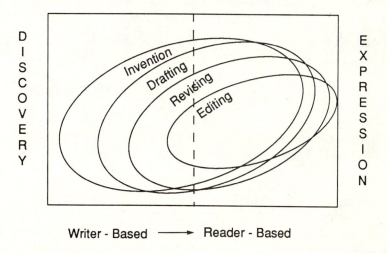

process are merely indications of what preoccupies the writer at any particular

As the diagram illustrates, each stage in the writing process brings us a clearer conception of what it is we want to say.

As we become more confident about the ideas we have discovered, we begin to shift our attention to expressing them. We can never predict when we will be confident enough to make this shift, but often the "inspiration" that writers wait for is really the result of active listening, reading, experiencing—that is, the discovery of so many ideas that we have to start writing them down to make sense of them. This writing stimulates new ideas, the new ideas alter the old ones, the writing is reshaped and polished—and always lurking behind the writer's thoughts is the reader. The composing process represents how we reason as we analyze, synthesize, and evaluate what we have heard others say. The questions we ask at each stage of our writing address an aspect of our relationship with our readers, and indicate how that relationship helps our reasoning progress: "What do others think?" (invention); "How does that fit with what I think?" (drafting); "What do I really think?" (revision); "How well have I presented what I think to my readers?" (editing).

EXERCISE

How do you respond to the following passage? Jot down your responses as you read, and then develop them into a paragraph or two, using the following four questions to help you invent, draft, revise, and edit what you think. (*Note:* These questions are to steer you through the composing process; do not simply string together answers to these questions for your response.) When you have finished, show your notes and draft(s) to one or two of your classmates and explain why you made the changes you did.

> It is thus that mutual cowardice keeps us in peace. Were one-half of mankind brave and one-half cowards, the brave would be always beating the cowards. Were all brave, they would lead a very uneasy life; all would be continually fighting; but being all cowards, we go on very well.
>
> —*Samuel Johnson* (1709–1784)

1. *Inventing.* What does the author say? What are the different ways other readers might respond to it, either emotionally or intellectually?
2. *Drafting.* How do these different responses fit with my own?
3. *Revising.* What is my real response to the passage, emotionally *and* intellectually?
4. *Editing.* How well have I presented this response to my readers? (Your readers are your classmates, who are also deliberating about the passage and will be interested in what you have to say.)

Although writing is a learned art, the composing process records the way we naturally reason. When writing to a deadline, however, we cannot indulge in the luxury of waiting for the "inspiration" that precedes each stage. To become effective time managers, we must develop writing techniques that make our thinking and writing more efficient. These techniques may be as conventional as the basic academic skills of taking notes and outlining, or they may be little tricks of habit that you have discovered from writing experience. No one can say what will work the best for you, because each writer is unique and each rhetorical situation is different. Your writing is a social act, an attempt to enter into a public discussion, and the way you write reflects how you view your relationship to those who are carrying on that discussion. At times you will be confident, and your drafts will come easily; at other times, you will feel insecure or too emotional, and you might draw diagrams, charts, or separate clusters of your conflicting and complex feelings. Whatever the technique, if it helps to distance you from your ideas so that you can test how reasonable they really are, it will make your writing more efficient.

Because you are constantly reinventing your ideas as you write and revise, you should continually remind yourself that your purpose is to contribute to a conversation that involves other perspectives. It is not enough just to distance yourself from your ideas; you need to evaluate them in the context of a particular discussion. "The world is a stage and we are merely players" makes sense in the context of a literary discussion, but would need a little translation at a conference on the proliferation of nuclear energy. This is not to say the idea has no value in that context, but it needs to be adapted to what others have said to show how it contributes to what nuclear scientists are talking about. Remembering your reader's concerns can help you to avoid overly creative, unnecessary digressions, help you to use your time more productively, and make the writing process easier. Following is a review of some ways you can keep that reader's perspective in mind at every stage of the composing process.

Knowing When to Write

There are several ways to invent what you are going to write about. Some writers brainstorm; others freewrite; some even invent, draft, revise, and edit their essay all at once (usually because they waited too long to begin the assignment!). None of these invention techniques are very helpful, however, if you have no purpose other than to fulfill an assignment. Without a sense of a conversation you are responding to, your brainstorming may be about everything and nothing. In the following example, one student tried freewriting, an invention technique where writers write rapidly without stopping, using the writing to direct their invention process. Paul's assignment was: "Write about something new you have learned since coming to college."

Paul's Freewrite

What am I going to write about? Let's see, have I learned anything? I learned that too much bleach makes your clothes smell like a janitor's closet. Could I get five paragraphs out of that? I could get three examples out of the different kinds of clothes—I wonder if there is a difference in the material that is used, I mean whether different materials hold the smell differently? Oh, I better get serious here. The only point to that lesson is to use less bleach and that has nothing to do with the type of clothes. . . . Let's see, what have I learned? I have learned that it is very hard to discover something to write about! Maybe I should do this. I could talk about how I have been "inspired" . . . maybe how I have been inspired by that graduate assistant in the Chemistry Lab. Boy, he has it hard! He has to translate Dr. Blake's lectures for us, and those lectures are doozies! But he does a good job—take the principle of chemical bonding. Before, I thought it merely referred to how superglue works, but after he explained. . . .

Although Paul finally discovered what he wanted to write about, the freewriting method he used was unproductive until he seized on a discussion he could respond to (the discussion in Chemistry Lab about chemical bonding). As soon as that rhetorical situation entered his thoughts, his purpose was no longer just to fulfill the assignment but to explain what chemical bonding is and why he feels it is an important principle to learn. The rest of Paul's freewrite (not included here) was well-focused and his writing more confident because he had established a relationship with his readers, who probably had not thought much about chemical bonding before. The discussion in Chemistry Lab, not his freewriting, was the source of his invention process.

This does not mean that you should not freewrite; in fact, it can be a very helpful invention technique when you begin sorting out your responses to a particular discussion. However, beginning freewriting before you have a conversation to respond to can be very inefficient: you force yourself to develop an idea out of nothing. As Paul discovered, if you begin with something others are discussing, you can build your argument from theirs. This can help you in two ways: the most obvious way is that it gives you a topic, something specific to talk about; the most important way is that it gives you a way to talk—that is, to reason—about that topic. Paul's half-serious initial topic, the problems of using too much bleach, failed mostly because he had no way to reason about it. He began to consider three examples that he might use for the body of his paper but even they were not clearly related to his topic. At that point in his freewrite, he was inventing not to communicate a new idea but to construct a neat and tidy five-paragraph theme. Any time you feel yourself searching for ways to pad the body of your essay, take it as a sign that you have lost sight of a real rhetorical situation, that you aren't engaged seriously in a discussion.

Invention: Reading and Listening

Academic discussions have no beginning and no end. They are always developing from what has gone on before, and the "last word" is always challenged by new perspectives, new voices that have entered the discussion. When you are asked to write in college, you are invited to contribute a new voice to the conversation. Unfortunately, students don't often take advantage of this opportunity; they cannot believe their instructors care about their inexpert opinions, and they view writing assignments as just another test to see how much they know. Usually this is due to a lack of confidence, a feeling that they cannot make an informed judgment about something they have only begun to study. What these students do not realize, however, is that they began making judgments the first time they read about the subject. Just making sense out of what others are talking about forces us to invent and compose arguments.

To make our arguments good ones, though, we need to listen well to that small part of the conversation we are exposed to. Although we may not understand everything that is being said, we pick up clues that will help us to make sense out of what is going on. How well we respond to the discussion will depend on how good a detective we are. We begin reinventing the conversation the first time we read: we interpret the words on the page to reconstruct what the writer is saying and why. Each of us reads differently. Although we sometimes reach agreement about what the author's main point is, we may disagree about how the author arrived at it or how significant it is.

How we perceive what we read is influenced by our past experiences, our value systems, our opinions, and our own rhetorical situation. When we read, we do not all receive the same knowledge; we converse with the author to develop our own understanding of the subject, to shape the words on the page into a kind of knowledge we can reason with. The act of reading becomes an act of composing an interpretation.

Reading as a Composing Act

Invention	*Drafting*	*Revising*
Predicting the argument:	Synthesizing ideas:	Evaluating the whole:
INTRODUCTION	BODY AND CONCLUSION	THE ESSAY
(Reading for expectations)	(Reading for clues)	(Rereading)

As you read, your perception of what you are reading changes so that you have invented, drafted, and revised the work by the time you have finished. Consider the following passage. As you read, pay attention to how your perceptions of the author's argument change:

(1) One of the many challenges in journalism is turning out serious articles about celebrities who say they served in Joan of Arc's army or strolled through Iran with Jesus Christ. (2) "Free spirit," "flamboyant," and "controversial" are not really up to the task. (3) In a profile of a well-known woman who insists that she has lived several times before, one journalese speaker came up with this deft line: "more than most people on this earth, she has found spiritual answers." (4) In crime journalese, the top thug in any urban area is always referred to as a "reputed Mafia chieftain" and generally depicted as an untutored but charismatic leader of a successful business operation. (5) The chieftain's apprentice thugs are his "associates." (6) This sort of coverage reflects the automatic respect and dignity accorded crime figures who know where reporters live and recognize the understandable desire of journalists everywhere to keep their kneecaps in good working order.

(7) As all users know, journalese is a formidable bulwark against libel, candor, and fresh utterance. (8) Any threat to its state-of-the-art ground-breaking terminology would have a chilling effect on everybody, especially us award-winning journalists.

(From John Leo's "Journalese: A Ground-breaking Study.")

Let me take you through one possible reading of this passage:

Just after reading the first sentence, we are anticipating what will follow, inventing what we think Leo's argument will be. At this point, he sounds quite serious, doesn't he? Leo appears to be addressing a very real problem: how to write seriously about celebrities we tend to laugh at. One reading of this opening might predict that he will give us good advice on how to keep our personal judgments out of our writing, or how to be objective and honest in our descriptions.

Fairly confident that we know how the argument will unfold, we begin drafting the argument in our minds as we read on. But it soon becomes a messy draft when the second sentence does not quite fit our expectations. Why is "controversial" not up to the task of being serious? As we read on, the next three sentences give us some clues that honesty isn't really Leo's concern: what he means by "serious" descriptions seems to be those that treat the subject with respect. Respect before honesty? Well, OK, still a noble endeavor, we might think, as we begin to restructure the draft in our minds and turn to the sixth sentence. Yes, there's the word "respect", but something doesn't sound quite noble: "crime figures"? "automatic respect"? "broken kneecaps"? What is his point, anyway?

We suspend our revision, looking to the concluding sentences for what Leo really thinks: Oh, he's worried about libel—that's noble . . . but "candor"? "fresh utterance"? Why is he championing language that avoids these? The only "chilling effect" we perceive is that which the reading has had on us. We have quite a rough draft of his argument in our minds at this point. So we reread the passage in view of those final sentences, revising our interpretation as we read.

EXERCISE

Reread the passage from Leo's essay. What interpretation have you composed for this passage? (Try to condense your answer into one sentence.) Compare your interpretation with a classmate's. How might you account for the differences in your interpretations?

Composing a mental interpretation of what we read is similar to how we make sense of conversations as we listen. Although oral discussions are less tangible than the books we read (we do not get the opportunity to hear them twice), they still give us clues that we use to construct our interpretation of what is being argued. But whether we are listening or reading, we should not depend on our memories to keep track of what is being said and what we think about it. Underlining and annotating the books you read helps you recover what you have invented; keeping a reading notebook to record your responses to the readings and the class discussions helps you sort through the many ideas you have encountered. When you sit down to write the first draft of your essay, your difficulty will not be that you have too little to write about but that you will have too much for one essay!

Drafting: Arranging Ideas into a Thesis Statement

When someone reads what you have written and responds with "What's the point?", you can assume that you have not clearly communicated something that your reader finds worthwhile. The "point" of your writing is the thesis of your argument: the idea you want to contribute to the discussion. As you read and listen to what others are saying, you continually test and revise what it is you want to say in response. Although your annotations and the notes in your reading notebook will probably contain several potential theses, some of them contradictory, there will be one that continually reappears. Review the entries in your notebook closely because this idea will be expressed in different ways, with each expression coming closer to the point you want to make.

You may find it helpful to freewrite at this time, to explore your idea by writing it in as many different ways as you can. Brainstorming and outlining may also work. Jot down the most prominent ideas in your notebook and then attempt to arrange them in some meaningful order. Sometimes you may have so many ideas that you cannot organize them without first writing an exploratory rough draft. The draft can help you to discover how your ideas relate to one another, how they all add up to one thesis. All of these activities have the same aim: they help you to discover exactly what your point will be and what you will need to say to prove it.

Drafting your thesis is a process of summarizing your main point and providing the primary reason you believe it is valid. When you boil your notes down to one statement that says "This is true because . . . ," you have established the reasoning you will use to develop your essay. For example, the reasoning behind Leo's argument above might be expressed in this way: "Journalese is a formidable bulwark against libel, candor, and fresh utterance because it disguises the journalist's true feelings." As you proceed through this text, you will discover how to test a two-clause statement logically, to ensure that the reasons you will use to support your position are good reasons. This testing is essential: your readers will not care what your thesis is if you cannot give them a good reason to believe it. (Do you think Leo gave good reasons?)

No matter how precisely you have articulated your point as a two-clause thesis statement, it still may change as you develop it into an essay. You should approach the first draft of your essay as a chance to test your thesis against what your readers have argued. It also gives you a chance to revise and modify your thesis as you discover new ideas while you write. For this reason, view your thesis statement as a *working thesis—a hypothesis.* If you view your thesis as inflexible, you will be tempted to manipulate your examples, your reasons, to fit the thesis (what Paul tried to do when he sought examples for his "bleach" essay). A working thesis, however, gives you an idea what kinds of reasons you need to explore while still having the freedom to let these reasons take you to the best possible conclusion. By the time of the drafting stage, you will have some sense of your audience and why you need to communicate with them, but you will still be focusing on discovering exactly what it is you want to say.

Revision: Shifting to Reader-Based Prose

Rewriting your draft is essential. Until this stage, you will have written primarily writer-based prose: prose that reveals the thinking process you went through to discover what you wanted to say. As you become more confident about your argument, though, you begin to shift your attention to how well you have expressed it.

During revision, you experiment with different ways to present your ideas to your readers. For example, you might rearrange the order of your paragraphs, clarify vague expressions, restate important points, choose better words, and/or delete irrelevant ideas. To revise well, you need to anticipate how your readers might interpret your writing. This might seem difficult because you know what you are trying to say and unconsciously supply logical connections that are not apparent on the page. However, you can more easily shift your essay from writer-based to reader-based prose (i.e., from writing for yourself to writing for others) if you explore questions that put your writing back in the context of the discussion: What was everyone talking about? Have you contributed to that discussion? Placing your ideas in the context of the discussion as you rewrite makes maintaining objectivity much easier, and helps you to remember to include your reader in the conversation.

Editing: Delivering Your Argument

Editing is the last stage of the composing process, the time when you groom your prose to make the best possible impression on your reader. You should edit only when satisfied that you have revised the ideas and structure of your argument to include your reader in the discussion. Although you still may want to revise words, sentences, or paragraphs, if you are fairly confident of the quality of your ideas, then you can revise and fine tune your writing. Any changes you make during editing should improve the delivery of your argument to the reader. Although your ideas may be excellent, if your grammar, spelling, or punctuation is flawed, then your reader can misinterpret your ideas or lose respect for the argument as a whole. Editing includes a final proofreading to recheck the little things—the spelling, punctuation, and typing—that can affect how your reader responds to your ideas.

WRITING IN THE DIFFERENT DISCIPLINES

The composing process outlined above can help you to discover how to make your writing respond to any conversation or rhetorical situation. As you will discover, though, the nature of the academic conversation and rhetorical situation will change what your writing looks like in fairly predictable ways. The subject under discussion, the type of knowledge the participants have, and the nature of the questions they are asking, all control how you will reason about the material. The writing you produce in a science class is quite different from the writing expected of you in a history course, because the questions scientists ask and the types of reasons they use to answer these questions are different in kind from those of a historian.

You can usually predict the kind of reasoning that will take place in different academic conversations. This book will introduce you to one way you can categorize the kinds of questions and reasons that shape writing in the different disciplines. It will not discuss all disciplines, but it will introduce you to the four basic types of arguments we use. As noted below, each of these four types represents a different question and reasoning process:

The Four Types of Argument

Policy: What should be done?
Value: Is it good or bad?
Consequence: Why did it occur? What effect will it have?
Definition: What is it?

Although we may address more than one of these questions in an argument, note how we cannot answer "What should be done?" or whether something is "good or bad" until we have answered "What effect will it have?" or even reached agreement about "What is it?" What we already know—or can assume is true—will affect the type of argument we address. On the other hand, different writers will shape their argument around one type of argument in order to limit their investigations to the kind of information their discipline provides. Recognizing what type of argument they need to construct is important because each question limits their reasoning process in some way.

Recognizing what kind of questions scientists, historians, or philosophers tend to ask can help you to enter into their conversations, to understand both what they say and how you can reason about it. Generally, each field focuses its attention on one or another of the four types of argument:

Representative of Policy Argument
Political Science: "What should be done?"
(questions of government and law)

Representative of Value Argument
Literature/Philosophy: "Is it good?"
(questions of truth, beauty, and ethics)

Representative of Consequence Argument
History/Economics/Psychology: "Why did it occur?"
or "What effect will it have?"
(questions of cause and effect)

Representative of Definition Argument
Natural Science: "What is it?"
(questions of observation)

Although no one can write an argument that is "purely" one type (people just can't think that way), much of our knowledge and technological advancement results from our attempts to do so. Consider the kinds of questions scientists ask. When Einstein wrote his argument that $E = MC^2$, he was asking "What is energy?" When other scientists responded to him, they turned their discussion to another question of fact: "What is the most powerful source of energy we can devise?" The requirements of their discipline led scientists who explored how to make an atomic bomb ("What is it?") to avoid addressing the policy arguments of the government officials who hired them to make the bomb ("How should it be used?") or the value arguments of advocacy groups ("Is it a good thing to make?"). After World War II, when the atomic bomb was used on Hiroshima and Nagasaki, Einstein regretted the development of atomic energy, sadly proclaiming that humankind was not ready to use it responsibly. However, the type of arguments scientists used to discover the bomb did not involve this question. Their purpose was to discover atomic energy, and the other questions would have led them away from that aim.

This book will introduce you to the different kinds of arguments that take place in academic discussions. As you read the essays, respond to them in your reading notebook, listen to class discussion, and contribute your written arguments, keep in mind the nature of the conversation you are addressing: Is it addressing matters of policy, value, consequence, or definition? You will want to address the same questions others are asking. At the same time, consider the implications that the kind of conversation has for other kinds. Once you know what something is, you can explore where it came from or the consequences it might have; this would, in turn, help you to determine whether it is a good thing and what you should—or should not—do with that knowledge. That is essentially what makes academic writing a rhetorical activity: when you put in your oar, you affect the course others will take.

CHAPTER TWO

Reasoning with Language

*F*or each subject you study there is an academic community that has developed a specific way of talking and reasoning about it. Learning a subject is learning how to talk about it, how to interpret what members of that community have to say, and how to use their language to develop your own understanding. Your teacher and the authors of your textbooks represent how members of a particular academic community use language to reason with one another about their common field. When you discuss your teacher's lectures and the assigned readings in class, you and your peers imitate this language and develop ways of talking that you have learned by hearing the experts talk. And when you write, you try on the language of the field to develop and share your understanding with the community in your classroom.

Although at times you may be asked to write to the teacher to demonstrate that you can discuss a subject reasonably well, your teacher won't expect you to write like an expert. Most often, your real audience will be what Kenneth Bruffee has called "knowledgeable peers": those classmates who have some experience with the language of the field but are just learning—as you are—how to think and talk like the experts. Just as you and your classmates in a French 101 course can use French to communicate with one another but would have difficulty carrying on a conversation with a Paris schoolboy, you and your peers can draw on your common knowledge of a scientist's language to discuss science together, although you might not be proficient enough to understand and talk with the specialized vocabulary of a nuclear scientist.

Although you cannot expect that one course will teach you how to talk and reason as the experts do, how much you learn depends on how well you understand the language of the discipline. How the community talks about the subject affects how you think about it, and how well you understand the community's language and can adopt it as your own affects how well you can think and write. Each academic community uses language to look at the world from a unique perspective, asking specific questions that require specific types of answers. Before you can discuss any subject reasonably well, you need to have some sense of how the community reasons with language. How do the speakers and writers formulate the questions they ask? What kinds of reasons do they use? You can find answers to these questions by analyzing the community's "voice" and the specialized vocabulary it uses.

An academic community's vocabulary consists of both its nouns and its verbs.

The prominent nouns pinpoint the subject under discussion; the verbs reveal the kinds of questions the community asks about that subject. Compare the voices of the following two paragraphs. The first represents how scientists discuss their subject, the second how historians do. (I have italicized the most prominent nouns and verbs.)

> Although *black holes are* almost invisible, we can search for observable phenomena that *may be characteristic* of them. The first of these *is* a large amount of *electromagnetic radiation.* A *black hole* continuously *attracts* hydrogen atoms, cosmic particles, and everything else to it. As these particles and objects *are drawn* to the *black hole,* they steadily accelerate through its gravitational field until they approach the velocity of light itself. This causes tremendous amounts of *electromagnetic radiation.* (From Gary Zukaw's *The Dancing Wu Li Masters.*)

Judging from the prominent nouns ("black hole," "electromagnetic radiation"), we can easily guess that the writer is speaking as a scientist, addressing the concerns of a physicist or astronomer. The first sentence suggests that he is discussing the question "What are black holes?" Notice how the verbs reinforce this reading. They are not dramatic verbs. They aren't even very memorable: "are invisible," "may be characteristic," "are drawn." These are all passive verbs—words that describe states of being (note the forms of the verb "to be"). They comment quietly on what occurs when black holes are around, directing our attention to what those holes are rather than to what they do or what we should do about them. Note how the speaker does not draw attention to himself or to what he is doing: we see no "then I saw" or "I believe. . . ." Phrases like these would make the scientist (not the black holes) the primary subject. If you have ever been told to avoid using "I" when you write, it was probably because your teacher thought that personal pronoun would lead you away from your real subject. Here, the speaker attempts to achieve objectivity by using inanimate nouns and passive verbs—the vocabulary of the science community.

Compare the next passage:

> *People who could agree* on few other facts about remote regions of the earth *somehow agreed* on the geography of the afterworlds. Even while the shape of most of the earth's surface *was still unknown,* the *Nether World was described* in vivid detail. The practice of burying the dead in the earth made it quite natural that *people should think* that the dead inhabited the *Nether World.* A subterranean topography *seemed to make* that afterlife possible and even plausible. *Tradition reported* that the Romans, at the foundation of their city, followed an old Etruscan custom and dug a pit in the city's center so that *ancestors* in the *Nether World could more easily communicate* with the world of the living. (From Daniel J. Boorstin's *The Discoverers.*)

Several clues tell us that this is a historian talking about the past, and that his specific subject in this passage is the Nether World. His question, however, is quite different from the scientist's. Instead of asking "What is (or was) the Nether World?", the historian is asking "How did the concept of a Nether World come about?" Note how the nouns indicate his concern. He talks about the "people" and "tradition" as much as the Nether World, indicating that he is looking at how people acted and reasoned.

Again, the verbs indicate the speaker's concern. Here they are quite prominent, intended to focus the discussion on how people reasoned about the Nether World (people "somehow agreed," tradition "reported," and the topography "seemed to make"). As we might expect from a historian, these active verbs are past tense, but what makes them even more distinctive as part of the historian's voice is their tentative and hypothetical nature (for example, his use of "somehow" and "seemed"). Whereas the scientific community speaks as objectively and factually as possible, historians use a vocabulary that emphasizes the speculative nature of their discussions.

To enter into a conversation with experts, you have to speak as the natives do. If you were to write an essay in response to one of these writers, you would have to adopt the rhetoric of a scientist or historian. But that does not mean simply to mimic the authors or to use the jargon of the discipline; to adopt a rhetoric, you need to adopt a particular perspective in order to introduce and explore a specific question that would be of interest to that community. By using the discipline's vocabulary to develop an argument around a specific question, you will discipline your thinking as a scientist or historian, and discover in the writing something (even if not "the" answer) that contributes meaningfully to the discussion.

The questions your textbook authors and your instructors deliberate about have no "yes" or "no" answers; if they did, no one would have to develop arguments to answer them. Similarly, when you write, you should address only those questions for which we have no definite answers. There are more of them than you probably realize. Many expert answers that we have accepted as fact are only beliefs, conclusions that we agree on as most probably true because of the way someone has argued for them. When you read to discover what questions you need to address, keep in mind that the way the authors *reason* about a subject is at least as important as their *answers.* And think of your own writing as a math test where you receive credit for how you attempt to solve a problem even when the answer is not completely persuasive.

CRITICAL READING: EVALUATING REASONS

Critical reading is reading not just for the answers but for the reasons the author uses to justify them. However, we are not always taught to read this way. When studying for a test or doing research for a term paper, we often skip the discussion and go straight to the answers. Reading just for the answers appears easy and safe. When we read to memorize information, we need merely to sit back and let the writer talk to us. But appearances can be deceptive. For example, when you prepare to study after a long day of classes, sitting back in the easy chair with a thick book, you feel quite good about yourself for being so industrious. You read the first few paragraphs, underline one or two key sentences (thinking, "Aha! I know this will be on the test!"). Soon you find your mind wandering; you are reading absolutely every word on the page, but you have trouble concentrating on what is being said. Perhaps you begin to worry about another course that you need to prepare for, or about what you will do Friday night. Determined as you are, you shake yourself back to the task at hand, back up a few pages and, with renewed determination, begin again. Within minutes, though, you are found curled snugly in your chair, overtaken by the demands of desperately needed sleep, while your book lies abandoned, open on the floor.

You have been quite diligent—attempting to stay awake while reading *is* hard work. But have you learned anything? Even if you have memorized all of the important points you underlined in your reading, and obediently regurgitated all of these facts on the tests, chances are, once the test is over, these facts no longer have meaning for you and are erased from your memory to make room for the next parcel of information.

Reading for information is passive. It implies that you are not part of the academic community the author is addressing but a tourist watching the natives. You may pause to admire the sound of their language and rituals, but you don't participate in their dance. Critical reading is active reading: instead of taking photographs of what the natives do, you ask them questions, listen to their answers (which may sound quite foreign at first), and soon find yourself drawn into their world. Although you may not be a native of the discipline, an expert in the subject, you have learned to understand and communicate with them. The more disciplines you become familiar with through active reading, the more cosmopolitan you become (or, as one of my students once said, you stop being a tourist and become a "cosmopolite").

EXERCISE

Here is the introduction to one of the essays you will read in this chapter. You will read it twice. This first time through, read it as a tourist, marking the terms that are most foreign to you. Then write two or three sentences translating what you think is going on.

> Metaphor is for most people a device of the poetic imagination and the rhetorical flourish—a matter of extraordinary rather than ordinary language. Moreover, metaphor is typically viewed as characteristic of language alone, a matter of words rather than thought or action. For this reason, most people think they can get along perfectly well without metaphor. We have found, on the contrary, that metaphor is pervasive in everyday life, not just in language but in thought and action. Our ordinary conceptual system, in terms of which we both think and act, is fundamentally metaphorical in nature.

Now reread the passage (using your dictionary when you are still unsure of the meaning of a word), analyzing the nouns and verbs to discover both the subject under consideration and the question the authors are asking about it. This time, write two or three sentences *in response* to the paragraph, stating the question and formulating an answer based on your own experiences. (Feel free to criticize the metaphors I have used in this chapter.)

When you actively participate in what you read, you can become part of the discussion, using your knowledge and experience to question and evaluate the argument. Everyone has a unique perspective to contribute to a discussion. If you feel you have no right to criticize what you read, then you will read (and write) like a tourist. You may get a sense about what the natives have said but won't be able to explain or discuss what they meant. To understand what you read, you need to participate in the author's discussion, question passages that do not make sense, and discover what ideas appear most valuable for you. While you read, you will be staking a claim in the argument, discovering where you can alter the discussion by phrasing things differently or highlighting different points. Later, it will be easier to write about that particular subject, because you will already have initiated yourself into the discussion and have a stake in how it turns out.

Although critical reading sounds like it would be more work than passive reading, in the long run it is less—and it is more productive and pleasurable than you might think. The reason is simple. To "learn," you do not have to memorize a mass of apparently unrelated facts, but can retrieve this information by duplicating the process of reasoning the author used to arrive at the conclusions that are most important. If you talk *with* the author as you read, you listen more closely to what the author is saying and how it is said. Instead of letting the author tell you what to think, instead of memorizing only the conclusions, you uncover the author's reasoning and analyze how he or she arrived at those conclusions. As you talk with the author, writing responses in the margins of the text, you train yourself to reason with the discipline's vocabulary, to write and think like a scientist or historian or economist.

Each of your courses is an invitation to join a specific academic community, perhaps not the community of experts (yet) but a community of peers who have learned how to discuss the subject intelligently and appear to have a good time doing it. Reading critically is an important first step in acquainting yourself with the language they use, the questions they ask, and the types of reasons they respect. Some important questions you will want to keep in mind as you read critically are:

1. Why does the author think this subject is important?
2. What are the different questions the author is asking about this subject?
3. How does the author attempt to answer these questions?
4. Why should I believe this author? Are the reasons he or she gives good reasons? Has he or she considered alternative views?
5. Why is the author telling me this? Why should I care about it?

Once you can answer that last question, you have stopped being a tourist. Responding actively to what you read leads you to understand the subject in a particular way that is meaningful for you, that is, to *care* about it. If you don't care when you start to read, a good author can make you care by the time you finish. He or she may do this by making you angry, making you laugh, making you question your own beliefs, or saying something that rings true to your own experience.

Reading with a Pencil

To change the lecture into a conversation, talk with the author by writing back to the text when you have questions or wish to add comments. Don't just underline, but annotate. Write questions in the margins, such as: "How does this relate to what

she says above?" or "But can't we also see it this way . . .?" When you read your book
with a pencil in hand, you leave a record of what you have or have not understood.
You also have begun to experiment with the community's voice, to express your
understanding of the subject with the vocabulary the author has used.

When you reread the book, you can use your annotations to focus on passages
that confused you earlier. And when you review your reading, either to prepare for
a test or to write a formal paper, you will have a record not only of what the book
says but of what you *learned* while reading it. (Have you been annotating this
chapter? If not, you might wish to go back to the beginning and reread it, jotting
down your responses in the margins.)

The Reading Notebook

Every good conversation allows you a chance to respond with more than nods,
isolated questions, and intermittent comments. At some point, someone will turn to
you and ask, "Do you see what I mean?" or "What do you think about that?" For this
reason, once you have finished reading (with a pencil) your assignment, you should
allow yourself time to speak at length about what you think of the reading—to
explore through your own writing what the author meant and what you have
learned from it. This is not unlike the feeling you have immediately after seeing a
good movie: you need to discuss what went on and why you are inclined to feel a
certain way about it. The best place to discuss what goes on in your mind as you
read is a reading notebook.

Like a journal, the reading notebook gives you a private place to explore ideas
and feelings, to take risks without exposing yourself to ridicule. Unlike a personal
journal, however, a reading notebook is limited to the reading you are doing. Treat
the notebook entries as extensions of the conversation you have already begun with
the authors of your assigned reading. As with any conversation, your notebook entry
should begin by summarizing and analyzing what you have just heard.

ANALYZE: TAKE NOTES, PARAPHRASE, SUMMARIZE

Everytime you read actively, you compose the author's argument from your perspective. Your past experience and previous knowledge leads you to read a little
differently than someone else. One of the author's ideas or examples might remind
you of something you have seen before, and this might prompt you to shape the rest
of the author's argument around that idea. On the other hand, some ideas or examples might escape your attention because they are less familiar to you. Although we
all read differently, some readings are better than others. To ensure that you have
read effectively, that you have not overlooked an important point that could change
how you interpret the author's argument, you need to analyze what you have read.

Analyzing involves taking the reading apart, interpreting the various sections,
and then recomposing the author's argument in your own words. You are already
analyzing when you begin to annotate what you are reading. When you underline
passages or jot down comments in the margins, you are dissecting the argument to
focus on different reasons the author has given to justify his or her conclusion. To

make sense of the whole, though, you still need to take notes on what you have read.

Note taking is not merely copying down the author's words; if it were, you would have to recopy the whole text to do it well. Rather, note taking is restating in your own words what you see as the most significant points of the reading. Your annotations can help you locate which passages were most significant. Usually, your restatements will boil down one or more paragraphs into a phrase or sentence that summarizes your understanding of the passage. Sometimes, though, mere summary is not enough; you may be able to restate the idea but not feel that you thoroughly understand it. This is when you may wish to explore the author's point further, to paraphrase it in terms you feel more comfortable with. Note the following ways a student has taken notes, summarized, and then paraphrased the passage on metaphor quoted on p. 22. Although Kirsten was analyzing only one paragraph, you will want to use a similar procedure when you analyze long passages.

Kirsten's Notebook Entry

Kirsten's Notes

1. Dictionary says metaphors are figures of speech that compare the thing you are talking about to something else ("evening of life").
2. Most people think we don't need metaphors because they are merely fancy ways of saying things.
3. Metaphors are all around us.
4. Everything we do and think is based on metaphor.

Her Summary

Although most people don't think we need metaphors, we really do. They affect what we think and how we act.

Her Paraphrase

I think the authors are saying that most of us think we can live without metaphors because we can say the same things without them. Like, if you say "I worked like a dog last night," you could just say "I worked very hard last night" and say the same thing. The authors, however, say these wouldn't mean the same thing, that somehow saying "I worked like a dog" would mean something different, change how people thought about me. I guess we say this because a dog works very hard, that he is a "beast of burden" (that's a metaphor, too!), and I would be saying I slaved (is that a metaphor?) rather than just worked hard. I guess that's different, and I somehow couldn't quite explain it without metaphors. That's what the author is getting at.

Although Kirsten's paraphrase is quite a bit longer than her summary, note how she didn't quite understand what she had read until she attempted to relate the ideas to something she was more familiar with. She still appears not to be completely sure of her interpretation of the reading, but she has a better idea why it troubles her. Although Kirsten was analyzing only a short paragraph, she used her note taking, summarizing, and paraphrasing skills to begin composing a response to the reading.

As we discussed in Chapter 1, the composing process can be broken down into three stages: analysis, synthesis, and evaluation. Kirsten's paraphrase both helps her become more confident of her analysis of what the authors meant and enables her to begin synthesizing her own experience and knowledge with the authors'. After writing this paraphrase, Kirsten was able to summarize the rest of the argument more quickly and felt more confident about her ability to evaluate it. After writing her summary and paraphrase of the reading, Kirsten concluded her notebook entry with the following evaluation:

> Although I agree with the authors that we should be more aware than we are of how metaphors affect what we think and do, I am not convinced that every metaphor has this power. One thing the authors don't discuss is how we overuse metaphors, how we can say something like "busy as a bee" so many times that no one actually thinks of a bee when we say it. I think the same goes for phrases like "how I spent my time"—we don't think about money when we say it, we just have no other words for that idea. Does that mean we are just unconscious of how we always use money to measure what we do? Perhaps, but if we are unconscious of it, then how will it hurt us?

Although Kirsten went on to modify her position somewhat as she drafted and revised her essay, her reading notebook entry had helped her enter the authors' conversation. If you are careful constructing the entries in your reading notebook, you will not only prepare yourself well for class discussion of the material but create a transcript of your thought processes—a very helpful, although very rough, first draft of the essay you will write. When you write your notebook entries for the essays in this chapter, be sure to take notes, summarize, and paraphrase. You might also keep in mind the questions for critical reading listed on pp. 23.

CRITICAL DISCUSSION: SYNTHESIS AND EVALUATION

As Kirsten's notebook entry reveals, the ideas you develop when you read critically and write your notebook entries are only tentatively synthesized and evaluated. Often, you cannot be completely sure how to evaluate the worth of an author's argument until you can test your ideas through critical discussion. When you begin to share your interpretations of the readings with your classmates, you may discover that what you assumed the author meant should not have been assumed at all. This does not mean that your reading is not "correct," but that you interpret what you read in the context of what you already know. As mentioned above, each of us reads differently. To distinguish one reading as better than another, we have to consider the reasons each of us uses to justify our interpretation as a good one.

Your interpretation is "wrong" only if you cannot justify it to another reader, and the only way you can justify your interpretation to another is to understand his or her perspective. By listening to the reasons others use to justify their understanding of the reading, even if you think their interpretation is wrong, you can discover new perspectives that could modify your own. And by responding to their arguments with your own, you can test your understanding of the reading and experiment with different reasons that might justify your evaluation of it. If you use class discussion as an opportunity to play with different ideas, then you can discover whether you have good reasons for evaluating the subject as you have. If you use class discussion well, then you can discover an argument that has the *best* reasons, reasons that not only justify the worth of the argument but can be used to persuade others that it is the better one.

Engaging actively in critical discussion can provide you with multiple ways of looking at the reading, helping you discover what is unique about your evaluation and why others need to hear it. You cannot assume your evaluation is the "right" or only one, but you can assume it is important. When you develop a thesis and essay that synthesizes the author's and your classmates' perspectives with your own, you can arrive at a new way to look at the subject. The best essay you can write will offer not only your own perspective but show how your ideas work with those of your audience to create a more complete understanding of the subject and its importance.

If you have used your reading notebook thoroughly and creatively, you will have discovered different ways to express your ideas. When you share these ideas with others, you may modify your ideas to some extent. After a class discussion, you might want to return to your reading notebook and continue your conversation there, summarizing what occurred in the class discussion: What significant new perspectives did your classmates offer? What ideas seemed particularly "wrong" to you? Although you might not have been able to think of a suitable response to these ideas in class, you could now use your reading notebook to discover ways to formulate what you wish you would have said.

Although it sounds peculiar, the most profitable class discussions can be those that leave you frustrated, that leave you with the nagging sense that you or your classmates are overlooking some fundamental truth. This frustration is good; it reveals that you have involved yourself with the subject and have a stake in how the conversation turns out.

To prepare yourself to engage actively in class discussion, you will need to read the following essays closely and critically. Read each essay at least twice. The first time through, listen in on the author's conversation, annotating the text when you have specific questions or comments. On second reading, be sure to use your dictionary to look up words you are still unsure of and take notes that will help you summarize the argument. After you are finished, respond to the author by writing a notebook entry. First, summarize what the author said, then analyze the reasons the author gave to justify it. Next, synthesize your previous knowledge with what you have learned from the essay. Finally, conclude by offering a tentative evaluation of the author's ideas. When you are finished, you might read your notebook entry to your classmates to ease your way into the discussion.

The following readings do not reveal the voice of just one academic community. They were chosen to introduce you to the different ways people view language. As you read, keep in mind that each essay is discussing a particular way that language affects what we think. Some of the essays, like Lakoff and Johnson's or Nilsen's, suggest that the language we take for granted actually shapes how we see the world and others. This is not just a question for people who study language (linguists), but a question you should consider every time you read. In fact, through this first set of readings, you will discover that if you do not examine *how* something is said before you accept it, you might be supporting ideas that you do not believe.

Examsmanship and the Liberal Arts: A Study in Educational Epistemology

William G. Perry, Jr. *(1913–   )*

The following essay was printed in 1964 as part of a collection of essays written by members of the Harvard faculty. Part of the purpose of this collection, Examining in Harvard College: A Collection of Essays, *was to investigate how teachers at Harvard evaluate student learning. One of the most valuable contributions of this collection was the revelation that Harvard teachers responded less favorably to students who could recall everything they had read than to students who could argue intelligently, whether or not they could demonstrate that they had read the material for the course. Perry's essay in particular explores why this was so. In 1968, he went on to explore the issue further, publishing* Forms of Intellectual and Ethical Development, *a speculation into the different stages of intellectual growth that college students must pass through to become independent thinkers. As you read this essay, try to identify which of the student writers Perry discusses is most like you.*

"But sir, I don't think I really deserve it, it was mostly bull, really." This disclaimer from a student whose examination we have awarded a straight "A" is wondrously depressing. Alfred North Whitehead invented its only possible rejoinder: "Yes, sir, what you wrote is nonsense, utter nonsense. But ah! Sir! It's the right *kind* of nonsense!"

Bull, in this university, is customarily a source of laughter, or a problem in ethics. I shall step a little out of fashion to use the subject as a take-off point for a study in comparative epistemology. The phenomenon of bull, in all the honor and opprobrium with which it is regarded by students and faculty, says something, I think, about our theories of knowledge. So too, the grades which we assign on examinations communicate to students what these theories may be.

We do not have to be out-and-out logical-positivists to suppose that we have something to learn about "what we think knowledge is" by having a good look at "what we do when we go about measuring it." We know the straight "A" examination when we see it, of course, and we have reason to hope that the student will understand why his work receives our recognition. He doesn't always. And those who receive lesser honor? Perhaps an understanding of certain anomalies in our customs of grading good bull will explain the students' confusion.

I must beg patience, then, both of the reader's humor and of his morals. Not that I ask him to suspend his sense of humor but that I shall ask him to go beyond it. In a great university the picture of a bright student attempting to outwit his professor while his professor takes pride in not being outwitted is certainly ridiculous. I shall report just such a scene, for its implications bear upon my point. Its comedy need not present a serious obstacle to thought.

As for the ethics of bull, I must ask for a suspension of judgment. I wish that students could suspend theirs. Unlike humor, moral commitment is hard to think beyond. Too early a moral judgment is precisely what stands between many able students and a liberal education. The stunning realization that the Harvard Faculty will often accept, as evidence of knowledge, the cerebrations of a student who has little data at his disposal, confronts every student with an ethical dilemma. For some it forms an academic focus for what used to be thought of as "adolescent disillusion." It is irrelevant that rumor inflates the phenomenon to mythical proportions. The students know that beneath the myth there remains a solid and haunting reality. The moral "bind" consequent on this awareness appears most poignantly in serious students who are reluctant to concede the competitive advantage to the bullster and who yet feel a deep personal shame when, having succumbed to "temptation," they themselves receive a high grade for work they consider "dishonest."

I have spent many hours with students caught in this unwelcome bitterness. These hours lend an urgency to my theme. I have found that students have been able to come to terms with the ethical problem, to the extent that it is real, only after a refined study of the true nature of bull and its relation to "knowledge." I shall submit grounds for my suspicion that we can be found guilty of sharing the student's confusion of moral and epistemological issues.

I

I present as my "premise," then, an amoral *fabliau.* Its hero-villain is the Abominable Mr. Metzger '47. Since I celebrate his virtuosity, I regret giving him a pseudonym, but the peculiar style of his bravado requires me to honor also his modesty. Bull in pure form is rare; there is usually some contamination by data. The community has reason to be grateful to Mr. Metzger for having created an instance of laboratory purity, free from any adulteration by matter. The more credit is due him, I think, because his act was free from premeditation, deliberation, or hope of personal gain.

Mr. Metzger stood one rainy November day in the lobby of Memorial Hall. A junior, concentrating in mathematics, he was fond of diverting himself by taking part in the drama, a penchant which may have had some influence on the events of the next hour. He was waiting to take part in a rehearsal in Sanders Theatre, but, as sometimes happens, no other players appeared. Perhaps the rehearsal had been canceled without his knowledge? He decided to wait another five minutes.

Students, meanwhile, were filing into the Great Hall opposite, and taking seats at the testing tables. Spying a friend crossing the lobby toward the Great Hall's door, Metzger greeted him and extended appropriate condolences. He inquired, too, what course his friend was being tested in. "Oh, Soc. Sci. something-or-other." "What's it all about?" asked Metzger, and this, as Homer remarked of Patroclus, was the beginning of evil for him.

"It's about Modern Perspectives on Man and Society and All That," said his friend. "Pretty interesting, really."

"Always wanted to take a course like that," said Metzger. "Any good reading?"

"Yeah, great. There's this book"—his friend did not have time to finish.

"Take your seats please" said a stern voice beside them. The idle conversation had somehow taken the two friends to one of the tables in the Great Hall. Both students automatically obeyed; the proctor put blue-books before them; another proctor presented them with copies of the printed hour-test.

Mr. Metzger remembered afterwards a brief misgiving that was suddenly overwhelmed by a surge of curiosity and puckish glee. He wrote "George Smith" on the blue book, opened it, and addressed the first question.

I must pause to exonerate the Management. The Faculty has a rule that no student may attend an examination in a course in which he is not enrolled. To the wisdom of this rule the outcome of this deplorable story stands witness. The Registrar, charged with the enforcement of the rule, has developed an organization with procedures which are certainly the finest to be devised. In November, however, class rosters are still shaky, and on this particular day another student, named Smith, was absent. As for the culprit, we can reduce his guilt no further than to suppose that he was ignorant of the rule, or, in the face of the momentous challenge before him, forgetful.

We need not be distracted by Metzger's performance on the "objective" or "spot" questions on the test. His D on these sections can be explained by those versed in the theory of probability. Our interest focuses on the quality of his essay. It appears that when Metzger's friend picked up his own blue book a few days later, he found himself in company with a large proportion of his section in having received on the essay a C. When he quietly picked up "George Smith's" blue book to return it to Metzger, he observed that the grade for the essay was A. In the margin was a note in the section man's hand. It read "Excellent work. Could you have pinned these observations down a bit more closely? Compare . . . in . . . pp. . . ."

Such news could hardly be kept quiet. There was a leak, and the whole scandal broke on the front page of Tuesday's *Crimson*. With the press Metzger was modest, as becomes a hero. He said that there had been nothing to it at all, really. The essay question had offered a choice of two books, Margaret Mead's *And Keep Your Powder Dry* or Geoffrey Gorer's *The American People*. Metzger reported that having read neither of them, he had chosen the second "because the title gave me some notion as to what the book might be about." On the test, two critical comments were offered on each book, one favorable, one unfavorable. The students were asked to "discuss." Metzger conceded that he had played safe in throwing his lot with the most laudatory of the two comments, "but I did not forget to be balanced."

I do not have Mr. Metzger's essay before me except in vivid memory. As I recall, he took his first cue from the name Geoffrey, and committed his strategy to the premise that Gorer was born into an "Anglo-Saxon" culture, probably English, but certainly "English speaking." Having heard that Margaret Mead was a social anthropologist, he inferred that Gorer was the same. He then entered upon his essay, centering his inquiry upon what he supposed might be the problems inherent in an anthropologist's observation of a culture which was his own, or nearly his own. Drawing in part from memories of table-talk on cultural relativity[1] and in part from creative logic, he rang changes on the relation of observer to observed, and assessed the kind and degree of objectivity which might accrue to an observer through training as an anthropologist. He concluded that the book in question did in fact contribute a considerable range of " 'objective', and even 'fresh'," insights into the nature of our culture. "At the same time," he warned, "these observations must be understood within the context of their generation by a person only partly freed from his embeddedness in the culture he is observing, and limited in his capacity to transcend those particular tendencies and biases which he has himself developed as a personality in his interraction with this culture since his birth. In this sense the book portrays as much the character of Geoffrey Gorer as it analyzes that of the American people." It is my regrettable duty to report that at this moment of triumph Mr. Metzger was carried away by the temptations of parody and added, "We are thus much the richer."

In any case, this was the essay for which Metzger received his honor grade and his public acclaim. He was now, of course, in serious trouble with the authorities.

I shall leave him for the moment to the mercy of the Administrative Board of Harvard College and turn the reader's attention to the section man who ascribed the grade. He was in much worse trouble. All the consternation in his immediate area of the Faculty and all the glee in other areas fell upon his unprotected head. I shall now undertake his defense.

I do so not simply because I was acquainted with him and feel a respect for his intelligence; I believe in the justice of his grade! Well, perhaps "justice" is the wrong word in a situation so manifestly absurd. This is more a case in "equity." That is, the grade is equitable if we accept other aspects of the situation which are equally absurd. My proposition is this: if we accept as valid those C grades which were accorded students who, like Metzger's friend, demonstrated a thorough familiarity with the details of the book without relating their critique to the methodological problems of social anthropology, then "George Smith" deserved not only the same, but better.

The reader may protest that the C's given to students who showed evidence only of diligence were indeed not valid and that both these students and "George Smith" should have received E's. To give the diligent E is of course not in accord with custom. I shall take up this matter later. For now, were I to allow the protest, I could only restate my thesis: that "George Smith's" E would, in a college of liberal arts, be properly a "better" E.

---

[1]"An important part of Harvard's education takes place during meals in the Houses." An Official Publication. AUTHOR'S NOTE: Houses are dormitories for upperclassmen.

At this point I need a short-hand. It is a curious fact that there is no academic slang for the presentation of evidence of diligence alone. "Parroting" won't do; it is possible to "parrot" bull. I must beg the reader's pardon, and, for reasons almost too obvious to bear, suggest "cow."

Stated as nouns, the concepts look simple enough:

cow (pure): data, however relevant, without relevancies.

bull (pure): relevancies, however relevant, without data.

The reader can see all too clearly where this simplicity would lead. I can assure him that I would not have imposed on him this way were I aiming to say that knowledge in this university is definable as some neuter compromise between cow and bull, some infertile hermaphrodite. This is precisely what many diligent students seem to believe: that what they must learn to do is to "find the right mean" between "amounts" of detail and "amounts" of generalities. Of course this is not the point at all. The problem is not quantitative, nor does its solution lie on a continuum between the particular and the general. Cow and bull are not poles of a single dimension. A clear notion of what they really are is essential to my inquiry, and for heuristic purposes I wish to observe them further in the celibate state.

When the pure concepts are translated into verbs, their complexities become apparent in the assumptions and purposes of the students as they write:

To cow (v. intrans.) or the act of cowing:
To list data (or perform operations) without awareness of, or comment upon, the contexts, frames of reference, or points of observation which determine the origin, nature, and meaning of the data (or procedures). To write on the assumption that "a fact is a fact." To present evidence of hard work as a substitute for understanding, without any intent to deceive.

To bull (v. intrans.) or the act of bulling:
To discourse upon the contexts, frames of reference and points of observation which would determine the origin, nature, and meaning of data if one had any. To present evidence of an understanding of form in the hope that the reader may be deceived into supporting a familiarity with content.

At the level of conscious intent, it is evident that cowing is more moral, or less immoral, than bulling. To speculate about unconscious intent would be either an injustice or a needless elaboration of my theme. It is enough that the impression left by cow is one of earnestness, diligence, and painful naiveté. The grader may feel disappointment or even irritation, but these feelings are usually balanced by pity, compassion, and a reluctance to hit a man when he's both down and moral. He may feel some challenge to his teaching, but none whatever to his one-ups-manship. He writes in the margin: "See me."

We are now in a position to understand the anomaly of custom: As instructors, we always assign bull an E, *when we detect it;* whereas we usually give cow a C, *even though it is always obvious.*

After all, we did not ask to be confronted with a choice between morals and understanding (or did we?). We evince a charming humanity, I think, in our decision to grade in favor of morals and pathos. "I simply *can't* give this student an E after he has *worked* so hard." At the same time we tacitly express our respect for the bullster's strength. We recognize a colleague. If he knows so well how to dish it out, we can be sure that he can also take it.

Of course it is just possible that we carry with us, perhaps from our own school-days, an assumption that if a student is willing to work hard and collect "good hard facts" he can always be taught to understand their relevance, whereas a student who has caught onto the forms of relevance without working at all is a lost scholar.

But this is not in accord with our experience.

It is not in accord either, as far as I can see, with the stated values of a liberal education. If a liberal education should teach students "how to think," not only in their own fields but in fields outside their own—that is, to understand "how the other fellow orders knowledge," then bulling, even in its purest form, expresses an important part of what a pluralist university holds dear, surely a more important part than the collecting of "facts that are facts" which schoolboys learn to do. Here then, good bull appears not as ignorance at all but as an aspect of knowledge. It is both relevant and "true." In a university setting good bull is therefore of more value than "facts," which, without a frame of reference, are not even "true" at all.

Perhaps this value accounts for the final anomaly: as instructors, we are inclined to reward bull highly, *where we do not detect its intent,* to the consternation of the bullster's acquaintances. And often we do not examine the matter too closely. After a long evening of reading blue books full of cow, the sudden meeting with a student who at least understands the problems of one's field provides a lift like a draught of refreshing wine, and a strong disposition toward trust.

This was, then, the sense of confidence that came to our unfortunate section man as he read "George Smith's" sympathetic considerations.

II

In my own years of watching over students' shoulders as they work, I have come to believe that this feeling of trust has a firmer basis than the confidence generated by evidence of diligence alone. I believe that the theory of a liberal education holds. Students who have dared to understand man's real relation to his knowledge have shown themselves to be in a strong position to learn content rapidly and meaningfully, and to retain it. I have learned to be less concerned about the education of a student who has come to understand the nature of man's knowledge, even though he has not yet committed himself to hard work, than I am about the education of the student who, after one or two terms at Harvard, is working desperately hard and still believes that collected "facts" constitute knowledge. The latter, when I try to explain to him, too often understands me to be saying that he "doesn't *put in enough generalities.*" Surely he has "put in *enough* facts."

I have come to see such quantitative statements as expressions of an entire, coherent epistemology. In grammar school the student is taught that Columbus discovered America in 1492. The *more* such items he gets "right" on a given test the more he is credited with "knowing." From years of this sort of thing it is not unnatural to develop the conviction that knowledge consists of the accretion of hard facts by hard work.

The student learns that the more facts and procedures he can get "right" in a given course, the better will be his grade. The more courses he takes, the more subjects he has "had," the more credits he accumulates, the more diplomas he will get, until, after graduate school, he will emerge with his doctorate, a member of the community of scholars.

The foundation of this entire life is the proposition that a fact is a fact. The necessary correlate of this proposition is that a fact is either right or wrong. This implies that the standard against which the rightness or wrongness of a fact may be judged exists *someplace*—perhaps graven upon a tablet in a Platonic world outside and above *this* cave of tears. In grammar school it is evident that the tablets which enshrine the spelling of a word or the answer to an arithmetic problem are visible to my teacher who need only compare my offerings to it. In high school I observe that my English teachers disagree. This can only mean that the tablets in such matters as the goodness of a poem are distant and obscured by clouds. They surely exist. The pleasing of befuddled English teachers degenerates into assessing their prejudices, a game in which I have no protection against my competitors more glib of tongue. I respect only my science teachers, authorities who *really know.* Later I learn from them that "this is only what we think *now.*" But eventually, surely. . . . Into this epistemology of education, apparently shared by teachers in such terms as "credits," "semester hours" and "years of French" the student may invest his ideals, his drive, his competitiveness, his safety, his self-esteem, and even his love.

College raises other questions: by whose calendar is it proper to say that Columbus discovered America in 1492? How, when and by whom was the year 1 established in this calendar? What of other calendars? In view of the evidence for Leif Ericson's previous visit (and the American Indians), what historical ethnocentrism is suggested by the use of the word "discover" in this sentence? As for Leif Ericson, in accord with what assumptions do you order the evidence?

These questions and their answers are not "more" knowledge. They are devastation. I do not need to elaborate upon the epistemology, or rather epistemologies, they imply. A fact has become at last "an observation or an operation performed in a frame of reference." A liberal education is founded in an awareness of frame of reference even in the most immediate and empirical examination of data. Its acquirement involves relinquishing hope of absolutes and of the protection they afford against doubt and the glib-tongued competitor. It demands an ever widening sophistication about systems of thought and observation. It leads, not away from, but *through* the arts of gamesmanship to a new trust.

This trust is in the value and integrity of systems, their varied character, and the way their apparently incompatible metaphors enlighten, from complementary facets, the particulars of human experience. As one student said to me: "I used to be cynical about intellectual games. Now I want to know them thoroughly. You see I came to realize that it was only when I knew the rules of the game cold that I could tell whether what I was saying was tripe."

We too often think of the bullster as cynical. He can be, and not always in a light-hearted way. We have failed to observe that there can lie behind cow the potential of a deeper and more dangerous despair. The moralism of sheer work and obedience can be an ethic that, unwilling to face a despair of its ends, glorifies its means. The implicit refusal to consider the relativity of both ends and means leaves the operator in an unconsidered proprietary absolutism. History bears witness that in the pinches this moral superiority has no recourse to negotiation, only to force.

A liberal education proposes that man's hope lies elsewhere: in the negotiability that can arise from an understanding of the integrity of systems and of their origins in man's address to his universe. The prerequisite is the courage to accept such a definition of knowledge. From then on, of course, there is nothing incompatible between such an epistemology and hard work. Rather the contrary.

I can now at last let bull and cow get together. The reader knows best how a productive wedding is arranged in his own field. This is the nuptial he celebrates with a straight A on examinations. The masculine context must embrace the feminine particular, though itself "born of woman." Such a union is knowledge itself, and it alone can generate new contexts and new data which can unite in their turn to form new knowledge.

In this happy setting we can congratulate in particular the Natural Sciences, long thought to be barren ground to the bullster. I have indeed drawn my examples of bull from the Social Sciences, and by analogy from the Humanities. Essay-writing in these fields has long been thought to nurture the art of bull to its prime. I feel, however, that the Natural Sciences have no reason to feel slighted. It is perhaps no accident that Metzger was a mathematician. As part of my researches for this paper, furthermore, a student of considerable talent has recently honored me with an impressive analysis of the art of amassing "partial credits" on examinations in advanced physics. Though beyond me in some respects, his presentation confirmed my impression that instructors of Physics frequently honor on examinations operations structurally similar to those requisite in a good essay.

The very qualities that make the Natural Sciences fields of delight for the eager gamesman have been essential to their marvelous fertility.

III

As priests of these mysteries, how can we make our rites more precisely expressive? The student who merely cows robs himself, without knowing it, of his education and his soul. The student who only bulls robs himself, as he knows full well, of the joys of inductive discovery—that is, of engagement. The introduction of frames of reference in the new curricula of Mathematics and Physics in the schools is a hopeful experiment. We do not know yet how much of these potent revelations the very young can stand, but I suspect they may rejoice in them more than we have supposed. I can't believe they have never wondered about Leif Ericson and that word "discovered," or even about 1492. They have simply been too wise to inquire.

Increasingly in recent years better students in the better high schools and preparatory schools are being allowed to inquire. In fact they appear to be receiving both encouragement and training in their inquiry. I have the evidence before me.

Each year for the past five years all freshmen entering Harvard and Radcliffe have been asked in freshman week to "grade" two essays answering an examination question in History. They are then asked to give their reasons for their grades. One essay, filled with dates, is 99% cow. The other, with hardly a date in it, is a good essay, easily mistaken for bull. The "official" grades of these essays are, for the first (alas!) C "because he has worked so hard," and for the second (soundly, I think) B. Each year a larger majority of freshmen evaluate these essays as would the majority of the faculty, and for the faculty's reasons, and each year a smaller minority give the higher honor to the essay offering data alone. Most interesting, a larger number of students each year, while not overrating the second essay, award the first the straight E appropriate to it in a college of liberal arts.

For us who must grade such students in a university, these developments imply a new urgency, did we not feel it already. Through our grades we describe for the students, in the showdown, what we believe about the nature of knowledge. The subtleties of bull are not peripheral to our academic concerns. That they penetrate to the center of our care is evident in our feelings when a student whose good work we have awarded a high grade reveals to us that he does not feel he deserves it. Whether he disqualifies himself because "there's too much bull in it," or worse because "I really don't think I've worked that hard," he presents a serious educational problem. Many students feel this sleaziness; only a few reveal it to us.

We can hardly allow a mistaken sense of fraudulence to undermine our students' achievements. We must lead students beyond their concept of bull so that they may honor relevancies that are really relevant. We can willingly acknowledge that, in lieu of the date 1492, a consideration of calendars and of the word "discovered," may well be offered with intent to deceive. We must insist that this does not make such considerations intrinsically immoral, and that, contrariwise, the date 1492 may be no substitute for them. Most of all, we must convey the impression that we grade understanding qua understanding. To be convincing, I suppose we must concede to ourselves in advance that a bright student's understanding is understanding even if he achieved it by osmosis rather than by hard work in our course.

These are delicate matters. As for cow, its complexities are not what need concern us. Unlike good bull, it does not represent partial knowledge at all.

It belongs to a different theory of knowledge entirely. In our theories of knowledge it represents total ignorance, or worse yet, a knowledge downright inimical to understanding. I even go so far as to propose that we award no more C's for cow. To do so is rarely, I feel, the act of mercy it seems. Mercy lies in clarity.

The reader may be afflicted by a lingering curiosity about the fate of Mr. Metzger. I hasten to reassure him. The Administrative Board of Harvard College, whatever its satanic reputation, is a benign body. Its members, to be sure, were on the spot. They delighted in Metzger's exploit, but they were responsible to the Faculty's rule. The hero stood in danger of probation. The debate was painful. Suddenly one member, of a refined legalistic sensibility, observed that the rule applied specifically to "examinations" and that the occasion had been simply an hour-test. Mr. Metzger was merely "admonished."

QUESTIONS FOR A CRITICAL REREADING

After you have read the essay through once (while noting your initial reactions in the margins of the text), use the following questions to begin your critical rereading of the argument. (*Helpful hint:* recording your answers in your reading notebook will help you write your essay later on.)

1. Paragraphs 1–6 of Perry's essay can be seen as his introduction. What is the subject he is introducing and what question does he appear to be asking about it?
2. In paragraphs 7–20, Perry illustrates how the question became an important issue for him. Can you explain why he thinks we need to answer this question? To whom is he writing?
3. The majority of Perry's essay is devoted to defining what he means by "bull" and "cow." Summarize what these terms mean. Why do you think Perry chose these particular metaphors?
4. In paragraph 25, he says that "some neuter compromise between cow and bull, some infertile hermaphrodite" is "not the point at all." What does this mean and why doesn't Perry think it is the point? (Note in paragraph 44 how he feels he can finally "let bull and cow get together" to make his real point. What has occurred between these two passages to make his thesis clearer?)
5. At the end of his essay, Perry assumes that he has answered the question that troubled him at the start of the essay. What is this answer (his thesis)? After writing out his thesis, try to give the primary reason he uses to justify it (ask yourself how Perry would complete the statement "This is true because . . . ").

POSSIBLE ISSUES FOR WRITING

Following are a few of the questions that you might find at issue in Perry's argument. Discuss these with your classmates to see whether your interpretation differs from theirs. During class discussion, listen closely for the difference in the answers your classmates give. Whenever the class disagrees, jot down in your notebook what appears to be at issue (it may be one of these questions or others that arise in the discussion). Be sure to listen carefully. After you have discussed all the essays in this chapter, you will use your notebook entry to discover what you want to say and who needs to hear it.

1. What would you feel like if you had spent a term attending and studying for a class, diligently preparing for the final, and then had a friend "drop in" to take the exam with you, only to receive a better grade? Would it be "just?" Would it be "equitable" (as Perry claims)? Explain your answer.

2. Are the metaphors "bull" and "cow" the best ones for Perry's argument? Brainstorm about other words he might have used. How do different metaphors change the argument?

3. Do you think Perry's essay will have any effect on how you write in college? Why or why not?

_____
_____
_____

Concepts We Live By

George Lakoff (1941–   ) and Mark Johnson (1949–   )

The following excerpt is taken from two chapters of Lakoff and Johnson's book-length study, Metaphors We Live By *(1980). This selection reveals how a linguist (George Lakoff) and a philosopher (Mark Johnson) worked together to arrive at a new under- standing of how language works. When they first met in early 1979, they found they shared a common concern: that both the philosopher's and the linguist's view of how language means "has very little to do with what people find meaningful in their lives" (from their preface). Their collaboration led them to focus on metaphor, traditionally viewed as a literary device by which we clarify abstract concepts by comparing them to something familiar (for example, Presidential campaigns become "races" with a lesser-known candidate as the "dark horse").*

Both Lakoff and Johnson were troubled that neither philosophers nor linguists had paid much attention to metaphors, that metaphors were usually seen as merely a way to dress up ordinary language. With a different hypothesis in mind—that metaphors affect not just what we say but how we think and act—Lakoff and Johnson collected linguistic evidence (the common phrases we use everyday) and analyzed it with the eye of a philosopher (looking at how language affects what we believe). As you read the following excerpt, be aware of how they are using language; because their terms are often drawn from the vocabulary of a philosopher or linguist, use your dictionary to clarify concepts that may at first appear confusing. To prepare yourself for the summary you will write, read with this question in mind: would the argument change signifi- cantly if Lakoff and Johnson used other terms?

Metaphor is for most people a device of the poetic imagination and the rhetorical flourish—a matter of extraordinary rather than ordinary language. Moreover, metaphor is typically viewed as characteristic of language alone, a matter of words rather than thought or action. For this reason, most people think they can get along perfectly well without metaphor. We have found, on the contrary, that metaphor is pervasive in everyday life, not just in language but in thought and action. Our ordinary conceptual system, in terms of which we both think and act, is fundamentally metaphorical in nature.

The concepts that govern our thought are not just matters of the intellect. They also govern our everyday functioning, down to the most mundane de- tails. Our concepts structure what we perceive, how we get around in the world, and how we relate to other people. Our conceptual system thus plays a central role in defining our everyday realities. If we are right in suggesting that our conceptual system is largely metaphorical, then the way we think, what we experience, and what we do every day is very much a matter of metaphor.

But our conceptual system is not something we are normally aware of. In most of the little things we do every day, we simply think and act more or less automatically along certain lines. Just what these lines are is by no means obvious. One way to find out is by looking at language. Since communication is based on the same conceptual system that we use in thinking and acting, language is an important source of evidence for what that system is like.

Primarily on the basis of linguistic evidence, we have found that most of our ordinary conceptual system is metaphorical in nature. And we have found a way to begin to identify in detail just what the metaphors are that structure how we perceive, how we think, and what we do.

To give some idea of what it could mean for a concept to be metaphorical and for such a concept to structure an everyday activity, let us start with the concept ARGUMENT and the conceptual metaphor ARGUMENT IS WAR. This metaphor is reflected in our everyday language by a wide variety of expressions:

Argument Is War

Your claims are *indefensible.*
He *attacked every weak point* in my argument.
His criticisms were *right on target.*
I *demolished* his argument.
I've never *won* an argument with him.
You disagree? Okay, *shoot!*
If you use that *strategy,* he'll *wipe you out.*
He *shot down* all of my arguments.

It is important to see that we don't just *talk* about arguments in terms of war. We can actually win or lose arguments. We see the person we are arguing with as an opponent. We attack his positions and we defend our own. We gain and lose ground. We plan and use strategies. If we find a position indefensible, we can abandon it and take a new line of attack. Many of the things we *do* in arguing are partially structured by the concept of war. Though there is no physical battle, there is a verbal battle, and the structure of an argument—attack, defense, counterattack, etc.—reflects this. It is in this sense that the ARGUMENT IS WAR metaphor is one that we live by in this culture; it structures the actions we perform in arguing.

Try to imagine a culture where arguments are not viewed in terms of war, where no one wins or loses, where there is no sense of attacking or defending, gaining or losing ground. Imagine a culture where an argument is viewed as a dance, the participants are seen as performers, and the goal is to perform in a balanced and aesthetically pleasing way. In such a culture, people would view arguments differently, experience them differently, carry them out differently, and talk about them differently. But *we* would probably not view them as arguing at all: they would simply be doing something different. It would seem strange even to call what they were doing "arguing." Perhaps the most neutral way of describing this difference between their culture and ours would be to say that we have a discourse form structured in terms of battle and they have one structured in terms of dance.

This is an example of what it means for a metaphorical concept, namely, ARGUMENT IS WAR, to structure (at least in part) what we do and how we understand what we are doing when we argue. *The essence of metaphor is understanding and experiencing one kind of thing in terms of another.* It is not that arguments are a subspecies of war. Arguments and wars are different kinds of things—verbal discourse and armed conflict—and the actions performed are different kinds of actions. But ARGUMENT is partially structured, understood, performed, and talked about in terms of WAR. The concept is metaphorically structured, the activity is metaphorically structured, and, consequently, the language is metaphorically structured.

Moreover, this is the *ordinary* way of having an argument and talking about one. The normal way for us to talk about attacking a position is to use the words "attack a position." Our conventional ways of talking about arguments presuppose a metaphor we are hardly ever conscious of. The metaphor is not merely in the words we use—it is in our very concept of an argument. The language of argument is not poetic, fanciful, or rhetorical; it is literal. We talk about arguments that way because we conceive of them that way—and we act according to the way we conceive of things.

The most important claim we have made so far is that metaphor is not just a matter of language, that is, of mere words. We shall argue that, on the contrary, human *thought processes* are largely metaphorical. This is what we mean when we say that the human conceptual system is metaphorically structured and defined. Metaphors as linguistic expressions are possible precisely because there are metaphors in a person's conceptual system. Therefore, whenever in this book we speak of metaphors, such as ARGUMENT IS WAR, it should be understood that *metaphor* means *metaphorical concept* . . .

. . . [The] metaphor [ARGUMENT IS WAR] allows us to conceptualize what a rational argument is in terms of something that we understand more readily, namely, physical conflict. Fighting is found everywhere in the animal kingdom and nowhere so much as among human animals. Animals fight to get what they want—food, sex, territory, control, etc.—because there are other animals who want the same thing or who want to stop them from getting it. The same is true of human animals, except that we have developed more sophisticated techniques for getting our way. Being "rational animals," we have institutionalized our fighting in a number of ways, one of them being war. Even though we have over the ages institutionalized physical conflict and have employed many of our finest minds to develop more effective means of carrying it out, its basic structure remains essentially unchanged. In fights between two brute animals, scientists have observed the practices of issuing challenges for the sake of intimidation, of establishing and defending territory, attacking, defending, counterattacking, retreating, and surrendering. Human fighting involves the same practices.

Part of being a rational animal, however, involves getting what you want without subjecting yourself to the dangers of actual physical conflict. As a result, we humans have evolved the social institution of verbal argument. We have arguments all the time in order to try to get what we want, and sometimes these "degenerate" into physical violence. Such verbal battles are comprehended in much the same terms as physical battles. Take a domestic quarrel, for instance. Husband and wife are both trying to get what each of them wants, such as getting the other to accept a certain viewpoint on some issue or at least to act according to that viewpoint. Each sees himself as having something to win and something to lose, territory to establish and territory to defend. In a no-holds-barred argument, you attack, defend, counterattack, etc., using whatever verbal means you have at your disposal—intimidation, threat, invoking authority, insult, belittling, challenging authority, evading issues, bargaining, flattering, and even trying to give "rational reasons." But all of these tactics can be, and often are, presented as *reasons;* for example:

. . . because I'm bigger than you. *(intimidation)*
. . . because if you don't, I'll . . . *(threat)*
. . . because I'm the boss. *(authority)*
. . . because you're stupid. *(insult)*
. . . because you usually do it wrong. *(belittling)*
. . . because I have as much right as you do. *(challenging authority)*
. . . because I love you. *(evading the issue)*
. . . because if you will . . . , I'll . . . *(bargaining)*
. . . because you're so much better at it. *(flattery)*

Arguments that use tactics like these are the most common in our culture, and because they are so much a part of our daily lives, we sometimes don't notice them. However, there are important and powerful segments of our culture where such tactics are, at least in principle, frowned upon because they are considered to be "irrational" and "unfair." The academic world, the legal world, the diplomatic world, the ecclesiastical world, and the world of journalism claim to present an ideal, or "higher," form of RATIONAL ARGUMENT, in which all of these tactics are forbidden. The only permissible tactics in this RATIONAL ARGUMENT are supposedly the stating of premises, the citing of supporting evidence, and the drawing of logical conclusions. But even in the most ideal cases, where all of these conditions hold, RATIONAL ARGUMENT is still comprehended and carried out in terms of WAR. There is still a position to be established and defended, you can win or lose, you have an opponent whose position you attack and try to destroy and whose argument you try to shoot down. If you are completely successful, you can wipe him out.

The point here is that not only our conception of an argument but the way we carry it out is grounded in our knowledge and experience of physical combat. Even if you have never fought a fistfight in your life, much less a war, but have been arguing from the time you began to talk, you still conceive of arguments, and execute them, according to the ARGUMENT IS WAR metaphor because the metaphor is built into the conceptual system of the culture in which you live. Not only are all the "rational" arguments that are assumed to actually live up to the ideal of RATIONAL ARGUMENT conceived of in terms of WAR, but almost all of them contain, in hidden form, the "irrational" and "unfair" tactics that rational arguments in their ideal form are supposed to transcend. Here are some typical examples:

It is plausible to assume that . . . *(intimidation)*
Clearly, . . .
Obviously, . . .

It would be unscientific to fail to . . . *(threat)*
To say that would be to commit the Fallacy of . . .

As Descartes showed, . . . *(authority)*
Hume observed that . . .
Footnote 374: cf. Verschlugenheimer, 1954.

The work lacks the necessary rigor for . . . *(insult)*
Let us call such a theory "Narrow" Rationalism.
In a display of "scholarly objectivity," . . .

The work will not lead to a formalized theory. *(belittling)*
His results cannot be quantified.
Few people today seriously hold that view.

Lest we succumb to the error of positivist approaches, . . . *(challenging authority)*
Behaviorism has led to . . .

He does not present any alternative theory. *(evading the issue)*
But that is a matter of . . .
The author does present some challenging facts, although . . .

Your position is right as far as it goes, . . . *(bargaining)*
If one takes a realist point of view, one can accept the claim that . . .

In his stimulating paper, . . . *(flattery)*
His paper raises some interesting issues.

Examples like these allow us to trace the lineage of our rational argument back through "irrational" argument (= *everyday arguing*) to its origins in physical combat. The tactics of intimidation, threat, appeal to authority, etc., though couched, perhaps, in more refined phrases, are just as present in rational argument as they are in everyday arguing and in war. Whether we are in a scientific, academic, or legal setting, aspiring to the ideal of rational argument, or whether we are just trying to get our way in our own household by haggling, the way we conceive of, carry out, and describe our arguments is grounded in the ARGUMENT IS WAR metaphor.

QUESTIONS FOR A CRITICAL REREADING

After you have read and annotated the essay, use the following questions to begin your critical rereading of the argument. (Don't forget to enter your answers in your reading notebook.)

1. The subject Lakoff and Johnson have chosen to examine is the metaphor. However, at the beginning of their essay they offer two different definitions for it. What is the definition they assume we already use? How do they extend that definition to expose how the subject is important?

2. Paragraphs 1–4 appear to introduce the general question Lakoff and Johnson are seeking to answer. Can you paraphrase what that question is? Why do they think it is important?

3. In the selections printed here, Lakoff and Johnson examine the metaphor "Argument is War" and arrive at the following claim: "Whether we are in a scientific,

academic, or legal setting, aspiring to the ideal of rational argument, or whether we are just trying to get our way in our own household by haggling, the way we conceive of, carry out, and describe our arguments is grounded in the ARGUMENT IS WAR metaphor." What does this mean? What do the authors imply about how this metaphor affects how we argue?

4. The authors suggest that we consider a culture where argument is viewed as a dance rather than as a battle. What would that society be like? Would Lakoff and Johnson think that our culture should start doing this?

5. Formulate a thesis for this excerpt, referring back to the general question you formulated in answer to question 1. As you did with the Perry essay, try to develop a "because" clause that isolates the primary reason Lakoff and Johnson use to justify this thesis.

POSSIBLE ISSUES FOR WRITING

Following are a few of the questions that you might find at issue in Lakoff and Johnson's argument. Discuss these with your classmates to see whether your interpretation differs from theirs. Again, listen closely for the difference in the answers your classmates give and keep a record in your notebook of what appears to be at issue. As before, these notes will help you discover and develop the essay you will write for this chapter.

1. Assuming that you have not thought much about metaphors before, do Lakoff and Johnson convince you that it is important to be aware of them? Why or why not?

2. Can you think of any other metaphors that might be a better way to shape what we do when we argue? What are they and why are they better?

3. Following are some of the other metaphors Lakoff and Johnson discuss in their book. What do these metaphor concepts appear to imply about our society?

Time Is Money

You're *wasting* my time.
This gadget will *save* you hours.
I don't *have* the time to *give* you.
How do you *spend* your time these days?
That flat tire *cost* me an hour.
I've *invested* a lot of time in her.
I don't *have enough* time to *spare* for that.
You're *running out* of time.
You need to *budget* your time.
Is that *worth your while?*

Ideas Are Fashions

That idea went *out of style* years ago.
I hear sociobiology *is in* these days.
Marxism is currently *fashionable* in western Europe.
That idea is *old hat!*
That's an *outdated* idea.
What are the new *trends* in English criticism?
Old-fashioned notions have no place in today's society.

Berkeley is a center of *avant-garde* thought.
Semiotics has become quite *chic*.

Love Is War

He is known for his many *conquests*.
She *fought* for him, but his mistress *won out*.
He *fled from* her *advances*.
He *won* her hand in marriage.
She is *beseiged* by suitors.
He has to *fend* them *off*.
He *enlisted the aid* of her friends.
He *made an ally* of her mother.
This is a *misalliance* if I've ever seen one.

Sexism in English:
A 1990s Update

Alleen Pace Nilsen (1936–   )

At present, Alleen Pace Nilsen is a Professor of English and Assistant Vice President for Academic Affairs at Arizona State University. As her essay reveals, though, it is her experience abroad that has led her to explore the relationship between cultural attitudes and language. As a linguist, Nilsen explores her subject by collecting, analyzing, and evaluating examples of current language usage. An earlier version of this essay appeared in 1972 as "Sexism in English: A Feminist View." At that time, Nilsen stated that her aim was to show "how really deep-seated sexism is in our communication system." Her purpose, in part, was to expose how we unconsciously perpetuate sexism in our culture with the language we use. Her revised version is a little different. Although she uses many of the same examples, she has tailored her argument to speak to the present. As you read the following essay, see if you can recognize how her purpose has changed.

Twenty years ago I embarked on a study of the sexism inherent in American English. I had just returned to Ann Arbor, Michigan, after living for two years (1967–1969) in Kabul, Afghanistan, where I had begun to look critically at the role society assigned to women. The Afghan version of the *chaderi* prescribed for Moslem women was particularly confining. Few women attended the American-built Kabul University where my husband was teaching linguistics because there were no women's dormitories, which meant that the only females who could attend were those whose families happened to live in the capital city. Afghan jokes and folklore were blatantly sexist; for example, this proverb: "If you see an old man, sit down and take a lesson; if you see an old woman, throw a stone."

But it wasn't only the native culture that made me question women's roles; it was also the American community. Nearly 600 Americans lived in Kabul, mostly supported by U. S. taxpayers. The single women were career secretaries, school teachers, or nurses. The three women who had jobs comparable to the American men's jobs were textbook editors with the assignment of developing reading books in Dari (Afghan Persian) for young children. They worked at the Ministry of Education, a large building in the center of the city. There were no women's restrooms so during their two-year assignment whenever they needed to go to the bathroom they had to walk across the street and down the block to the Kabul Hotel.

The rest of the American women were like myself—wives and mothers whose husbands were either career diplomats, employees of USAID, or college professors teaching at Kabul University. These were the women who were most influential in changing my way of thinking because we were suddenly bereft of our traditional roles. Servants worked for $1.00 a day and our lives revolved around supervising these men (women were not allowed to work for foreigners). One woman's husband grew so tired of hearing her stories that he scheduled an hour a week for listening to complaints. The rest of the time he wanted to keep his mind clear to focus on working with his Afghan counterparts and with the president of the University and the Minister of Education. He was going to make a difference in this country, while in the great eternal scheme of things it mattered little that the servant stole the batteries out of the flashlight or put chili powder instead of paprika on the eggs.

I continued to ponder this dramatic contrast between men's and women's work, and when we finished our contract and returned in the fall of 1969 to the University of Michigan in Ann Arbor I was surprised to find that many other women were also questioning the expectations that they had grown up with. I attended a campus women's conference, but I returned home more troubled than ever. Now that I knew housework was worth only a dollar a day, I couldn't take it seriously, but I wasn't angry in the same way these women were. Their militancy frightened me. I wasn't ready for a revolution, so I decided I would have my own feminist movement. I would study the English language and see what it could tell me about sexism. I started reading a desk dictionary and making notecards on every entry that seemed to tell something about male and female. I soon had a dog-eared dictionary, along with a collection of notecards filling two shoe boxes.

Ironically, I started reading the dictionary because I wanted to avoid getting involved in social issues, but what happened was that my notecards brought me right back to looking at society. Language and society are as intertwined as a chicken and an egg. ~~The language that a culture uses is telltale evidence of the values and beliefs of that cult~~ure. And because there is a lag in how fast a language changes—new words can easily be introduced, but it takes a long time for old words and usages to disappear—a careful look at English will reveal the attitudes that our ancestors held and that we as a culture are therefore predisposed to hold. My notecards revealed three main points. Friends have offered the opinion that I didn't need to read the dictionary to learn such obvious facts. Nevertheless, it was interesting to have linguistic evidence of sociological observations.

WOMEN ARE SEXY; MEN ARE SUCCESSFUL

First, in American culture a woman is valued for the attractiveness and sexiness of her body, while a man is valued for his physical strength and accomplishments. A woman is sexy. A man is successful.

A persuasive piece of evidence supporting this view are the eponyms—words that have come from someone's name—found in English. I had a two-and-a-half-inch stack of cards taken from men's names, but less than a half-inch stack from women's names, and most of those came from Greek mythology. In the words that came into American English since we separated from Britain, there are many eponyms based on the names of famous American men: bartlett pear, boysenberry, diesel engine, franklin stove, ferris wheel, gatling gun, mason jar, sideburns, sousaphone, schick test, and winchester rifle. The only common eponyms taken from American women's names are *Alice blue* (after Alice Roosevelt Longworth), bloomers (after Amelia Jenks Bloomer) and *Mae West jacket* (after the buxom actress). Two out of the three feminine eponyms relate closely to a woman's physical anatomy, while the masculine eponyms (except for *sideburns* after General Burnsides) have nothing to do with the namesake's body, but instead honor the man for an accomplishment of some kind.

Although in Greek mythology women played a bigger role than they did in the biblical stories of the Judeo-Christian cultures and so the names of goddesses are accepted parts of the language in such place names as Pomona from the goddess of fruit and Athens from Athena, and in such common words as *cereal* from Ceres, *psychology* from Psyche, and *arachnoid* from Arachne, the same tendency to think of women in relation to sexuality is seen in the eponyms *aphrodisiac* from Aphrodite, the Greek name for the goddess of love and beauty, and *venereal disease,* from Venus, the Roman name for Aphrodite.

Another interesting word from Greek mythology is *Amazon.* According to Greek folk etymology, the *a* means "without" as in *atypical* or *amoral* while *mazon* comes from *mazos* meaning *breast* as still seen in *mastectomy.* In the Greek legend, Amazon women cut off their right breasts so that they could better shoot their bows. Apparently, the storytellers had a feeling that for women to play the active "masculine" role that the Amazons adopted for themselves, they had to trade in part of their femininity.

This preoccupation with women's breasts is not limited to ancient stories. As a volunteer for the University of Wisconsin's *Dictionary of American Regional English (DARE),* I read a western trapper's diary from the 1830s. I was to make notes of any unusual usages or language patterns. My most interesting finding was that he referred to a range of mountains as *The Teats,* a metaphor based on the similarity between the shapes of the mountains and women's breasts. Because today we use the French wording, *The Grand Tetons,* the metaphor isn't as obvious, but I wrote to mapmakers and found the following listings: *Nippletop* and *Little Nipple Top* near Mt. Marcy in the Adirondacks; *Nipple Mountain* in Archuleta County, Colorado; *Nipple Peak* in Coke County, Texas; *Nipple Butte* in Pennington, South Dakota; *Squaw Peak* in Placer County, California (and many other locations); *Maiden's Peak* and *Squaw Tit* (they're the same mountain) in the Cascade Range in Oregon; *Mary's Nipple* near Salt Lake City, Utah; and *Jane Russell Peaks* near Stark, New Hampshire.

Except for the movie star Jane Russell, the women being referred to are anonymous—it's only a sexual part of their body that is mentioned. When topographical features are named after men, it's probably not going to be to draw attention to a sexual part of their bodies but instead to honor individuals for an accomplishment. For example, no one thinks of a part of the male body when hearing a reference to Pike's Peak, Colorado, or Jackson Hole, Wyoming.

Going back to what I learned from my dictionary cards, I was surprised to realize how many pairs of words we have in which the feminine word has acquired sexual connotations while the masculine word retains a serious businesslike aura. For example, a *callboy* is the person who calls actors when it is time for them to go on stage, but a *callgirl* is a prostitute. Compare *sir* and *madam. Sir* is a term of respect while *madam* has acquired the specialized meaning of a brothel manager. Something similar has happened to *master* and *mistress.* Would you rather have a painting by *an old master* or *an old mistress?*

It's because the word *woman* had sexual connotations as in "She's his woman," that people began avoiding its use, hence such terminology as *ladies room, lady of the house,* and *girls' school* or *school for young ladies.* Feminists, who ask that people use the term *woman* rather than *girl* or *lady,* are rejecting the idea that *woman* is primarily a sexual term. They have been at least partially successful in that today *woman* is commonly used to communicate gender without intending implications about sexuality.

I found 200 pairs of words with masculine and feminine forms, for example, *heir/heiress, hero/heroine, steward/stewardess, usher/usherette,* etc. In nearly all such pairs, the masculine word is considered the base with some kind of a feminine suffix being added. The masculine form is the one from which compounds are made; for example, from *king/queen* comes *kingdom* but not *queendom,* from *sportsman/sportslady* comes *sportsmanship* but not *sports/ladyship.* There is one—and only one—semantic area in which the masculine word is not the base or more powerful word. This is in the area dealing with sex and marriage. When someone refers to a *virgin,* a listener will probably think of a female unless the speaker specifies *male* or uses a masculine pronoun. The same is true for *prostitute.*

In relation to marriage, there is much linguistic evidence showing that weddings are more important to women than to men. A woman cherishes the wedding and is considered a bride for a whole year, but a man is referred to as a groom only on the day of the wedding. The word *bride* appears in *bridal attendant, bridal gown, bridesmaid, bridal shower,* and even *bridegroom. Groom* comes from the Middle English *grom,* meaning "man," and in this sense is seldom used outside of a wedding. With most pairs of male/female words, people habitually put the masculine word first, *Mr. and Mrs., his and hers, boys and girls, men and women, kings and queens,* brothers and sisters, *guys and dolls,* and *host and hostess,* but it is the *bride and groom* who are talked about, not the *groom and bride.*

The importance of marriage to a woman is also shown by the fact that when a marriage ends in death, the woman gets the title of *widow.* A man gets the derived title of *widower.* This term is not used in other phrases or contexts, but *widow* is seen in *widowhood, widow's peak,* and *widow's walk.* A *widow* in a card game is an extra hand of cards, while in typesetting it is an extra line of type.

How changing cultural ideas bring changes to language is clearly visible in this semantic area. The feminist movement has caused the differences between the sexes to be downplayed, and since I did my dictionary study two decades ago the word *singles* has largely replaced such sex specific and value-laden terms as *bachelor, old maid, spinster, divorcee, widow,* and *widower.*

And in 1970, I wrote that when a man is called *a professional* he is thought to be a doctor or a lawyer, but when people hear a woman referred to as *a professional* they are likely to think of a prostitute. That's not as true today because so many women have become doctors and lawyers that it's no longer incongruous to think of women in those professional roles.

Another change that has taken place is in wedding announcements. They used to be sent out from the bride's parents and did not even give the name of the groom's parents. Today, most couples choose to list either all or none of the parents' names. Also, it is now much more likely that both the bride and groom's picture will be in the newspaper, while a decade ago only the bride's picture was published on the "Women's" or the "Society" page. Even the traditional wording of the wedding ceremony is being changed. Many officials now pronounce the couple "husband and wife" instead of the old "man and wife," and they ask the bride if she promises "to love, honor, and cherish," instead of "to love, honor, and obey."

WOMEN ARE PASSIVE; MEN ARE ACTIVE

The wording of the wedding ceremony also relates to the second point that my cards showed, which is that women are expected to play a passive or weak role while men play an active or strong role. In the traditional ceremony, the official asks "Who gives the bride away?" and the father answers "I do." Some fathers answer "Her mother and I do," but that doesn't solve the problem inherent in the question. The idea that a bride is something to be handed over from one man to another bothers people because it goes back to the days when a man's servants, his children, and his wife were all considered to be his property. They were known by his name because they belonged to him and he was responsible for their actions and their debts.

The grammar used in talking or writing about weddings as well as other sexual relationships shows the expectation of men playing the active role. Men *wed* women while women *become* brides of men. A man *possesses* a woman; he *deflowers* her; he *performs;* he *scores;* he *takes away* her virginity. Although a woman can *seduce* a man, she cannot offer him her virginity. When talking about virginity, the only way to make the woman the actor in the sentence is to say that "She lost her virginity," but people lose things by accident rather than by purposeful actions and so she's only the grammatical, not the real-life, actor.

The reason that women tried to bring the term *Ms.* into the language to replace *Miss* and *Mrs.* relates to this point. Married women resented being identified only under their husband's names. For example, when Susan Glascoe did something newsworthy she would be identified in the newspaper only as Mrs. John Glascoe. The dictionary cards showed what appeared to be an attitude on the part of editors that it was almost indecent to let a respectable woman's name march unaccompanied across the pages of a dictionary. Women were listed with male names whether or not the male contributed to the woman's reason for being in the dictionary or in his own right was as famous as the woman. For example, Charlotte Brontë was identified as Mrs.

Arthur B. Nicholls, Amelia Earhart as Mrs. George Palmer Putnam, Helen Hayes as Mrs. Charles MacArthur, Jenny Lind as Mme. Otto Goldschmit, Cornelia Otis Skinner as the daughter of Otis, Harriet Beecher Stowe as the sister of Henry Ward Beecher, and Edith Sitwell as the sister of Osbert and Sacheverell. A very small number of women got into the dictionary without the benefit of a masculine escort. They were rebels and crusaders: temperance leaders Frances Elizabeth Caroline Willard and Carry Nation, women's rights leaders Carrie Chapman Catt and Elizabeth Cady Stanton, birth control educator Margaret Sanger, religious leader Mary Baker Eddy, and slaves Harriet Tubman and Phillis Wheatley.

Etiquette books used to teach that if a woman had *Mrs.* in front of her name, then the husband's name should follow because *Mrs.* is an abbreviated form of *Mistress* and a woman couldn't be a mistress of herself. As with many arguments about "correct" language usage, this isn't very logical because *Miss* is also an abbreviation of *Mistress.* Feminists hoped to simplify matters by introducing *Ms.* as an alternative to both *Mrs.* and *Ms.,* but what happened is that *Ms.* largely replaced *Miss* to became a catchall business title for women. Many married women still prefer the title *Mrs.,* and some resent being addressed with the term *Ms.* As one frustrated newspaper reporter complained, "Before I can write about a woman, I have to know not only her marital status but also her political philosophy." The result of such complications may contribute to the demise of titles which are already being ignored by many computer programmers who find it more efficient to simply use names, for example, in a business letter, "Dear Joan Garcia," instead of "Dear Mrs. Joan Garcia," "Dear Ms. Garcia," or "Dear Mrs. Louis Garcia."

The titles given to royalty provide an example of how males can be disadvantaged by the assumption that they are always to play the more powerful role. In British royalty, when a male holds a title, his wife is automatically given the feminine equivalent. But the reverse is not true. For example, a *count* is a high political officer with a *countess* being his wife. The same is true for a *duke* and a *duchess* and a *king* and a *queen.* But when a female holds the royal title, the man she marries does not automatically acquire the matching title. For example, Queen Elizabeth's husband has the title of *prince* rather than *king,* but if Prince Charles should become king while he is still married to Lady or Princess Diana, she will be known as the queen. The reasoning appears to be that since masculine words are stronger, they are reserved for true heirs and withheld from males coming into the royal family by marriage. If Prince Phillip were called *King Phillip,* it would be much easier for British subjects to forget where the true power lies.

The names that people give their children show the hopes and dreams they have for them, and when we look at the differences between male and female names in a culture we can see the cumulative expectations of that culture. In our culture girls often have names taken from small, aesthetically pleasing items, for example, *Ruby, Jewel,* and *Pearl. Esther,* and *Stella* mean "star," *Ada* means "ornament," and *Vanessa* means "butterfly." Boys are more likely to be given names with meanings of power and strength; for example, *Neil* means "champion," *Martin* is from Mars, the God of War, *Raymond* means "wise protection," *Harold* means "chief of the army," *Ira* means "vigilant," *Rex* means "king," and *Richard* means "strong king."

We see similar differences in food metaphors. Food is a passive substance just sitting there waiting to be eaten. Many people have recognized this and so no longer feel comfortable describing women as "delectable morsels." However, when I was a teenager, it was considered a compliment to refer to a girl (we didn't call anyone a *woman* until she was middle-aged) as *a cute tomato, a peach, a dish, a cookie, honey, sugar,* or *sweetie-pie.* When being affectionate, women will occasionally call a man *honey* or *sweetie,* but, in general, food metaphors are used much less often with men than with women. If a man is called *a fruit,* his masculinity is being questioned. But it's perfectly acceptable to use a food metaphor if the food is heavier and more substantive than that used for women. For example, pinup pictures of women have long been known as *cheesecake,* but when Burt Reynolds posed for a nude centerfold the picture was immediately dubbed *beefcake,* that is, *a hunk of meat.* That such sexual references to men have come into the general language is another reflection of how society is beginning to lessen the differences between their attitudes toward men and women.

Something similar to the *fruit* metaphor happens with references to plants. We insult a man by calling him *a pansy,* but it wasn't considered particularly insulting to talk about a girl being a *wallflower,* a *clinging vine,* or a *shrinking violet,* or to give girls such names as *Ivy, Rose, Lily, Iris, Daisy, Camellia, Heather,* or *Flora.* A plant metaphor can be used with a man if the plant is big and strong, for example, Andrew Jackson's nickname of *Old Hickory.* Also, the phrases *blooming idiots* and *budding geniuses* can be used with either sex, but notice how they are based on the most active thing a plant can do, which is to bloom or bud.

Animal metaphors also illustrate the different expectations for males and females. Men are referred to as *studs, bucks,* and *wolves* while women are referred to with such metaphors as *kitten, bunny, beaver, bird, chick,* or *lamb.* In the 1950s, we said that boys went *tomcatting,* but today it's just *catting around* and both boys and girls do it. When the term *foxy,* meaning that someone was sexy, first became popular it was used only for girls, but now someone of either sex can be described as *a fox.* Some animal metaphors that are used predominantly with men have negative connotations based on the size and/or strength of the animals, for example, *beast, bullheaded, jackass, rat, loanshark,* and *vulture.* Negative metaphors used with women are based on smaller animals, for example, *social butterfly, mousy, catty,* and *vixen.* The feminine terms connote action, but not the same kind of large-scale action as with the masculine terms.

WOMEN ARE CONNECTED WITH NEGATIVE CONNOTATIONS, MEN WITH POSITIVE CONNOTATIONS

The final point that my notecards illustrated was how many positive connotations are associated with the concept of masculine, while there are either trivial or negative connotations connected with the corresponding feminine concept. An example from the animal metaphors makes a good illustration. The word *shrew* taken from the name of a small but especially vicious animal was defined in my dictionary as "an ill tempered scolding woman," but the word *shrewd* taken from the same root was defined as "marked by clever, discerning awareness" and was illustrated with the phrase "a shrewd businessman."

Early in life, children are conditioned to the superiority of the masculine role. As child psychologists point out, little girls have much more freedom to experiement with sex roles than do little boys. If a little girl acts like a *tomboy,* most parents have mixed feelings, being at least partially proud. But if their little boy acts like a *sissy* (derived from *sister*), they call a psychologist. It's perfectly acceptable for a little girl to sleep in the crib that was purchased for her brother, to wear his hand-me-down jeans and shirts, and to ride the bicycle that he has outgrown. But few parents would put a boy baby in a white and gold crib decorated with frills and lace, and virtually no parents would have their little boy wears his sister's hand-me-down dresses, nor would they have their son ride a girl's pink bicycle with a flower-bedecked basket. The proper names given to girls and boys show this same attitude. Girls can have "boy" names—*Chris, Craig, Jo, Kelly, Shawn, Teri, Toni,* and *Sam*—but it doesn't work the other way around. A couple of generations ago, *Beverley, Frances, Hazel, Marion,* and *Shirley* were common boys' names. As parents gave these names to more and more girls, they fell into disuse for males, and some older men who have these names prefer to go by their initials or by such abbreviated forms as *Haze* or *Shirl.*

When a little girl is told to *be a lady,* she is being told to sit with her knees together and to be quiet and dainty. But when a little boy is told to *be a man* he is being told to be noble, strong, and virtuous—to have all the qualities that the speaker looks on as desirable. The concept of manliness has such positive connotations that it used to be a compliment to call someone a *he-man,* to say that he was doubly a man. Today, many people are more ambivalent about this term and respond to it much as they do to the word *macho.* But calling someone a *manly man* or a *virile man* is nearly always meant as a compliment. *Virile* comes from the Indo-European *vir* meaning "man," which is also the basis of *virtuous.* Contrast the positive connotations of both *virile* and *virtuous* with the negative connotations of *hysterical.* The Greeks took this latter word from their name for *uterus* (as still seen in *hysterectomy*). They thought that women were the only ones who experienced uncontrolled emotional outbursts and so the condition must have something to do with a part of the body that only women have.

Differences between positive male connotations and negative female connotations can be seen in several pairs of words which differ denotatively only in the matter of sex. *Bachelor* as compared to *spinster* or *old maid* has such positive connotations that women try to adopt them by using the term *bachelor-girl* or *bachelorette. Old maid* is so negative that it's the basis for metaphors: pretentious and fussy old men are called *old maids* as are the leftover kernels of unpopped popcorn and the last card in a popular children's game.

Patron and *matron* (Middle English for *father* and *mother*) have such different levels of prestige that women try to borrow the more positive masculine connotations with the word *patroness,* literally "female father." Such a peculiar term came about because of the high prestige attached to *patron* in such phrases as *a patron of the arts* or *a patron saint. Matron* is more apt to be used in talking about a woman in charge of a jail or a public restroom.

When men are doing jobs that women often do, we apparently try to pay the men extra by giving them fancy titles; for example, a male cook is more likely to be called a *chef* while a male seamstress will get the title of *tailor.* The Armed Forces have a special problem in that they recruit under such slogans as "The Marine Corps builds men!" and "Join the Army! Become a Man." Once the recruits are enlisted, they find themselves doing much of the work that has been traditionally thought of as "women's work." The solution to getting the work done and not insulting anyone's masculinity was to change the titles as shown below:

waitress	orderly
nurse	medic or corpsman
secretary	clerk-typist
assistant	adjutant
dishwasher or kitchen helper	KP (kitchen police)

Compare *brave* and *squaw.* Early settlers in America truly admired Indian men and hence named them with a word that carried connotations of youth, vigor, and courage. But they used the Algonquin's name for "woman," and over the years it developed almost opposite connotations to those of *brave. Wizard* and *witch* contrast almost as much. The masculine *wizard* implies skill and wisdom combined with magic, while the feminine *witch* implies evil intentions combined with magic. Part of the unattractiveness of both *witch* and *squaw* is that they have been used so often to refer to old women, something with which our culture is particularly uncomfortable, just as the Afghans were. Imagine my surprise, when I ran across the phrases *grandfatherly advice* and *old wives' tales* and realized that the underlying implication is the same as the Afghan proverb about old men being worth listening to while old women talk only foolishness.

Other terms that show how negatively we view old women as compared to young women are *old nag* as compared to *filly, old crow* or *old bat* as compared to *bird,* and being *catty* as compared to being *kittenish.* There is no matching set of metaphors for men. The chicken metaphor tells the whole story of a woman's life. In her youth she is a *chick.* Then she marries and begins *feathering her nest.* Soon she begins feeling *cooped up,* so she goes to *hen parties* where she *cackles* with her friends. Then she has her *brood,* begins to *henpeck* her husband, and finally turns into *an old biddy.*

I embarked on my study of the dictionary not with the intention of prescribing language change but simply to see what the language would tell me about sexism. Nevertheless, I have been both surprised and pleased as I've watched the changes that have occurred over the past two decades. I'm one of those linguists who believes that new language customs will cause a new generation of speakers to grow up with different expectations. This is why I'm happy about people's efforts to use inclusive language, to say *he or she* or *they* when speaking about individuals whose names they do not know. I'm glad that leading publishers have developed guidelines to help writers use language that is fair to both sexes and I'm glad that most newspapers and magazines list women by their own names instead of only by their husbands' names and that educated and thoughtful people no longer begin their business letters with "Dear Sir" or "Gentlemen" but instead use a memo form or begin with such salutations as "Dear Colleagues," "Dear Reader," or "Dear Committee Members." I'm also glad that such words as *poetess, authoress, conductress,* and *aviatrix* now sound quaint and old fashioned and that *chairman* is giving way to *chair* or *head, mailman* to *mail carrier, clergyman* to *clergy,* and *stewardess* to *flight attendant.* I was also pleased when the National Oceanic and Atmospheric Administration bowed to feminist complaints and in the late seventies began to alternate men's and women's names for hurricanes. However, I wasn't so pleased to discover that the change did not immediately erase sexist thoughts from everyone's mind as shown by a headline about Hurricane David in a 1979 New York tabloid, "David Rapes Virgin Islands." More recently, a similar metaphor appeared in a headline in the *Arizona Republic* about Hurricane Charlie, "Charlie Quits Carolinas, Flirts with Virginia."

What these incidents show is that sexism is not something existing independently in American English or in the particular dictionary that I happened to read. Rather, it exists in people's minds. Language is like an x-ray in providing visible evidence of invisible thoughts. The best thing about people being interested in and discussing sexist language is that as they make conscious decisions about what pronouns they will use, what jokes they will tell or laugh at, how they will write their names, or how they will begin their letters, they are forced to think about the underlying issue of sexism. This is good because as a problem that begins in people's assumptions and expectations, it's a problem that will be solved only when a great many people have given it a great deal of thought.

QUESTIONS FOR A CRITICAL REREADING

After you have read the essay through once, use the following questions to begin your critical rereading of the argument. Continue to use your reading notebook to develop your responses.

1. At the beginning of her essay, Nilsen describes how she developed interest in the feminist movements of the late sixties. To explore the nature of sexism in our culture, why does she turn to the English dictionary?

2. Nilson concludes her introduction with the fifth paragraph. What question do you expect the rest of her essay to answer? Why does she think it is important?

3. What are the three main points Nilsen discusses? Why do you think she discusses them in the order she does?

4. Implicit in Nilsen's discussion is the question "Does culture shape language, or does language shape culture?" Or, more particularly, are we sexist because our language is, or is our language sexist because we are? Looking specifically at her discussion of the title *Ms.*, how do you think Nilsen would answer this question?

5. In her conclusion, Nilsen mentions that she is pleased in the changes she has observed in our language. Why is she pleased? What do you think is her real thesis? (*Hint:* Her last two sentences can be paraphrased to state her thesis and the primary reason she uses to justify it—"I am pleased that . . . because. . . .")

POSSIBLE ISSUES FOR WRITING

Following are a few of the questions that you and your classmates might find at issue in Nilsen's argument. Discuss these with your classmates to see how your response to the essay may differ from theirs. Remember to keep your notebook handy so you can keep notes about what your classmates think and jot down the new ideas you may want to contribute to the discussion. Be sure to listen carefully and test your ideas orally when you can; after this discussion, you will be asked to write an essay that presents your view on language.

1. The three main points Nilsen uses in the body of her essay are, by necessity, generalizations. Note the examples she uses to justify them. Can they be interpreted differently? How? Can you think of any examples that would prove one of her generalizations faulty? What are they? (Remember that there are some exceptions to any generalization, so your examples need to be compelling ones.)

2. Nilsen bases her argument on several unexamined claims:

   "The language that a culture uses is tell-tale evidence of the values and beliefs of that culture."

   ". . . new words can be easily introduced, but it takes a long time for old words and usages to disappear—a careful look at English will reveal the attitudes that our ancestors held and that we as a culture are therefore predisposed to hold."

   ". . . new language customs will cause a new generation of speakers to grow up with different expectations."

   Discuss whether Lakoff and Johnson would agree with each of these claims. Do you agree with them? Why or why not?

3. What might Nilsen say about Perry's choice of the words "cow" and "bull" to describe different types of writing (see p. 29–38)? Even if his choice of metaphors was not sexist intentionally, do you think he is being irresponsible in using such language? Why or why not? What effect might these metaphors have on our culture?

4. Our current guidelines for nonsexist language encourage writers to avoid using masculine terms to refer to indefinite persons. For example, it is no longer acceptable to say "One should always bring *his* book" or "A linguist always says what *he* believes." Our alternatives, however, are often clumsy: "A linguist always says what he or she (or 'he/she' or 's/he') believes." Sometimes we can avoid problems

by making the noun plural ("Linguists always say what they believe."), but not always. Some writers have even suggested new genderless pronouns (Marge Piercy has written a futuristic novel where "per"—short for "person"—is used throughout as a genderless pronoun). What do you think should be done?

WRITING YOUR ESSAY

Now that you have read and discussed different ways we can view language, you are prepared to write an essay that will justify your opinion of the subject to your classmates. You may choose to respond to one of the issues the class discussed or you may wish to argue that none of these issues is really very important. Whatever you choose to argue, though, you need to give good reasons why your classmates should respect your opinion. This means that you will have to review your notebook entries and discussion notes to discover both the reasons others have used to support their position *and* how they differ from those derived from your own reading and experience. To begin your essay, summarize what others have had to say, using their arguments to develop your own. Following is an example of one way you might organize your notes to help you do this. To finish drafting and revising your essay, refer to the discussion on drafting and revising in Chapter 1.

THE WORKING SENTENCE OUTLINE

You might already be familiar with standard outlines. They are a formal way of summarizing what your paper will look like. A thorough standard outline will attempt to detail the function of each paragraph in your essay in the following manner:

   I. Introductory paragraph
     A. Thesis
     B. Summary of the main points used to support the thesis
  II. Main point of the second body paragraph
     A. Supporting example #1
     B. Supporting example #2
 III. Main point of the third body paragraph
     A. Supporting example #1
     B. Supporting example #2
  IV. Main point of the fourth body paragraph
     A. Supporting example #1
     B. Supporting example #2
   V. Concluding paragraph
     A. Summary of the main points
     B. Thesis

This type of outline describes an essay that is almost impossible to write. If you were to write an essay around it, you would be forced to simplify—perhaps even misrepresent—the ideas you want to discuss. Although you might be able to use a standard outline to describe what a finished essay looks like, it probably won't do justice to what an essay *says.* Standard outlines represent the form rather than the content of an argument.

On the other hand, working sentence outlines are often messy. Although, like standard outlines, they detail the introduction, body, and conclusion of your essay, they define those divisions not by how many paragraphs are devoted to each section but by the ideas they contain, and they express these ideas in complete sentences. Working outlines are also subject to much revision. As you draft your essay, you may think of new ideas, and new connections between old ideas, that will alter the organization—and the outline—of your paper. A good way of thinking about working outlines is to consider them "trial runs" of the paper you will write. They enable you to see where the ideas of others might take you, if you were to reason about them in a certain way.

Consider the following example, the working sentence outline a student named Steven used to fuel his "trial run" with ideas from a class discussion on Perry's use of metaphors:

Steven's Working Sentence Outline

INTRODUCTION

(Question we are discussing)

1. We are talking about Perry's use of "bull" and "cow" to discuss types of academic writing.

2. Some people believe these metaphors are sexist, that Perry's use of "cow" to describe an inferior type of writing implies that he believes women are not independent thinkers.

(Introducing working thesis)

BODY

(Testing thesis-answer)

3. I think that Perry probably did not mean that, that somehow the metaphor conveys more than he intended.
(Could I consider here different, asexual metaphors? "Rock" and "clay" for "cow" and "bull"?)

CONCLUSION
(My new answer   after   test?)

4. Hence, Perry's metaphors are not intentionally sexist because nonsexist metaphors can be used to express the same ideas (?).

This working outline helped Steven sift through the notes in his reading notebook. He first asked himself what question most of his notes addressed, what specific issue both he and his classmates were attempting to resolve (1). He then summarized how some of his classmates felt about this issue (2). In response to what his classmates think, Steven then posed a general statement of his position, his working thesis, and discovered possible ways to test and prove it (3). (Note how the outline identifies this part of his argument as the "body" of his essay—the ideas that will require the most discussion when he writes out his argument.) Finally, Steven arrived at a clearer statement of what his thesis-answer was (4). It is still a working thesis—a hypothesis—at this stage, but it gives him a better idea of what he will have to test when he drafts his essay around this outline.

This student's working outline has helped him make sense out of his notes and arrive at a possible thesis. It also has given him a tentative structure to the essay he will write. Essays are not merely statements of what you believe. They are representations of a conversation you are having with your reader. To communicate your different perspective on an issue, you need to take your reader on a mental journey that begins from his or her point of view and ends with yours:

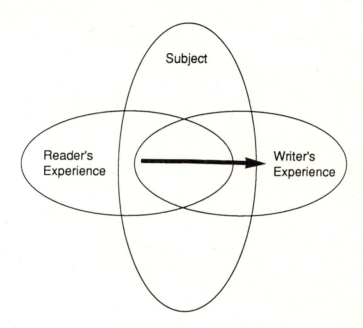

The mental journey mapped out above illustrates how you can structure your essay to lead your readers from their perspective on the subject to yours. This requires that you not only use your readers' perspective as a point of departure, but that you identify what parts of your past experience have led you to a new point of view so you can help your readers see the path of reasoning you used to arrive at your conclusion. Again, you support your point of view not because you think it is more correct than your readers' but because it is different and worth considering.

Working outlines can help you sift through your notes, develop a tentative argument and thesis from others' ideas, and discover what is and isn't important for the argument you want to make. They also can help you write. They give you the signposts that can help you decide when to discuss each of your points. After you draft your essay, you might wish to refer to Chapter 1 for help in revising and editing it. Most importantly, when you have finished revising and editing your essay, and before you turn it in, let someone read it.

Unit Two

CHAPTER THREE

Discovering Your Argument

*A*ll knowledge is a product of social interaction: you learn by listening to what others are saying, by making sense out of their interpretation of the facts, and by using their knowledge to develop your own informed perspective on the subject. Although you might feel sometimes that you have discovered your ideas on your own, they are always products of your past experience, conclusions you have drawn based on previous encounters. To communicate these ideas to others, you need to take your audience on a mental journey that traces the path you took to make sense out of the world around you. Your written arguments are maps that show your readers how to arrive at the same insights you have. This means that, to discover what your written argument should look like, you need to resurrect the social influences that shaped your thinking. In each academic course, as you read and listen to what others are saying, you are becoming acquainted with a social community that will help you discover the argument you will want to make in your writing.

As this course progresses, you will discover how the social community of each discipline helps shape what you discover and learn. The social community—the authors you read, the lecturers you hear, and the fellow students you talk with—is the audience your writing addresses. It is this informed audience that helps you discover and test what you need to learn because they are the ones who influence what you will say and how you will say it.

Writing is both a *process* of learning how to use written language to inquire about a subject and a *product* that reveals to your readers what you have discovered and learned. At both stages, you are writing to communicate. When you write, your primary motivation is to clarify for yourself what others know and how you have begun to make sense of and evaluate that knowledge. For example, when you explore ideas in your reading notebook, you argue with yourself, indulging in self-deliberation that alternately says "But that doesn't make any sense . . ." and "Perhaps that's why I want to say this. . . ." When you begin to shape your writing into a formal essay, you communicate to others how you have worked with their knowledge about the subject to make new knowledge. You make "new knowledge" whenever you clearly communicate a new way of understanding and evaluating the information your reader already has. The written product you are aiming for will present an argument that uses your audience's knowledge to develop and justify your thesis—the new knowledge that helps both you and your readers learn a little more about the subject.

To discover the best argument for your finished product, you need to view the writing process as moving through two stages that involve different audiences. The earlier stages of the writing process involve writer-based prose: you first write to yourself to externalize the self-deliberation process you are going through to make sense out of what you have learned. The latter stages of the writing process (and your final product) are reader-based prose: you write to informed readers to communicate and justify how you have made sense of the subject. To help you understand how this course leads you through the process of moving from a writer-based to a reader-based argument, here are examples of how one student first used her reading notebook to discover the argument she wished to make and then reshaped that argument to present it persuasively to her readers:

Julia's Notebook Entry

R. J. Smith's essay presents us with a lot of figures. He gives us lists of college test scores and results of a poll taken on how much television college students watch. These figures appear to indicate that college tests scores have declined since 1963 and that students are spending more time watching T.V. than doing homework. Smith's thesis appears to be that students are watching too much television today, that if they spent more time doing homework or just reading for pleasure, their test scores would be better. He has some good facts to support his argument, statistics from respectable authorities. I wonder, though, if his is the only way to interpret them?

For example, maybe the tests have gotten harder—or just less effective. Wouldn't that have little to do with whether students watch T.V. too much? Except, I guess, spending time watching T.V. would have some impact—even if the tests were harder, students would probably do better if they watched less T.V. Or would they? Not all T.V. is bad. There are many good educational shows these days, and the popularity of talk shows indicates that we are not looking for mere entertainment but ways to explore current issues. Shouldn't that count for something? Current issues are more relevant to our education than some homework assignments. Can he prove homework assignments—or reading for pleasure—are keys to success in these same tests?

It seems I have two issues here: Is the decline in scores caused by too much T.V. or by the increasing unreliability of the tests? I certainly could not answer the second one; there are few statistics to work with. Using Smith's own sets of statistics, though, I could probably address the first issue. He seems to make this an either/or issue: homework or T.V. But don't other factors come into it? What other aspects of students' lives have changed? I would think overcrowding and crime in the schools would count for something—as would the increasing number of students who must work part-time to earn money for college. (Would I need stats for that? Probably not, most would agree there has been a substantial rise in college costs making part-time work necessary.) Now I see why Smith's essay bothered me! I need to write an argument to those readers who support Smith's view, to convince them that we need more evidence before we make television the scapegoat of student illiteracy!

Julia's Final Essay

Just Say "No" to Television?

R. J. Smith's "Are We Breeding a Nation of Illiterates?" offers us shocking statistics about the decline in student test scores. He exposes a very urgent problem: How can we improve student performance on these tests? Assuming that these tests have some validity in assessing student intellectual development, we need to explore how students' study habits have changed in the last two decades.

Certainly the rise in the number of hours students spend watching television (which Smith so carefully documents) would have some impact on student study habits. However, how much impact does television have, and is its influence necessarily detrimental? We need more information about the types of shows students watch, and a more objective analysis that explores the good as well as the bad effects of television before we tell students to "just say 'no'" to television. Pulling the plug on our T.V. sets won't turn off other social influences that could be affecting the change in students' study habits. Could it be that Smith is just making television the scapegoat?

During the last two decades, society has changed dramatically, and certainly in ways that prevent us from developing good study habits. Unlike the young Lincoln, if we have no money, little formal education, and meager living quarters, we cannot devote ourselves to diligent and constant study by candlelight. The problems students face today cannot be ignored or merely thrown out with the T.V. set: day or night, they actively threaten a student's freedom to learn.

Unlike Lincoln, we cannot replace formal education with independent study. To succeed today, students need more than a high school degree. Even secretarial positions are looking for college graduates these days. Although more and more students are completing high school and going on to college, they might not be learning as much (as Smith's test scores reveal). The pressure to go to college is directly affected by the rapidly rising costs of higher education. More and more students find it necessary to hold part-time jobs while in high school to ensure they can afford college. Students may be watching more T.V., but that might be because they are too exhausted to study after putting in four hours of work after school each day!

Even for those students who do not work, there are other recent social changes that can affect their ability to develop good study habits. Many schools just cannot provide an environment that would produce good study habits; they are increasingly overcrowded, and this overcrowding means less discipline. Students are being forced to grow up faster, to solve social problems on their own. Many schools have seen an increase in teenage pregnancy, drug use, and gang pressure. Students cannot be expected to work on their study habits while they are fighting for their lives!

Just saying "no" to television won't help; students have to say "no" to drugs, sex, and peer pressure as well. But is this humanely possible? Perhaps the real source of our problems in the increase in student illiteracy is the educational system itself because, without more discipline and student support in the school environment, students will not be free from the social pressures that make developing the ability to read and write a low priority. Pulling the plug on our T.V. sets is easy to do, but will it solve or only compound the problem of student illiteracy?

In Julia's final essay, she has addressed her comments to those readers who are ready to accept and act on Smith's proposal to pull the plug. She acknowledges the worth of his statistics, and the urgency of the literacy problem they expose. Although she disagrees with Smith's solution, she clearly focuses on what is at issue both for him and for her readers—how to solve the problem of the decline in student test scores. By starting on this point of agreement about what is at issue, she leads her readers through an analysis of Smith's argument to show them that changing television habits is not the only—or even the best—solution.

Julia's formal essay is a good example of reader-based prose: she has clearly reasoned with her readers to lead them to question the validity of Smith's thesis. This argument, though, would have been substantially different if she had not gone through the exploratory writing of her reading notebook entry. The writer-based prose of her notebook entry helped her discover what was really at issue. Her initial response to Smith's essay was to say that "No! Television can be good! The tests are bad!" By testing this initial response, through self-deliberation that constantly questioned her evidence, she realized that the quality of television or the tests was not the real issue. What Smith and her readers cared about was how to solve the problem of illiteracy. By engaging in a writer-based argument before she attempted to communicate her perspective to her readers, Julia was able to discover more about her readers and what they cared about, while learning more about the issues involved. By identifying the rhetorical situation, she discovered her real audience— the social community that had stimulated her thinking and could shape her ideas into a worthwhile argument.

As Julia's essay demonstrates, written arguments are not little "wars" where we attempt to "win" by defeating the reasoning of an "enemy." Instead, they are peacemaking missions, social acts by which we work with readers who have different opinions so that we can find the best possible solution to problems we all care about. Cooperative argumentation is how we have furthered our knowledge in any field of study. The ongoing dialogue about the "missing links" in Darwin's theory has led to more sophisticated theories of the evolutionary process; ongoing arguments about the causes of World War II have led us to consider the dangerous power of mob psychology as much as the despotic leadership of Hitler.

Cooperative argumentation is quite different from the type of argument Julia might have written had she not first explored the issue in her reading notebook. Her initial, and quite emotional, response to Smith's essay exaggerated where she and her readers disagreed: "Not all T.V. is bad!" Constructing an essay around this thesis would have done little to correct the problem of illiteracy; an essay written around this thesis would merely rationalize her position by presenting interesting but probably not overwhelming examples of how television can be good for you. These examples would not have explained why college test scores have been declining, but they would have inspired her readers to think of all the ways television is bad and to argue *against* her. Writing before you have reflected on what your readers know and on what really disturbs you about it can only produce a defensive argument where you fight against the social community that should be helping you develop new ideas.

Defensive arguments are not always destructive; they are quite often what we see in courts of law when the issue is clearly evident ("Did this man kill his neighbor's dog out of spite or in self-defense?"). Lawyers are hired to argue one side or another, and the judge or jury is left to arbitrate the disagreement. However, there are no objective judges or juries to arbitrate academic arguments. We can arrive at the best argument only by working together, by constantly judging the worth of the arguments we want to make, and by acknowledging how our audience would pass judgment on our ideas. When you review the Supreme Court's decision on the Bakke case in the next chapter, keep in mind how carefully the writer must work with the opinions of his fellow justices to make an informed argument that helps all of them discover further how to resolve the issue.

EXERCISE

To practice using your audience to discover the argument you wish to make, try writing the different arguments that might be presented in small claims court when the following case is deliberated. Once you have written out the positions of the prosecutor and the defense attorney, then you be the judge, constructing an informed argument to resolve the case.

The Facts of "The Case of the Neighbor's Dog"

Mr. Mitchell discovered the body of his 4-year old dog, Ruff, on the front lawn of his home, June 17th at 3:30 P.M. An autopsy revealed that the dog had died from a common garden poison. Mr. Wilson, an avid gardener who had recently won several prizes for his hybrid roses, had recently switched to using the same poison on the flower bed in his front lawn. Mitchell claims Wilson switched poisons specifically with the intent to murder Mitchell's dog; Wilson claims he switched poisons to defend his garden from destruction, either from bugs or dogs. Mitchell's dog was licensed, and, although there was a city "leash-law" forbidding owners to let their dogs run freely, it had seldom been enforced. The question being deliberated is whether Mitchell's dog was poisoned by Wilson out of spite or justifiably out of self-defense. The judge for the case is a well-known cat lover.

We have discussed how the argument you will make in your written essays is shaped by the social community you are addressing, how your ideas are necessarily influenced by what your readers already know and how you can contribute to their knowledge. You can contribute meaningfully to this academic community only after you have come to terms with what your readers already know and care about.

To help make the most of your writing process, you need to be aware of what it is you are discovering as you move from the self-deliberation of your reading notebook to sharpen and revise your ideas into a reader-based argument. To do this, you need to read your notebook entries critically, to discover not only the academic community you are addressing but the specific rhetorical situation within that community that inspired your response. As we mentioned in Chapter One, there are five questions you should be able to answer if you are to accurately distinguish the rhetorical situation that will make your writing meaningful for your reader:

1. Who are you talking to?
2. Where and when does the conversation take place?
3. What are you discussing?
4. What does your audience think?
5. How does your perspective differ?

As you read your notebook entries and prepare to shape them into a formal argument, try to identify the answers to these five questions. They represent information essential for discovering and focussing the argument you are trying to make.

RECOGNIZING YOUR AUDIENCE

The answers to all of the questions involved in identifying the rhetorical situation hinge on your understanding of your audience. Your audience is not identified just by your relationship to them (whether they are your superiors or your friends) but by how much knowledge they have about the subject (whether they are specialists or nonspecialists), by their attitude toward the subject (how much they have invested in a certain interpretation), and by what questions they still seek answers to. Whether you wish to persuade someone to change an opinion or merely intend to report information to a nonspecialist, you will need to identify your audience and what they already know or believe. No matter what your main intention is, your essay will lead your readers through the mental journey that begins with what they know and concludes with your new perspective. Your relationship with your readers will differ depending on how much either of you knows about the subject.

Persuasive Writing

The essay you wrote for your classmates in Unit One probably represents writing that assumes your readers know as much about the subject as you do. As peers, you and your classmates were equally informed (or equally baffled) by the subject of language. To communicate with one another, you had to share opinions, and your essay became a means of persuading your peers that your opinion was at least as valid as theirs, that it could contribute in some way to their understanding of the subject. Your writing probably spent less time informing your readers, because you could assume they had access to the same information you had, and spent most of its time persuading your readers to accept your interpretation of that information. Writing that is primarily persuasive in this way is the kind produced by one "specialist" for another.

By arguing with the authors of the essays you read in Chapter 2 and with your classmates as you discussed those essays, you developed a common body of knowledge that you could share with your readers. You developed a specialized community that shares some attitudes about the subject and differs about others. The social community of your classroom is a mirror of the disciplinary community that shapes the making of knowledge in the different subjects you study. Each course you take will introduce you to the types of conversations different disciplinary communities have, and as you learn to enter into these conversations, you will learn how to make sense of these subjects as the specialists have.

When you write for readers who have as much as or more knowledge about the subject than you do, you will find yourself producing primarily persuasive essays.

Expository Writing

Your formal essays will not always be attempts to persuade a reader who has as much as or at least the same kind of knowledge about the subject as you have. Sometimes you have more authority to speak on a subject than your readers do. This changes your relationship with your audience: instead of speaking to them as colleagues, you must give them basic information before you argue for a particular interpretation of the subject.

When you write to inform your readers of something they do not already know, you are producing what many writers call expository writing. Expository writing exposes something new to the reader rather than offers a new perspective on the reader's prior knowledge. When you write to someone who has evaluated a subject in a way that you do not completely agree with, sometimes it is because he or she does not have access to the same information you have. For example, Julia, in the essay that began this chapter, discovered that when R. J. Smith drew conclusions about why college tests scores were declining, he either was not aware of or did not adequately acknowledge information about the present condition of America's schools. Although Julia could not claim she was more of an authority on educational statistics than Smith was, she was more of an authority on the type of academic environment that today's students confront at school and at home. To persuade readers of Smith's argument to consider her different evaluation of the issue, she had to expose them to information they had not previously considered—for example, information about the economic and peer pressures that affect how well students study.

Because Julia's audience was composed of students, she did not have to give that much information; she could assume a few concrete details would be sufficient to inform her readers of the knowledge she was basing her argument on. If she were writing directly to Smith, though, she would have had to expand the expository section of her essay. Because he has no first-hand experience of what it is like to be a student in today's schools, she would have had to include even more details to show the kind of pressures today's students face. Whether her essay would be primarily expository or persuasive depended on how much information she could assume her reader already had about the subject she was addressing.

EXERCISE

To understand how your audience determines whether your essay will be primarily expository or persuasive, turn to the judicial opinion you wrote for "The Case of the Neighbor's Dog" (see exercise on p. 67). Because that essay was written to the Court, that is, to an audience that already knew the facts of the case, the essay represents writing that is primarily persuasive. To understand how that essay might become primarily expository, rewrite it as if you were a newspaper reporter, an eyewitness of the court proceedings whose purpose is to inform the general public of the case and the argument the judge used to resolve it.

The more authority you have over your reader, the more expository your writing will be. However, even when your essay's primary purpose is to inform your readers of something they did not already know, your essay is still attempting to persuade your readers to accept a particular evaluation of that information. What you decide to inform your readers about depends not just on *what* they already know but also on *why* they need to know more. No matter how important the information is to you, it has no value to your readers unless you can persuade them that it affects what they already know and believe. For this reason, whenever you choose to develop an expository section in your essay, you need to remember to relate it clearly to what your readers already care about.

RECOGNIZING THE ISSUES

To identify what your audience cares about, you need to recognize the real issue behind their argument. As we have discussed earlier, the real issue is the point at which you and your readers are not in agreement, either because you disagree or because you have not yet agreed upon a satisfactory answer. When a teenage boy tells his parents "but I have to have a Porsche because everyone else does," he is avoiding what the parents will most likely see as the real issue: "It's not how you can be like everyone else, but what is best for you and the family." If he really wants the Porsche, he will have to prove that he and his family will profit from his having this very expensive car. Just as his parents do not want to hear an argument that avoids the real issue, your readers will not want to read an essay that argues an irrelevant point. The thesis of your essay will be worthwhile for your readers only if it clearly answers a question that is at issue for them.

Most often, you will identify what is at issue by listening critically to what others have to say, whether they say it in the articles you read or in the classroom.

You will need to be aware how the issue changes each time someone advances a new argument. For example, you might have identified the issue behind Nilsen's essay, "Sexism in English: A 1990s Update," as "how can we change language to reform our culture?" When you began to explore Nilsen's argument, first through self-deliberation and then with others in your class discussion, you might have seen different questions emerge. These questions often address points the author assumed we would agree with: "Do we need to reform our culture?" "Is culture really a product of our use of language?" "Is our language really that sexist?" "What do we mean by culture anyway?" If any of these questions are at issue for your classmate-readers, they would have to be answered before your readers would care to explore the issue you saw in Nilsen's essay.

The less you know about your readers, the more difficult it will be for you to identify exactly what might be at issue for them. When you are in doubt, the best way to begin discovering your argument is to explore how the knowledge you have in common with your readers shapes the questions we still need to ask to develop that knowledge further. For example, Freud's work on how the mother–son relationship affects an individual's psychological development would naturally lead us to questions about the effects of the father–daughter, mother–daughter, or father–son relationship. If you wrote on any of these issues, you would be clearly working with the knowledge of your readers to help improve both your and their understanding of Freud's theories.

Even if you do not have a thorough understanding of your reader, your understanding of the social community that your writing addresses will help you discover the issue you need to address. Besides working with the knowledge that you and your prospective readers have in common, you can also anticipate the kinds of questions specialists in different subjects might ask. Whenever you produce academic writing, you can assume that your audience is relatively well-informed, that they have a specialized knowledge they have acquired from the texts for the course, and that they have some interest in exploring that subject matter further. To help you produce written arguments that would appeal to a specialized audience, there are specific ways you can formulate the issues you might address to ensure that your writing will reflect the reasoning process a specialist audience would expect.

In Chapter 1, we briefly introduced you to the four types of arguments that can be found in academic writing. Often you can anticipate the kind of questions your readers might explore by identifying which of these types of arguments is most prevalent in the academic writing you have read in a particular course. For ease in reference, here are the four types again, identified by the general form of the questions they explore:

Policy:	What should be done?
Value:	Is it good or bad?
Consequence:	How did it come about?
	What will it produce?
Definition ("Fact"):	What is it?

Recognizing which type of argument a specific subject area requires can help you identify and formulate the issue you want your essay to address. To identify the type of argument being used (either in your reading or in the comments made during class discussion), you need to first write out the specific question being addressed and then analyze that question to discover which of the four arguments it reflects.

To help you recognize how a specific issue reflects the general issue behind one of the four types of arguments, following is an abbreviated dialogue among specialists from four different subject areas who are discussing the question, "What will we be like in the 21st century?" Note how these specialists use the knowledge of their subject to build different hypotheses, answers that do not necessarily disagree with one another but do reveal how the speakers have reinterpreted the question to fit the kind of argument they use in their field of expertise:

[*A political scientist*] "What will we be like? The spreading of democracy should produce individuals who are more socially responsible."

[*A scientist*] "I'm not sure we can predict. There is currently an environmental crisis—the depletion of the ozone layer, the pollution of our air and water, the unchecked epidemics of AIDS and cancer—who knows what type of organism the human being will become."

[*A psychologist*] "It's difficult to predict how societies will develop when each individual is psychologically unique. Currently, the demise of the nuclear family unit makes many of us more neurotic and less predictable."

[*A historian*] "We just need to look to the past. Although our environment might change, how we act as a society is constant and predictable."

[*A philosopher*] "What we do is not as important as what we think. Although our bodies, our environment, even our physiology might change, our fates will still be determined by an absolute Good, the eternal Truths we constantly seek."

To identify the issues behind the different responses, you need to formulate the answers into specific questions. For example, the political scientist's answer ("The rise of democratic governments should produce individuals who are more socially responsible.") answers the specific question, "What effect will future governments have on the behavior of the citizenry?" Although this issue reflects the consequence argument embodied in the general question "What will we be like in the 21st century?" it has been reformulated to accommodate the political scientist's need to establish effective governmental policies. Behind all political arguments is the general policy issue of "what should be done?" and here the political scientist is exploring the specialized issue, "Should we encourage the spreading of democracy?"

EXERCISE

Try to identify the real issue behind the other specialists' answers listed above. Your inquiry should take the following three steps:

1. Phrase the speaker's comment into a specific question.
2. Identify which of the four kinds of argument the speaker appears to be addressing.

> **3.** Reformulate the specific question identified in step 1 into a question that reflects the real issue the speaker wishes to address.

When you read and discuss the selected readings in this book, you need to continually ask yourself what questions the authors are attempting to answer and what kinds of arguments they use to reason about them. Often, your reading notebook will be the place where you discover what these real questions are and how you might formulate your own questions to develop the kind of argument that can contribute to the conversation in that discipline. When you discuss the selected readings in class, you will need to listen quite carefully to the real issues your classmates' comments address. By applying your understanding of the four kinds of arguments, you can discover how to phrase the issue you will want to explore in your writing and be better prepared to discover the argument you will advance to answer it.

DISCOVERING YOUR STANCE

Your stance is your position on the issue, and is most clearly expressed in a two-clause thesis that implies your answer and the main reason you use to support it ("This is right because . . ."). Once you have identified what is at issue for your audience and have formulated the real issue you want to explore in your paper, you will have a general sense of your stance—a potential thesis that contains the seeds of the idea that has prompted you to respond to this issue. Your real thesis, though, will emerge most clearly only when you use your writing to clarify how it differs from the arguments you have already heard.

From your experience of the various arguments you have read or listened to in class, you can anticipate the stances your readers might take on the issue you wish to address. For instance, if you wished to respond to the political scientist in the above discussion, you could anticipate that his or her stance on the specific issue ("Should we encourage the spreading of democracy?") would be: "The spreading of democracy should produce individuals who are more socially responsible because democracy gives everyone an equal voice in deciding how the people should be governed." Articulating the political scientist's thesis in this way could help you use your writing to explore what you wished to say in response. Here is one possible response to the political scientist's thesis:

> But does giving everyone an equal voice ensure that they will use it, and if they do, use it responsibly? The American voting system doesn't always encourage me to become socially responsible; often I feel as if my vote won't make a difference. It is always the powerful majority that makes the social policy in our system, and that majority often looks out for its own interests.

To discover your real thesis (where you stand on the issue of whether we should encourage the spreading of democracy), you will need to synthesize your newly discovered stance with that of a specific reader (here, the individual who believes democracy encourages social responsibility). Your first draft should explore the relationship between the two stances, help you discover if your point means you completely disagree with your specific reader or if you can accommodate his or her argument. Based on what you discovered above, you probably would decide at the end of your paper that we should encourage the spreading of democracy, but we should also explore ways to ensure that individuals use their voting power responsibly. The most important aspect of your real stance is that it reveals how you have contributed a valuable new perspective on the issue.

To ensure that your thesis represents a position that has something new to offer your readers, you need to direct your writing to those whose stance has prompted your desire to respond. As we discussed earlier, the audience for an academic essay is well-informed about the subject and is aware of the stances you are responding to. Once you identify the real issue you wish to respond to, you become aware of the specific readers you have in mind: they are not only well-informed about the issue but have a definite opinion about it. You will develop a clearer idea of what your stance and thesis should be as you recognize the most specific audience that can gain from what you have to say.

Although your essay will be read by a wider audience, the specific reader who holds a different stance from yours is the one whose argument can most help you discover what you want to say. Once you have discovered your thesis, you might still wish to revise your writing with that specific reader in mind; if you can persuade those most inclined to disagree with you, you can persuade almost anyone who reads your essay.

Following is a sequence of steps you can use to develop the argument of your draft so that it can help you discover your specific audience and thesis:

1. What is the real issue I am addressing?
2. What are the possible stances?
3. What position do I most disagree with?
4. Why do I disagree with it?
5. How can I formulate my position to show readers who hold the position I disagree with that my stance is valid?

You might wish to answer these questions in your reading notebook, when you are brainstorming ideas before you construct your draft, and/or as you are composing the first exploratory draft of your essay. All writers work differently, but this invention stage requires that you discover what you will write about by considering why you wish to write it and who needs to hear it.

As you participate in the conversations about political science that follow in Chapter 4, keep in mind that the audience for your essay (the authors of the readings as well as your classmates) will influence what you will write about. The issue you address and the stance you use to answer it can only be determined if you first discover what your reader's stance is and why you felt a need to respond to it. By first recognizing the social context and specific rhetorical situation that gave rise to your ideas, you can discover how your audience reasons about the subject and how you will be able to reason with them. Only then will you discover how to contribute meaningfully to the conversation.

CHAPTER FOUR

Reasoning About Political Science

*P*olitical science is one of a number of subjects that make up the social sciences; among the others are sociology, anthropology, religious studies, economics, education, psychology, linguistics, and women's studies. The social sciences focus their interest on the social nature of human behavior. Most specifically, they examine the cultural institutions that regulate how humans behave within a particular community. For example, economics studies the market system (i.e., how we earn and spend our money); anthropology observes cultural rituals (e.g., marriage ceremonies and funerals); and religious studies examines organized religions (i.e., how we worship). Political science investigates the forms of government—that is, how we govern ourselves. More specifically, it investigates how individuals behave when they interact in society, and within those other cultural institutions listed above, and how government should regulate that behavior.

The term "political science" conjures up visions of eloquent politicians, cunning lawyers, or even our country's revered forefathers. You may be quite surprised, then, when I tell you that you reason like a political scientist everyday. Political scientists—whether they be political theorists, congressional lawmakers, or Supreme Court justices—all concern themselves with governmental policy and the laws that state what we should or should not do. Whenever you deliberate about what you should do, or about what someone else should do, you are also reasoning about policies for action. Whenever you attempt to persuade someone to act, you use the rhetoric of policy: "You should wash the dishes because it is your turn" implies an established policy that everyone should take turns washing the dishes. It may be difficult to imagine George Washington—or even George Bush—arguing about how the dirty dishes need to be done, but the type of issues they have addressed are similarly about matters of policy, about what should be done.

We reason about the politics of our private affairs as political scientists do about the politics of government. Unfortunately, we also abuse the rhetoric of private policy just as badly as the most cunning politician can abuse political rhetoric during a campaign. When a politician claims "we should reduce taxes," we wonder if his or her pronouncement is based on sound economic policies or on the desire to be elected. Similarly, when you claim "I should be allowed to take this course," your instructor will wonder if your pronouncement is based on an established policy about the prerequisites for the course or on your personal desire. The former we might call an example of "mere politics," the latter "mere rhetoric." Both phrases refer to the way we are prone to make hasty judgments based on what we want rather than what we know. The armchair football critic, the rebellious teenager, the unrequited lover, all have advice for what "should" be done, but they often do not have a thorough understanding of the policies that would make their pronouncements responsible judgments. However, that does not stop them from voicing their opinions.

Learning how to reason like a political scientist can help you distinguish the rhetoric of "mere politics" from the rhetoric of informed policy, as well as help you transform the "mere rhetoric" of your armchair opinions into informed judgments. To learn to reason about political science, you need to restrain your desire to voice an opinion until you have listened to the types of conversations political scientists have. In this chapter, you will be able to listen to three different kinds of political arguments: one from the point of view of a politician, one from a private citizen, and one from a Supreme Court justice. As you read these essays, listen for the three primary features that distinguish the type of reasoning they use. You can identify them by answering the following questions:

1. What is the real question at issue?
2. What is the proposed answer?
3. What is the established policy they are basing their answer on?

Keep in mind that the questions the authors ask will be concerned with how government should or should not regulate how individuals interact in society. Also keep in mind that their answers tend to take the form of "(something) should be done because people tend to act (in some particular way)." You will have to read very carefully to discern the policy the answer is based on; this might be stated overtly early in the essay, or merely implied throughout.

Helpful Hints for Reading: Most often the answer to number 1 above can be found in the introductory section of the essay; the answer to number 2 near the conclusion. As you read an essay the first time through, you might note in the margins which paragraphs make up the introduction to the question at issue and possible answers, which paragraphs make up the body of the essay, and which begin the conclusion or statement of the author's thesis-answer.

When you read the essay through a second time, first read the introduction and conclusion together to discover how they relate to each other. At this time, you might enter in your reading notebook what you interpret as the real issue and thesis behind the work. Once you have done that, then reread the body of the essay to discover how the author reasons from the question to arrive at his or her thesis. During this second reading, note carefully in your notebook any questions you still have, either about particular claims the author makes or about confusing passages.

You might also list words you have had to look up in your dictionary to help you remember them.

PRACTICE READING

Following is the introduction and conclusion to the "Declaration of Independence." Note how Jefferson moves clearly from an introduction of the question (which presents the issue, established policy, and working hypothesis) through his proof (not included here) to arrive at an answer (his thesis). Also note the underlined words (primarily verbs) that clearly indicate that Jefferson is reasoning on the level of policy.

The Declaration of Independence

In Congress, July 4, 1776
The Unanimous Declaration of the Thirteen
United States of America

Issue: Why should the states dissolve relations with Britain?

When in the Course of human events, it becomes necessary for one people to dissolve the political bands which have connected them with another, and to assume among the Powers of the earth, the separate and equal station to which the Laws of Nature and of Nature's God entitle them, a decent respect to the opinions of mankind requires that they <u>should</u> declare the causes which <u>impel</u> them to the separation.

Established policy

Working hypothesis

We hold these truths to be self-evident, that all men are created equal, that they are endowed by their Creator with certain unalienable Rights, that among these are Life, Liberty and the pursuit of Happiness. That to secure these rights, Governments are instituted among Men, deriving their just powers from the consent of the governed. That whenever any Form of Government becomes destructive of these ends, it is the Right of the People to alter or to abolish it, and to institute a new Government, laying its foundation on such principles and organizing its powers in such form, as to them shall seem most likely to effect their Safety and Happiness. Prudence, indeed, will <u>dictate</u> that Governments long established <u>should</u> not be changed for light and transient causes; and accordingly all experience hath shown, that mankind are more disposed to suffer, while evils are sufferable, than to right themselves by abolishing the forms to which they are accustomed. But when a long train of abuses and usurpations, pursuing invariably the same Object evinces a design to reduce them under absolute Despotism, it is their right, it is their <u>duty,</u> to throw off such Government, and to provide new Guards for their future security.—<u>Such has been the patient sufferance of these Colonies; and such is now the necessity which constrains them to alter their former Systems of Government.</u> The history of the present King of Great Britain is a history of repeated injuries and usurpations, all having in direct object the establishment of an absolute

Tyranny over these States. To prove this, let Facts be submitted to a candid world.

. . . .

Answer/Thesis introduced by "therefore"

Answer as a new policy for action

> We, therefore, the Representatives of the united States of America, in General Congress, Assembled, appealing to the Supreme Judge of the world for the rectitude of our intentions, do, in the Name, and by Authority of the good People of these Colonies, solemnly publish and declare, That these United Colonies are, and of Right <u>ought</u> to be Free and Independent States, that they are Absolved from all Allegiance to the British Crown, and that all political connection between them and the State of Great Britain, is and <u>ought</u> to be totally dissolved, and that as Free and Independent States, they have full Power to levy War, conclude Peace, contract Alliances, establish Commerce, and to do all other Acts and Things which Independent States may of right do. And for the support of this Declaration, with a firm reliance on the Protection of Divine Providence, we mutually <u>pledge</u> to each other our Lives, our Fortunes and our sacred Honor.

If you were to summarize Jefferson's argument in your reading notebook, it might look something like this:

1. It is the duty of any people to dissolve relations with a government that reduces their unalienable rights under "absolute Despotism."
2. Great Britain has attempted to establish an "absolute Tyranny over these states."
3. Hence, these states should dissolve relations with Great Britain.

Jefferson's reasoning is representative of the type of reasoning used by political scientists in that it clearly moves from (1) establishing agreement on a general policy through (2) proving that current conditions warrant application of that policy to (3) conclude with a specific policy for action in the current situation.

As Americans, we find Jefferson's reasoning quite persuasive because we have been brought up to expect the individual rights Jefferson is championing. However, not all governments—nor all peoples—have recognized these rights as "self-evident Truths." Even in the course of American history, there have been times when individuals felt "tyrannized" by the government but believed they had no right—least of all "duty"—to question the policies and actions of this government. If they were to do so, however, they would find themselves reasoning as a political scientist would, basing their grievances and demands for compensation on their understanding of how the government should maintain an ideal relationship with its people.

As you read the following essays, observe how the essayists arrive at different answers to questions about the relationship between the individual and his or her government, whether they be questions about governmental policy (i.e., political issues that address what the government should do) or questions about individual policy (i.e., legal issues that govern what we should—or should not—do). Try to distinguish how the different answers result from conflicting views of how we exercise freedoms when they are granted to us. As you pull out the specific question that appears to be at issue for the authors, note their reasoning—the various stances and established policies they consider in addressing these issues. Although these essays represent the subject of political science, note how the "subject" is not represented by the *answers* these authors give as much as by the *questions* they have asked and the *reasoning* they have used to arrive at those answers.

On Things for Which Princes Are Praised or Blamed

Niccolo Machiavelli (1469–1527)

The following excerpt is taken from The Prince *(1513), Niccolo Machiavelli's most famous work. If for nothing else, Machiavelli is worth reading for his rhetoric: the argument is remarkable in its apparent simplicity and clarity. We can even better appreciate the practical sophistication of Machiavelli's reasoning when we consider the social context that prompted him to write it.*

Machiavelli invented his Prince to argue for the practical policies that he felt were urgently needed in Renaissance Italy. At the time, the country was divided into independent city-states ruled by vulnerable princes with uncertain power. Machiavelli's probable audience, the Medici brothers, had just returned to power in 1512 after being banished for eighteen years, and the volatility of the city-states was making Italy particularly vulnerable to invasions from France and Spain. Machiavelli responded to this unstable political climate with practical political advice for how Italy's present and future rulers should act. As a policy argument, the reasoning of The Prince *is based on established policies and historical precedent; note, though, how the weakened condition of Italy's government led Machiavelli to draw his examples from military history in particular.*

Machiavelli was also responding to a more specific rhetorical situation that could affect our reading of his argument. Machiavelli's interest in political policy was not an unselfish one. He had enjoyed a politically influential position in civil service until, upon the return of the Medici brothers, he was imprisoned for alleged crimes against the state. With the Medicis as the specific audience Machiavelli had in mind, The Prince *is as much a rhetorical defense of Machiavelli's dedication to the state as it is an astute, pragmatic discussion of governmental policy. Perhaps his rhetoric was effective, for Machiavelli was allowed to resume his career.*

As you read the selection below, keep in mind Machiavelli's dual purpose. Does he sound sincere or is he merely saying what he hopes the Medici brothers want to hear? (Could he be doing both?)

CHAPTER XV

On Things for Which Men, and Particularly Princes, Are Praised or Blamed

We now have left to consider what should be the manners and attitudes of a prince toward his subjects and his friends. As I know that many have written on this subject I feel that I may be held presumptuous in what I have to say, if in my comments I do not follow the lines laid down by others. Since, however, it has been my intention to write something which may be of use to the understanding reader, it has seemed wiser to me to follow the real truth of the matter rather than what we imagine it to be. For imagination has created many principalities and republics that have never been seen or known to have any real existence, for how we live is so different from how we ought to live that he who studies what ought to be done rather than what is done will learn the way to his downfall rather than to his preservation. A man striving in every way to be good will meet his ruin among the great number who are not good. Hence it is necessary for a prince, if he wishes to remain in power, to learn how not to be good and to use his knowledge or refrain from using it as he may need.

Putting aside then the things imagined as pertaining to a prince and considering those that really do, I will say that all men, and particularly princes because of their prominence, when comment is made of them, are noted as having some characteristics deserving either praise or blame. One is accounted liberal, another stingy, to use a Tuscan term—for in our speech avaricious *(avaro)* is applied to such as are desirous of acquiring by rapine whereas stingy *(misero)* is the term used for those who are reluctant to part with their own—one is considered bountiful, another rapacious; one cruel, another tenderhearted; one false to his word, another trustworthy; one effeminate and pusillanimous, another wild and spirited; one humane, another haughty; one lascivious, another chaste; one a man of integrity and another sly; one tough and another plaint; one serious and another frivolous; one religious and another skeptical, and so on. Everyone will agree, I know, that it would be a most praiseworthy thing if all the qualities accounted as good in the above enumeration were found in a Prince. But since they cannot be so possessed nor observed because of human conditions which do not allow of it, what is necessary for the prince is to be prudent enough to escape the infamy of such vices as would result in the loss of his state; as for the others which would not have that effect, he must guard himself from them as far as possible but if he cannot, he may overlook them as being of less importance. Further, he should have no concern about incurring the infamy of such vices without which the preservation of his state would be difficult. For, if the matter be well considered, it will be seen that some habits which appear virtuous, if adopted would signify ruin, and others that seem vices lead to security and the well-being of the prince.

CHAPTER XVI

Generosity and Meanness

To begin then with the first characteristic set forth above, I will say that it would be well always to be considered generous, yet generosity used in such a way as not to bring you honor does you harm, for if it is practiced virtuously and as it is meant to be practiced it will not be publicly known and you will not lose the name of being just the opposite of generous. Hence to preserve the reputation of being generous among your friends you must not neglect any kind of lavish display, yet a prince of this sort will consume all his property in such gestures and, if he wishes to preserve his reputation for generosity, he will be forced to levy heavy taxes on his subjects and turn to fiscal measures and do everything possible to get money. Thus he will begin to be regarded with hatred by his subjects and should he become poor he will be held in scant esteem; having by his prodigality given offense to many and rewarded only a few, he will suffer at the first hint of adversity, and the first danger will be critical for him. Yet when he realizes this and tries to reform he will immediately get the name of being a miser. So a prince, as he is unable to adopt the virtue of generosity without danger to himself, must, if he is a wise man, accept with indifference the name of miser. For with the passage of time he will be regarded as increasingly generous when it is seen that, by virtue of his parsimony, his income suffices for him to defend himself in wartime and undertake his enterprises without heavily taxing his people. For in that way he practices generosity towards all from whom he refrains from taking money, who are many, and stinginess only toward those from whom he withholds gifts, who are few.

In our times we have seen great things accomplished only by such as have had the name of misers; all others have come to naught. Pope Julius made use of his reputation for generosity to make himself Pope but later, in order to carry on his war against the King of France, he made no effort to maintain it; and he has waged a great number of wars without having had recourse to heavy taxation because his persistent parsimony has made up for the extra expenses. The present King of Spain, had he had any reputation for generosity, would never have carried through to victory so many enterprises.

A prince then, if he wishes not to rob his subjects but to be able to defend himself and not to become poor and despised nor to be obliged to become rapacious, must consider it a matter of small importance to incur the name of miser, for this is one of the vices which keep him on his throne. Some may say Caesar through generosity won his way to the purple, and others either through being generous or being accounted so have risen to the highest ranks. But I will answer by pointing out that either you are already a prince or you are on the way to becoming one and in the first case generosity is harmful while in the second it is very necessary to be considered open-handed. Caesar was seeking to arrive at the domination of Rome but if he had survived after reaching his goal and had not moderated his lavishness he would certainly have destroyed the empire.

It might also be objected that there have been many princes, accomplishing great things with their armies, who have been acclaimed for their generosity. To which I would answer that the prince either spends his own (or his subjects') money or that of others; in the first case he must be very sparing but in the second he should overlook no aspect of open-handedness. So the prince who leads his armies and lives on looting and extortion and booty, thus handling the wealth of others, must indeed have this quality of generosity for otherwise his soldiers will not follow him. You can be very free with wealth not belonging to yourself or your subjects, in the fashion of Cyrus, Caesar, or Alexander, for spending what belongs to others rather enhances your reputation than detracts from it; it is only spending your own wealth that is danger-

~~ous.~~ There is nothing that consumes itself as does prodigality; even as you practice it you lose the faculty of practicing it and either you become poor and despicable or, in order to escape poverty, rapacious and unpopular. And among the things a prince must guard against is precisely the danger of becoming an object either of contempt or of hatred. Generosity leads you to both these evils, wherefore it is wiser to accept the name of miserly, since the reproach it brings is without hatred, than to seek a reputation for generosity and thus perforce acquire the name of rapacious, which breeds hatred as well as infamy.

CHAPTER XVII

Cruelty and Clemency and Whether It Is Better to Be Loved or Feared

Now to continue with the list of characteristics. It should be the desire of every prince to be considered merciful and not cruel, yet he should take care not to make poor use of his clemency. Cesare Borgia was regarded as cruel, yet his cruelty reorganized Romagna and united it in peace and loyalty. Indeed, if we reflect, we shall see that this man was more merciful than the Florentines who, to avoid the charge of cruelty, allowed Pistoia to be destroyed.[1] A prince should care nothing for the accusation of cruelty so long as he keeps his subjects united and loyal; by making a very few examples he can be more truly merciful than those who through too much tender-heartedness allow disorders to arise whence come killings and rapine. For these offend an entire community, while the few executions ordered by the prince affect only a few individuals. For a new prince above all it is impossible not to earn a reputation for cruelty since new states are full of dangers. Virgil indeed has Dido apologize for the inhumanity of her rule because it is new, in the words:

> Res dura et regni novitas me talia cogunt
>
> Moliri et late fines custode tueri.[2]

Nevertheless a prince should not be too ready to listen to talebearers nor to act on suspicion, nor should he allow himself to be easily frightened. He should proceed with a mixture of prudence and humanity in such a way as not to be made incautious by overconfidence nor yet intolerable by excessive mistrust.

Here the question arises; whether it is better to be loved than feared or feared than loved. The answer is that it would be desirable to be both but, since that is difficult, it is much safer to be feared than to be loved, if one must choose. For on men in general this observation may be made: they are un-

---

[1] By unchecked rioting between opposing factions (1502).

[2] . . . my cruel fate
And doubts attending an unsettled state
Force me to guard my coast from foreign foes. (Dryden)

grateful, fickle, and deceitful, eager to avoid dangers, and avid for gain, and while you are useful to them they are all with you, offering you their blood, their property, their lives, and their sons so long as danger is remote, as we noted above, but when it approaches they turn on you. Any prince, trusting only in their words and having no other preparations made, will fall to his ruin, for friendships that are bought at a price and not by greatness and nobility of soul are paid for indeed, but they are not owned and cannot be called upon in time of need. Men have less hesitation in offending a man who is loved than one who is feared, for love is held by a bond of obligation which, as men are wicked, is broken whenever personal advantage suggests it, but fear is accompanied by the dread of punishment which never relaxes.

Yet a prince should make himself feared in such a way that, if he does not thereby merit love, at least he may escape odium, for being feared and not hated may well go together. And indeed the prince may attain this end if he but respect the property and the women of his subjects and citizens. And if it should become necessary to seek the death of someone, he should find a proper justification and a public cause, and above all he should keep his hands off another's property, for men forget more readily the death of their father than the loss of their patrimony. Besides, pretexts for seizing property are never lacking, and when a prince begins to live by means of rapine he will always find some excuse for plundering others, and conversely pretexts for execution are rarer and are more quickly exhausted.

A prince at the head of his armies and with a vast number of soldiers under his command should give not the slightest heed if he is esteemed cruel, for without such a reputation he will not be able to keep his army united and ready for action. Among the marvelous things told of Hannibal is that, having a vast army under his command made up of all kinds and races of men and waging war far from his own country, he never allowed any dissension to arise either as between the troops and their leaders or among the troops themselves, and this both in times of good fortune and bad. This could only have come about through his most inhuman cruelty which, taken in conjunction with his great valor, kept him always an object of respect and terror in the eyes of his soldiers. And without the cruelty his other characteristics would not have achieved this effect. Thoughtless writers have admired his actions and at the same time deplored the cruelty which was the basis of them. As evidence of the truth of our statement that his other virtues would have been insufficient let us examine the case of Scipio, an extraordinary leader not only in his own day but for all recorded history. His army in Spain revolted and for no other reason than because of his kindheartedness, which had allowed more license to his soldiery than military discipline properly permits. His policy was attacked in the Senate by Fabius Maximus, who called him a corrupter of the Roman arms. When the Locrians had been mishandled by one of his lieutenants, his easy-going nature prevented him from avenging them or disciplining his officer, and it was à propos of this incident that one of the senators remarked, wishing to find an excuse for him, that there were many men who knew better how to avoid error themselves than to correct it in others. This characteristic of Scipio would have clouded his fame and glory had he continued in authority, but as he lived under the government of the Senate, its harmful aspect was hidden and it reflected credit on him.

Hence, on the subject of being loved or feared I will conclude that since love depends on the subjects, but the prince has it in his own hands to create fear, a wise prince will rely on what is his own, remembering at the same time that he must avoid arousing hatred, as we have said.

CHAPTER XVIII

In What Manner Princes Should Keep Their Word

How laudable it is for a prince to keep his word and govern his actions by integrity rather than trickery will be understood by all. Nonetheless we have in our times seen great things accomplished by many princes who have thought little of keeping their promises and have known the art of mystifying the minds of men. Such princes have won out over those whose actions were based on fidelity to their word.

It must be understood that there are two ways of fighting, one with laws and the other with arms. The first is the way of men, the second is the style of beasts, but since very often the first does not suffice it is necessary to turn to the second. Therefore a prince must know how to play the beast as well as the man. This lesson was taught allegorically by the ancient writers who related that Achilles and many other princes were brought up by Chiron the Centaur, who took them under his discipline. The clear significance of this half-man and half-beast preceptorship is that a prince must know how to use either of these two natures and that one without the other has no enduring strength. Now since the prince must make use of the characteristics of beasts he should choose those of the fox and the lion, though the lion cannot defend himself against snares and the fox is helpless against wolves. One must be a fox in avoiding traps and a lion in frightening wolves. Such as choose simply the rôle of a lion do not rightly understand the matter. Hence a wise leader cannot and should not keep his word when keeping it is not to his advantage or when the reasons that made him give it are no longer valid. If men were good, this would not be a good precept, but since they are wicked and will not keep faith with you, you are not bound to keep faith with them.

A prince has never lacked legitimate reasons to justify his breach of faith. We could give countless recent examples and show how any number of peace treaties or promises have been broken and rendered meaningless by the faithlessness of princes, and how success has fallen to the one who best knows how to counterfeit the fox. But it is necessary to know how to disguise this nature well and how to pretend and dissemble. Men are so simple and so ready to follow the needs of the moment that the deceiver will always find some one to deceive. Of recent examples I shall mention one. Alexander VI did nothing but deceive and never thought of anything else and always found some occasion for it. Never was there a man more convincing in his asseverations nor more willing to offer the most solemn oaths nor less likely to observe them. Yet his deceptions were always successful for he was an expert in this field.

So a prince need not have all the aforementioned good qualities, but it is most essential that he appear to have them. Indeed, I should go so far as to say that having them and always practicing them is harmful, while seeming to have them is useful. It is good to appear clement, trustworthy, humane, religious, and honest, and also to be so, but always with the mind so disposed that, when the occasion arises not to be so, you can become the opposite. It must be understood that a prince and particularly a new prince cannot practise all the virtues for which men are accounted good, for the necessity of preserving the state often compels him to take actions which are opposed to loyalty, charity, humanity, and religion. Hence he must have a spirit ready to adapt itself as the varying winds of fortune command him. As I have said, so far as he is able, a prince should stick to the path of good but, if the necessity arises, he should know how to follow evil.

A prince must take great care that no word ever passes his lips that is not full of the above mentioned five good qualities, and he must seem to all who see and hear him a model of piety, loyalty, integrity, humanity, and religion. Nothing is more necessary than to seem to possess this last quality, for men in general judge more by the eye than the hand, as all can see but few can feel. Everyone sees what you seem to be, few experience what you really are and these few do not dare to set themselves up against the opinion of the majority supported by the majesty of the state. In the actions of all men and especially princes, where there is no court of appeal, the end is all that counts. Let a prince then concern himself with the acquisition or the maintenance of a state; the means employed will always be considered honorable and praised by all, for the mass of mankind is always swayed by appearances and by the outcome of an enterprise. And in the world there is only the mass, for the few find their place only when the majority has no base of support. A certain prince of our own times, whom it would not be well to name, preaches nothing but peace and faith and yet is the enemy of both, and if he had observed either he would already on numerous occasions have lost both his state and his renown.

QUESTIONS FOR A CRITICAL REREADING

After you have read the essay through once (while noting your initial reactions in the margins of the text), answer the following questions in your reading notebook as you reread the essay more critically.

1. To begin rereading this excerpt, identify which paragraphs make up the introduction and which the conclusion. What appears to be the real policy issue he is addressing? What is his proposed answer? Who is his audience and what would their initial stance be?
2. For Machiavelli's argument to work, he would have to base it on a general policy

that his audience would be predisposed to agree with. Just looking at the introduction and the conclusion, what might this established policy be?

3. To prove why a prince should learn how not to be good, Machiavelli divides the body of his essay into three separate sections. To test whether his argument is valid, analyze each section as a mini-essay in itself. What more specific question does each section raise, and is the answer arrived at the conclusion of each section valid? Looking at both the reasoning (i.e., the assumed policy he bases his arguments on) and the examples he uses to prove his claims, which section appears the strongest? Which the weakest?

4. After rereading the whole essay, do you find Machiavelli's argument *more* or *less* acceptable than it appeared at the beginning? Does your answer depend on whether or not you are his intended audience? Why or why not?

POSSIBLE ISSUES FOR WRITING

Following are a few of the questions that you might find at issue in Machiavelli's work. Discuss these with your classmates to see whether your interpretation differs from theirs. During class discussion, listen closely for the types of answers and stances that are being expressed and jot them down in your notebook (keep in mind that the discussion may uncover issues other than those listed below). This will help you write your essay at the end of this chapter, an essay that will contribute to the discussion by resolving a problem your audience cares about.

1. Can we summarize Machiavelli's argument by saying the ruler should always do whatever is necessary to accomplish his purpose—that, for the prince, the end always justifies the means? Justify your answer.

2. What does Machiavelli assume is the end the prince should always strive to accomplish? Should a president of the United States serve this same end? Why or why not? _always appear to have good qualities but when time_

3. As an argument about governmental policy, this essay discusses the relationship between a ruler and his or her subjects. How does Machiavelli define this relationship? In what ways is it similar to the relationship between the President and the American people? How does it differ? Should it? Why or why not?

4. As a social science, the field of political science bases its reasoning on general statements about how humans behave in social situations. Are Machiavelli's claims that men act primarily out of their own self-interest accurate? Based on your own assessment of how we tend to balance our civic duties with our own interests, are there any current laws that you feel should be changed? Consider particularly laws that affect your own behavior, like those limiting the drinking age, the speed limit, or smoking areas.

———————
———————
———————

Letter from Birmingham Jail

Martin Luther King, Jr. *(1929–1968)*

Martin Luther King, Jr., is best remembered as the charismatic, inspirational leader of the black civil rights movement in America. In the late 1950s and 1960s, black Americans began to fight for basic rights long denied them by state laws and city ordinances that were blatantly unconstitutional. Their demands were often quite simple—such as the right to drink from public fountains or eat alongside whites in public restaurants— but they often met bitter resistance from local officials and the white population. After King successfully led the boycott of segregated buses in Montgomery, Alabama, he used the Southern Christian Leadership Conference to organize the fight for civil rights into a national movement.

Although King organized the sit-ins, boycotts, and other demonstrations on a policy of passive resistance, the public response to these activities became increasingly violent. King himself fell victim to an assassin's bullet in Memphis, Tennessee, in 1968. He had received the Nobel Peace Prize in 1964.

King wrote the following letter in 1963, when many were criticizing King's methods of passive resistance. Writing from jail after being arrested during a sit-in at a luncheon counter, King directed his comments specifically to eight clergymen who had called his policy for nonviolent direct action "unwise and untimely." Being a clergyman himself and obviously aware of his specific audience, King drew most of his supporting examples from the Bible. King, however, was also aware that his comments had larger social significance, and revised his letter for publication. Clearly part of a tradition that includes Thoreau and Gandhi, this work has become the best representation of King's argument for a policy of passive, nonviolent resistance.

As you read King's argument, try to identify where it goes beyond the specific rhetorical requirements of a response to the clergymen's letter. How does he formulate the issue so that his letter can become a political policy argument?*

April 16, 1963

MY DEAR FELLOW CLERGYMEN:

While confined here in the Birmingham city jail, I came across your recent statement calling my present activities "unwise and untimely." Seldom do I pause to answer criticism of my work and ideas. If I sought to answer

---

*AUTHOR'S NOTE: This response to a published statement by eight fellow clergymen from Alabama (Bishop C. C. J. Carpenter, Bishop Joseph A. Durick, Rabbi Hilton L. Grafman, Bishop Paul Hardin, Bishop Holan B. Harmon, the Reverend George M. Murray, the Reverend Edward V. Ramage and the Reverend Earl Stallings) was composed under somewhat constricting circumstances. Begun on the margins of the newspaper in which the statement appeared while I was in jail, the letter was continued on scraps of writing paper supplied by a friendly Negro trusty, and concluded on a pad my attorneys were eventually permitted to leave me. Although the text remains in substance unaltered, I have indulged in the author's prerogative of polishing it for publication.

all the criticisms that cross my desk, my secretaries would have little time for anything other than such correspondence in the course of the day, and I would have no time for constructive work. But since I feel that you are men of genuine good will and that your criticisms are sincerely set forth, I want to try to answer your statement in what I hope will be patient and reasonable terms.

I think I should indicate why I am here in Birmingham, since you have been influenced by the view which argues against "outsiders coming in." I have the honor of serving as president of the Southern Christian Leadership Conference, an organization operating in every southern state, with headquarters in Atlanta, Georgia. We have some eighty-five affiliated organizations across the South, and one of them is the Alabama Christian Movement for Human Rights. Frequently we share staff, educational and financial resources with our affiliates. Several months ago the affiliate here in Birmingham asked us to be on call to engage in a nonviolent direct-action program if such were deemed necessary. We readily consented, and when the hour came we lived up to our promise. So I, along with several members of my staff, am here because I was invited here. I am here because I have organizational ties here.

But more basically, I am in Birmingham because injustice is here. Just as the prophets of the eighth century B.C. left their villages and carried their "thus saith the Lord" far beyond the boundaries of their home towns, and just as the Apostle Paul left his village of Tarsus and carried the gospel of Jesus Christ to the far corners of the Greco-Roman world, so am I compelled to carry the gospel of freedom beyond my own home town. Like Paul, I must constantly respond to the Macedonian call for aid.

Moreover, I am cognizant of the interrelatedness of all communities and states. I cannot sit idly by in Atlanta and not be concerned about what happens in Birmingham. Injustice anywhere is a threat to justice everywhere. We are caught in an inescapable network of mutuality, tied in a single garment of destiny. Whatever affects one directly, affects all indirectly. Never again can we afford to live with the narrow, provincial "outside agitator" idea. Anyone who lives inside the United States can never be considered an outsider anywhere within its bounds.

You deplore the demonstrations taking place in Birmingham. But your statement, I am sorry to say, fails to express a similar concern for the conditions that brought about the demonstrations. I am sure that none of you would want to rest content with the superficial kind of social analysis that deals merely with effects and does not grapple with underlying causes. It is unfortunate that demonstrations are taking place in Birmingham, but it is even more unfortunate that the city's white power structure left the Negro community with no alternative.

In any nonviolent campaign there are four basic steps: collection of the facts to determine whether injustices exist; negotiation; self-purification; and direct action. We have gone through all these steps in Birmingham. There can be no gainsaying the fact that racial injustice engulfs this community. Birmingham is probably the most thoroughly segregated city in the United

States. Its ugly record of brutality is widely known. Negroes have experienced grossly unjust treatment in the courts. There have been more unsolved bombings of Negro homes and churches in Birmingham than in any other city in the nation. These are the hard, brutal facts of the case. On the basis of these conditions, Negro leaders sought to negotiate with the city fathers. But the latter consistently refused to engage in good-faith negotiation.

Then, last September, came the opportunity to talk with leaders of Birmingham's economic community. In the course of the negotiations, certain promises were made by the merchants—for example, to remove the stores' humiliating racial signs. On the basis of these promises, the Reverend Fred Shuttlesworth and the leaders of the Alabama Christian Movement for Human Rights agreed to a moratorium on all demonstrations. As the weeks and months went by, we realized that we were the victims of a broken promise. A few signs, briefly removed, returned; the others remained.

As in so many past experiences, our hopes had been blasted, and the shadow of deep disappointment settled upon us. We had no alternative except to prepare for direct action, whereby we would present our very bodies as a means of laying our case before the conscience of the local and the national community. Mindful of the difficulties involved, we decided to undertake a process of self-purification. We began a series of workshops on nonviolence, and we repeatedly asked ourselves: "Are you able to accept blows without retaliating?" "Are you able to endure the ordeal of jail?" We decided to schedule our direct-action program for the Easter season, realizing that except for Christmas, this is the main shopping period of the year. Knowing that a strong economic-withdrawal program would be the by-product of direct action, we felt that this would be the best time to bring pressure to bear on the merchants for the needed change.

Then it occurred to us that Birmingham's mayoral election was coming up in March, and we speedily decided to postpone action until after election day. When we discovered that the Commissioner of Public Safety, Eugene "Bull" Connor, had piled up enough votes to be in the run-off, we decided again to postpone action until the day after the run-off so that the demonstrations could not be used to cloud the issues. Like many others, we waited to see Mr. Connor defeated, and to this end we endured postponement after postponement. Having aided in this community need, we felt that our direct-action program could be delayed no longer.

You may well ask: "Why direct action? Why sit-ins, marches and so forth? Isn't negotiation a better path?" You are quite right in calling for negotiation. Indeed, this is the very purpose of direct action. Nonviolent direct action seeks to create such a crisis and foster such a tension that a community which has constantly refused to negotiate is forced to confront the issue. It seeks so to dramatize the issue that it can no longer be ignored. My citing the creation of tension as part of the work of the nonviolent-resister may sound rather shocking. But I must confess that I am not afraid of the word "tension." I have earnestly opposed violent tension, but there is a type of constructive, nonviolent tension which is necessary for growth. Just as

Socrates felt that it was necessary to create a tension in the mind so that individuals could rise from the bondage of myths and half-truths to the unfettered realm of creative analysis and objective appraisal, so must we see the need for nonviolent gadflies to create the kind of tension in society that will help men rise from the dark depths of prejudice and racism to the majestic heights of understanding and brotherhood.

The purpose of our direct-action program is to create a situation so crisis-packed that it will inevitably open the door to negotiation. I therefore concur with you in your call for negotiation. Too long has our beloved Southland been bogged down in a tragic effort to live in monologue rather than dialogue.

One of the basic points in your statement is that the action that I and my associates have taken in Birmingham is untimely. Some have asked: "Why didn't you give the new city administration time to act?" The only answer that I can give to this query is that the new Birmingham administration must be prodded about as much as the outgoing one, before it will act. We are sadly mistaken if we feel that the election of Albert Boutwell as mayor will bring the millennium to Birmingham. While Mr. Boutwell is a much more gentle person than Mr. Connor, they are both segregationists, dedicated to maintenance of the status quo. I have hope that Mr. Boutwell will be reasonable enough to see the futility of massive resistance to desegregation. But he will not see this without pressure from devotees of civil rights. My friends, I must say to you that we have not made a single gain in civil rights without determined legal and nonviolent pressure. Lamentably, it is an historical fact that privileged groups seldom give up their privileges voluntarily. Individuals may see the moral light and voluntarily give up their unjust posture; but, as Reinhold Niebuhr has reminded us, groups tend to be more immoral than individuals.

We know through painful experience that freedom is never voluntarily given by the oppressor; it must be demanded by the oppressed. Frankly, I have yet to engage in a direct-action campaign that was "well timed" in the view of those who have not suffered unduly from the disease of segregation. For years now I have heard the word "Wait!" It rings in the ear of every Negro with piercing familiarity. This "Wait" has almost always meant "Never." We must come to see, with one of our distinguished jurists, that "justice too long delayed is justice denied."

We have waited for more than 340 years for our constitutional and God-given rights. The nations of Asia and Africa are moving with jetlike speed toward gaining political independence, but we still creep at horse-and-buggy pace toward gaining a cup of coffee at a lunch counter. Perhaps it is easy for those who have never felt the stinging darts of segregation to say, "Wait." But when you have seen vicious mobs lynch your mothers and fathers at will and drown your sisters and brothers at whim; when you have seen hate-filled policemen curse, kick and even kill your black brothers and sisters; when you see the vast majority of your twenty million Negro brothers smothering in an airtight cage of poverty in the midst of an affluent society; when you suddenly find your tongue twisted and your speech stammering as you seek to explain to your six-year-old daughter why she can't go to the public amusement park that has just been advertised on television, and see tears welling up in her eyes when she is told that Funtown is closed to colored children, and see ominous clouds of inferiority beginning to form in her little mental sky, and see her beginning to distort her personality by developing an unconscious bitterness toward white people; when you have to concoct an answer for a five-year-old son who is asking: "Daddy, why do white people treat colored people so mean?"; when you take a cross-country drive and find it necessary to sleep night after night in the uncomfortable corners of your automobile because no motel will accept you; when you are humiliated day in and day out by nagging signs reading "white" and "colored"; when your first name becomes "nigger," your middle name becomes "boy" (however old you are) and your last name becomes "John," and your wife and mother are never given the respected title "Mrs."; when you are harried by day and haunted by night by the fact that you are a Negro, living constantly at tiptoe stance, never quite knowing what to expect next, and are plagued with inner fears and outer resentments; when you are forever fighting a degenerating sense of "nobodiness"—then you will understand why we find it difficult to wait. There comes a time when the cup of endurance runs over, and men are no longer willing to be plunged into the abyss of despair. I hope, sirs, you can understand our legitimate and unavoidable impatience.

You express a great deal of anxiety over our willingness to break laws. This is certainly a legitimate concern. Since we so diligently urge people to obey the Supreme Court's decision of 1954 outlawing segregation in the public schools, at first glance it may seem rather paradoxical for us consciously to break laws. One may well ask: "How can you advocate breaking some laws and obeying others?" The answer lies in the fact that there are two types of laws: just and unjust. I would be the first to advocate obeying just laws. One has not only a legal but a moral responsibility to obey just laws. Conversely, one has a moral responsibility to disobey unjust laws. I would agree with St. Augustine that "an unjust law is no law at all."

Now, what is the difference between the two? How does one determine whether a law is just or unjust? A just law is a man-made code that squares with the moral law or the law of God. An unjust law is a code that is out of harmony with the moral law. To put it in the terms of St. Thomas Aquinas: An unjust law is a human law that is not rooted in eternal law and natural law. Any law that uplifts human personality is just. Any law that degrades human personality is unjust. All segregation statutes are unjust because segregation distorts the soul and damages the personality. It gives the segregator a false sense of superiority and the segregated a false sense of inferiority. Segregation, to use the terminology of the Jewish philosopher Martin Buber, substitutes an "I-it" relationship for an "I-thou" relationship and ends up relegating persons to the status of things. Hence segregation is not only politically, economically and sociologically unsound, it is morally wrong and sinful. Paul Tillich has said that sin is separation. Is not segregation an existential expression of man's tragic separation, his awful estrangement, his terrible sinfulness? Thus it is that I can urge men to obey the 1954 decision of the Supreme Court, for it is morally right; and I can urge them to disobey segregation ordinances, for they are morally wrong.

Let us consider a more concrete example of just and unjust laws. An unjust law is a code that a numerical or power majority group compels a minority group to obey but does not make binding on itself. This is *difference* made legal. By the same token, a just law is a code that a majority compels a minority to follow and that it is willing to follow itself. This is *sameness* made legal.

Let me give another explanation. A law is unjust if it is inflicted on a minority that, as a result of being denied the right to vote, had no part in enacting or devising the law. Who can say that the legislature of Alabama which set up that state's segregation laws was democratically elected? Throughout Alabama all sorts of devious methods are used to prevent Negroes from becoming registered voters, and there are some counties in which, even though Negroes constitute a majority of the population, not a single Negro is registered. Can any law enacted under such circumstances be considered democratically structured?

Sometimes a law is just on its face and unjust in its application. For instance, I have been arrested on a charge of parading without a permit. Now, there is nothing wrong in having an ordinance which requires a permit for a parade. But such an ordinance becomes unjust when it is used to maintain segregation and to deny citizens the First-Amendment privilege of peaceful assembly and protest.

I hope you are able to see the distinction I am trying to point out. In no sense do I advocate evading or defying the law, as would the rabid segregationist. That would lead to anarchy. One who breaks an unjust law must do so openly, lovingly, and with a willingness to accept the penalty. I submit that an individual who breaks a law that conscience tells him is unjust, and who willingly accepts the penalty of imprisonment in order to arouse the conscience of the community over its injustice, is in reality expressing the highest respect for law.

Of course, there is nothing new about this kind of civil disobedience. It was evidenced sublimely in the refusal of Shadrach, Meshach and Abednego to obey the laws of Nebuchadnezzar, on the ground that a higher moral law was at stake. It was practiced superbly by the early Christians, who were willing to face hungry lions and the excruciating pain of chopping blocks rather than submit to certain unjust laws of the Roman Empire. To a degree, academic freedom is a reality today because Socrates practiced civil disobedience. In our own nation, the Boston Tea Party represented a massive act of civil disobedience.

We should never forget that everything Adolf Hitler did in Germany was "legal" and everything the Hungarian freedom fighters did in Hungary was "illegal." It was "illegal" to aid and comfort a Jew in Hitler's Germany. Even so, I am sure that, had I lived in Germany at the time, I would have aided and comforted my Jewish brothers. If today I lived in a Communist country where certain principles dear to the Christian faith are suppressed, I would openly advocate disobeying that country's antireligious laws.

I must make two honest confessions to you, my Christian and Jewish brothers. First, I must confess that over the past few years I have been gravely disappointed with the white moderate. I have almost reached the regrettable conclusion that the Negro's great stumbling block in his stride toward freedom is not the White Citizen's Councilor or the Ku Klux Klanner, but the white moderate, who is more devoted to "order" than to justice; who prefers a negative peace which is the absence of tension to a positive peace which is the presence of justice; who constantly says: "I agree with you in the goal you seek, but I cannot agree with your methods of direct action"; who paternalistically believes he can set the timetable for another man's freedom; who lives by a mythical concept of time and who constantly advises the Negro to wait for a "more convenient season." Shallow understanding from people of good will is more frustrating than absolute misunderstanding from people of ill will. Lukewarm acceptance is much more bewildering than outright rejection.

I had hoped that the white moderate would understand that law and order exist for the purpose of establishing justice and that when they fail in this purpose they become the dangerously structured dams that block the flow of social progress. I had hoped that the white moderate would understand that the present tension in the South is a necessary phase of the transition from an obnoxious negative peace, in which the Negro passively accepted his unjust plight, to a substantive and positive peace, in which all men will respect the dignity and worth of human personality. Actually, we who engage in nonviolent direct action are not the creators of tension. We merely bring to the surface the hidden tension that is already alive. We bring it out in the open, where it can be seen and dealt with. Like a boil that can never be cured so long as it is covered up but must be opened with all its ugliness to the natural medicines of air and light, injustice must be exposed, with all the tension its exposure creates, to the light of human conscience and the air of national opinion before it can be cured.

In your statement you assert that our actions, even though peaceful, must be condemned because they precipitate violence. But is this a logical assertion? Isn't this like condemning a robbed man because his possession of money precipitated the evil act of robbery? Isn't this like condemning Socrates because his unswerving commitment to truth and his philosophical inquiries precipitated the act by the misguided populace in which they made him drink hemlock? Isn't this like condemning Jesus because his unique God-consciousness and never-ceasing devotion to God's will precipitated the evil act of crucifixion? We must come to see that, as the federal courts have consistently affirmed, it is wrong to urge an individual to cease his efforts to gain his basic constitutional rights because the quest may precipitate violence. Society must protect the robbed and punish the robber.

I had also hoped that the white moderate would reject the myth concerning time in relation to the struggle for freedom. I have just received a letter from a white brother in Texas. He writes: "All Christians know that the colored people will receive equal rights eventually, but it is possible that you are in too great a religious hurry. It has taken Christianity almost two thousand years to accomplish what it has. The teachings of Christ take time to come to earth." Such an attitude stems from a tragic misconception of time, from the strangely irrational notion that there is something in the very flow of time that will inevitably cure all ills. Actually, time itself is neutral; it can be used either destructively or constructively. More and more I feel that the people of ill will have used time much more effectively than have the people of good will. We will have to repent in this generation not merely for the hateful words and actions of the bad people but for the appalling silence of the good people. Human progress never rolls in on wheels of inevitability; it comes through the tireless efforts of men willing to be co-workers with God, and without this hard work, time itself becomes an ally of the forces of social stagnation. We must use time creatively, in the knowledge that the time is always ripe to do right. Now is the time to make real the promise of democracy and transform our pending national elegy into a creative psalm of brotherhood. Now is the time to lift our national policy from the quicksand of racial injustice to the solid rock of human dignity.

You speak of our activity in Birmingham as extreme. At first I was rather disappointed that fellow clergymen would see my nonviolent efforts as those of an extremist. I began thinking about the fact that I stand in the middle of two opposing forces in the Negro community. One is a force of complacency, made up in part of Negroes who, as a result of long years of oppression, are so drained of self-respect and a sense of "somebodiness" that they have adjusted to segregation; and in part of a few middle-class Negroes who, because of a degree of academic and economic security and because in some ways they profit by segregation, have become insensitive to the problems of the masses. The other force is one of bitterness and hatred, and it comes perilously close to advocating violence. It is expressed in the various black nationalist groups that are springing up across the nation, the largest and best-known being Elijah Muhammad's Muslim movement. Nourished by the Negro's frustration over the continued existence of racial discrimination, this movement is made up of people who have lost faith in America, who have absolutely repudiated Christianity, and who have concluded that the white man is an incorrigible "devil."

I have tried to stand between these two forces, saying that we need emulate neither the "do-nothingism" of the complacent nor the hatred and despair of the black nationalist. For there is the more excellent way of love and nonviolent protest. I am grateful to God that, through the influence of the Negro church, the way of nonviolence became an integral part of our struggle.

If this philosophy had not emerged, by now many streets of the South would, I am convinced, be flowing with blood. And I am further convinced that if our white brothers dismiss as "rabble-rousers" and "outside agitators" those of us who employ nonviolent direct action, and if they refuse to support our nonviolent efforts, millions of Negroes will, out of frustration and despair, seek solace and security in black-nationalist ideologies—a development that would inevitably lead to a frightening racial nightmare.

Oppressed people cannot remain oppressed forever. The yearning for freedom eventually manifests itself, and that is what has happened to the American Negro. Something within has reminded him of his birthright of freedom, and something without has reminded him that it can be gained. Consciously or unconsciously, he has been caught up by the *Zeitgeist,* and with his black brothers of Africa and his brown and yellow brothers of Asia, South America and the Caribbean, the United States Negro is moving with a sense of great urgency toward the promised land of racial justice. If one recognizes this vital urge that has engulfed the Negro community, one should readily understand why public demonstrations are taking place. The Negro has many pent-up resentments and latent frustrations, and he must release them. So let him march; let him make prayer pilgrimages to the city hall; let him go on freedom rides—and try to understand why he must do so. If his repressed emotions are not released in nonviolent ways, they will seek expression through violence; this is not a threat but a fact of history. So I have not said to my people: "Get rid of your discontent." Rather, I have tried to say that this normal and healthy discontent can be channeled into the creative outlet of nonviolent direct action. And now this approach is being termed extremist.

But though I was initially disappointed at being categorized as an extremist, as I continued to think about the matter I gradually gained a measure of satisfaction from the label. Was not Jesus an extremist for love: "Love your enemies, bless them that curse you, do good to them that hate you, and pray for them which despitefully use you, and persecute you." Was not Amos an extremist for justice: "Let justice roll down like waters and righteousness like an ever-flowing stream." Was not Paul an extremist for the Christian gospel: "I bear in my body the marks of the Lord Jesus." Was not Martin Luther an extremist: "Here I stand; I cannot do otherwise, so help me God." And John Bunyan: "I will stay in jail to the end of my days before I make a butchery of my conscience." And Abraham Lincoln: "This nation cannot survive half slave and half free." And Thomas Jefferson: "We hold these truths to be self-evident, that all men are created equal . . ." So the question is not whether we will be extremists, but what kind of extremists we will be. Will we be extremists for hate or for love? Will we be extremists for the preservation of injustice or for the extension of justice? In that dramatic scene on Calvary's hill three men were crucified. We must never forget that all three men crucified for the same crime—the crime of extremism. Two were extremists for immorality, and thus fell below their environment. The other, Jesus Christ, was an extremist for love, truth and goodness, and thereby rose above his environment. Perhaps the South, the nation and the world are in dire need of creative extremists.

I had hoped that the white moderate would see this need. Perhaps I was too optimistic; perhaps I expected too much. I suppose I should have realized that few members of the oppressor race can understand the deep groans and passionate yearnings of the oppressed race, and still fewer have the vision to see that injustice must be rooted out by strong, persistent and determined action. I am thankful, however, that some of our white brothers in the South have grasped the meaning of this social revolution and committed themselves to it. They are still all too few in quantity, but they are big in quality. Some—such as Ralph McGill, Lillian Smith, Harry Golden, James McBride Dabbs, Ann Braden and Sarah Patton Boyle—have written about our struggle in eloquent and prophetic terms. Others have marched with us down nameless streets of the South. They have languished in filthy, roach-infested jails, suffering the abuse and brutality of policemen who view them as "dirty nigger-lovers." Unlike so many of their moderate brothers and sisters, they have recognized the urgency of the moment and sensed the need for powerful "action" antidotes to combat the disease of segregation.

Let me take note of my other major disappointment. I have been so greatly disappointed with the white church and its leadership. Of course, there are some notable exceptions. I am not unmindful of the fact that each of you has taken some significant stands on this issue. I commend you, Reverend Stallings, for your Christian stand on this past Sunday, in welcoming Negroes to your worship service on a nonsegregated basis. I commend the Catholic leaders of this state for integrating Spring Hill College several years ago.

But despite these notable exceptions, I must honestly reiterate that I have been disappointed with the church. I do not say this as one of those negative critics who can always find something wrong with the church. I say this as a minister of the gospel, who loves the church; who was nurtured in its bosom; who has been sustained by its spiritual blessings and who will remain true to it as long as the cord of life shall lengthen.

When I was suddenly catapulted into the leadership of the bus protest in Montgomery, Alabama, a few years ago, I felt we would be supported by the white church. I felt that the white ministers, priests and rabbis of the South would be among our strongest allies. Instead, some have been outright opponents, refusing to understand the freedom movement and misrepresenting its leaders; all too many others have been more cautious than courageous and have remained silent behind the anesthetizing security of stained-glass windows.

In spite of my shattered dreams, I came to Birmingham with the hope that the white religious leadership of this community would see the justice of our cause and, with deep moral concern, would serve as the channel through which our just grievances could reach the power structure. I had hoped that each of you would understand. But again I have been disappointed.

I have heard numerous southern religious leaders admonish their worshipers to comply with a desegregation decision because it is the law, but I have longed to hear white ministers declare: "Follow this decree because integration is morally right and because the Negro is your brother." In the midst of blatant injustices inflicted upon the Negro, I have watched white

churchmen stand on the sideline and mouth pious irrelevancies and sanc-
timonious trivialities. In the midst of a mighty struggle to rid our nation of
racial and economic injustice, I have heard many ministers say: "Those are
social issues, with which the gospel has no real concern." And I have watched
many churches commit themselves to a completely otherworldly religion
which makes a strange, un-Biblical distinction between body and soul, between the sacred and the secular.

I have traveled the length and breadth of Alabama, Mississippi and all
the other southern states. On sweltering summer days and crisp autumn
mornings I have looked at the South's beautiful churches with their lofty
spires pointing heavenward. I have beheld the impressive outlines of her
massive religious-education buildings. Over and over I have found myself
asking: "What kind of people worship here? Who is their God? Where were
their voices when the lips of Governor Barnett dripped with words of interpo-
sition and nullification? Where were they when Governor Wallace gave a
clarion call for defiance and hatred? Where were their voices of support when
bruised and weary Negro men and women decided to rise from the dark
dungeons of complacency to the bright hills of creative protest?"

Yes, these questions are still in my mind. In deep disappointment I have
wept over the laxity of the church. But be assured that my tears have been
tears of love. There can be no deep disappointment where there is not deep
love. Yes, I love the church. How could I do otherwise? I am in the rather
unique position of being the son, the grandson and the great-grandson of
preachers. Yes, I see the church as the body of Christ. But, oh! How we have
blemished and scarred that body through social neglect and through fear of
being nonconformists.

There was a time when the church was very powerful—in the time when
the early Christians rejoiced at being deemed worthy to suffer for what they
believed. In those days the church was not merely a thermometer that recorded the ideas and principles of popular opinion; it was a thermostat that
transformed the mores of society. Whenever the early Christians entered a
town, the people in power became disturbed and immediately sought to
convict the Christians for being "disturbers of the peace" and "outside agitators." But the Christians pressed on, in the conviction that they were "a colony
of heaven," called to obey God rather than man. Small in number, they were
big in commitment. They were too God-intoxicated to be "astronomically
intimidated." By their effort and example they brought an end to such ancient
evils as infanticide and gladiatorial contests.

Things are different now. So often the contemporary church is a weak,
ineffectual voice with an uncertain sound. So often it is an archdefender of
the status quo. Far from being disturbed by the presence of the church, the
power structure of the average community is consoled by the church's silent—and often even vocal—sanction of things as they are.

But the judgment of God is upon the church as never before. If today's
church does not recapture the sacrificial spirit of the early church, it will lose
its authenticity, forfeit the loyalty of millions, and be dismissed as an irrele-

vant social club with no meaning for the twentieth century. Every day I meet young people whose disappointment with the church has turned into outright disgust.

Perhaps I have once again been too optimistic. Is organized religion too inextricably bound to the status quo to save our nation and the world? Perhaps I must turn my faith to the inner spiritual church, the church within the church, as the true *ekklesia* and the hope of the world. But again I am thankful to God that some noble souls from the ranks of organized religion have broken loose from the paralyzing chains of conformity and joined us as active partners in the struggle for freedom. They have left their secure congregations and walked the streets of Albany, Georgia, with us. They have gone down the highways of the South on tortuous rides for freedom. Yes, they have gone to jail with us. Some have been dismissed from their churches, have lost the support of their bishops and fellow ministers. But they have acted in the faith that right defeated is stronger than evil triumphant. Their witness has been the spiritual salt that has preserved the true meaning of the gospel in these troubled times. They have carved a tunnel of hope through the dark mountain of disappointment.

I hope the church as a whole will meet the challenge of this decisive hour. But even if the church does not come to the aid of justice, I have no despair about the future. I have no fear about the outcome of our struggle in Birmingham, even if our motives are at present misunderstood. We will reach the goal of freedom in Birmingham and all over the nation, because the goal of America is freedom. Abused and scorned though we may be, our destiny is tied up with America's destiny. Before the pilgrims landed at Plymouth, we were here. Before the pen of Jefferson etched the majestic words of the Declaration of Independence across the pages of history, we were here. For more than two centuries our forebears labored in this country without wages; they made cotton king; they built the homes of their masters while suffering gross injustice and shameful humiliation—and yet out of a bottomless vitality they continued to thrive and develop. If the inexpressible cruelties of slavery could not stop us, the opposition we now face will surely fail. We will win our freedom because the sacred heritage of our nation and the eternal will of God are embodied in our echoing demands.

Before closing I feel impelled to mention one other point in your statement that has troubled me profoundly. You warmly commended the Birmingham police force for keeping "order" and "preventing violence." I doubt that you would have so warmly commended the police force if you had seen its dogs sinking their teeth into unarmed, nonviolent Negroes. I doubt that you would so quickly commend the policemen if you were to observe their ugly and inhumane treatment of Negroes here in the city jail; if you were to watch them push and curse old Negro women and young Negro girls; if you were to see them slap and kick old Negro men and young boys; if you were to observe them, as they did on two occasions, refuse to give us food because we wanted to sing our grace together. I cannot join you in your praise of the Birmingham police department.

It is true that the police have exercised a degree of discipline in handling the demonstrators. In this sense they have conducted themselves rather "nonviolently" in public. But for what purpose? To preserve the evil system of segregation. Over the past few years I have consistently preached that nonviolence demands that the means we use must be as pure as the ends we seek. I have tried to make clear that it is wrong to use immoral means to attain moral ends. But now I must affirm that it is just as wrong, or perhaps even more so, to use moral means to preserve immoral ends. Perhaps Mr. Connor and his policemen have been rather nonviolent in public, as was Chief Pritchett in Albany, Georgia, but they have used the moral means of nonviolence to maintain the immoral end of racial injustice. As T. S. Eliot has said: "The last temptation is the greatest treason: To do the right deed for the wrong reason."

I wish you had commended the Negro sit-inners and demonstrators of Birmingham for their sublime courage, their willingness to suffer and their amazing discipline in the midst of great provocation. One day the South will recognize its real heroes. They will be the James Merediths, with the noble sense of purpose that enables them to face jeering and hostile mobs, and with the agonizing loneliness that characterizes the life of the pioneer. They will be old, oppressed, battered Negro women, symbolized in a seventy-two-year-old woman in Montgomery, Alabama, who rose up with a sense of dignity and with her people decided not to ride segregated buses, and who responded with ungrammatical profundity to one who inquired about her weariness: "My feets is tired, but my soul is at rest." They will be the young high school and college students, the young ministers of the gospel and a host of their elders, courageously and nonviolently sitting in at lunch counters and willingly going to jail for conscience' sake. One day the South will know that when these disinherited children of God sat down at lunch counters, they were in reality standing up for what is best in the American dream and for the most sacred values in our Judeo-Christian heritage, thereby bringing our nation back to those great wells of democracy which were dug deep by the founding fathers in their formulation of the Constitution and the Declaration of Independence.

Never before have I written so long a letter. I'm afraid it is much too long to take your precious time. I can assure you that it would have been much shorter if I had been writing from a comfortable desk, but what else can one do when he is alone in a narrow jail cell, other than write long letters, think long thoughts and pray long prayers?

If I have said anything in this letter that overstates the truth and indicates an unreasonable impatience, I beg you to forgive me. If I have said anything that understates the truth and indicates my having a patience that allows me to settle for anything less than brotherhood, I beg God to forgive me.

I hope this letter finds you strong in the faith. I also hope that circumstances will soon make it possible for me to meet each of you, not as an integrationist or a civil-rights leader but as a fellow clergyman and a Christian brother. Let us all hope that the dark clouds of racial prejudice will soon pass away and the deep fog of misunderstanding will be lifted from our fear-drenched communities, and in some not too distant tomorrow the radiant stars of love and brotherhood will shine over our great nation with all their scintillating beauty.

Yours for the cause of Peace and Brotherhood,
Martin Luther King, Jr.

QUESTIONS FOR A CRITICAL REREADING

After you have read the essay through, use the following questions to begin your critical rereading of the argument. Write your answers in your reading notebook and be prepared to defend them.

1. To begin your rereading of King's letter, identify the introductory and concluding sections of his argument and read them together. What appears to be the real issue King is addressing? What is his stance and thesis? Although he is specifically responding to the eight clergymen, how would you describe the larger audience he is attempting to reach? Describe how your answers reveal that King is reasoning about political science.

2. The first five paragraphs of King's letter introduce several related questions that were posed by the clergymen: "Why is Nonviolent Direct Action the only alternative?" "Won't it lead to anarchy?" "Isn't it as immoral as the laws it is addressing?" How does King set up these questions to prepare his audience to see them from his perspective? Do you think he has been fair in the way he has presented his specific audience's position? Why or why not?

3. Most of King's letter is devoted to defining what he means by Nonviolent Direct Action (NVDA), the policy he is basing his argument on. In paragraphs 6–9, he outlines the four steps of any nonviolent campaign. What are these steps? How do they agree with the policies upon which our nation was founded?

4. King's primary argument is that direct action was the only alternative the civil rights movement had at the time. Based on the evidence he cites, how does he attempt to convince you that all other means of communication had failed?

5. The second half of King's letter offers further justification by citing historical precedents for NVDA. Would these examples be acceptable to his audience? Are they persuasive to you? Can you think of any others? What historical incidents might be used to argue that we do *not* have a right to break what we feel is an unjust law?

POSSIBLE ISSUES FOR WRITING

Discuss the following possible issues with your classmates. As before, try to record in your reading notebook the different stances that are being expressed during the discussion. Also, jot down comments that particularly bother you—you might wish to respond to them when you write your essay at the end of this chapter.

1. Martin Luther King clarifies the purpose of NVDA as seeking "to create such a crisis and foster such a tension that a community which has constantly refused to negotiate is forced to confront the issue." Do you agree that fostering tension

and forcing society to confront this issue is a nonviolent act? Is the individual or group that demonstrates in a nonviolent way not responsible for any violence that might result? What specific incidents can you cite to support your answer? (You might consider here the fairly recent incident where the American Nazi Party marched through the predominately Jewish neighborhood of Skokie, Illinois. They were granted a permit to march but enjoined not to display the Nazi emblem because that action was construed as an attempt to "incite to riot.")

2. King argues: "One has not only a legal but a moral responsibility to obey just laws. Conversely, one has a moral responsibility to disobey unjust laws." What does his reasoning imply about the individual's role in government? Would Thomas Jefferson have endorsed King's reasoning? Under what circumstances would you feel a moral obligation to disobey the law?

3. A general issue implied by arguments in political science is, "What is the ideal relationship between the government and the people it governs?" What do you think would be King's stance? What would be Machiavelli's? Compare and contrast the two positions keeping in mind their different rhetorical situations. Which stance do you most agree with? Why?

University of California Regents v. Bakke

Excerpted from the Supreme Court Majority Opinion by Associate Justice Lewis F. Powell, Jr.

The federal Supreme Court's judicial opinions represent a highly sophisticated, comprehensive form of reasoning about governmental policy. Although often mistakenly assumed to be lawmakers, the Supreme Court justices are actually only responsible for interpreting the laws we already have. They can overrule state or local laws, but only by basing their opinions on the foremost law of the land, the American Constitution. However, the wording of the Constituion is often ambiguous, no doubt intentionally so, and needs to be reinterpreted in light of the specific political and social climates of each generation. The Supreme Court's opinions often appear as law because they establish precedent for future decisions, but the Court always reserves the right to reverse a previous decision when the situation requires it.

One such precedent for the landmark case between the University of California Regents and Allan Bakke was Brown v. Board of Education *(1954). In this earlier decision, the Supreme Court ruled that segregation of public schools denied minority children their basic right to equal protection under the law, effectively making it illegal to use race to deny equal educational opportunities to public school children. Under provisions of the Civil Rights Act of 1964, the right to equal educational opportunity was extended to affect admissions policies at public institutions for higher education. It required any educational institution that received federal funds to implement affirmative action programs. As the following opinion points out, the purpose of affirmative action programs was often viewed as a temporary corrective for past injustices. Because minority college applicants had not received an equal opportunity to prepare for college, they would receive special consideration to gain admission even though this would cause some white applicants with better academic records to be denied admission.*

Allan Bakke's case against the Medical School at the University of California at Davis charged that the university's affirmative action quota system was, in effect, reverse discrimination. A white male, Allan Bakke was denied admission to the University for two years in a row. Although he met all the academic requirements, he was told his application came at a time when all spaces in the freshman class had been filled. What he was not told was that there were available spaces reserved for minorities through a special admissions program. Bakke took his case to the Supreme Court, claiming that, since minority candidates could compete for both the regular and special admissions programs and he could only compete for the former, the University was denying his right to equal opportunity.

There were actually two policy issues involved in the case. The specific rhetorical situation addressed whether the affirmative action admissions program at Davis was unconstitutional; the larger issue that presented some conflict on the Bench was whether affirmative action programs in general (and, hence, the provisions under the Civil Rights Act) were also unconstitutional. The Court was split in its judgment. It voted 5-4 that the Davis affirmative action policy was unconstitutional and ordered the Uni-

versity to admit Bakke; however, it also voted 5-4 that some affirmative action programs did not engage in reverse discrimination, and the policy outlined in the Civil Rights Act was allowed to stand.

As you read the excerpt from the majority opinion as written by Justice Powell, take special note of the rhetoric he uses. How is this judicial opinion similar to the other political science arguments you have read? In what ways does it differ?

The Medical School of the University of California at Davis opened in 1968 with an entering class of 50 students. In 1971, the size of the entering class was increased to 100 students, a level at which it remains. No admissions program for disadvantaged or minority students existed when the school opened, and the first class contained three Asians but no blacks, no Mexican-Americans, and no American Indians. Over the next two years, the faculty devised a special admissions program to increase the representation of "disadvantaged" students in each medical school class. The special program consisted of a separate admissions system operating in coordination with the regular admissions process.

Under the regular admissions procedure, a candidate could submit his application to the Medical School beginning in July of the year preceding the academic year for which admission was sought. Because of the large number of applications, the admissions committee screened each one to select candidates for further consideration. Candidates whose overall undergraduate grade point averages fell below 2.5 on a scale of 4.0 were summarily rejected. About one out of six applicants was invited for a personal interview. Following the interviews, each candidate was rated on a scale of 1 to 100 by his interviewers and four other members of the admissions committee. The rating embraced the interviewers' summaries, the candidate's overall grade point average, grade point average in science courses, scores on the Medical College Admissions Test (MCAT), letters of recommendation, extracurricular activities, and other biographical data. . . . The chairman was responsible for placing names on the waiting list. They were not placed in strict numerical order; instead, the chairman had discretion to include persons with "special skills."

The special admissions program operated with a separate committee, a majority of whom were members of minority groups. On the 1973 application form, candidates were asked to indicate whether they wished to be considered as "economically and/or educationally disadvantaged" applicants; on the 1974 form the question was whether they wished to be considered as members of a "minority group," which the Medical School apparently viewed as "Blacks," "Chicanos," "Asians," and "American Indian." If these questions were answered affirmatively, the application was forwarded to the special admissions committee. No formal definition of "disadvantaged" was ever produced, but the chairman of the special committee screened each application to see whether it reflected economic or educational deprivation. Having passed this initial hurdle, the applications then were rated by the special committee in a fashion similar to that used by the general admissions committee, except that special candidates did not have to meet the 2.5 grade point average cutoff applied to regular applicants.

. . . The special committee continued to recommend special applicants until a number prescribed by faculty vote were admitted. While the overall class size was still 50, the prescribed number was 8; in 1973 and 1974, when the class size had doubled to 100, the prescribed number of special admissions also doubled, to 16. . . . Although disadvantaged whites applied to the special program in large numbers, none received an offer of admission through that process. Indeed, in 1974, at least, the special committee explicitly considered only "disadvantaged" special applicants who were members of one of the designated minority groups.

Allan Bakke is a white male who applied to the Davis Medical School in both 1973 and 1974. In both years Bakke's application was considered under the general admissions program, and he received an interview. His 1973 interview was with Dr. Theodore C. West, who considered Bakke "a very desirable applicant to [the] medical school." Despite a strong benchmark score of 468 out of 500, Bakke was rejected. His application had come late in the year, and no applicants in the general admissions process with scores below 470 were accepted after Bakke's application was completed. There were four special admissions slots unfilled at that time, however, for which Bakke was not considered. After his 1973 rejection, Bakke wrote to Dr. George H. Lowrey, Associate Dean and Chairman of the Admissions Committee, protesting that the special admissions program operated as a racial and ethnic quota.

Bakke's 1974 application was completed early in the year. His student interviewer gave him an overall rating of 94, finding him "friendly, well tempered, conscientious and delightful to speak with." His faculty interviewer was, by coincidence, the same Dr. Lowrey to whom he had written in protest of the special admissions program. Dr. Lowrey found Bakke "rather limited in his approach" to the problems of the medical profession and found disturbing Bakke's "very definite opinions which were based more on his personal viewpoints than upon a study of the total problem." Dr. Lowrey gave Bakke the lowest of his six ratings, an 86; his total was 549 out of 600. Again, Bakke's application was rejected. In neither year did the chairman of the admissions committee, Dr. Lowrey, exercise his discretion to place Bakke on the waiting list. In both years, applicants were admitted under the special program with grade point averages, MCAT scores, and benchmark scores significantly lower than Bakke's.

After the second rejection, Bakke filed the instant suit in the Superior Court of California. He sought mandatory, injunctive, and declaratory relief compelling his admission to the Medical School. He alleged that the Medical School's special admissions program operated to exclude him from the school on the basis of his race, in violation of his rights under the Equal Protection Clause of the Fourteenth Amendment,[1] Art. I, § 21, of the California Constitution,[2] and § 601 of Title VI of the Civil Rights Act of 1964, 78 Stat. 252, 42 U. S. C. § 2000d.[3] The University cross-complained for a declaration that its special admissions program was lawful. The trial court found that the special program operated as a racial quota, because minority applicants in the special program were rated only against one another, and 16 places in the class of 100 were reserved for them. Declaring that the University could not take race into account in making admissions decisions, the trial court held the challenged program violative of the Federal Constitution, the state constitution, and Title VI. The court refused to order Bakke's admission, however, holding that he had failed to carry his burden of proving that he would have been admitted but for the existence of the special program.

Bakke appealed from the portion of the trial court judgment denying him admission, and the University appealed from the decision that its special admissions program was unlawful and the order enjoining it from considering race in the processing of applications. The Supreme Court of California transferred the case directly from the trial court, "because of the importance of the issues involved."

. . . . It then turned to the goals the University presented as justifying the special program. Although the court agreed that the goals of integrating the medical profession and increasing the number of physicians willing to serve members of minority groups were compelling state interests, it concluded that the special admissions program was not the least intrusive means of achieving those goals. Without passing on the state constitutional or the federal statutory grounds cited in the trial court's judgment, the California court held that the Equal Protection Clause of the Fourteenth Amendment required that "no applicant may be rejected because of his race, in favor of another who is less qualified, as measured by standards applied without regard to race."

Turning to Bakke's appeal, the court ruled that since Bakke had established that the University had discriminated against him on the basis of his race, the burden of proof shifted to the University to demonstrate that he would not have been admitted even in the absence of the special admissions program. . . .

. . . . Although many of the Framers of the Fourteenth Amendment conceived of its primary function as bridging the vast distance between mem-

---

[1] "[N]or shall any State . . . deny to any person within its jurisdiction the equal protection of the laws."

[2] "No special privileges or immunities shall ever be granted which may not be altered, revoked, or repealed by the Legislature; nor shall any citizen, or class of citizens, be granted privileges or immunities which, upon the same terms, shall not be granted to all citizens."

This section was recently repealed and its provisions added to Art. I, § 7, of the state constitution."

[3] Section 601 of Title VI, 78 Stat. 252, provides as follows:

"No person in the United States shall, on the ground of race, color, or national origin, be excluded from participation in, be denied the benefits of, or be subjected to discrimination under any program or activity receiving Federal financial assistance."

bers of the Negro race and the white "majority," the Amendment itself was framed in universal terms, without reference to color, ethnic origin, or condition of prior servitude. . . . Indeed, it is not unlikely that among the Framers were many who would have applauded a reading of the Equal Protection Clause that states a principle of universal application and is responsive to the racial, ethnic, and cultural diversity of the Nation. . . .

Over the past 30 years, this Court has embarked upon the crucial mission of interpreting the Equal Protection Clause with the view of assuring to all persons "the protection of equal laws," in a Nation confronting a legacy of slavery and racial discrimination. See, *e. g., Shelley v. Kraemer*, 334 U. S. 1 (1948); *Brown v. Board of Education*, 347 U. S. 483 (1954); *Hills v. Gautreaux*, 425 U. S. 284 (1976). Because the landmark decisions in this area arose in response to the continued exclusion of Negroes from the mainstream of American society, they could be characterized as involving discrimination by the "majority" white race against the Negro minority. But they need not be read as depending upon that characterization for their results. It suffices to say that "[o]ver the years, this Court has consistently repudiated '[d]istinctions between citizens solely because of their ancestry' as being 'odious to a free people whose institutions are founded upon the doctrine of equality.' ". . . .

Petitioner urges us to adopt for the first time a more restrictive view of the Equal Protection Clause and hold that discrimination against members of the white "majority" cannot be suspect if its purpose can be characterized as "benign." The clock of our liberties, however, cannot be turned back to 1868. It is far too late to argue that the guarantee of equal protection to *all* persons permits the recognition of special wards entitled to a degree of protection greater than that accorded others. "The Fourteenth Amendment is not directed solely against discrimination due to a 'two-class theory'—that is, based upon differences between 'white' and Negro."

If petitioner's purpose is to assure within its student body some specified percentage of a particular group merely because of its race or ethnic origin, such a preferential purpose must be rejected not as insubstantial but as facially invalid. Preferring members of any one group for no reason other than race or ethnic origin is discrimination for its own sake. This the Constitution forbids. *E. g., Loving v. Virginia, McLaughlin v. Florida, Brown v. Board of Education.*

The State certainly has a legitimate and substantial interest in ameliorating, or eliminating where feasible, the disabling effects of identified discrimination. The line of school desegregation cases, commencing with *Brown*, attests to the importance of this state goal and the commitment of the judiciary to affirm all lawful means toward its attainment. In the school cases, the States were required by court order to redress the wrongs worked by specific instances of racial discrimination. That goal was far more focused than the remedying of the effects of "societal discrimination," an amorphous concept of injury that may be ageless in its reach into the past.

. . . . Hence, the purpose of helping certain groups whom the faculty of the Davis Medical School perceived as victims of "societal discrimination" does not justify a classification that imposes disadvantages upon persons like respondent, who bear no responsibility for whatever harm the beneficiaries of the special admissions program are thought to have suffered. To hold otherwise would be to convert a remedy heretofore reserved for violations of legal rights into a privilege that all institutions throughout the Nation could grant at their pleasure to whatever groups are perceived as victims of societal discrimination. That is a step we have never approved.

In summary, it is evident that the Davis special admissions program involves the use of an explicit racial classification never before countenanced by this Court. It tells applicants who are not Negro, Asian, or Chicano that they are totally excluded from a specific percentage of the seats in an entering class. No matter how strong their qualifications, quantitative and extracurricular, including their own potential for contribution to educational diversity, they are never afforded the chance to compete with applicants from the preferred groups for the special admissions seats. At the same time, the preferred applicants have the opportunity to compete for every seat in the class.

The fatal flaw in petitioner's preferential program is its disregard of individual rights as guaranteed by the Fourteenth Amendment. Such rights are not absolute. But when a State's distribution of benefits or imposition of burdens hinges on ancestry or the color of a person's skin or ancestry, that individual is entitled to a demonstration that the challenged classification is necessary to promote a substantial state interest. Petitioner has failed to carry this burden. For this reason, that portion of the California court's judgment holding petitioner's special admissions program invalid under the Fourteenth Amendment must be affirmed.

In enjoining petitioner from ever considering the race of any applicant, however, the courts below failed to recognize that the State has a substantial interest that legitimately may be served by a properly devised admissions program involving the competitive consideration of race and ethnic origin. For this reason, so much of the California court's judgment as enjoins petitioner from any consideration of the race of any applicant must be reversed.

With respect to respondent's entitlement to an injunction directing his admission to the Medical School, petitioner has conceded that it could not carry its burden of proving that, but for the existence of its unlawful special admissions program, respondent still would not have been admitted. Hence, respondent is entitled to the injunction, and that portion of the judgment must be affirmed.

QUESTIONS FOR A CRITICAL REREADING

After you have read Justice Powell's opinion through once, use the following questions to help you analyze what it says. As you reread the opinion, jot down your answers to these questions in your notebook, and include any questions you have about other aspects of the argument and what it means.

1. As a judicial opinion, this argument attempts to balance the arguments of the two parties involved (Bakke and the Davis Medical School) before passing judgment.

How does this argument differ from the others you have read in this chapter? (Note in particular the language throughout, the nature of the introduction, and the type of supporting examples.) Based on the differences you see, what aspects of this argument would you say are common to all legal writing—that is, what are the rhetorical conventions that Powell observes? Why do you think lawyers and judges have accepted this way of talking to one another?

2. Reread the section that you have marked off as the introduction to the argument. What appear to be the issues Justice Powell will address? What are the various stances involved (i.e., those held by the two parties in the case)? Referring to Powell's concluding statements, what stances did the Court take?

3. As you begin to reread the body of the argument, what issue becomes primary? Why do you think Powell spent most of his time addressing it?

4. The established policy that Powell uses to reason about the case is the Equal Protection Clause of the Fourteenth Amendment to the Constitution: "No applicant may be rejected because of his race, in favor of another who is less qualified, as measured by standards applied without regard to race." What does this amendment mean? How did the Davis Medical School interpret it? How does Justice Powell?

POSSIBLE ISSUES FOR WRITING

Because the Court's ruling in the Bakke case was by no means a unanimous decision, the issues involved remain controversial. Following are a few of the questions that are still being deliberated. Discuss these with your classmates to see whether you all agree, and, as before, keep a record in your notebook of other possible issues that arise during the discussion.

1. Powell states that Davis Medical School "urges us to adopt for the first time a more restrictive view of the Equal Protection Clause and hold that discrimination against members of the white 'majority' cannot be suspect if its purpose can be characterized as 'benign.' " How did Davis perceive their special admissions program as "benigh," and, hence, not an instance of reverse discrimination? Would you agree? Why or why not?

2. Although the Court ruled that the special admissions program at Davis was indeed discriminatory to whites and, hence, unconstitutional, it also ruled that affirmative action programs are not in general discriminatory and should be reviewed on a case by case basis. What type of race-conscious affirmative action program would be constitutional in light of the Court's decision? Or would you argue that special consideration of one's race or sex is always discriminatory?

3. Let's say that Davis's special admissions program is adjusted to accommodate the Court's decision. Instead of holding spaces only for nonwhite candidates, they also consider less-advantaged whites. How well would this correct the problem?

4. Affirmative action programs are one response our nation has given to Martin Luther King, Jr. and the civil rights movement. What others can you think of? Which, in your view, have been the most effective? Why? If King were alive today, do you think he would feel a need for Nonviolent Direct Action?

5. Compare how the three arguments you have read in this chapter reflect a different relationship between the government and the people it governs. Which author— Machiavelli, King, or Powell—best reflects your own attitude toward government? In your opinion, in what ways could our government improve?

WRITING YOUR ESSAY

Now that you have listened in on the conversations selected authors have had about political science and you have continued these conversations informally with your classmates, you are prepared to make a more formal contribution to the discussion. Write an essay that responds to one of the political arguments your classmates have offered. To decide what you will need to write, determine who in the class would benefit from hearing your position on the issue and analyze how their stance differs from yours. Review your notes from class discussions of the essays on political science, noting in particular those questions most at issue for the class. Choose from these issues one that you feel most strongly about because of something someone said; your specific audience will be the classmate(s) that expressed a stance different from your own, although you will also be writing for a broader audience of informed readers.

To make drafting your argument easier, pretend that you are talking directly to your specific audience. Introduce the issue in the context of the discussion you have had and carefully present your opponent's point of view before developing the new points that you are arguing for. If necessary, draw up a working outline first (you might want to review the example in Chapter 2), and use the outline to shape your ideas into a political argument before you draft your essay.

Here are some hints on how to reason through a political argument. Be sure to phrase the question you are addressing as a policy issue (something "should" or "should not" be done because . . .). Also, as you present your audience's position, try to recognize what established policy both you and your audience agree with (e.g., the Fourteenth Amendment, or that the ruler should always act for the safety of the state). You will need to use this established policy to reason your readers from their stance to yours. Also, as you offer proof in the body of your argument, consider the types of historical examples you use as precedent, always asking yourself how your specific audience would respond to each of them.

As you draft and revise your argument, refer to the following discussion for special help.

REVIEW: WRITING TO AUDIENCE AND ISSUE

Recall from Chapter 3 that the audience you are writing to will affect what you have to say and how you will say it. Let's review Machiavelli's argument to see how his audience shaped both the issue he addressed and the way he sought to answer it.

Because Machiavelli was writing to instruct the youth of the elite classes on how to become effective rulers, he addressed only those issues that concerned them. The issues were necessarily pragmatic and the way we formulate the general question he sought to answer reflects this pragmatic concern: Should a prince always act virtuously when attempting to preserve the state? He recognized in his audience what he perceived as a naive idealism—an innocent view of human nature that assumed the people being ruled would respect a prince who acted virtuously. He sought to dispel this idealism by exposing how a prince's subjects are primarily self-interested and hypocritical, leading his audience to see that a prince must act not according to an ideal standard of behavior but according to how people really are.

However, if Machiavelli had been writing to the common people, he might have posed a different question: How should the public ensure that the prince remain ethical? Had the people been his audience and this last question his issue, he probably would have addressed how we are primarily self-interested and how our behavior forces our rulers to act less virtuously than we might wish. However, because he did not write his essay to the public but to its rulers, his generalizations about how self-interested and fickle we are as subjects is most likely to make us view his thesis as merely a way to rationalize the right for rulers to manipulate and deceive us.

This analysis of Machiavelli's audience emphasizes how a writer's argument will most likely fail if he or she does not consider how the audience should shape both the issue and the reasoning involved in answering it. If you choose to write about the general issue of what is the ideal relationship between the ruler and his or her subjects, you will need to consider how your audience might answer the question. Suppose that someone in your class has mentioned that a government of the people (as Jefferson has described it) is unrealistic and that we need to let presidents act independently of public opinion in the interests of the state. Your answer would have to consider the practical, realistic consequences of any "ideal" relationship you discuss. You might discover, while exploring the issue from first your audience's and then your perspective, that Jefferson's definition does accommodate the exceptions your classmate has cited. From this perspective, your new thesis might assert that Jefferson's definition of government would create an ideal relationship between a ruler and his subjects *because* it is practical in some way.

Remember that to argue well you need to have listened well, both to the authors whose essays have stimulated the discussion and to your classmates as they discussed the readings. Always review your notes to remind yourself of what others had to say. The process of learning through writing about a subject begins with an attempt to identify exactly what concerns your readers and what is unique about your position. The issue you address in your essay should reflect the questions both you and your audience are asking, and the answer you arrive at should follow from the type of reasoning that is appropriate for both the subject and your audience. Often you will discover that your essay is not an act of persuading your audience to change their minds; instead, it is a means of cooperating with them to reach a conclusion that both of you can accept. Your essay should attempt to expose what is the best, most probable, answer in light of what you and your audience believe at this time.

USING YOUR DRAFT TO DISCOVER YOUR STANCE

As with the essays you have read, the essay you write should begin with an introductory section that presents both the issue you will address and what others have thought about it. Sometimes merely recounting the ideas from your class discussion will help you discover what is precisely at issue. Whether you start your essay with a quotation from the readings or with an example from your own experience, you should make the issue urgent for your readers, specifically by giving them a general idea how your position might differ (you might want to go so far as to introduce your working thesis).

A good way of getting your readers' attention is to focus on what they have said about the subject. Not only does this begin your argument on a point of agreement with your reader, it also helps determine what you should say next and what should be the first step in the body of your argument. Reasoning from issue to answer is not just a matter of making a statement and then offering three different examples to support it. It is a process of testing different stances, possible thesis statements, discovering where they disagree and which appears the most plausible. The body of your argument should begin this reasoning process by analyzing where your stance differs from your reader's and continue your reasoning by proving how and why that difference is important.

The conclusion you arrive at may be different from the thesis you had in mind when you began to write. Take that as a good sign. It reveals that you seriously considered the differing perspectives and reasoned carefully as you wrote. The best conclusions are ones we did not quite expect. The worst are those we arranged—conclusions that merely repeat what we said all along.

REVISING YOUR DRAFT: CRITICAL READING AND PEER RESPONSE

No matter how careful you were when you drafted your argument, it will need to be revised to better accommodate your reader. Particularly on the first writing of an essay, we are all guilty of stereotyping our audience, of oversimplifying their position. This is only natural. Eager to get our ideas on paper before we forget them, we avoid alternative ideas that may confuse us. Once an argument is drafted, though, we can step back and analyze the hasty conclusions and vague generalizations—that is, read the draft more critically.

To read your own work critically, you need to put yourself into the minds and hearts of your specific readers, see your draft through their eyes. This is when you need to develop your awareness of the specific audience: What is their investment in the subject? Have you identified what is at issue for them, or clearly made the issue you address urgent enough so they will read on? Do you represent their stance(s) fairly?

A very helpful audience awareness exercise is to write what you think your reader would say in response to your essay—or, better yet, have a classmate write it for you. Only if it is written out can a self-critique or peer response objectify the reasoning process your audience would use to criticize your argument. Following are some questions you need to consider when you read a draft critically and prepare an audience response:

1. What is the question at issue? How does the author answer it?
2. Is the issue important to the reader? Is it a question the reader is also asking?
3. Does the draft acknowledge the reader's perspective? How will it change what the reader already knows or thinks? What stances does the author still need to consider?

Ideally, a peer response or self-critique should be written quickly (your instructor may even assign the draft exchange and peer response as an in-class writing). The point is not to edit the draft but to respond to the ideas. When you receive a peer response to your draft, determine whether it is an accurate portrayal of the reader you have in mind; however, even if it isn't, that information can be helpful because it indicates how your essay can be misread.

REVISION CHECKLIST

After you receive a peer response or write a self-critique that presents your reader's argument, you will most likely revise major features of your essay—either the question at issue, your summary of possible stances, and/or your own thesis. You may choose to delete unnecessary sections of your argument, or choose to add important clarifications and examples. Before you leave this stage of revising your essay to begin editing for punctuation, spelling, and grammar, though, test how well you have restricted your argument to the kind of reasoning used in political science:

1. Does your essay address an issue of policy (i.e., either ask directly or imply a question about what should be done)?
2. Does it clearly begin (either explicitly or by implication) on a point of established policy—a general belief that certain conditions dictate certain actions?
3. Does it reserve its discussion of human action to how we tend to behave as a society? (That is, does it contain enough examples before making generalizations about how all people act?)
4. Do the examples generally establish a historical or legal precedent for the main ideas?

Unit Three

CHAPTER FIVE

Creating a Logical Thesis Statement

*I*n this chapter, you will explore the reasoning process—how authors put ideas together to create a logical thesis. The best thesis is complete enough to be a map of the author's argument. It shows the route an essay takes as the author leads the reader from a question at issue to arrive at its reasonable answer. When you create a logical thesis to summarize an essay you have read, you discover how the author put ideas together into a reasonable answer. When you create a logical thesis to summarize what you want to write about, you discover how to reason about the ideas you had as you heard others discuss the issue.

To create a logical thesis statement for something you read, you must consider two primary questions about how an essay is put together:

1. What question does it offer an answer to?
2. What kind of information is used to arrive at the answer?

Asking these questions can help you define the type of reasoning the author has used and what kind of argument you need to write in response. Every field you study has a way of asking questions and a specific kind of information it uses to answer them. Learning to write about political science is learning how to put ideas together into a picture of the world that is slightly different from that painted by a natural scientist. Both pictures can be quite reasonable, but they represent the different perspectives that result from asking different kinds of questions and using different kinds of information to answer them.

REVIEW: THE REASONING PROCESS OF POLITICAL SCIENCE

When you learn to reason about governmental policy as Machiavelli or Jefferson did, you learn to ask questions political scientists ask and to work with the kind of evidence they use to discover answers to these questions. These two writers offered different answers for what the ideal relationship between a government and its subjects might be, and each used different reasons to justify their answers. Still, their reasoning process was the same because they based their reasons on the same kind of evidence. Consider the following summaries of their arguments:

Machiavelli

(Thesis)   A Prince should not attempt to be virtuous

(Primary reason)   *because*, more often than not, acting virtuously will prevent him from preserving the state.

Jefferson

(Thesis)   The colonies have a duty to dissolve their allegiance to the British Crown

(Primary reason)   *because* the King has proven that he intends to establish an absolute tyranny over them.

Although Machiavelli focuses on the ruler and Jefferson on the people, note how each of them chose to support their thesis with a reason that is based on what is best for the state. (Machiavelli believes the state needs to be preserved at all costs; Jefferson believes that the state—the colonies—would not be preserved by a tyrant.) Both arguments represent how political scientists construct written arguments to reason in a specific way. They both answer questions about what should be done in response to a particular political situation, and they both develop primary reasons from evidence about what is best for the state.

CREATING THESIS STATEMENTS FROM YOUR READING

As illustrated above, summarizing an argument in the form of *thesis + the primary reason* is a helpful way to identify and test the argument an author is making. For the sake of distinction, I will call this extended thesis the author's *logical thesis statement*. Here are three steps to help you derive a logical thesis statement from someone else's argument:

1. Formulate the question you see the author addressing.

Begin with a general question. For example, you might begin by articulating Machiavelli's question as "How should a Prince behave?" Then look at how you might revise the question to make it as specific as possible without overlooking essential points in the argument. You might revise the general question behind Machiavelli's argument to say, "Should a Prince be virtuous?" This is more specific but still embodies the major points in the selection from Machiavelli. However, if you revised it to say "Should a Prince tell the truth?" the question would no longer address Machiavelli's extensive discussion of other virtues.

2. Express the author's answer to this question as a complete clause.

A complete clause contains both a subject and a predicate. The subject is the topic—the primary term expressed as a noun (or noun phrase). The predicate expresses an evaluation of that topic (through a verb and another major term). You can take your cues for both the noun and predicate from the question you have formulated. For example, the revised question for Machiavelli's essay ("Should a Prince be virtuous?") introduces "a Prince" as the primary term, "should be" (which could be paraphrased as "should act") as the verb, and "virtuous" (or some form of "virtue") as the other major term. You might begin phrasing Machiavelli's answer with a simple reordering of these elements: "A Prince should not be virtuous." However, you would probably want to revise this statement to express Machiavelli's point more accurately: "A Prince should not *attempt to* be virtuous."

3. Summarize the bulk of the essay into a "because" clause that represents the primary reason the author uses to justify his or her answer.

This is the most important part of the thesis statement. In pulling out a "because" clause that summarizes the kind of proof the author has given throughout the argument, you are forced to identify how that author has reasoned toward his or her answer. Be certain this second clause does not merely restate the first clause you have written. To accurately reflect a reason, the "because" clause should contain some information that is not present in the first.

Consider the following paraphrase of Machiavelli's thesis: "A Prince should not attempt to be virtuous *because* he should not attempt to be generous, benevolent, or honest." The "because" clause appears to give new information, but it actually gives only a definition for what it means to be virtuous (virtuous = generous, benevolent, and honest). A "because" clause that gives a real reason why a prince cannot be virtuous (or generous, or honest) would contain the criteria Machiavelli uses to judge these virtues: "because virtuous behavior will prevent him from preserving the state." Again, after you have formulated your clause, you might wish to revise it to make it a more precise reflection of the author's point: "because virtuous behavior, *more often than not,* will prevent him from preserving the state."

EXAMINING THE ARGUMENT BEHIND THE LOGICAL THESIS

To test a logical thesis statement, ask yourself whether it accurately reflects the question the author was addressing and whether the "because" clause represents a real reason. You will also want to test the thesis against the rhetorical situation. Does the thesis answer a question that is primary for both the author and readers? Does the "because" clause focus on information that the author and readers would respect as evidence? For example, Machiavelli wouldn't ask "Is virtue good for a Prince's soul?" Nor would he argue, "A Prince should not attempt to be virtuous because virtuous behavior is not rewarded in an afterlife." Either of these examples would require the kind of speculative evidence a theologian or philosopher would use, a different kind of information than the political and historical examples that Machiavelli used.

Consider the political argument behind Jefferson's "Declaration of Independence":

(Thesis)	The colonies have a duty to dissolve their allegiance to the British Crown
(Primary reason)	because the King has proven that he intends to establish an absolute tyranny over them.

The first clause represents the answer Jefferson is offering to the question "What should the colonies do about their relationship to the British Crown?" It is a political question because its major terms concern governmental bodies and because it asks a question of policy ("What should be done?"). The "because" clause similarly requires that the author focus on the King's political behavior as evidence. You could summarize the kind of reasoning Jefferson has used as a political conversation: "The colonies must dissolve their allegiance." "Why must they do so?" "Because the King is a tyrant."

E X E R C I S E

Using your notebook entries, try to formulate a logical thesis statement for one or two of the other essays you have read in this course. Remember to follow these three steps:

1. Formulate the question you see the author addressing.
2. Express the author's answer to this question as a complete clause.
3. Summarize the bulk of the essay into a "because" clause that represents the primary reason the author uses to justify his or her answer.

When you have finished, compare your statements with your classmates'. Why may the class come up with many different ways of stating the thesis for any one essay? Look at the kinds of questions and evidence being addressed by the thesis statements. Do some thesis statements represent an author's argument better than others? Why or why not?

TESTING THE LOGIC BEHIND YOUR THESIS

You have been practicing using a logical thesis statement to discover how others have reasoned in their essays. Now let's examine how you can create your own for the arguments you want to make.

Although you may not be aware of it, the form of the logical thesis statement is behind many of your daily statements. It is how you develop reasonable opinions based on your past experiences. For example, if you said, "I think I will take my umbrella because those are angry storm clouds," you would be using your past experience with angry storm clouds to determine whether it will rain today. Or when you tell yourself, "I better prepare well for class today because my teacher hasn't called on me in a long time," you are using your experience of your teacher's habits and what has recently gone on in class to conclude what will probably happen the next time class meets.

Sometimes, though, statements may sound logical but, on examination, prove to be quite unreasonable. Consider this comment, "I might as well not study for the test because it is scheduled for Friday the thirteenth." For the sake of argument, let's call this student Jane and assume she has a history of bad luck on Friday the thirteenth. She may even sincerely believe that day brings her bad luck. Does she still have a good reason for not preparing for the test? No matter how well she studies for any test, does her performance ever depend *primarily* on luck? If she studied and still did poorly, having studied for the wrong questions, she might blame her "bad luck," but her method of studying would probably have more to do with it. By saying she will not study at all because of fear of "bad luck," Jane is merely making it easier to avoid taking responsibility for her failure. If she examined the reasoning behind her statement, she might recognize how she was setting herself up for "bad luck." What is worse, she would not learn much from the experience; she would see failing the test as just another reason to act the same way when Friday the thirteenth came around again.

No matter how many past experiences seem to justify your beliefs, you need to examine them anew each time you use them to reach a decision. An easy way to do this is to become conscious of the reasoning process you go through with every decision you make.

Inductive Reasoning

There are basically two types of reasoning: inductive and deductive. Although we will discuss them separately, keep in mind how you seldom use one type independent of the other.

You reason inductively whenever you generalize about your experiences. For example, if you did well in your math classes in grade school, junior high, and high school, you might conclude that you are always good at math. However, if you fare less well in a college math course, you will need to reconsider your earlier generalization. Following is a diagram of this inductive process:

First Experience: X led to Y.
Second Experience: X led to Y.
Third Experience: X led to Y.
Conclusion: *X will always lead to Y.*

Fourth Experience: X did not lead to Y.
Revised Conclusion: *X won't always lead to Y. (Either not all X's are the same or the first conclusion was faulty.)*

The quality of conclusions reached inductively depends on two conditions: (1) how many similar experiences you have to draw upon (e.g., in the first conclusion, you might have not had enough experience of the different kinds of math to safely conclude you are good at it), and (2) whether each experience is an example of the same thing (e.g., in the revised conclusion, you might decide that there is a distinct difference between college calculus and the arithmetic, geometry, and algebra you studied before). Of course, there may also be other variables at work (e.g., the college course may have been too advanced for you, you were taking too many courses, or you were ill that semester). These variables should make you cautious in the conclusions you draw (e.g., here you might revise your conclusion to say, "I am *usually* good at math").

Deductive Reasoning

When you demonstrate the worth of your argument by citing a series of examples, you are reasoning inductively, that is, you are using numerous past experiences to conclude that something is or is not most probably true. Many of the maxims you live by are the result of inductive reasoning, for example, "A lie will always haunt you." Although you can probably think of exceptions to this statement, the voice of past experience advises you as to what *usually* happens. It is an inductive conclusion, but to apply it to your own life would require a kind of reasoning that is both speculative and more certain: deduction.

Deductive reasoning is how we arrive at opinions by applying past knowledge to new situations:

(Old knowledge)	Lies come back to haunt you.
(New knowledge)	I told a lie.
(Conclusion)	*It will come back to haunt me.*

In this example, if you didn't have the wisdom of the first statement, you wouldn't be able to predict the consequences of your telling a lie. Any deduction requires some prior knowledge derived either from deductive or inductive reasoning. This example is a syllogism, the common form for illustrating deductive reasoning. The "old knowledge" is technically called the *major premise,* the "new knowledge" the *minor premise.* Either premise may be proven inductively or deductively. However, the conclusion to a syllogism can only be arrived at deductively.

Let's consider another example using the technical terms:

(Major premise)	Birds fly south for the winter.
(Minor premise)	It is winter now.
(Conclusion)	*The birds fly south now.*

There are two tests you must make to test whether a deductive conclusion is valid: (1) is the syllogism logical? and (2) are the premises true?

Is it logical? To be logical, a syllogism must restrict itself to three primary terms. The primary terms in this example are "birds fly south," "winter," and "now". Each statement must share one, but only one, term with each of the other statements. Because "birds fly south" is shared by statements 1 and 3, "winter" is shared by statements 1 and 2, and "now" is shared by 2 and 3, the syllogism is logical.

Are the premises true? The minor premise ("It is winter now.") is probably difficult to dispute. We can rely on fairly certain evidence (the calendar, the weather) to agree on the time of year. The major premise, although it looks quite self-evident, may not be as certain as you think. It is a commonplace truth based on inductive reasoning: we have seen or heard about how most birds fly south for the winter and so we conclude that they do. However, this is a generalization based on inductive reasoning, a probable truth that cannot be as certain as the minor premise in this example. If we agree that the major premise (and, thus, the conclusion) is talking only about *most* birds, then we won't make hasty judgments about the penguins, turkeys, or pet canaries. To make certain your conclusion is true, be sure to qualify your statements, using "all" or "none" if they apply, and "most" or "few" when warranted. (Avoid qualifiers like "some" because it is difficult to draw a probable truth from a wishy-washy premise like "some do and some don't.")

EXERCISE

Test whether the conclusions to the following syllogisms are valid. Remember, for a deductive conclusion to be valid, the syllogism must be logical and the premises must be true.

1. Mammals are warm blooded.
   Reptiles are cold blooded.
   Reptiles are not mammals.

2. Virtuous people have many virtues.
   Vices are not virtues.
   Virtuous people do not have many vices.

3. Flibbers gyre in the gimble.
   Zaylias are flibbers.
   Zaylias gyre in the gimble.

4. Most working couples own a VCR.
   Steve and Lavon are a couple.
   They probably own a VCR.

5. Saturday morning television shows are violent.
   Pee Wee's Clubhouse is on Saturday morning T.V.
   Pee Wee's Clubhouse is violent.

6. All students in the class received an A.
   Yolanda received an A.
   Yolanda was in the class.

7. True Americans exercise their right to vote.
   My baby brother is a true American.
   My baby brother votes.

8. Blondes have more fun.
   Cinderella is a blonde.
   Cinderella has more fun.

9. Some students don't eat breakfast.
   Hollis is a student.
   Hollis doesn't eat breakfast.

RHETORICAL SYLLOGISMS AND ENTHYMEMES

Sometimes you cannot assess whether a syllogism is valid until you have more information about the claims made in the premises. Consider the following example, slightly revised from your previous exercise:

> True Americans exercise their right to vote.
> My baby brother is a true American.
> My baby brother exercises his right to vote.

On face value, the conclusion appears outrageous (a baby can't vote!). However, the syllogism is logical: each term ("True American," "my baby brother," and "exercises the right to vote") is properly distributed among the statements. The confusion lies in the meaning of those terms. The primary term that requires some explanation is "true American." The major premise implies that a true American is someone who actively participates in our democratic system; the minor premise implies that a true American is anyone born (or just living) in America. You cannot judge the validity of the minor premise unless you are certain what the speaker means. (Would the syllogism be valid if the speaker clarified "exercises the right to vote" by saying that the child's "right" is the right to abstain until he is 21?)

Syllogisms with uncertain premises require further explanation before they can be assessed. They represent the kind of argument that needs to be extended into an essay. When you write an extended argument, you need to identify what parts of your reasoning would not be self-evident to your reader. Constructing the syllogism behind your ideas can help you identify which terms and which premise you need to develop and explain so your reader will accept the logic of your argument.

The logical thesis statements you pulled out from your readings represent how the different authors developed their writing around the least certain premise in their argument. The technical term for the logical thesis statement is an *enthymeme* or *rhetorical syllogism.* It represents the conclusion of a syllogism in the first clause and the least acceptable premise in the "because" clause. Consider this example:

Syllogism

1. Our civil rights include the right to privacy.
2. Affirmative action programs invade our right to privacy.
3. Therefore, affirmative action programs violate our civil rights.

Enthymeme

> Affirmative action programs violate our civil rights because they invade upon our right to privacy.

This enthymeme represents the conclusion and the minor premise of the author's syllogism (listed after "because"). The bulk of the author's essay was devoted to an explanation of what affirmative action programs are, specifically those aspects of the programs that required applicants to disclose personal information unrelated to the duties of the job the applicants were applying for. The author spent very little time discussing the major premise of the syllogism because she felt that her readers already accepted it as true. Because the missing premise behind her enthymeme is the statement that she *assumed* her readers would accept without much clarification, it represents the major *assumption* behind her argument. (Most often, the assumption will be the major premise of the syllogism because it represents the more general, prior knowledge that you and your reader are likely to share.)

Testing Assumptions

The assumption behind the author's logical thesis statement represents what the author assumed you would agree with. Often arguments you read may appear valid, and you may be persuaded to believe them, but they are based on an assumption you would not want to agree with. Consider the argument that Tim developed from the following two-clause thesis:

> Dropping the bomb on Hiroshima preserved the dignity of the United States because it put an end to that dreadful war.

The argument is quite appealing, particularly because Tim included the adjective "dreadful" to emphasize how tragic continuation of World War II would have been. Although the reader would probably agree that the dropping of the atomic bomb was at least a major factor in the ending of the war, Tim spent the bulk of his essay reminding the reader of how devastating the war was to everyone involved, particularly emphasizing the horror faced daily by thousands of young American soldiers, many just teenagers. The argument was effective, but was it valid?

Because Tim spent his time discussing a premise you would most likely aready agree with, you should probably be suspicious of his assumption, the unstated premise that he did not prove in his essay. To identify the major assumption behind his argument, you need to reconstruct the syllogism behind his two-clause thesis statement. Remember that a syllogism must have at least three—but only three—primary terms to be logical, and these terms must be distributed evenly among the premises and the conclusion. To reconstruct the premise left out of an enthymeme, then, you need to identify which two of the three terms it contains. Here is the enthymeme again with the primary terms identified:

(1)	Dropping the bomb on Hiroshima
(2)	preserved the dignity of the United States
	because
(1 again)	it
(3)	put an end to that dreadful war.

Because term 1 is already repeated, the missing premise must repeat terms 2 and 3. To put these terms together into a statement, replace the shared term ("dropping the bomb") with an indefinite one ("anything") and, beginning with the remaining information in the "because" clause, recreate the logical relationship between the remaining two terms:

> (*Anything* that the United States did to) put an end to that dreadful war (would have) preserved her dignity.

Now that you have the assumed premise before you, do you accept it? Would *anything* that the United States did to stop the war have been dignified? (The United States actually bombed two Japanese cities, Hiroshima and Nagasaki. Would it have been dignified to bomb three—or four—or destroy the whole country?) This premise is obviously less valid than the one Tim chose to write about.

To make the written argument stronger, Tim should either make the missing premise his "because" clause (if he can prove it in his essay) or modify his enthymeme to make the assumption more valid. Here is a possible revision of his enthymeme:

> Dropping the bomb on Hiroshima preserved the dignity of the United States because it put an end to that dreadful war in the least destructive way.

> (*Assumption:* Anything the United States did to put an end to the war in the least destructive way would preserve her dignity.)

EXERCISE

Following are some possible two-clause thesis statements (enthymemes) for a few of the essays you have read in earlier chapters. Discuss the three thesis statements in each set and justify why one is a better representation of the essay than the other two. Then, test the thesis you have chosen by identifying the assumption (the missing premise) and examining whether you are willing to accept it without proof. (Remember, to pull out the assumed premise, you need to relate the two *unshared* terms.)

1.a. Students should write "bull" rather than "cow" because restating facts is boring.

1.b. Students who write "bull" will pass their exams because how they think is more important than what they know.

1.c. "Cow" not "bull" represents total ignorance because it represents a knowledge downright inimical to understanding.

2.a. Referring to argument as "war" prevents compromise because that metaphor makes us think we do not have to listen to what others say.

2.b. The metaphors we use play a central role in defining our everyday realities because they affect how we think and act.

2.c. We should avoid using metaphors because they control what we can think.

3.a. The American language is sexist because language reflects the attitudes of the society that uses it.

3.b. We should avoid using sexist language because that will prevent sexist attitudes in future generations.

3.c. Sexist attitudes cannot be changed by changing language because they lurk behind words that we do not consciously recognize as sexist.

4.a. The colonies have a duty to dissolve their allegiance to the British Crown because it has acted with the direct object to establish an absolute tyranny over them.

4.b. Creating the United States of America through revolution is our only option because only that action will establish government by the people.

4.c. The colonies have a duty to overthrow the King's authority over them because the King is a fink.

5.a. Nonviolent Direct Action will lead to a more Christian government because passive resistance does not lead to anarchy.

5.b. Nonviolent Direct Action displays the highest respect for law because conscientious violation of an unjust law arouses the conscience of the community over its injustice.

5.c. As Christians, we have no choice but to pursue a policy of nonviolent direct action because passive violation of unjust laws allows us to "turn the other cheek" while following our conscience.

6.a. Recognizing the enthymeme behind an argument makes it easier to accept what the author is saying because the enthymeme reveals the logic the author has used.

6.b. Recognizing the enthymeme behind an argument makes it easier to disagree with the author because it reveals how the author's position is not universally true.

6.c. Recognizing the enthymeme behind an argument can help you discover whether to believe the author's thesis because the enthymeme can expose what the author assumes you will believe without proof.

CREATING YOUR OWN LOGICAL THESIS STATEMENT

Although you have been practicing how to test the logic behind arguments you read, you can use this same procedure to test any argument you wish to make. Ideally, you will want to create a logical thesis statement for your essay *before* you write. If you don't, you might waste time and energy writing a draft around an argument that is either illogical (because it is based on an illogical syllogism) or invalid (because it does not give attention to the premise that your reader needs clarified). Here are some steps that can help you create a logical thesis statement:

1. Identify the question at issue for you and your readers, and state your answer as a complete clause.
2. Ask yourself why your answer is true, and state your reason as a complete "because" clause. Make sure your "because" clause makes a claim you can prove by offering information that is new to your reader. This "new information" may consist of examples drawn from your past experiences and reading for other courses, or may just be a new way to interpret an argument you and your reader have both read.
3. Analyze your two-clause statement as an enthymeme. Discover the syllogism

behind it by using the first clause as the conclusion, listing the "because" clause as one of the premises, and formulating the missing premise.

4. Ask yourself which premise your reader would be least likely to accept.
5. Adjust your enthymeme, if necessary, to make the "because" clause contain the premise you most need to clarify for your reader.

EXERCISE

Before you prepare to write your essay in response to the readings about science in the next chapter, practice creating your own logical thesis by addressing the issues listed below. Also try reading the map contained in your proposed enthymemes, considering how you might develop the proof for your "because" clause.

1. Would mandatory drug testing in the schools violate a student's rights?
2. Do schools place too much emphasis on sports?
3. What is the most important book we should read?
4. What is the most pressing problem facing society today?
5. How did it come about?
6. What should we do about it?

CHAPTER SIX

Reasoning About Science

"**S**cience" can be a confusing term. For example, in many colleges, political science, psychology, history, and anthropology all call themselves "social sciences" because they investigate *behavior,* that is, they hypothesize about how animals, primarily humans, tend to act in response to certain stimuli. Behavior is examined in the context of political, interpersonal, historical, or religious situations. On the other hand, in these same colleges, geology, chemistry, physics, and biology call themselves "natural sciences" because they look at *physical nature* (which includes, but is certainly not restricted to, the human animal). In this chapter, you will be introduced to how natural scientists reason. You will also become aware of some ways the community of natural scientists differs from the community of social scientists, both in the kinds of questions it explores and in the type of information it uses to answer them. To help you discover these essential differences, let's review what you learned about syllogisms and enthymemes in Chapter 5.

HOW THE QUESTIONS DIFFER FROM DISCIPLINE TO DISCIPLINE

Although some fields may rely more on inductive than deductive processes (you will see that natural science is one), almost every kind of written argument reflects the deductive process you must use to convey your findings to an audience. In Chapter 5, you learned how testing an author's two-clause thesis statement as an enthymeme (or rhetorical syllogism) can help you identify the question an author is addressing and the kinds of premises he or she uses to reason toward its answer. Both the stated "because" clause and the assumption behind the author's argument reflect what kind of information the author uses to justify his or her thesis. For this reason, the enthymeme is a particularly helpful tool for identifying which kinds of questions and information are respected by the different disciplines.

From Chapter 4, you already know the types of questions political scientists ask: "What should be the relationship between the government and the people?" "What should a ruler do to establish and preserve this ideal relationship?" What makes this type of reasoning particular to political science is not the subjects it addresses (i.e., the nouns "rulers" or "individuals") but the verbs (e.g., "should be"

and "govern"). The verbs imply a relationship between the subjects under consideration, a relationship respected by other political scientists as a valid way to establish
public policy.

     To understand how a natural scientist's questions differ from a political scien-
tist's, you need to analyze how the verbs in their respective questions differ. Behind
every specific question a scientist asks is a more general question that represents
what is important to a scientist. Consider scientists who ask, "How can we cure
cancer?" To find a cure, they have to address the more general question, "What is
cancer?" To develop any new solutions to a scientific problem, the natural scientist
must identify the nature of the thing that created the problem in the first place (e.g.,
What *is* a quasar? a bagworm? a brain?). Their questions are questions of definition,
all based on a copulative verb like "is."

     The verb "is" focuses the scientist's argument on a particular type of reasoning.
Let's review the four types of argument you were introduced to in Chapter 1:

The Four Types of Argument

Policy:	What should be done?
Value:	Is it good?
Consequence:	Why did it occur?
	What effect did it have?
Definition:	What is it?

Although natural scientists may address other questions rather than just questions
of definition, their primary argument focuses on an investigation of "what is it?" For
example, although a chemist may discuss in his or her lab report what happened
when the AIDS virus came into contact with a certain gene, the discussion of what
came about as a consequence is important primarily because it gives us a partial
answer to the question "What is AIDS?"

     Once the chemist has answered the question of definition, though, he or she
may also make some suggestions about the implications of the finding, considering
question such as: "Then is the AIDS virus more or less destructive than we thought,
and what course of action should we take to eradicate it?" Once scientists can
determine what the AIDS virus *is,* they have a better idea what *effects* it has on the
body, just how *bad* it is, and what we *should do* to cure it.

     Sometimes, though, the other types of reasoning are beyond the specialization
of science. For example, some social and moral philosophers may see the chemist's
answer to "What is the value of the AIDS virus?" as avoiding a more important value
argument: that the AIDS virus is "good" or "bad" based on the effect its presence has
had on our behavior and quality of life. Similarly, politicians would argue that, in
terms of policy, how we should respond to the AIDS epidemic depends less on which
chemical procedure would ensure its eradication than on which is most cost efficient, or even whether a social program that addresses prevention rather than a cure
might be better overall for the nation. However, although the chemist might be
ill-equipped to address these other types of arguments, no one could reason as well
about them without some knowledge of what the AIDS virus is, the chemist's specialized contribution to the discussion.

On the other hand, there are some disciplines that do not need to begin their investigation with a definition question. Political scientists specializing in American government, for example, do not need to define what democracy is, how it came about, or whether it is good. The answers to these questions can be assumed. What they need to investigate, though, is what governments should do to preserve democracy. Because political science reasons primarily about a question of policy, it represents an extreme contrast to the type of reasoning used by a natural scientist.

You can determine which type of argument is primary for a writer by analyzing the verbs of both the questions asked and the assertions made to answer these questions. Consider once again the list given you in Chapter 1, this time paired with representatives of different disciplines that tend to focus their reasoning on each type of argument:

Policy
Political science: "What should be done?"
(questions of government and law)

Value
Literature/Philosophy: "Is it good?"
(questions of truth, beauty, and ethics)

Consequence
History/Economics/Psychology: "Why did it occur?" or "What effect will it have?"
(questions of cause and effect)

Definition
Natural science: "What is it?"
(questions of observation)

Although this book will not survey all the different disciplines, it does introduce you to arguments in these fields to give you practice identifying and writing on each type of argument.

HOW INFORMATION DIFFERS FROM DISCIPLINE TO DISCIPLINE

In addition to the kinds of questions it asks, each discipline is distinctive in the kind of information it uses to reason toward an answer. There are two kinds of information at operation in the syllogism. The assumed premise behind the enthymeme (usually the major premise of the syllogism), if it is valid for readers in the discipline, represents *old information.* It is usually what we refer to as a "fact" because those knowledgeable in the subject agree that it has already been proven to be true. (For example, since political scientists in American government agree upon their definition of democracy, they would view that definition as old information.) The "because" clause of the enthymeme (usually the minor premise of the syllogism) represents new information that a writer brings into the conversation to help further understanding of the subject. To develop a conclusion about what the new information means, a writer needs to synthesize the new information with the old:

$$\text{Major premise} + \text{minor premise} = \text{Conclusion}$$
$$\text{Old information} + \text{new information} = \text{New Knowledge}$$

Consider how scientists might use old information to reason about the new information that earth's seasons have been increasingly warmer (what has become known as "The Greenhouse Effect"):

Processing Information as a Scientist

Old information: The ozone layer in the atmosphere protects the earth from the sun's harmful rays.

New information: The earth is experiencing a dangerous global warming.

Conclusion: Something must be causing the deterioration of the ozone layer.

How scientists use new information about the earth's warmer temperatures is shaped by the information they already have.

Note how the new information of a global warming might be used differently in the reasoning of a psychologist:

Processing Information as a Psychologist

Old information: When confronted with increased stress in one area of their lives, individuals move to decrease stress in other areas.

New information: A global warming is increasing stress on our physical wellbeing.

Conclusion: The global warming is moving individuals to decrease stress in their interpersonal relationships, perhaps even responsible for the defusing of Cold War tensions.

Note how psychologists would shape information about the rise in global temperatures to apply it to the old information in their field. Because the information that makes up the field of psychology addresses individual behavior, psychologists would have to define the new information of a global warming as a human phenomenon in order to draw a significant conclusion about what it means. Both fields would be addressing the same new discovery, but the old information in their fields of study would require them to provide different information about it. The difference in the kind of new information they use to develop their argument is reflected both in the old information they use to interpret it and in the nature of the questions they ultimately address. Scientists ask, "What is the physical cause of this global warming?" whereas psychologists investigate "Why are individuals behaving less confrontational in their interpersonal relationships?"

SCIENTIFIC REASONING

As you have learned, natural scientists ask general questions of definition. To answer questions about what something is, they rely upon a specific kind of information—inductive reasoning from concrete observation. Sir Francis Bacon, a seventeenth-century English philosopher, strongly influenced the development of modern scientific method by proving how we can mistake the true nature of something outside of us if we do not test our immediate impressions with repeated observations. Today, scientific reasoning is primarily inductive; it relies primarily on systematic experimentation, where the greater the number of similar results the more valid the conclusion.

A good example of how natural scientists reason from induction to deduction is the reasoning process Sir Isaac Newton (1642–1727) might have used to develop his theory of gravity. After too many apples fell on his head, Newton realized that apples never seemed to fall up. By watching several apples drop from the tree, he felt he could safely conclude that apples *always* would do so. As Newton thought about the apples that hit him, he remembered all of the inanimate objects that could move only if someone or something pushed or pulled them in some way. By synthesizing his inductive conclusion about apples with this old information, he could deduce a theory of gravity:

A Possible Syllogism for Newton's Reasoning

Nothing can move without some force acting on it.
Apples, when released from above, always fall down.
Therefore, some force (I'll call it gravity) must be acting on apples to make them fall down.

A Possible Enthymeme for Newton's Reasoning

Some force ("gravity") makes apples fall down to the ground *because* apples when released from trees always fall to the ground.

If Newton were to write a paper to propose his theory of gravity, he could *assume* his colleague knew the conditions under which objects could move, but he would have to cite repeated evidence of apples falling out of trees to justify his inductive conclusion ("apples when released from trees always fall down"). His argument would answer the question "What is gravity?" And he would be using information based on inductive reasoning to justify his definition.

Following are three essays that introduce you to the kind of discussions scientists have and the way they reason with one another in their writing. All three overtly discuss the method behind their scientific reasoning and how it differs from other fields of inquiry. Although they all discuss the natural sciences, they each represent a different way to talk about the subject. The first essay, Sherburne Cook's investigation into the human ecology that caused the population decline of the California Indians, represents the analytical method behind technical scientific reports. The second essay, by Harvard scientist Stephen Jay Gould, represents applied scientific theory. He applies his theory of scientific method to reason differently than other scientists have about the data they have compiled on the ichneumon fly. The last essay, by Thomas S. Kuhn, represents the philosophy of science. Kuhn addresses a question about the nature of scientific inquiry in order to suggest how it produces new ideas, how it is valuable, and how we should teach it. All include some discussion of scientific theory, the method by which knowledge is made in the field, and draw some conclusions about how it distinguishes itself from other fields of inquiry. As you read these essays and discuss them with your classmates, try to determine whether the authors practice the scientific theory they preach.

A Study in Human Ecology: The Conflict Between the California Indian and White Civilization

Sherburne F. Cook *(1896–1974)*

Sherburne Cook was a professor of human physiology at the University of California. His work was a blend of population biology and what he describes here as "human ecology"—the environmental factors affecting the survival of a race. In the 1940s, his painstaking statistical work on the causes of the disintegration of the California Indian population led to several startling conclusions, conclusions that appeared to pass judgment on the Anglo-American settlers and their responsibility for the destruction of a whole population.

The following is a synthesis of the introduction and conclusion of Cook's book-length report of his findings, The Conflict Between the California Indian and White Civilization. *Much of the detailed data he used in the body of his book is left out, but you can get a sense from his conclusion how thorough his examination was. As you read this selection, note how his argument focuses on a question of definition: "What was the racial impact, first of the Spanish missionaries and, later, of the Anglo-American settlers, on the decline of the primitive Indian population?" Does he convince you his analysis is objective, or does his argument appear to be primarily fashioned around another type of argument, for example, a value question such as "Were the American settlers good people?" or the policy question still being explored today, "What should we do for the American Indian people?" As you read, underline specific words or phrases that might help you decide.*

The present work consists of an examination of the reaction of a primitive human population to a new and disturbing environment. As such it constitutes a study in human ecology, the word ecology being used to denote all the relations of a biological group with its physical and social surroundings. In other terms, it concerns itself with the factors and responses inherent in, and resulting from, the interaction of two civilizations, the one old and static, the other new and dynamic. In particular, those factors are considered which lend themselves to at least semiquantitative treatment.

The investigation concerns the disintegration of the aboriginal Indian stock of the middle Pacific coast of the United States under the influence of Spanish and American culture. This particular example has been selected for various reasons.

1. The effect of racial impact and competition was here unusually complete. It resulted in the substantial disappearance of the primitive population and the utter extinction of its civilization. The weaker established race gave way with little opposition to the stronger invading race. This response may

be advantageously contrasted with two analogous biological competitions which occurred on our continent, the Spanish-Apache contact in the Southwest and the Spanish-Aztec contact in Central Mexico. In the former, the primitive race suffered little diminution of population and no weakening of culture in the course of three centuries. In the latter, there was but a moderate effect on population, although the civilization was radically altered. In the Mexican area, however, in contrast to the other two regions, the established race, largely through interbreeding, extensively assimilated the invader, with the eventual emergence of a new, composite race and civilization. We have thus before us examples of three fundamentally distinct types of human adaptation to a newly introduced and in all respects similar invading civilization.

2. The replacement, historically, of the Spanish by American political control affords the opportunity of comparing the response on the part of one human group to contact with two other quite different groups. This situation has not been duplicated elsewhere in North America except, perhaps, in the southwestern states.

3. There is a relatively large body of information readily available in the libraries and archives of California.[1]

4. The extensive number of individuals concerned makes it possible in certain connections to utilize large enough masses to warrant employment of statistical methods. This could not be done if the populations were small or their approximate numerical value unknown.

The wide field for investigation presented by any comprehensive problem in human biology with its physical, social, and psychological ramifications, obviously makes it necessary to restrict discussion and detailed consideration to various specific topics, particularly to those which lend themselves, at least partially, to concrete treatment. Facility in handling factual material, if nothing else, demands that certain perhaps artificial restrictions be imposed for the sake of clarity in presentation. Consequently, this study has been arranged along the lines of a few leading ideas even at the sacrifice of omitting or suppressing matters which might otherwise appear pertinent.

Finally, it should be pointed out that, since we are dealing with events which occurred in the past, it is necessary to employ what may be termed the historical method rather than the field or observational method. The latter is, of course, the one universally favored by the animal biologist, but it is very rarely available for the study of the human species over a long period of time. Still more unutilizable is the experimental method, in the course of which the organisms may be deliberately subjected to all sorts of treatment and in which controls for comparison may be maintained. Nevertheless, the fact that these two avenues of approach are closed to us should not prevent us from

---

[1]All citations to manuscripts, unless otherwise stated, refer to documents contained in the Bancroft Library of the University of California, Berkeley. Many of these are in the form of transcripts. The "Bancroft compilation" referred to in connection with mission population is a tabular compilation of annual statistics taken by Hubert Howe Bancroft from original sources now lost.

using the sources of knowledge which are open, that is to say, the records of what human beings, the organisms concerned in our study, have actually done and how they have reacted under definite conditions. . . .

. . . . The fundamental clue to success in interracial competition is the change in population. Under the relatively favorable control of the missions the natives suffered considerable diminution. From the mission records it is ascertained that approximately 53,600 Indians underwent conversion. At the end of the mission period (1834) there were 14,900 left, a reduction of 72 per cent. This signifies a mean annual reduction of 0.9 per cent. The six wild tribes which came into direct contact with the California civil and military civilization between 1800 and 1848 were reduced from approximately 58,900 to 35,950, or 0.8 percent annually. The surviving mission Indians together with the remainder of the wild tribes which were subjected to Anglo-American influence from 1848 to 1865 diminished from 72,000 to 23,000, a mean annual depletion of 2.9 per cent. From these figures alone, it is apparent that the impact of the settlement from the United States was three times as severe as that of pre-American colonization.

The triad of factors which brings about a decline in population is war, disease, and starvation. In the missions, war was of negligible consequence. A study of expeditions and sporadic fighting shows that for the six wild tribes mentioned above, roughly 11.5 per cent of the decline may be attributed to casualties suffered in armed conflict. The corresponding value for the period after 1848 is 8.6 per cent. Hence, although the absolute effect of warfare was greater in the American period, its relative influence population decline was substantially the same as in the years of Ibero-American domination.

The relative effect of disease was also quite uniform, since in the missions, in the valley before 1848, and generally after 1848, approximately 60 per cent of the decline may be attributed to this cause. Such a result is not surprising, since most of the mortality was due to introduced epidemic maladies and the action of these upon a nonimmune population is entirely independent of the culture which introduces them. It is probable that the spread of disease was intensified in the missions by the crowded living conditions there but, on the other hand, this factor may have been nullified by the hygienic, sanitary, and curative measures adopted by the missionaries.

The effect of dietary maladjustment cannot be evaluated in strictly numerical terms. This factor operates on both birth rate and death rate; moreover, very few persons actually died of direct starvation. In the missions the subsistence level seems to have been low, and, because of a tendency to rely upon cereal crops, there may have been vitamin and mineral deficiencies. The nonconverted Indians encountered the problem of depletion rather than alteration of diet. Until 1848, the reduction of food supply was not serious because the few settlers in the interior did not materially alter the natural flora and fauna. After the gold rush, however, the universal conversion of fertile valleys into farms, the widespread cattle ranching on the hills, and the pollution of the streams all combined to destroy the animal and plant species used for food. The transition to a white dietary, although ultimately accomplished, was rendered difficult by economic and social obstacles. During the interim a great deal of malnutrition was present. From the nutritional standpoint, therefore, the natives suffered most under Anglo-Saxon domination.

Certain quasicultural items were undoubtedly significant in intensifying the effect of the primary lethal factors. Among these were, in particular, labor and sex relations. In the missions a great deal of unrest and maladjustment was caused by the current system of forced labor and of drastically restricted liberty in sex matters. In both these, the basic difficulty was not physical but emotional and was derived from the compulsion which forced activity into new and unaccustomed channels. Under the Americans, compulsion was of a different character, but even more disruptive in its effects. The native was compelled to labor by economic necessity rather than by personal command. In acquiring the tools and the facility for work he was obstructed by a hostile society, rather than aided by a paternal government. Hence his progress was slow and his entire material welfare—diet and health—suffered in consequence. From the sexual inhibitions of the mission environment he was carried by the Americans to the most violent and brutal excesses and his women subjected to universal outrage. The hatred and despair thus generated found expression in still further retardation of his material adjustment.

On the whole, therefore, and for many causes, the conflict of the native with the settlers from the United States was characterized by far greater violence than the conflict with the invaders from Latin America. This violence was reflected in greater relative population decline and in more difficult adjustment in all material respects under the American occupation.

QUESTIONS FOR A CRITICAL REREADING

Use the following questions to help you reread Cook's argument critically. As you enter your answers in your reading notebook, try to keep your answers objective, citing evidence from the text when you need to justify your answer. You will be able to reason about the consequences, value, and policy implications of Cook's argument later, when you discuss possible issues behind Cook's argument with your classmates.

1. Read Cook's first two paragraphs, underlining the verbs he uses. What type of argument do they imply Cook will be making? What other features of his rhetoric—both what he says and how he says it—help focus his argument on that type of reasoning?

2. As in most scientific reports, Cook's initial statement of the problem is followed by a discussion of the method he used to solve it. What portion of the selection presents Cook's method? Do you agree with his argument that it was scientifically sound?

3. In the body of his argument, Cook classifies his data according to three categories: statistics of deaths caused by war, by disease, and by starvation. Later, he adds two more, labor and sex relations, which he calls "quasicultural." What does he mean by that term? How would the data for these categories differ from that of the other three? Is his use of them in his scientific analysis justified? Why or why not?

4. Cook's concluding paragraph clearly presents the thesis behind his argument. Rephrase his conclusion as an enthymemic thesis. What is the missing premise that he assumes you agree with? Do you agree with it? Why or why not? Does it represent old knowledge in the field of science? Explain your answer.

POSSIBLE ISSUES FOR WRITING

Following are some of the possible issues behind Cook's argument. As you discuss these with your classmates and jot down in your notebook the different positions you hear, try to keep in mind the type of argument the discussion is addressing. Sometimes, shifting the discussion from a question of definition to a question of value or policy can expose the real differences between you and your classmates and make it easier to write your essay later on.

1. Why do you think Cook's study upset so many in the 1940s? What type of argument might they have used against him? Who might object to Cook's study today? Would they use the same argument against him? Why or why not?
2. Under his discussion of the methodology he used, Cook mentions that he used "the records of what human beings, the organisms concerned in our study, have actually done. . . ." How appropriate is his use of the word "organisms"? What does it imply about his attitude toward the Indians? Are there any other uses of language in the selection that imply his attitude toward his subject? What are they? Do they hinder or support his attempt to reason scientifically?
3. Today we are attempting to correct any injustices done to Native Americans. Museums are being forced to return artifacts from burial sites to their resting places; tribes earlier forced to relocate to reservation lands are seeking recompense for the land that was taken from them. In view of Cook's argument, do you think we are doing too little, too much, or just enough? Why or why not?
4. What is America's attitude toward the Native American today? Consider how the Indian is portrayed in history books, movies, and advertising. How do they and games such as "Cowboys and Indians" affect our interpretation of the past? Assuming that Cook's study presents us with the fact and these traditional attitudes present the myth, which is most valuable for us to believe? Why?

Nonmoral Nature

Stephen Jay Gould (1941–   )

Stephen Jay Gould is one of today's most popular science writers. A professor of geology at Harvard University, he is author of several books and collections of essays taken from Natural History. *"Nonmoral Nature" was originally published in that magazine in 1982.* Natural History *is read by specialists and nonspecialists alike, and this essay, as most of Gould's work, is directed to a wide audience. Part of Gould's appeal is his ability to express with clarity and simplicity the most complex scientific principles, making his findings accessible to all.*

In this essay, Gould surveys different approaches scientists have taken to explain the existence of the ichneumon fly. In the course of this survey, though, Gould argues for a particular theory of scientific reasoning that he feels earlier scientists have failed to follow. As you read his essay, ask yourself whether Gould's own writing lives up to the ideal standard of scientific reasoning that he uses to criticize other scientists.

When the Right Honorable and Reverend Francis Henry, earl of Bridgewater, died in February, 1829, he left £8,000 to support a series of books "on the power, wisdom and goodness of God, as manifested in the creation." William Buckland, England's first official academic geologist and later dean of Westminster, was invited to compose one of the nine Bridgewater Treatises. In it he discussed the most pressing problem of natural theology: if God is benevolent and the Creation displays his "power, wisdom and goodness," then why are we surrounded with pain, suffering, and apparently senseless cruelty in the animal world?

Buckland considered the depredation of "carnivorous races" as the primary challenge to an idealized world in which the lion might dwell with the lamb. He resolved the issue to his satisfaction by arguing that carnivores actually increase "the aggregate of animal enjoyment" and "diminish that of pain." The death of victims, after all, is swift and relatively painless, victims are spared the ravages of decrepitude and senility, and populations do not outrun their food supply to the greater sorrow of all. God knew what he was doing when he made lions. Buckland concluded in hardly concealed rapture:

> The appointment of death by the agency of carnivora, as the ordinary termination of animal existence, appears therefore in its main results to be a dispensation of benevolence; it deducts much from the aggregate amount of the pain of universal death; it abridges, and almost annihilates, throughout the brute creation, the misery of disease, and accidental injuries, and lingering decay; and imposes such salutary restraint upon excessive increase of numbers, that the supply of food maintains perpetually a due ratio to the demand. The result is, that the surface of the land and depths of the waters

are ever crowded with myriads of animated beings, the pleasures of whose life are co-extensive with its duration; and which throughout the little day of existence that is allotted to them, fulfill with joy the functions for which they were created.

We may find a certain amusing charm in Buckland's vision today, but such arguments did begin to address "the problem of evil" for many of Buckland's contemporaries—how could a benevolent God create such a world of carnage and bloodshed? Yet these claims could not abolish the problem of evil entirely, for nature includes many phenomena far more horrible in our eyes than simple predation. I suspect that nothing evokes greater disgust in most of us than slow destruction of a host by an internal parasite—slow ingestion, bit by bit, from the inside. In no other way can I explain why *Alien,* an uninspired, grade-C, formula horror film, should have won such a following. That single scene of Mr. Alien, popping forth as a baby parasite from the body of a human host, was both sickening and stunning. Our nineteenth-century forebears maintained similar feelings. Their greatest challenge to the concept of a benevolent deity was not simple predation—for one can admire quick and efficient butcheries, especially since we strive to construct them ourselves—but slow death by parasitic ingestion. The classic case, treated at length by all the great naturalists, involved the so-called ichneumon fly. Buckland had sidestepped the major issue.

The ichneumon fly, which provoked such concern among natural theologians, was a composite creature representing the habits of an enormous tribe. The Ichneumonoidea are a group of wasps, not flies, that include more species than all the vertebrates combined (wasps, with ants and bees, constitute the order Hymenoptera; flies, with their two wings—wasps have four—form the order Diptera). In addition, many related wasps of similar habits were often cited for the same grisly details. Thus, the famous story did not merely implicate a single aberrant species (perhaps a perverse leakage from Satan's realm), but perhaps hundreds of thousands of them—a large chunk of what could only be God's creation.

The ichneumons, like most wasps, generally live freely as adults but pass their larval life as parasites feeding on the bodies of other animals, almost invariably members of their own phylum, Arthropoda. The most common victims are caterpillars (butterfly and moth larvae), but some ichneumons prefer aphids and others attack spiders. Most hosts are parasitized as larvae, but some adults are attacked, and many tiny ichneumons inject their brood directly into the egg of their host.

The free-flying females locate an appropriate host and then convert it to a food factory for their own young. Parasitologists speak of ectoparasitism when the uninvited guest lives on the surface of its host, and endoparasitism when the parasite dwells within. Among endoparasitic ichneumons, adult females pierce the host with their ovipositor and deposit eggs within it. (The ovipositor, a thin tube extending backward from the wasp's rear end, may be many times as long as the body itself.) Usually, the host is not otherwise

inconvenienced for the moment, at least until the eggs hatch and the ichneumon larvae begin their grim work of interior excavation. Among ectopara-
sites, however, many females lay their eggs directly upon the host's body.
Since an active host would easily dislodge the egg, the ichneumon mother
often simultaneously injects a toxin that paralyzes the caterpillar or other
victim. The paralysis may be permanent, and the caterpillar lies, alive but
immobile, with the agent of its future destruction secure on its belly. The egg
hatches, the helpless caterpillar twitches, the wasp larva pierces and begins
its grisly feast.

Since a dead and decaying caterpillar will do the wasp larva no good,
it eats in a pattern that cannot help but recall, in our inappropriate, anthropocentric interpretation, the ancient English penalty for treason—drawing and
quartering, with its explicit object of extracting as much torment as possible
by keeping the victim alive and sentient. As the king's executioner drew out
and burned his client's entrails, so does the ichneumon larva eat fat bodies
and digestive organs first, keeping the caterpillar alive by preserving intact
the essential heart and central nervous system. Finally, the larva completes
its work and kills its victim, leaving behind the caterpillar's empty shell. Is
it any wonder that ichneumons, not snakes or lions, stood as the paramount
challenge to God's benevolence during the heyday of natural theology?

As I read through the nineteenth- and twentieth-century literature on
ichneumons, nothing amused me more than the tension between an intellectual knowledge that wasps should not be described in human terms and a
literary or emotional inability to avoid the familiar categories of epic and
narrative, pain and destruction, victim and vanquisher. We seem to be caught
in the mythic structures of our own cultural sagas, quite unable, even in our
basic descriptions, to use any other language than the metaphors of battle and
conquest. We cannot render this corner of natural history as anything but
story, combining the themes of grim horror and fascination and usually
ending not so much with pity for the caterpillar as with admiration for the
efficiency of the ichneumon.

I detect two basic themes in most epic descriptions: the struggles of prey
and the ruthless efficiency of parasites. Although we acknowledge that we
witness little more than automatic instinct or physiological reaction, still we
describe the defenses of hosts as though they represented conscious struggles.
Thus, aphids kick and caterpillars may wriggle violently as wasps attempt to
insert their ovipositors. The pupa of the tortoise-shell butterfly (usually considered an inert creature silently awaiting its conversion from duckling to
swan) may contort its abdominal region so sharply that attacking wasps are
thrown into the air. The caterpillars of *Hapalia,* when attacked by the wasp
Apanteles machaeralis, drop suddenly from their leaves and suspend themselves in air by a silken thread. But the wasp may run down the thread and
insert its eggs nonetheless. Some hosts can encapsulate the injected egg with
blood cells that aggregate and harden, thus suffocating the parasite.

J. H. Fabre, the great nineteenth-century French entomologist, who remains to this day the preeminently literate natural historian of insects, made

a special study of parasitic wasps and wrote with an unabashed anthropocentrism about the struggles of paralyzed victims (see his books *Insect Life* and *The Wonders of Instinct*). He describes some imperfectly paralyzed caterpillars that struggle so violently every time a parasite approaches that the wasp larvae must feed with unusual caution. They attach themselves to a silken strand from the roof of their burrow and descend upon a safe and exposed part of the caterpillar:

> The grub is at dinner: head downwards, it is digging into the limp belly of one of the caterpillars. . . . At the least sign of danger in the heap of caterpillars, the larva retreats . . . and climbs back to the ceiling, where the swarming rabble cannot reach it. When peace is restored, it slides down [its silken cord] and returns to table, with its head over the viands and its rear upturned and ready to withdraw in case of need.

In another chapter, he describes the fate of a paralyzed cricket:

> One may see the cricket, bitten to the quick, vainly move its antennae and abdominal styles, open and close its empty jaws, and even move a foot, but the larva is safe and searches its vitals with impunity. What an awful nightmare for the paralyzed cricket!

Fabre even learned to feed some paralyzed victims by placing a syrup of sugar and water on their mouthparts—thus showing that they remained alive, sentient, and (by implication) grateful for any palliation of their inevitable fate. If Jesus, immobile and thirsting on the cross, received only vinegar from his tormentors, Fabre at least could make an ending bittersweet.

The second theme, ruthless efficiency of the parasites, leads to the opposite conclusion—grudging admiration for the victors. We learn of their skill in capturing dangerous hosts often many times larger than themselves. Caterpillars may be easy game, but the psammocharid wasps prefer spiders. They must insert their ovipositors in a safe and precise spot. Some leave a paralyzed spider in its own burrow. *Planiceps hirsutus,* for example, parasitizes a California trapdoor spider. It searches for spider tubes on sand dunes, then digs into nearby sand to disturb the spider's home and drive it out. When the spider emerges, the wasp attacks, paralyzes its victim, drags it back into its own tube, shuts and fastens the trapdoor, and deposits a single egg upon the spider's abdomen. Other psammocharids will drag a heavy spider back to a previously prepared cluster of clay or mud cells. Some amputate a spider's legs to make the passage easier. Others fly back over water, skimming a buoyant spider along the surface.

Some wasps must battle with other parasites over a host's body. *Rhyssella curvipes* can detect the larvae of wood wasps deep within alder wood and drill down to its potential victims with its sharply ridged ovipositor. *Pseudorhyssa alpestris,* a related parasite, cannot drill directly into wood since its slender ovipositor bears only rudimentary cutting ridges. It locates the holes made by *Rhyssella,* inserts its ovipositor, and lays an egg on the host (already conveniently paralyzed by *Rhyssella*), right next to the egg deposited by its relative. The two eggs hatch at about the same time, but the larva of *Pseudorhyssa* has a bigger head bearing much larger mandibles. *Pseudorhyssa* seizes the smaller *Rhyssella* larva, destroys it, and proceeds to feast upon a banquet already well prepared.

Other praises for the efficiency of mothers invoke the themes of early, quick, and often. Many ichneumons don't even wait for their hosts to develop into larvae, but parasitize the egg directly (larval wasps may then either drain the egg itself or enter the developing host larva). Others simply move fast. *Apanteles militaris* can deposit up to seventy-two eggs in a single second. Still others are doggedly persistent. *Aphidius gomezi* females produce up to 1,500 eggs and can parasitize as many as 600 aphids in a single working day. In a bizarre twist upon "often," some wasps indulge in polyembryony, a kind of iterated supertwinning. A single egg divides into cells that aggregate into as many as 500 individuals. Since some polyembryonic wasps parasitize caterpillars much larger than themselves and may lay up to six eggs in each, as many as 3,000 larvae may develop within, and feed upon, a single host. These wasps are endoparasites and do not paralyze their victims. The caterpillars writhe back and forth, not (one suspects) from pain, but merely in response to the commotion induced by thousands of wasp larvae feeding within.

The efficiency of mothers is matched by their larval offspring. I have already mentioned the pattern of eating less essential parts first, thus keeping the host alive and fresh to its final and merciful dispatch. After the larva digests every edible morsel of its victim (if only to prevent later fouling of its abode by decaying tissue), it may still use the outer shell of its host. One aphid parasite cuts a hole in the belly of its victim's shell, glues the skeleton to a leaf by sticky secretions from its salivary gland, and then spins a cocoon to pupate within the aphid's shell.

In using inappropriate anthropocentric language in this romp through the natural history of ichneumons, I have tried to emphasize just why these wasps became a preeminent challenge to natural theology—the antiquated doctrine that attempted to infer God's essence from the products of his creation. I have used twentieth-century examples for the most part, but all themes were known and stressed by the great nineteenth-century natural theologians. How then did they square the habits of these wasps with the goodness of God? How did they extract themselves from this dilemma of their own making?

The strategies were as varied as the practitioners; they shared only the theme of special pleading for an a priori doctrine—they knew that God's benevolence was lurking somewhere behind all these tales of apparent horror. Charles Lyell, for example, in the first edition of his epochal *Principles of Geology* (1830–1833), decided that caterpillars posed such a threat to vegetation that any natural checks upon them could only reflect well upon a creating deity, for caterpillars would destroy human agriculture "did not Providence put causes in operation to keep them in due bounds."

The Reverend William Kirby, rector of Barham and Britain's foremost entomologist, chose to ignore the plight of caterpillars and focused instead upon the virtue of mother love displayed by wasps in provisioning their young with such care.

> The great object of the female is to discover a proper nidus for her eggs. In search of this she is in constant motion. Is the caterpillar of a butterfly or moth the appropriate food for her young? You see her alight upon the plants where they are most usually to be met with, run quickly over them, carefully examining every leaf, and, having found the unfortunate object of her search, insert her sting into its flesh, and there deposit an egg. . . . The active Ichneumon braves every danger, and does not desist until her courage and address have insured subsistence for one of her future progeny.

Kirby found this solicitude all the more remarkable because the female wasp will never see her child and enjoy the pleasures of parenthood. Yet her love compels her to danger nonetheless:

> A very large proportion of them are doomed to die before their young come into existence. But in these the passion is not extinguished. . . . When you witness the solicitude with which they provide for the security and sustenance of their future young, you can scarcely deny to them love for a progeny they are never destined to behold.

Kirby also put in a good word for the marauding larvae, praising them for their forbearance in eating selectively to keep their caterpillar prey alive. Would we all husband our resources with such care!

> In this strange and apparently cruel operation one circumstance is truly remarkable. The larva of the Ichneumon, though every day, perhaps for months, it gnaws the inside of the caterpillar, and though at last it has devoured almost every part of it except the skin and intestines, carefully all this time it avoids injuring the vital organs, as if aware that its own existence depends on that of the insect upon which it preys! . . . What would be the impression which a similar instance amongst the race of quadrupeds would make upon us? If, for example, an animal . . . should be found to feed upon the inside of a dog, devouring only those parts not essential to life, while it cautiously left uninjured the heart, arteries, lungs, and intestines,—should we not regard such an instance as a perfect prodigy, as an example of instinctive forbearance almost miraculous? [The last three quotes come from the 1856, and last pre-Darwinian, edition of Kirby and Spence's *Introduction to Entomology*.]

This tradition of attempting to read moral meaning from nature did not cease with the triumph of evolutionary theory after Darwin published *On the Origin of Species* in 1859—for evolution could be read as God's chosen method of peopling our planet, and ethical messages might still populate nature. Thus, St. George Mivart, one of Darwin's most effective evolutionary critics and a devout Catholic, argued that "many amiable and excellent people" had been misled by the apparent suffering of animals for two reasons. First, however much it might hurt, "physical suffering and moral evil are simply incommensurable." Since beasts are not moral agents, their feelings cannot bear any ethical message. But secondly, lest our visceral sensitivities still be aroused, Mivart assures us that animals must feel little, if any, pain. Using a favorite racist argument of the time—that "primitive" people suffer far less than advanced and cultured people—Mivart extrapolated further down the ladder of life into a realm of very limited pain indeed: Physical suffering, he argued,

> depends greatly upon the mental condition of the sufferer. Only during consciousness does it exist, and only in the most highly organized men does it reach its acme. The author has been assured that lower races of men appear less keenly sensitive to physical suffering than do more cultivated and refined human beings. Thus only in man can there really be any intense degree of suffering, because only in him is there that intellectual recollection of past moments and that anticipation of future ones, which constitute in great part the bitterness of suffering. The momentary pang, the present pain, which beasts endure, though real enough, is yet, doubtless, not to be compared as to its intensity with the suffering which is produced in man through his high prerogative of self-consciousness [from *Genesis of Species*, 1871].

It took Darwin himself to derail this ancient tradition—in that gentle way so characteristic of his radical intellectual approach to nearly everything. The ichneumons also troubled Darwin greatly and he wrote of them to Asa Gray in 1860:

> I own that I cannot see as plainly as others do, and as I should wish to do, evidence of design and beneficence on all sides of us. There seems to me too much misery in the world. I cannot persuade myself that a beneficent and omnipotent God would have designedly created the Ichneumonidae with the express intention of their feeding within the living bodies of Caterpillars, or that a cat should play with mice.

Indeed, he had written with more passion to Joseph Hooker in 1856: "What a book a devil's chaplain might write on the clumsy, wasteful, blundering, low, and horribly cruel works of nature!"

This honest admission—that nature is often (by our standards) cruel and that all previous attempts to find a lurking goodness behind everything represent just so much absurd special pleading—can lead in two directions. One might retain the principle that nature holds moral messages for humans, but reverse the usual perspective and claim that morality consists in understanding the ways of nature and doing the opposite. Thomas Henry Huxley advanced this argument in his famous essay on *Evolution and Ethics* (1893):

> The practice of that which is ethically best—what we call goodness or virtue—involves a course of conduct which, in all respects, is opposed to that which leads to success in the cosmic struggle for existence. In place of ruthless self-assertion it demands self-restraint; in place of thrusting aside, or treading down, all competitors, it requires that the individual shall not merely respect, but shall help his fellows. . . . It repudiates the gladiatorial theory of existence. . . . Laws and moral precepts are directed to the end of curbing the cosmic process.

The other argument, more radical in Darwin's day but common now, holds that nature simply is as we find it. Our failure to discern the universal good we once expected does not record our lack of insight or ingenuity but merely demonstrates that nature contains no moral messages framed in human terms. Morality is a subject for philosophers, theologians, students of the humanities, indeed for all thinking people. The answers will not be read passively from nature; they do not, and cannot, arise from the data of science. The factual state of the world does not teach us how we, with our powers for good and evil, should alter or preserve it in the most ethical manner.

Darwin himself tended toward this view, although he could not, as a man of his time, thoroughly abandon the idea that laws of nature might reflect some higher purpose. He clearly recognized that the specific manifestations of those laws—cats playing with mice, and ichneumon larvae eating caterpillars—could not embody ethical messages, but he somehow hoped that unknown higher laws might exist "with the details, whether good or bad, left to the working out of what we may call chance."

Since ichneumons are a detail, and since natural selection is a law regulating details, the answer to the ancient dilemma of why such cruelty (in our terms) exists in nature can only be that there isn't any answer—and that the framing of the question "in our terms" is thoroughly inappropriate in a natural world neither made for us nor ruled by us. It just plain happens. It is a strategy that works for ichneumons and that natural selection has programmed into their behavioral repertoire. Caterpillars are not suffering to teach us something; they have simply been outmaneuvered, for now, in the evolutionary game. Perhaps they will evolve a set of adequate defenses sometime in the future, thus sealing the fate of ichneumons. And perhaps, indeed probably, they will not.

Another Huxley, Thomas's grandson Julian, spoke for this position, using as an example—yes, you guessed it—the ubiquitous ichneumons:

> Natural selection, in fact, though like the mills of God in grinding slowly and grinding small, has few other attributes that a civilized religion would call divine. . . . Its products are just as likely to be aesthetically, morally, or intellectually repulsive to us as they are to be attractive. We need only think of the ugliness of *Sacculina* or a bladder-worm, the stupidity of a rhinoceros or a stegasaur, the horror of a female mantis devouring its mate or a brood of ichneumon flies slowly eating out a caterpillar.

It is amusing in this context, or rather ironic since it is too serious to be amusing, that modern creationists accuse evolutionists of preaching a specific ethical doctrine called secular humanism and thereby demand equal time for their unscientific and discredited views. If nature is nonmoral, then evolution cannot teach any ethical theory at all. The assumption that it can has abetted a panoply of social evils that ideologues falsely read into nature from their beliefs—eugenics and (misnamed) social Darwinism prominently among them. Not only did Darwin eschew any attempt to discover an antireligious ethic in nature, he also expressly stated his personal bewilderment about such deep issues as the problem of evil. Just a few sentences after invoking the ichneumons, and in words that express both the modesty of this splendid man and the compatibility, through lack of contact, between science and true religion, Darwin wrote to Asa Gray,

> I feel most deeply that the whole subject is too profound for the human intellect. A dog might as well speculate on the mind of Newton. Let each man hope and believe what he can.

QUESTIONS FOR A CRITICAL REREADING

Use the following questions to help you reread Gould's argument critically. As you note your answers in your notebook, you may also wish to identify any of Gould's terms or examples that you are unsure about. Later, when you discuss the essay with your classmates, you may discover that Gould's rhetoric is really what is at issue.

1. Gould's essay can be viewed as addressing two arguments. The first half explores how scientists in the past have reasoned about the ichneumon fly; the second half is Gould's argument for how they should have reasoned. Can you identify where the shift in issue occurs? Why do you think Gould set up his essay in this way? Would scientists respect this method of reasoning?

2. The first half of Gould's essay, although an argument in itself, can be viewed as the introduction to his main argument. He reviews the logic others had used to analyze the ichneumon fly and concludes that they were addressing a question improper for a scientific investigation. The logic they had used can be summarized as a syllogism:

> Nature reveals God's benevolence.
> The ichneumon fly is a part of nature.
> Therefore, the ichneumon fly reveals God's benevolence.

What is the question they were addressing with this reasoning? What is the question Gould is asking about this argument?

3. In paragraph nine, Gould introduces "two basic themes" in the arguments about the ichneuman parasite. Note how these themes represent two different perspectives scientists attempted to use to resolve the issue. Which perspective was best able to "square the habits of these wasps with the goodness of God?" Can you articulate the enthymeme that represents the reasoning used?

4. In paragraph 17, Gould says that he has used "inappropriate anthropocentric language in this romp through the natural history of ichneumons" to expose why scientists had difficulty seeing the fly for what it was. What does "anthropocentric" mean and how does that type of language inhibit scientific inquiry?

5. Gould's thesis is most evident in paragraph 27:

> Since ichneumons are a detail, and since natural selection is a law regulating details, the answer to the ancient dilemma of why such cruelty (in our terms) exists in nature can only be that there isn't any answer—and that the framing of the question "in our terms" is thoroughly inappropriate in a natural world neither made for us nor ruled by us.

Try to formulate this statement into an enthymeme. What are Gould's assumptions? How does he think scientists should frame their questions?

POSSIBLE ISSUES FOR WRITING

Following are a few of the questions that you might find at issue in Gould's argument. Discuss these with your classmates to see how your interpretation differs from theirs. As before, keep in mind the type of argument different classmates use, and whether the issue is a question of definition, consequence, value, or policy. This will help you identify the audience for the essay you will write later.

1. Could Gould's argument be used to defend inductive over deductive reasoning in scientific writing? Why or why not? Consider both what he says is ideal for scientific investigation and the type of reasoning he himself uses.

2. In "Nonmoral Nature," Gould implies that different fields like religion and science cannot talk with each other, that the human mind is essentially not perfect enough to reconcile apparent contradictions like the benevolence of the evil parasite. Would Cook agree? What kind of argument might a theologian use to reason about the data Cook gives us? How would it make a difference in the thesis Cook gives us? Would it be less authoritative or merely different?

3. Gould introduces Darwin's theory of evolution to expose how a "nonmoral" approach to scientific investigation can help further our understanding of nature. Do you believe this kind of knowledge is valuable? Why or why not?

4. Gould is essentially arguing for scientists to restrict their investigations to a question of definition (i.e., ask only "What is the ichneumon fly?" not "Is the ichneumon fly good?" or "What should we do about it?"). Consider whether scientists should also avoid asking moral or policy questions about the following areas of scientific investigation:
   A. nuclear energy
   B. artificial respiration
   C. genetic cloning
   D. artificial reproduction
   E. the abortion pill

The Essential Tension: Tradition and Innovation in Scientific Research

Thomas S. Kuhn *(1922–   )*

Thomas Kuhn's writings on the history of science have had a major impact on twentieth-century thought. Although his work is on science, his theories have been adapted to explain how revolutionary ideas occur in all fields of academic reasoning. "The Essential Tension" is an early lecture, delivered in 1959 at the Third University of Utah Research Conference on the Identification of Scientific Talent. His theories here later developed into his landmark work, The Structure of Scientific Revolutions *(published in 1962; revised in 1970; and republished in its third edition in 1982).*

For "The Essential Tension," Kuhn's audience was composed of teachers and scholars seeking to make their students more creative scientific thinkers. They believed the conventional scientific method was not preparing their students to create revolutionary new theories. They were hoping Kuhn would give them a way to identify and develop scientific talent by defining the method of the nonconformist, what he calls "divergent", scientific thinker. As you read, note how cautious he is, how he is aware that what he has to tell them is probably not what they had expected to hear.

I am grateful for the invitation to participate in this important conference, and I interpret it as evidence that students of creativity themselves possess the sensitivity to divergent approaches that they seek to identify in others. But I am not altogether sanguine about the outcome of your experiment with me. As most of you already know, I am no psychologist, but rather an ex-physicist now working in the history of science. Probably my concern is no less with creativity than your own, but my goals, my techniques, and my sources of evidence are so very different from yours that I am far from sure how much we do, or even *should,* have to say to each other. These reservations imply no apology; rather they hint at my central thesis. In the sciences, as I shall suggest below, it is often better to do one's best with the tools at hand than to pause for contemplation of divergent approaches.

If a person of my background and interests has anything relevant to suggest to this conference, it will not be about your central concerns, the creative personality and its early identification. But implicit in the numerous working papers distributed to participants in this conference is an image of the scientific process and of the scientist; that image almost certainly conditions many of the experiments you try as well as the conclusions you draw; and about it the physicist-historian may well have something to say. I shall restrict my attention to one aspect of this image—an aspect epitomized as follows in one of the working papers: The basic scientist "must lack prejudice to a degree where he can look at the most 'self-evident' facts or concepts without necessarily accepting them, and, conversely, allow his imagination to play with the most unlikely possibilities" (Selye, 1959). In the more technical language supplied by other working papers (Getzels and Jackson), this aspect of the image recurs as an emphasis upon "divergent thinking, . . . the freedom to go off in different directions, . . . rejecting the old solution and striking out in some new direction."

I do not at all doubt that this description of "divergent thinking" and the concomitant search for those able to do it are entirely proper. Some divergence characterizes all scientific work, and gigantic divergences lie at the core of the most significant episodes in scientific development. But both my own experience in scientific research and my reading of the history of sciences lead me to wonder whether flexibility and open-mindedness have not been too exclusively emphasized as the characteristics requisite for basic research. I shall therefore suggest below that something like "convergent thinking" is just as essential to scientific advance as is divergent. Since these two modes of thought are inevitably in conflict, it will follow that the ability to support a tension that can occasionally become almost unbearable is one of the prime requisites for the very best sort of scientific research.

I am elsewhere studying these points more historically, with emphasis on the importance to scientific development of "revolutions."[1] These are episodes—exemplified in their most extreme and readily recognized form by the advent of Copernicanism, Darwinism, or Einsteinianism—in which a scientific community abandons one time-honored way of regarding the world and of pursuing science in favor of some other, usually incompatible, approach to its discipline. I have argued in the draft that the historian constantly encounters many far smaller but structurally similar revolutionary episodes and that they are central to scientific advance. Contrary to a prevalent impression, most new discoveries and theories in the sciences are not merely additions to the existing stockpile of scientific knowledge. To assimilate them the scientist must usually rearrange the intellectual and manipulative equipment he has previously relied upon, discarding some elements of his prior belief and practice while finding new significances in and new relationships between many others. Because the old must be revalued and reordered when assimilating the new, discovery and invention in the sciences are usually intrinsically revolutionary. Therefore, they do demand just that flexibility and open-mindedness that characterize, or indeed define, the divergent thinker. Let us henceforth take for granted the need for these characteristics. Unless many scientists possessed them to a marked degree, there would be no scientific revolutions and very little scientific advance.

Yet flexibility is not enough, and what remains is not obviously compatible with it. Drawing from various fragments of a project still in progress, I must now emphasize that revolutions are but one of two complementary

[1] *The Structure of Scientific Revolutions* (Chicago, 1962).

aspects of scientific advance. Almost none of the research undertaken by even the greatest scientists is designed to be revolutionary, and very little of it has any such effect. On the contrary, normal research, even the best of it, is a highly convergent activity based firmly upon a settled consensus acquired from scientific education and reinforced by subsequent life in the profession. Typically, to be sure, this convergent or consensus-bound research ultimately results in revolution. Then, traditional techniques and beliefs are abandoned and replaced by new ones. But revolutionary shifts of a scientific tradition are relatively rare, and extended periods of convergent research are the necessary preliminary to them. As I shall indicate below, only investigations firmly rooted in the contemporary scientific tradition are likely to break that tradition and give rise to a new one. That is why I speak of an "essential tension" implicit in scientific research. To do his job the scientist must undertake a complex set of intellectual and manipulative commitments. Yet his claim to fame, if he has the talent and good luck to gain one, may finally rest upon his ability to abandon this net of commitments in favor of another of his own invention. Very often the successful scientist must simultaneously display the characteristics of the traditionalist and of the iconoclast.[2]

The multiple historical examples upon which any full documentation of these points must depend are prohibited by the time limitations of the conference. But another approach will introduce you to at least part of what I have in mind—an examination of the nature of education in the natural sciences. One of the working papers for this conference (Getzels and Jackson) quotes Guilford's very apt description of scientific education as follows: "[It] has emphasized abilities in the areas of convergent thinking and evaluation, often at the expense of development in the area of divergent thinking. We have attempted to teach students how to arrive at 'correct' answers that our civilization has taught us are correct. . . . Outside the arts [and I should include most of the social sciences] we have generally discouraged the development of divergent-thinking abilities, unintentionally." That characterization seems to me eminently just, but I wonder whether it is equally just to deplore the product that results. Without defending plain bad teaching, and granting that in this country the trend to convergent thinking in all education may have proceeded entirely too far, we may nevertheless recognize that a rigorous training in convergent thought has been intrinsic to the sciences almost from their origin. I suggest that they could not have achieved their present state or status without it.

Let me try briefly to epitomize the nature of education in the natural

---

[2]Strictly speaking, it is the professional group rather than the individual scientist that must display both these characteristics simultaneously. In a fuller account of the ground covered in this paper that distinction between individual and group characteristics would be basic. Here I can only note that, though recognition of the distinction weakens the conflict or tension referred to above, it does not eliminate it. Within the group some individuals may be more traditionalistic, others more iconoclastic, and their contributions may differ accordingly. Yet education, institutional norms, and the nature of the job to be done will inevitably combine to insure that all group members will, to a greater or lesser extent, be pulled in both directions.

sciences, ignoring the many significant yet minor differences between the various sciences and between the approaches of different educational institutions. The single most striking feature of this education is that, to an extent totally unknown in other creative fields, it is conducted entirely through textbooks. Typically, undergraduate *and* graduate students of chemistry, physics, astronomy, geology, or biology acquire the substance of their fields from books written especially for students. Until they are ready, or very nearly ready, to commence work on their own dissertations, they are neither asked to attempt trial research projects nor exposed to the immediate products of research done by others, that is, to the professional communications that scientists write for each other. There are no collections of "readings" in the natural sciences. Nor are science students encouraged to read the historical classics of their fields—works in which they might discover other ways of regarding the problems discussed in their textbooks, but in which they would also meet problems, concepts, and standards of solution that their future professions have long since discarded and replaced.

In contrast, the various textbooks that the student does encounter display different subject matters, rather than, as in many of the social sciences, exemplifying different approaches to a single problem field. Even books that compete for adoption in a single course differ mainly in level and in pedagogic detail, not in substance or conceptual structure. Last, but most important of all, is the characteristic technique of textbook presentation. Except in their occasional introductions, science textbooks do not describe the sorts of problems that the professional may be asked to solve and the variety of techniques available for their solution. Rather, these books exhibit concrete problem solutions that the profession has come to accept as paradigms, and they then ask the student, either with a pencil and paper or in the laboratory, to solve for himself problems very closely related in both method and substance to those through which the textbook or the accompanying lecture has led him. Nothing could be better calculated to produce "mental sets" or *Einstellungen.* Only in their most elementary courses do other academic fields offer as much as a partial parallel.

Even the most faintly liberal educational theory must view this pedagogic technique as anathema. Students, we would all agree, must begin by learning a good deal of what is already known, but we also insist that education give them vastly more. They must, we say, learn to recognize and evaluate problems to which no unequivocal solution has yet been given; they must be supplied with an arsenal of techniques for approaching these future problems; and they must learn to judge the relevance of these techniques and to evaluate the possibly partial solutions which they can provide. In many respects these attitudes toward education seem to me entirely right, and yet we must recognize two things about them. First, education in the natural sciences seems to have been totally unaffected by their existence. It remains a dogmatic initiation in a pre-established tradition that the student is not equipped to evaluate. Second, at least in the period when it was followed by a term in an apprenticeship relation, this technique of exclusive exposure to a rigid tradition has been immensely productive of the most consequential sorts of innovations.

I shall shortly inquire about the pattern of scientific practice that grows out of this educational initiation and will then attempt to say why that pattern proves quite so successful. But first, an historical excursion will reinforce what has just been said and prepare the way for what is to follow. I should like to suggest that the various fields of natural science have not always been characterized by rigid education in exclusive paradigms, but that each of them acquired something like that technique at precisely the point when the field began to make rapid and systematic progress. If one asks about the origin of our contemporary knowledge of chemical composition, of earthquakes, of biological reproduction, of motion through space, or of any other subject matter known to the natural sciences, one immediately encounters a characteristic pattern that I shall here illustrate with a single example.

Today, physics textbooks tell us that light exhibits some properties of a wave and some of a particle: both textbook problems and research problems are designed accordingly. But both this view and these textbooks are products of an early twentieth-century revolution. (One characteristic of scientific revolutions is that they call for the rewriting of science textbooks.) For more than half a century before 1900, the books employed in scientific education had been equally unequivocal in stating that light was wave motion. Under those circumstances scientists worked on somewhat different problems and often embraced rather different sorts of solutions to them. The nineteenth-century textbook tradition does not, however, mark the beginning of our subject matter. Throughout the eighteenth century and into the early nineteenth, Newton's *Opticks* and the other books from which men learned science taught almost all students that light was particles, and research guided by this tradition was again different from that which succeeded it. Ignoring a variety of subsidiary changes within these three successive traditions, we may therefore say that our views derive historically from Newton's views by way of two revolutions in optical thought, each of which replaced one tradition of convergent research with another. If we make appropriate allowances for changes in the locus and materials of scientific education, we may say that each of these three traditions was embodied in the sort of education by exposure to unequivocal paradigms that I briefly epitomized above. Since Newton, education and research in physical optics have normally been highly convergent.

The history of theories of light does not, however, begin with Newton. If we ask about knowledge in the field before his time, we encounter a significantly different pattern—a pattern still familiar in the arts and in some social sciences, but one which has largely disappeared in the natural sciences. From remote antiquity until the end of the seventeenth century there was no single set of paradigms for the study of physical optics. Instead, many men advanced a large number of different views about the nature of light. Some of these views found few adherents, but a number of them gave rise to continuing schools of optical thought. Although the historian can note the emergence of new points of view as well as changes in the relative popularity of older ones, there was never anything resembling consensus. As a result, a new man entering the field was inevitably exposed to a variety of conflicting viewpoints: he was forced to examine the evidence for each, and there always was good evidence. The fact that he made a choice and conducted himself accordingly could not entirely prevent his awareness of other possibilities. This earlier mode of education was obviously more suited to produce a scientist without prejudice, alert to novel phenomena, and flexible in his approach to his field. On the other hand, one can scarcely escape the impression that, during the period characterized by this more liberal educational practice, physical optics made very little progress.[3]

The preconsensus (we might here call it the divergent) phase in the development of physical optics is, I believe, duplicated in the history of all other scientific specialties, excepting only those that were born by the subdivision and recombination of pre-existing disciplines. In some fields, like mathematics and astronomy, the first firm consensus is prehistoric. In others, like dynamics, geometric optics, and parts of physiology, the paradigms that produced a first consensus date from classical antiquity. Most other natural sciences, though their problems were often discussed in antiquity, did not achieve a first consensus until after the Renaissance. In physical optics, as we have seen, the first firm consensus dates only from the end of the seventeenth century; in electricity, chemistry, and the study of heat, it dates from the eighteenth; while in geology and the nontaxonomic parts of biology no very real consensus developed until after the first third of the nineteenth century. This century appears to be characterized by the emergence of a first consensus in parts of a few of the social sciences.

In all the fields named above, important work was done before the achievement of the maturity produced by consensus. Neither the nature nor the timing of the first consensus in these fields can be understood without a careful examination of both the intellectual and the manipulative techniques developed before the existence of unique paradigms. But the transition to maturity is not less significant because individuals practiced science before it occurred. On the contrary, history strongly suggests that, though one can practice science—as one does philosophy or art or political science—without a firm consensus, this more flexible practice will not produce the pattern of rapid consequential scientific advance to which recent centuries have accustomed us. In that pattern, development occurs from one consensus to another, and alternate approaches are not ordinarily in competition. Except

[3]The history of physical optics before Newton has recently been well described by Vasco Ronchi in *Histoire de la lumière*, trans. J. Taton (Paris, 1956). His account does justice to the element I elaborate too little above. Many fundamental contributions to physical optics were made in the two millennia before Newton's work. Consensus is not prerequisite to a sort of progress in the natural sciences, any more than it is to progress in the social sciences or the arts. It is, however, prerequisite to the sort of progress that we now generally refer to when distinguishing the natural sciences from the arts and from most social sciences.

under quite special conditions, the practitioner of a mature science does not pause to examine divergent modes of explanation or experimentation.

I shall shortly ask how this can be so—how a firm orientation toward an apparently unique tradition can be compatible with the practice of the disciplines most noted for the persistent production of novel ideas and techniques. But it will help first to ask what the education that so successfully transmits such a tradition leaves to be done. What can a scientist working within a deeply rooted tradition and little trained in the perception of significant alternatives hope to do in his professional career? Once again limits of time force me to drastic simplification, but the following remarks will at least suggest a position that I am sure can be documented in detail.

In pure or basic science—that somewhat ephemeral category of research undertaken by men whose most immediate goal is to increase understanding rather than control of nature—the characteristic problems are almost always repetitions, with minor modifications, of problems that have been undertaken and partially resolved before. For example, much of the research undertaken within a scientific tradition is an attempt to adjust existing theory or existing observation in order to bring the two into closer and closer agreement. The constant examination of atomic and molecular spectra during the years since the birth of wave mechanics, together with the design of theoretical approximations for the prediction of complex spectra, provides one important instance of this typical sort of work. Another was provided by the remarks about the eighteenth-century development of Newtonian dynamics in the paper on measurement supplied to you in advance of the conference.[4] The attempt to make existing theory and observation conform more closely is not, of course, the only standard sort of research problem in the basic sciences. The development of chemical thermodynamics or the continuing attempts to unravel organic structure illustrate another type—the extension of existing theory to areas that it is expected to cover but in which it has never before been tried. In addition, to mention a third common sort of research problem, many scientists constantly collect the concrete data (e.g., atomic weights, nuclear moments) required for the application and extension of existing theory.

These are normal research projects in the basic sciences, and they illustrate the sorts of work on which all scientists, even the greatest, spend most of their professional lives and on which many spend all. Clearly their pursuit is neither intended nor likely to produce fundamental discoveries or revolutionary changes in scientific theory. Only if the validity of the contemporary scientific tradition is assumed do these problems make much theoretical or any practical sense. The man who suspected the existence of a totally new type of phenomenon or who had basic doubts about the validity of existing theory would not think problems so closely modeled on textbook paradigms worth undertaking. It follows that the man who does undertake a problem of this sort—and that means all scientists at most times—aims to elucidate the scien-

---

[4]A revised version appeared in *Isis* 52 (1961): 161–93 (pp. 178–224 above).

tific tradition in which he was raised rather than to change it. Furthermore, the fascination of his work lies in the difficulties of elucidation rather than in any surprises that the work is likely to produce. Under normal conditions the research scientist is not an innovator but a solver of puzzles, and the puzzles upon which he concentrates are just those which he believes can be both stated and solved within the existing scientific tradition.

Yet—and this is the point—the ultimate effect of this tradition-bound work has invariably been to change the tradition. Again and again the continuing attempt to elucidate a currently received tradition has at last produced one of those shifts in fundamental theory, in problem field, and in scientific standards to which I previously referred as scientific revolutions. At least for the scientific community as a whole, work within a well-defined and deeply ingrained tradition seems more productive of tradition-shattering novelties than work in which no similarly convergent standards are involved. How can this be so? I think it is because no other sort of work is nearly so well suited to isolate for continuing and concentrated attention those loci of trouble or causes of crisis upon whose recognition the most fundamental advances in basic science depend.

As I have indicated in the first of my working papers, new theories and, to an increasing extent, novel discoveries in the mature sciences are not born *de novo.* On the contrary, they emerge from old theories and within a matrix of old beliefs about the phenomena that the world does *and does not* contain. Ordinarily such novelties are far too esoteric and recondite to be noted by the man without a great deal of scientific training. And even the man with considerable training can seldom afford simply to go out and look for them, let us say by exploring those areas in which existing data and theory have failed to produce understanding. Even in a mature science there are always far too many such areas, areas in which no existing paradigms seem obviously to apply and for whose exploration few tools and standards are available. More likely than not the scientist who ventured into them, relying merely upon his receptivity to new phenomena and his flexibility to new patterns of organization, would get nowhere at all. He would rather return his science to its preconsensus or natural history phase.

Instead, the practitioner of a mature science, from the beginning of his doctoral research, continues to work in the regions for which the paradigms derived from his education and from the research of his contemporaries seem adequate. He tries, that is, to elucidate topographical detail on a map whose main outlines are available in advance, and he hopes—if he is wise enough to recognize the nature of his field—that he will some day undertake a problem in which the anticipated does *not* occur, a problem that goes wrong in ways suggestive of a fundamental weakness in the paradigm itself. In the mature sciences the prelude to much discovery and to all novel theory is not ignorance, but the recognition that something has gone wrong with existing knowledge and beliefs.

What I have said so far may indicate that it is sufficient for the productive scientist to adopt existing theory as a lightly held tentative hypothesis, employ it *faute de mieux* in order to get a start in his research, and then abandon it as soon as it leads him to a trouble spot, a point at which something has gone wrong. But though the ability to recognize trouble when confronted by it is surely a requisite for scientific advance, trouble must not be too easily recognized. The scientist requires a thoroughgoing commitment to the tradition with which, if he is fully successful, he will break. In part this commitment is demanded by the nature of the problems the scientist normally undertakes. These, as we have seen, are usually esoteric puzzles whose challenge lies less in the information disclosed by their solutions (all but its details are often known in advance) than in the difficulties of technique to be surmounted in providing any solution at all. Problems of this sort are undertaken only by men assured that there is a solution which ingenuity can disclose, and only current theory could possibly provide assurance of that sort. That theory alone gives meaning to most of the problems of normal research. To doubt it is often to doubt that the complex technical puzzles which constitute normal research have any solutions at all. Who, for example, would have developed the elaborate mathematical techniques required for the study of the effects of interplanetary attractions upon basic Keplerian orbits if he had not assumed that Newtonian dynamics, applied to the planets then known, would explain the last details of astronomical observation? But without that assurance, how would Neptune have been discovered and the list of planets changed?

In addition, there are pressing practical reasons for commitment. Every research problem confronts the scientist with anomalies whose sources he cannot quite identify. His theories and observations never quite agree; successive observations never yield quite the same results; his experiments have both theoretical and phenomenological by-products which it would take another research project to unravel. Each of these anomalies or incompletely understood phenomena could conceivably be the clue to a fundamental innovation in scientific theory or technique, but the man who pauses to examine them one by one never completes his first project. Reports of effective research repeatedly imply that all but the most striking and central discrepancies could be taken care of by current theory if only there were time to take them on. The men who make these reports find most discrepancies trivial or uninteresting, an evaluation that they can ordinarily base only upon their faith in current theory. Without that faith their work would be wasteful of time and talent.

Besides, lack of commitment too often results in the scientist's undertaking problems that he has little chance of solving. Pursuit of an anomaly is fruitful only if the anomaly is more than nontrivial. Having discovered it, the scientist's first efforts and those of his profession are to do what nuclear physicists are now doing. They strive to generalize the anomaly, to discover other and more revealing manifestations of the same effect, to give it structure by examining its complex interrelationships with phenomena they still feel they understand. Very few anomalies are susceptible to this sort of treatment. To be so they must be in explicit and unequivocal conflict with some structurally central tenet of current scientific belief. Therefore, their recognition and evaluation once again depend upon a firm commitment to the contemporary scientific tradition.

This central role of an elaborate and often esoteric tradition is what I have principally had in mind when speaking of the essential tension in scientific research. I do not doubt that the scientist must be, at least potentially, an innovator, that he must possess mental flexibility, and that he must be prepared to recognize troubles where they exist. That much of the popular stereotype is surely correct, and it is important accordingly to search for indices of the corresponding personality characteristics. But what is no part of our stereotype and what appears to need careful integration with it is the other face of this same coin. We are, I think, more likely fully to exploit our potential scientific talent if we recognize the extent to which the basic scientist must also be a firm traditionalist, or, if I am using your vocabulary at all correctly, a convergent thinker. Most important of all, we must seek to understand how these two superficially discordant modes of problem solving can be reconciled both within the individual and within the group.

Everything said above needs both elaboration and documentation. Very likely some of it will change in the process. This paper is a report on work in progress. But, though I insist that much of it is tentative and all of it incomplete, I still hope that the paper has indicated why an educational system best described as an initiation into an unequivocal tradition should be thoroughly compatible with successful scientific work. And I hope, in addition, to have made plausible the historical thesis that no part of science has progressed very far or very rapidly before this convergent education and correspondingly convergent normal practice became possible. Finally, though it is beyond my competence to derive personality correlates from this view of scientific development, I hope to have made meaningful the view that the productive scientist must be a traditionalist who enjoys playing intricate games by pre-established rules in order to be a successful innovator who discovers new rules and new pieces with which to play them.

As first planned, my paper was to have ended at this point. But work on it, against the background supplied by the working papers distributed to conference participants, has suggested the need for a postscript. Let me therefore briefly try to eliminate a likely ground of misunderstanding and simultaneously suggest a problem that urgently needs a great deal of investigation.

Everything said above was intended to apply strictly only to basic science, an enterprise whose practitioners have ordinarily been relatively free to choose their own problems. Characteristically, as I have indicated, these problems have been selected in areas where paradigms were clearly applicable but where exciting puzzles remained about how to apply them and how to make nature conform to the results of the application. Clearly the inventor and applied scientist are not generally free to choose puzzles of this sort. The problems among which they may choose are likely to be largely determined by social, economic, or military circumstances external to the sciences. Often the decision to seek a cure for a virulent disease, a new source of household illumination, or an alloy able to withstand the intense heat of rocket engines must be made with little reference to the state of the relevant science. It is, I think, by no means clear that the personality characteristics requisite for pre-eminence in this more immediately practical sort of work are altogether the same as those required for a great achievement in basic science. History indicates that only a few individuals, most of whom worked in readily demarcated areas, have achieved eminence in both.

I am by no means clear where this suggestion leads us. The troublesome distinctions between basic research, applied research, and invention need far more investigation. Nevertheless, it seems likely, for example, that the applied scientist, to whose problems no scientific paradigm need be fully relevant, may profit by a far broader and less rigid education than that to which the pure scientist has characteristically been exposed. Certainly there are many episodes in the history of technology in which lack of more than the most rudimentary scientific education has proved to be an immense help. This group scarcely needs to be reminded that Edison's electric light was produced in the face of unanimous scientific opinion that the arc light could not be "subdivided," and there are many other episodes of this sort.

This must not suggest, however, that mere differences in education will transform the applied scientist into a basic scientist or vice versa. One could at least argue that Edison's personality, ideal for the inventor and perhaps also for the "oddball" in applied science, barred him from fundamental achievements in the basic sciences. He himself expressed great scorn for scientists and thought of them as wooly-headed people to be hired when needed. But this did not prevent his occasionally arriving at the most sweeping and irresponsible scientific theories of his own. (The pattern recurs in the early history of electrical technology: both Tesla and Gramme advanced absurd cosmic schemes that they thought deserved to replace the current scientific knowledge of their day.) Episodes like this reinforce an impression that the personality requisites of the pure scientist and of the inventor may be quite different, perhaps with those of the applied scientist lying somewhere between.[5]

Is there a further conclusion to be drawn from all this? One speculative thought forces itself upon me. If I read the working papers correctly, they suggest that most of you are really in search of the *inventive* personality, a sort of person who does emphasize divergent thinking but whom the United States has already produced in abundance. In the process you may be ignoring certain of the essential requisites of the basic scientist, a rather different sort of person, to whose ranks America's contributions have as yet been

---

[5]For the attitude of scientists toward the technical possibility of the incandescent light see Francis A. Jones, *Thomas Alva Edison* (New York, 1908). pp. 99–100, and Harold C. Passer, *The Electrical Manufacturers, 1875–1900* (Cambridge, Mass., 1953). pp. 82–83. For Edison's attitude toward scientists see Passer, ibid., pp. 180–81. For a sample of Edison's theorizing in realms otherwise subject to scientific treatments see Dagobert D. Runes, ed., *The Diary and Sundry Observations of Thomas Alva Edison* (New York, 1948), pp. 205–44, passim.

notoriously sparse. Since most of you are, in fact, Americans, this correlation may not be entirely coincidental.

QUESTIONS FOR A CRITICAL REREADING

After reading Kuhn's essay through once, use the following questions to help you reread it more critically. As you enter your answers in your notebook, you may also wish to include any observations you have about how Kuhn's approach to scientific inquiry differs from that of the other two scientists you have read in this chapter. This will help you synthesize what you know about scientific reasoning before you write your essay.

1. The key to understanding Kuhn's essay is identifying its rhetorical situation. The essay is a revised version of a speech he presented at a conference at the University of Utah in 1959. The purpose of this conference was to discuss how educators might help their students be more creative, innovative scientists. In the first three paragraphs, Kuhn implies that the conference is addressing the wrong issue. What is the real issue that Kuhn presents for discussion?
2. In paragraphs 2–5, Kuhn redefines "tradition" and "innovation" as "convergent" and "divergent" thinking and then illustrates the roles each plays in scientific revolutions. Why do you think he does this? Which type of thinking is his audience predisposed to value? Which does he think is most valuable (note well his argument in paragraphs 6–14)?
3. Kuhn's argument turns on the key words "paradigm" and "anomaly." What do these words mean and what do they have to do with scientific innovation?
4. Kuhn's thesis might be paraphrased as the following enthymeme:

    To be a successful innovator, the scientist first must be a committed tradition-alist *because* a traditionalist is the only one who can recognize the anomalies that could lead to new paradigms.

    What is the assumption behind this thesis? Can he assume his audience would agree?
5. What aspects of Kuhn's argument make you aware that he is a scientist? What aspects of his reasoning are particularly scientific?

POSSIBLE ISSUES FOR WRITING

Following are a few of the questions that you might find at issue in Kuhn's argument. Discuss these with your classmates, again noting what type of arguments are at issue for the class. Try to use the class discussion to test different types of arguments to help you discover what kind of reasoning you will need to use in your own essay.

1. Using Kuhn's definition of "paradigm," what paradigms do we use today? What kind of influence do they have over what we think and do?
2. A paradigm in scientific thought is often represented as the organizing model we use to synthesize the information we have, resulting in a kind of old knowledge from which a scientist reasons about new findings. What kind of paradigm were the scientists in Gould's essay using? Does Gould's argument against this paradigm conform to Kuhn's definition of a scientific revolution where a paradigm fails to accommodate an anomaly?
3. Kuhn claims that a student of science should be trained to be a convergent thinker

and that divergent thinking or innovation will naturally result. Do you think this is true for other fields? Are there some subjects for which this type of education would not work?

4. How would Cook feel about Kuhn's argument? Do you think he thought of himself as a "divergent" thinker? Why or why not? What kind of paradigm would you say Cook used to analyze his data? What kind of paradigm did his critics use? Who, in your opinion, was right?

WRITING YOUR ESSAY

Now that you have listened in on the conversations selected authors have had about science and have continued these conversations informally with your classmates, you are prepared to make a more formal contribution to the discussion. Write an essay that responds to the scientific arguments your classmates have offered. To decide what you will write on, you will need to discover who your primary audience is and what they need to know.

Review your notes from class discussion, noting in particular those questions most at issue for the class. Choose from these issues one that you feel most strongly about because of something someone said. Your specific audience will be the classmate(s) that expressed a stance different from your own, although you will be writing for the broader audience of informed readers.

Because your essay is to be reasoned as a scientific argument, be sure to rephrase any questions that were at issue during the class discussions so that they focus on a question of definition (something "is" something because . . .). Then construct a logical thesis statement in answer to the question. Be certain your "because" clause contains the new information that you need to give your reader. This new information may be a reinterpretation of Cook's data, an interpretation of the examples used by Gould and Kuhn, or information you have acquired through experience and reading you have done for other courses or on your own.

Before drafting your essay, you will need to test your enthymeme by identifying what old information you are assuming your reader already has (it will probably be some idea that arose in the readings or class discussion). If you have difficulty doing this, refer to the following discussion for special help.

RECOGNIZING ASSUMPTIONS IN CLASS DISCUSSIONS

It is important to be aware of the assumptions writers make about what their audience already believes. Recognizing the assumptions behind a specialist's reasoning process can introduce you to information that is considered valid in the field. We might refer to these assumptions as reflecting the "facts" you must know. As you attempt to enter into different conversations, you need to identify these assumed facts as the point from which you can develop your own answers to the questions the discipline poses.

However, as you collaborate with your classmates to inquire about the essays you have read, you cannot trust that the assumptions are always true. Just as Gould's perplexed scientists were led astray by the assumptions they based their reasoning on, you might be led astray by what sounds like a good argument. Arguments may be weakened not by what they say but by what they assume to be true. For this reason, when you discuss issues with your classmates (your potential readers), you need to listen closely to the types of reasons they give for their beliefs. It is helpful to construct their arguments in enthymemic form so you can identify the basis for their arguments. This means taking good notes during class discussion. There are three questions you will always need to ask to evaluate their arguments:

1. What question does their assertion answer? Is it really the issue?
2. What is the primary reason they give to support their answer?
3. What is the major assumption they are making? Will I let them assume I agree?

You will need to analyze the answer to number three very closely. Sometimes you will discover that the premise they are assuming is already true is really what they should be proving. To respond to them, either during class discussion or in your writing, you might make that assumed premise the issue you address in your argument.

WHEN "WINNING AN ARGUMENT" IS LOSING

As we discovered in Gould's essay, there are times when sincere inquirers are blinded by the weaknesses of the assumptions they make when they reason. However, there are also times (as we often discover in political speeches or advertisements) when speakers attempt to manipulate us by reasoning from an obviously false assumption. We often elect officials or buy products for the wrong reasons. For example, if we were told not to vote for a candidate because he or she would raise taxes, the assumption is that anyone who raised taxes should not be president. The assumption is not necessarily true; the real issue is what the taxes would be used for. Similarly, if an advertiser claims that we should buy a new soap because it will make our skin look younger, and we later discover that, although it makes us look younger, it also causes cancer and pollutes the water, we realize the assumption "anything that makes us look younger is good" is false. If we recognize our error in judgment, we might claim we were deceived. However, it would partly be our fault because we failed to analyze the reasoning the politician or advertiser used to "win the argument."

When you argue with others to further their understanding of a subject, though, there is no way to "win" if you attempt to manipulate others to buy a faulty argument. Everyone loses. The conclusions scholars come to accept as valid conclusions soon become the accepted truths from which other conclusions will be made. Even in a writing class, the issues you discuss and the conclusions you share with others may affect what others believe. As we noted at the beginning of this chapter, most arguments imply what we should believe is good or bad, and how we should act as a consequence. Thus, the stances you lead your classmates to take will ultimately have an effect on how they act in the future.

For this reason, every time you analyze another person's argument—when you read an essay, discuss positions in class, or write a peer response to a classmate's essay—you need to test the assumption fairly and thoroughly. Criticize when criticism is warranted; you are the kindest to your fellow students when you point out the weaknesses in their arguments. And when you receive criticism, weigh it honestly. Do not consider a peer's objections to your arguments as "fighting words" that you should always refute. Instead, see the discussion as a way to test ideas independent of the individuals expressing them, and use criticism to discover what it is you really should believe. It is only when argument is seen as a collaborative endeavor in which we cooperate to further everyone's understanding that we can "win" the argument.

Unit Four

CHAPTER SEVEN

The Thesis and Logical Structure

As you learned in Chapter 5, expressing a writer's thesis as an enthymeme can help you test the validity of the argument. It helps you identify both the issue being addressed and the reasoning process the writer used to answer it. Even more specifically, the "because" clause of an enthymemic thesis contains the most important new information in the argument and can be used to uncover what old information the author assumed you would accept. You need to consider all of these aspects of an argument if you are to become a critical reader. In this chapter, you will discover another benefit of the enthymemic thesis: how expressing your own argument as a logical thesis statement can help you predict the logical structure your own writing should take.

HOW THE ENTHYMEMIC THESIS PREDICTS LOGICAL STRUCTURE

The logical thesis statement (or enthymemic thesis) is a miniature outline of the logical steps a writer needs to use to structure a written argument. These logical steps are similar to what you probably already know as the introduction, body, and conclusion of an essay. As any writer knows, it is not easy to decide where to begin an essay. Having an idea what you want to say and knowing how to say it in a written argument are two very different skills. Often we have that moment of inspiration ("Aha! That's the answer!") but have difficulty retracing the logical steps we used to arrive at it. Summarizing your answer as an enthymeme, though, can help you rediscover those steps, giving you a map of the logical structure your essay should take to inform your reader just how inspired your answer is.

To discover the logical structure behind your thesis statement, you need to identify and label its essential parts. The essential parts of the enthymeme include the primary terms (i.e., the shared terms in the syllogism) and the verbs of both clauses. Your essay will need to treat each term as a significant step in the logic of the argument. Consider how the essential parts of the following enthymeme might be labelled:

The Labels for the Essential Parts of the Thesis

Enthymeme

A		V1		B
(first term)	+	(first verb)	+	(second term)
WHALES		**ARE**		**MAMMALS**

BECAUSE

A*		V2		C
(first term repeated)	+	(second verb)	+	(third term)
THEY		**ARE**		**WARM-BLOODED.**

Assumption

B		C
(second term)	+	(third term)
ONLY MAMMALS	**ARE**	**WARM-BLOODED.**

Although this enthymeme probably needs little clarification for most of us, if you were talking to an elementary school student, you would want to develop a logical explanation by clarifying each of the essential parts in turn. You would also want to begin with those terms that the student was most familiar with so he or she could follow your reasoning. Here is a brief outline of the logical steps you might take:

Introduction   You want to know if whales are fish or mammals?

Body

A–A*   Whales certainly look and act like fish, don't they? They swim in the ocean, have slippery skin, and eat other fish.

A*–V2   But, you know, they are also different than fish. They don't lay eggs like fish do.

C   And their body temperature stays fairly warm even when the ocean is very, very cold. They are warm-blooded.

B–C   As you know, this isn't true for fish. Their temperature changes with their surroundings. Only mammals are warm-blooded.

Conclusion

A–B   That means the answer to your question is that whales are mammals not fish.

Note how this extended discussion is structured around the enthymeme. You would introduce the question the first clause answers, begin the body with a general definition of the shared term (A–A*), move to give some new information about this shared term (A*–V2: "they are also . . . "), and then focus on the primary new information (C). You would then remind the child of what he or she needs to remember to evaluate this new information (B–C), and then give the answer to the question as a logical conclusion (A–B).

Not all arguments will develop in the same way, and many discuss information not summarized in the enthymemic thesis statement. However, although additional information may clearly strengthen your argument, it is not as essential as the steps in your reasoning. The enthymeme reveals the primary terms that are the bare bones of your argument, and you will have to discuss each term fully *at some point* in your essay to ensure that your reader follows your reasoning. You will also discover that you will spend more time discussing the essential parts of your "because" clause, because they contain the new information your reader needs to know. Let's examine another thesis, this time one for a more complicated argument, Thomas Kuhn's "The Essential Tension":

KUHN'S THESIS

(A) Scientists who are committed traditionalists

   (V1) are the only ones who can be

   (B) successful innovators

because

(A*) a traditionalist

   (V2) is the only one who can recognize

   (C) the anomalies that lead to new paradigms.

Assumption: (B) Successful innovators
             (C) develop new paradigms.

OUTLINE FOR THE LOGICAL STRUCTURE OF KUHN'S ARGUMENT

Q: How can a scientist be a successful innovator?

B–C: As we know, scientists are innovative only when they can create new paradigms, new ways of thinking about the evidence they have.

A–A*:   Most scientists, though, are trained to be traditionalists. They study and practice a scientific method based on a cautious examination of the evidence from the perspective of what scientists already know. They are trained to work within the accepted paradigms of the discipline.

A*–V*: Because they are trained in the accepted paradigms, they are the only ones who can recognize when the evidence doesn't seem to fit what they thought should occur. That is, they are the only ones who can identify the anomalies.

C: The anomalies, though, need to be accounted for. Even the best traditionalist will want to account for the discrepancy between evidence and expectation. If, after questioning the evidence, the anomaly still is apparent, the traditionalist will question the paradigm, readjusting it to accommodate the new evidence.

C*:   And since the best new paradigms are not spun out of whole cloth, but built on the best that has been thought in the discipline,

A—B: scientists who are committed traditionalists are the only ones who can be successful innovators.

The above example illustrates the logical steps Kuhn took to move from an introduction of the question at issue (Q) through the body of his essay (the discussion of his "because" clause: A*–C) to arrive at his conclusion (the first clause of his thesis: A–B). Note the extra attention given to term C of the "because" clause; the primary term in the "because" clause that is not shared with the first clause will always require the most discussion because it represents what is new about the information contained in your "because" clause.

The most important feature of the logical structure behind Kuhn's argument is the way it begins with a discussion of points that his audience was most likely to agree with (e.g., the question they had asked him to address; the assumed definition of what they meant by "innovators"; and a clarification of the training of "traditionalists") and then moves to discuss in greater detail the new information his audience didn't already understand (i.e., that the best innovations are founded on old paradigms). It is also important to note that Kuhn's thesis (the enthymeme itself) is not the introduction but the conclusion to his argument.

EXERCISE

Practice recognizing the logical structure behind an enthymemic thesis by outlining arguments for the following thesis statements. Remember to identify the essential parts of the thesis first, and then decide which of those parts will require extended explanation.

1. Pit bulls do not make good pets because they have been bred to kill.
2. Cockroaches are an anomaly because they have not evolved since they first appeared on earth.
3. San Francisco is a safer place to live than New York because the chance of being killed during an earthquake in California is much less than that of being killed on the streets of New York.
4. The current usage of the word "discrimination" is making us less responsible thinkers because using "discrimination" to refer only to distinctions we should not make leads us to avoid making distinctions of any kind.
5. We should not let the government search our houses without a permit because, as Americans, we have a duty to protect our right to privacy.

INTRODUCTIONS: STARTING ON A POINT OF AGREEMENT

Recognizing the logical steps in your argument can help you discover what to say in your essay, but you do have to be careful how you order them. The way to ensure that you communicate with your reader is to work from what your reader already knows. For this reason, your audience affects both what you are going to discuss and how you should do so. You need to approach your readers with information they already understand before you take them on the mental journey that will lead them to see things from a new perspective. For example, if Gould had begun his essay by saying, "We should not let religious questions blind our ability to understand nature as it is," you might have misunderstood his intention, thinking that Gould was arguing against religion itself. You might have stopped reading, or, if you had continued, you may have looked only for ways to argue *against* him—not work *with* him to understand what he really meant. Instead, Gould began with a point his readers understood, how nature can be baffling when it does not immediately reflect the hand of a benevolent creator. By doing this, Gould showed he had listened to and understood his readers' view of the subject.

There are several different points of agreement you can use to begin an argument. The most obvious is the issue you are addressing. If you and your reader agree on little else, at least you agree that there is disagreement about something. For example, Kuhn agreed with his audience that there was no established theory for how to train scientists to be original thinkers. He then promised his audience that he would give them an answer how it might be done, even though they may not like it. He was aware his audience did not believe traditional educational methods could teach creativity, even though that was what he was going to argue, so he suggested just enough of his stance on the issue—a very general working thesis—to encourage them that the issue was important to him, too.

Although you may never explicitly pose the question at issue in your writing, your introduction should imply it. Posing your thesis as a hypothesis you are going to test is a popular way to present the issue, because the thesis is being proposed as an answer to a question worth exploring. The question at issue is the starting point for every discussion, because it lets your readers know what they will learn if they continue reading. It establishes a writer/reader contract. Introducing the question at issue, whether directly posed or implied through a general statement of your thesis, promises your reader what problem your essay will attempt to solve. Because every introduction should at least imply what the essay will address, we can call the question at issue the primary point of agreement.

Another valid point of agreement is the major assumption behind your logical thesis statement. If your thesis is good, the premise that you assume your readers will accept without proof is a point that your readers want to believe. If you introduce it at the beginning of your essay, your readers will be likely to accept you as someone they respect and want to listen to. Kuhn's thesis assumed that his audience defined "innovators" as those who successfully developed new ways of thinking about the subject. He might have avoided mentioning this because it didn't require proof, but because he was aware that his audience also thought innovators were different from traditionalists, he spent time early in his essay letting his readers know how much he agreed with them so they would be more likely to understand the distinction he would make later on.

Sometimes a point of agreement might be what you and your readers mean by a term, a particular definition that both of you rely on when discussing the issue. Kuhn's assumed definition of "innovators" worked this way, but he also carefully defined "traditionalists" before moving to his real point. As Kuhn's essay reflects, an extended definition of the primary terms of your argument can often help you lead your reader from a point of agreement to start viewing the subject from your unique perspective.

As Kuhn's essay illustrates, your essay will begin ideally with all of these points of agreement: question at issue, clarification of assumption, and definition of terms. A natural way to introduce each of these steps is to start your essay by resurrecting the conversation that generated the particular issue you will address. To reconstruct this conversation (the rhetorical situation) you will want to review what the authors have said and what your classmates have said in response. This will help you introduce a particular question everyone seems to be asking and the types of answers you have heard them offer. When you begin your essay at this type of point of agreement, you are using your writing not only to clarify what others have said and why they believe what they do, but also to discover the precise point where communication has broken down.

CONCLUSIONS: ASSERTING YOUR THESIS

Starting your essay with a question (e.g., "Do superstitions help us live better lives?") or a hypothesis (e.g., "Perhaps there is something about superstitutions that can help us live better lives") is better than asserting a premature thesis statement as the only answer (e.g., "Superstitions help us live better lives because they give us hope that there is meaning in the world"). A question or hypothesis enables you to take your readers with you as you work with their ideas to justify your own perspective.

Although you will read and enjoy some essays because they express ideas similar to your own, their theses will still be different from ones you would have written, and the reasons used to justify them will be different from those you would give. The pleasure you gain from the essay is the new information that leads you to see the subject from a slightly different perspective. The author might prepare you for the thesis by merely introducing the question it will answer or by stating it early as a *hypothesis* to be examined in the rest of the essay. However, the thesis is primarily an answer, and as such, should be reserved for near the end of the essay, as the natural conclusion to the reasoning process.

The concluding section of the essays you read and the essays you write will vary in length, depending on how clearly the introduction presents the issue under examination and how well the body of the essay leads the reader through the reasoning process used to arrive at a thesis. Sometimes, if the logical structure of the essay is obvious, there will be no apparent concluding section at all—the writer can assume the reader will be able to deduce the underlying thesis. However, conclusions are not confined to mere statements (or restatements) of the thesis.

They are an opportunity to take your point further, to suggest what your reader might do with the knowledge you have arrived at.

THE BODY: "EARNING" THE RIGHT TO ASSERT YOURSELF

Every time you put pencil to paper (or fingers to your computer keyboard) you are actively engaging with the subjects you are learning. To "earn" the right to share that learning with others, you need to be honest with yourself, to recognize when you might be rationalizing or when your readers might interpret the evidence differently from the way you have. Considering your readers' perspectives makes the process of discovering your thesis much easier. You do not have to invent what you are going to say all by yourself: anticipating your readers' questions will tell you what you have to say. You will also know when you have said enough, for once you have "earned" the right to assert a conclusion (your thesis), you will know your essay has reached its intended destination.

The body of your essay should clarify and support the validity of the "because" clause in your enthymemic thesis. If you formulate your logical thesis statement before you draft your argument, you will have an idea what points you will need to develop. However, keep in mind that while drafting your argument, you may discover you need to modify or change your enthymeme in some way. It is still a working thesis until you prove to yourself that your argument is defensible in light of all the evidence. Sometimes you may wish to draft your argument before formulating a thesis. You would then have to analyze the body of your essay to discover how you had "earned" the conclusion you arrived at. Formulating an enthymeme from a rough draft can help you construct an outline that will guide your revision process, indicating where you have omitted or hidden essential steps in the logical structure of your argument.

As you read the essays in the following chapter, try to recognize the introduction (this might be as short as a title or as long as several paragraphs). Once you have done this, try to articulate the terms of the writer's contract: what is the issue the writer will address and what does he or she imply about the way this question will be explored? Once you have identified the terms of the writer/reader contract, you can test whether the body of the essay earns the writer the right to assert his or her concluding thesis. (The "because" clause you pull out for their thesis should represent the primary point they make to earn this right.) To help you do this, Chapter 8 will also discuss different ways you can use an outline of the logical structure behind the enthymeme to read more critically.

CHAPTER EIGHT

Reasoning About Psychology

*I*n Chapter 7, you learned how the logical thesis statement can be used to predict the logical structure of an essay. This knowledge can help you at each stage of the composing process, whether you are composing someone else's argument as you read or composing your own as you write. In this chapter, you will practice each of these stages by using a logical outline to (1) formalize your reading of an essay, (2) predict how to structure your rough draft, and (3) identify the structure behind your rough draft before you revise. Most importantly, though, as you go through these stages of the reading and writing process, you will learn how the logical structure of an argument reveals what is unique about the particular reasoning process used in a specific field. You will practice identifying the reasoning process used in psychology, but remember that the method of analyzing logical structure that you use in the chapter can be a helpful tool for identifying the reasoning processes used by other disciplines as well.

USING QUESTIONS AND INFORMATION IN PSYCHOLOGY

As you have learned, the most obvious distinction between the types of writing done in different fields is reflected in the specific ways disciplines formulate the questions they ask and in the specific kinds of information they use to answer them. You have discovered that political scientists address questions of policy (e.g., "What should be done?") by applying new information to previously established policies. For example, the following thesis depends on the policies stated in the United States Constitution for its reasoning to be valid: "The American Government should make mandatory retirement illegal *because* mandatory retirement policies violate the people's constitutional rights." (*Assumption:* "No policy should violate the people's constitutional rights.")

You have also discovered that natural scientists tend to address questions of definition (e.g., "What is it?") by applying new information based on observation to old information which is also primarily the result of inductive observation. Consider this thesis from medical science: "Alzheimer's disease is not a normal result of the aging process because it causes a breakdown in the brain's transmission system." Note how the assumption ("A breakdown in the brain's transmission system is not the normal result of the aging process.") is old information developed from an earlier inductive study.

Similar to the natural scientist, the psychologist often asks questions about "what is." In the following essay, B.F. Skinner's title asks "What is man?" The psychologist's question, though, implies a different type of argument than the scientist's. When scientists address "What is man?" they look at physical evidence within the human body to answer the question. When Skinner asks "What is man?" he is really addressing a question of human behavior: "Why does man behave as he does?"

Instead of asking a question of definition, the psychologist is really asking a question of consequence (e.g., "What causes man to behave in certain ways?"). To answer this question, psychology looks at intangible evidence and speculates about what stimulates humans to feel and behave as they do. This is different from psychiatry, the medical science that studies the human mind. As a natural science, psychiatry examines tangible evidence, the physical make-up of the human brain, to explain human behavior. Psychology, though, does not examine the physical mechanics of human thought processes, or *how* humans think; instead, it investigates *what* humans think, what makes them think it, and how it affects their behavior.

Rephrasing the questions psychologists pose can also help you recognize the connections between their field and political science. Whereas the latter generalizes about human behavior to reason how it should be governed, the former generalizes about human behavior to reason why this behavior occurs. The type of reasoning the question "why" requires, forces psychologists to direct their inquiry with a question of consequence: "What observable conditions clearly influence how we behave, and, hence, make us who we are?" Notice the verbs that will be used to answer questions of consequence—they are active and transitive, implying how something "produces" or "leads to" something else.

Reviewing the Types of Argument

POLICY: "What should be done?"
  (representative discipline: political science)

VALUE: "Is it good?"
  (representative disciplines: philosophy and literature)

CONSEQUENCE: "Why did it occur?"
    "What effect did it have?"
    (representative discipline: psychology)

DEFINITION: "What is it?"
  (representative discipline: natural science)

As you remember from Chapter 6, the questions that disciplines ask and the information they use to arrive at an answer reflect the type of argument they use. To better understand how different types of questions alter the reasoning process, note how a political scientist, a natural scientist, and a psychologist might reason differently about the following situation:

There was an earthquake in San Francisco in 1989 that registered 7.0 on the Richter scale. A lengthy portion of the Nimitz freeway collapsed. Because the earthquake hit at rush hour and the Nimitz was a double-decker freeway (the lanes heading toward San Francisco built directly above those heading away from the city), hundreds of motorists were feared dead. However, the rescue and clean-up efforts revealed that the casualty figure was under fifty because many commuters had left work early to attend the World Series game scheduled for that evening in Candlestick Park.

A Political Scientist's Analysis

Question: What should the state do to prevent this kind of tragedy in the future?

Answer: The state should redirect funds to improve the ability of older structures to withstand earthquakes because taxpayers have a right to expect reasonable protection when using public facilities.

A Natural Scientist's Analysis

Question: How damaging is an earthquake of 7.0 magnitude?

Answer: The damage to the Nimitz freeway is not representative of earthquakes of a 7.0 magnitude because the freeway had been built on an unstable landmass.

A Psychologist's Analysis

Question: How will this tragedy affect the behavior of the people in the Bay area?

Answer: The people of the Bay area will not change their behavior in response to the Nimitz disaster because the fact that the casualty figure was much lower than originally expected confirms their desire to dismiss official predictions that an even more devastating earthquake will occur in the near future.

USING SENTENCE OUTLINES TO READ

Before you read the following essays from the field of psychology, let's review how you might use your first readings to prepare for a critical rereading of the arguments. Although upon initial reading you might have a sense of the kind of arguments the authors are making, to discover their logical thesis statements you will need to pay close attention to the logical structure of the essay. Keeping an informal sentence outline as you read an essay for the first time helps you analyze the logical structure more efficiently when you reread it. A sentence outline is an informal list of statements that reflect the primary steps in the argument.

As you learned in Chapter 7, when you begin reading an essay, you look for some indication of what the essay will be about, for the question the author promises to answer. This question might be explicitly posed (as in Skinner's title) or reflected in a general statement of the thesis. Your sentence outline should identify this question (which is usually not posed directly but implied in the introductory paragraphs) and then list the primary points as the author moves from this question to earn the right to assert the answer (the thesis). Here is a rough outline of the first few pages of Skinner's essay:

Sentence Outline for "What Is Man?"

Para. 1–3:   Why does man behave as he does?

Para. 4–7:   Behavior can be perceived as initiated by the individual or as influenced by the environment.

Para. 8–11:   The environment affects behavior through "contingencies of reinforcement." (The dictionary defines "contingency" as "a possibility that must be prepared against"—I guess that means we use past experiences to determine how to act in new situations.)

Para. 12–18:   We are not really aware of why we do what we do. Self-knowledge is a response to how society has taught us to think about ourselves.

As this example illustrates, a sentence outline is an informal record of what you are thinking as you read. (Note how this student included what she had found in the dictionary and how she applied that definition to her vague understanding of the essay at that point.) Avoid being too mechanical as you take notes. Make your sentences reflect only those ideas that attract your attention. As this student did, indicate where these ideas are discussed, noting paragraphs or page numbers. Do not describe each paragraph independently, as if each paragraph were equally interesting. Just as the introduction of an essay may be as short as the title of the work or as long as several pages, each step in the logical structure of the argument takes a different amount of discussion to establish. Sometimes a logical step may be stated in one sentence; sometimes it may take four or five pages to establish.

As you read, try to identify each time the essay moves from one point (and its proof) to another. Sometimes, these transitions are easy to identify. Key words like "thus" or "to summarize" indicate that the author is preparing to move to the next logical point in the argument. (Note how Skinner uses "Let us consider some examples . . ." to begin paragraph 4 and links the next two paragraphs by beginning with "Another example . . ." and "A third example. . . .") Sometimes, the author might pose a rhetorical question to direct the next stage of the inquiry ("But what does this mean for . . . ?"). Sometimes the author will make it even easier, leaving spaces between the last paragraph of one section and the first paragraph of the next (note how Skinner does this). As you develop your ability to read critically, you will find these transitions between logical steps in the argument fairly easy to identify.

As you read the following essays, keep a sentence outline in your reading notebook by first indicating where the writer/reader contract is introduced, and formulating the question, either overt or implied, that the author promises to answer. As you proceed into the body of the essay, try to summarize each logical step by paraphrasing it into one sentence and indicating the paragraphs and/or sentences devoted to it. The last sentence in your outline should reflect how the author has fulfilled the terms of the contract, and is best formulated as the thesis-statement earned by the author's discussion and emphasized in the essay's concluding section.

What Is Man?

B. F. Skinner (1904–   )

B. F. Skinner's "What is Man?" is taken from his longer work, Beyond Freedom and Dignity, *published in 1971. As the title of his book implies, Skinner was interested in the issue of individual freedom, and whether human dignity actually depends on how much freedom individuals have to control their own behavior. He has become a major figure in behavioral psychology because of his unique position that individuals are not autonomous beings, that they cannot act independent from the physical and psychological environments that surround them.*

As you read the following essay, recognize how Skinner uses evidence. Although he is not a natural scientist, and does not rely solely on physical evidence, his discussion of humans relies partly on examples of other animals' behavior, utilizing scientific information about their biological similarities. Skinner's argument is the result of extensive experimentation, some of which included placing his own daughter in a box to experiment with how changes in environment might affect behavior. In 1976, he published Walden II, *patterned after Henry David Thoreau's account of the years he had spent living alone in the woods near Walden Pond. Although Thoreau's* Walden *(1854) exposed a world where individuals could be naturally free from the negative influences of society, Skinner's response was a vision of a world where children are programmed through controlled environmental influences so that individual behavior would lead to an ideal society.*

As a science of behavior adopts the strategy of physics and biology, the autonomous agent to which behavior has traditionally been attributed is replaced by the environment—the environment in which the species evolved and in which the behavior of the individual is shaped and maintained. The vicissitudes of "environmentalism" show how difficult it has been to make this change. That a man's behavior owes something to antecedent events and that the environment is a more promising point of attack than man himself has long been recognized. As Crane Brinton observed, "a program to change things not just to convert people" was a significant part of the English, French, and Russian revolutions. It was Robert Owen, according to Trevelyan, who first "clearly grasped and taught that environment makes character and that environment is under human control" or, as Gilbert Seldes wrote, "that man is a creature of circumstance, that if you changed the environments of thirty little Hottentots and thirty little aristocratic English children, the aristocrats would become Hottentots, for all practical purposes, and the Hottentots little conservatives."

The evidence for a crude environmentalism is clear enough. People are extraordinarily different in different places, and possibly just because of the places. The nomad on horseback in Outer Mongolia and the astronaut in outer space are different people, but, as far as we know, if they had been exchanged at birth, they would have taken each other's place. (The expression "change places" shows how closely we identify a person's behavior with the environment in which it occurs.) But we need to know a great deal more before that fact becomes useful. What is it about the environment that produces a Hottentot? And what would need to be changed to produce an English conservative instead?

Both the enthusiasm of the environmentalist and his usually ignominious failure are illustrated by Owen's utopian experiment at New Harmony. A long history of environmental reform—in education, penology, industry, and family life, not to mention government and religion—has shown the same pattern. Environments are constructed on the model of environments in which good behavior has been observed, but the behavior fails to appear. Two hundred years of this kind of environmentalism has very little to show for itself, and for a simple reason. We must know how the environment works before we can change it to change behavior. A mere shift in emphasis from man to environment means very little.

Let us consider some examples in which the environment takes over the function and role of autonomous man. The first, often said to involve human nature, is *aggression.* Men often act in such a way that they harm others, and they often seem to be reinforced by signs of damage to others. The ethologists have emphasized contingencies of survival which would contribute these features to the genetic endowment of the species, but the contingencies of reinforcement in the lifetime of the individual are also significant, since anyone who acts aggressively to harm others is likely to be reinforced in other ways—for example, by taking possession of goods. The contingencies explain the behavior quite apart from any state or feeling of aggression or any initiating act by autonomous man.

Another example involving a so-called "trait of character" is *industry.* Some people are industrious in the sense that they work energetically for long periods of time, while others are lazy and idle in the sense that they do not. "Industry" and "laziness" are among thousands of so-called "traits." The behavior they refer to can be explained in other ways. Some of it may be attributed to genetic idiosyncrasies (and subject to change only through genetic measures), and the rest to environmental contingencies, which are much more important than is usually realized. Regardless of any normal genetic endowment, an organism will range between vigorous activity and complete quiescence depending upon the schedules on which it has been reinforced. The explanation shifts from a trait of character to an environmental history of reinforcement.

A third example, a "cognitive" activity, is *attention.* A person responds only to a small part of the stimuli impinging upon him. The traditional view is that he himself determines which stimuli are to be effective by "paying attention" to them. Some kind of inner gatekeeper is said to allow some stimuli to enter and to keep all others out. A sudden or strong stimulus may break through and "attract" attention, but the person himself seems otherwise to be in control. An analysis of the environmental circumstances reverses the relation. The kinds of stimuli which break through by "attracting attention" do so because they have been associated in the evolutionary history of the species or the personal history of the individual with important—e.g., danger-ous—things. Less forceful stimuli attract attention only to the extent that they have figured in contingencies of reinforcement. We can arrange contingen-cies which ensure that an organism—even such a "simple" organism as a pigeon—will attend to one object and not to another, or to one property of an object, such as its color, and not to another, such as its shape. The inner gatekeeper is replaced by the contingencies to which the organism has been exposed and which select the stimuli to which it reacts.

In the traditional view a person perceives the world around him and acts upon it to make it known to him. In a sense he reaches out and grasps it. He "takes it in" and possesses it. He "knows" it in the Biblical sense in which a man knows a woman. It has even been argued that the world would not exist if no one perceived it. The action is exactly reversed in an environmental analysis. There would, of course, be no perception if there were no world to be perceived, but an existing world would not be perceived if there were no appropriate contingencies. We say that a baby perceives his mother's face and knows it. Our evidence is that the baby responds in one way to his mother's face and in other ways to other faces or other things. He makes this distinc-tion not through some mental act of perception but because of prior contin-gencies. Some of these may be contingencies of survival. Physical features of a species are particularly stable parts of the environment in which a species evolves. (That is why courtship and sex and relations between parent and offspring are given such a prominent place by ethologists.) The face and facial expressions of the human mother have been associated with security, warmth, food, and other important things, during both the evolution of the species and the life of the child.

We learn to perceive in the sense that we learn to respond to things in particular ways because of the contingencies of which they are a part. We may perceive the sun, for example, simply because it is an extremely powerful stimulus, but it has been a permanent part of the environment of the species throughout its evolution and more specific behavior with respect to it could have been selected by contingencies of survival (as it has been in many other species). The sun also figures in many current contingencies of reinforce-ment: we move into or out of sunlight depending on the temperature; we wait for the sun to rise or set to take practical action; we talk about the sun and its effects; and we eventually study the sun with the instruments and methods of science. Our perception of the sun depends on what we do with respect to it. Whatever we do, and hence however we perceive it, the fact remains that it is the environment which acts upon the perceiving person, not the perceiv-ing person who acts upon the environment.

The perceiving and knowing which arise from verbal contingencies are even more obviously products of the environment. We react to an object in many practical ways because of its color; thus, we pick and eat red apples of a particular variety but not green. It is clear that we can "tell the difference" between red and green, but something more is involved when we say that we *know* that one apple is red and the other green. It is tempting to say that knowing is a cognitive process altogether divorced from action, but the contingencies provide a more useful distinction. When someone asks about the color of an object which he cannot see, and we tell him that it is red, *we* do nothing about the object in any other way. It is the person who has questioned us and heard our answer who makes a practical response which depends on color. Only under verbal contingencies can a speaker respond to an isolated property to which a nonverbal response cannot be made. A response made to the property of an object without responding to the object in any other way is called *abstract.* Abstract thinking is the product of a particular kind of environment, not of a cognitive faculty.

As listeners we acquire a kind of knowledge from the verbal behavior of others which may be extremely valuable in permitting us to avoid direct exposure to contingencies. We learn from the experience of others by responding to what they say about contingencies. When we are warned against doing something or are advised to do something, there may be no point in speaking of knowledge, but when we learn more durable kinds of warnings and advice in the form of maxims or rules, we may be said to have a special kind of knowledge about the contingencies to which they apply. The laws of science are descriptions of contingencies of reinforcement, and one who knows a scientific law may behave effectively without being exposed to the contingencies it describes. (He will, of course, have very different feelings about the contingencies, depending on whether he is following a rule or has been directly exposed to them. Scientific knowledge is "cold," but the behavior to which it gives rise is as effective as the "warm" knowledge which comes from personal experience.)

Isaiah Berlin has referred to a particular sense of knowing, said to have been discovered by Giambattista Vico. It is "the sense in which I know what it is to be poor, to fight for a cause, belong to a nation, to join or abandon a church or a party, to feel nostalgia, terror, the omnipresence of a god, to understand a gesture, a work of art, a joke, a man's character, that one is transformed or lying to oneself." These are the kinds of things one is likely to learn through direct contact with contingencies rather than from the verbal behavior of others, and special kinds of feelings are no doubt associated with them, but, even so, the knowledge is not somehow directly given. A person can know what it is to fight for a cause only after a long history during which he has learned to perceive and to know that state of affairs called fighting for a cause.

The role of the environment is particularly subtle when what is known is the knower himself. If there is no external world to initiate knowing, must we not then say that the knower himself acts first? This is, of course, the field of consciousness, or awareness, a field which a scientific analysis of behavior is often accused of ignoring. The charge is a serious one and should be taken seriously. Man is said to differ from the other animals mainly because he is "aware of his own existence." He knows what he is doing; he knows that he has had a past and will have a future; he "reflects on his own nature"; he alone follows the classical injunction "Know thyself." Any analysis of human behavior which neglected these facts would be defective indeed. And some analyses do. What is called "methodological behaviorism" limits itself to what can be publicly observed; mental processes may exist, but they are ruled out of scientific consideration by their nature. The "behavioralists" in political science and many logical positivists in philosophy have followed a similar line. But self-observation can be studied, and it must be included in any reasonably complete account of human behavior. Rather than ignore consciousness, an experimental analysis of behavior has stressed certain crucial issues. The question is not whether a man can know himself but what he knows when he does so.

The problem arises in part from the indisputable fact of privacy: a small part of the universe is enclosed within a human skin. It would be foolish to deny the existence of that private world, but it is also foolish to assert that because it is private it is of a different nature from the world outside. The difference is not in the stuff of which the private world is composed, but in its accessibility. There is an exclusive intimacy about a headache, or heartache, or a silent soliloquy. The intimacy is sometimes distressing (one cannot shut one's eyes to a headache), but it need not be, and it has seemed to support the doctrine that knowing is a kind of possession.

The difficulty is that although privacy may bring the knower closer to what he knows, it interferes with the process through which he comes to know anything. As we saw in Chapter 6, the contingencies under which a child learns to describe his feelings are necessarily defective; the verbal community cannot use the procedures with which it teaches a child to describe objects. There are, of course, natural contingencies under which we learn to respond to private stimuli, and they generate behavior of great precision; we could not jump or walk or turn a handspring if we were not being stimulated by parts of our own body. But very little awareness is associated with this kind of behavior and, in fact, we behave in these ways most of the time without being aware of the stimuli to which we are responding. We do not attribute awareness to other species which obviously use similar private stimuli. To "know" private stimuli is more than to respond to them.

The verbal community specializes in self-descriptive contingencies. It asks such questions as: What did you do yesterday? What are you doing now? What will you do tomorrow? Why did you do that? Do you really want to do that? How do you feel about that? The answers help people to adjust to each other effectively. And it is because such questions are asked that a person responds to himself and his behavior in the special way called knowing or being aware. Without the help of a verbal community all behavior would be unconscious. Consciousness is a social product. It is not only *not* the special field of autonomous man, it is not within range of a solitary man.

And it is not within the range of accuracy of anyone. The privacy which seems to confer intimacy upon self-knowledge makes it impossible for the verbal community to maintain precise contingencies. Introspective vocabularies are by nature inaccurate, and that is one reason why they have varied so widely among schools of philosophy and psychology. Even a carefully trained observer runs into trouble when new private stimuli are studied. (Independent evidence of private stimulation—for example, through physiological measures—would make it possible to sharpen the contingencies which generate self-observation and would, incidentally, confirm the present interpretation. Such evidence would not, as we noted in Chapter I, offer any support for a theory which attributed human behavior to an observable inner agent.)

Theories of psychotherapy which emphasize awareness assign a role to autonomous man which is properly, and much more effectively, reserved for contingencies of reinforcement. Awareness may help if the problem is in part a lack of awareness, and "insight" into one's condition may help if one then takes remedial action, but awareness or insight alone is not always enough, and it may be too much. One need not be aware of one's behavior or the conditions controlling it in order to behave effectively—or ineffectively. On the contrary, as the toad's inquiry of the centipede demonstrates, constant self-observation may be a handicap. The accomplished pianist would perform badly if he were as clearly aware of his behavior as the student who is just learning to play.

Cultures are often judged by the extent to which they encourage self-observation. Some cultures are said to breed unthinking men, and Socrates has been admired for inducing men to inquire into their own nature, but self-observation is only a preliminary to action. The extent to which a man *should* be aware of himself depends upon the importance of self-observation for effective behavior. Self-knowledge is valuable only to the extent that it helps to meet the contingencies under which it has arisen.

Perhaps the last stronghold of autonomous man is that complex "cognitive" activity called thinking. Because it is complex, it has yielded only slowly to explanation in terms of contingencies of reinforcement. When we say that a person *discriminates* between red and orange, we imply that discrimination is a kind of mental act. The person himself does not seem to be doing anything; he responds in different ways to red and orange stimuli, but this is the result of discrimination rather than the act. Similarly, we say that a person *generalizes*—say, from his own limited experience to the world at large—but all we see is that he responds to the world at large as he has learned to respond to his own small world. We say that a person *forms a concept or an abstraction,* but all we see is that certain kinds of contingencies of reinforcement have brought a response under the control of a single property of a stimulus. We say that a person *recalls* or *remembers* what he has seen or heard, but all we see is that the present occasion evokes a response, possibly in weakened or altered form, acquired on another occasion. We say that a person *associates* one word with another, but all we observe is that one verbal stimulus evokes the response previously made to another. Rather than suppose that it is therefore autonomous man who discriminates, generalizes, forms concepts or abstractions, recalls or remembers, and associates, we can put matters in good order simply by noting that these terms do not refer to forms of behavior.

A person may take explicit action, however, when he solves a problem. In putting a jigsaw puzzle together he may move the pieces around to improve his chances of finding a fit. In solving an equation he may transpose, clear fractions, and extract roots to improve his chances of finding a form of the equation he has already learned how to solve. The creative artist may manipulate a medium until something of interest turns up. Much of this can be done covertly, and it is then likely to be assigned to a different dimensional system, but it can always be done overtly, perhaps more slowly but also often more effectively, and with rare exceptions it must have been learned in overt form. The culture promotes thinking by constructing special contingencies. It teaches a person to make fine discriminations by making differential reinforcement more precise. It provides rules which make it unnecessary to be exposed to the contingencies from which the rules are derived, and it provides rules for finding rules.

Self-control, or self-management, is a special kind of problem solving which, like self-knowledge, raises all the issues associated with privacy. We have discussed some techniques in connection with aversive control in Chapter 4. It is always the environment which builds the behavior with which problems are solved, even when the problems are to be found in the private world inside the skin. None of this has been investigated in a very productive way, but the inadequacy of our analysis is no reason to fall back on a miracle-working mind. If our understanding of contingencies of reinforcement is not yet sufficient to explain all kinds of thinking, we must remember that the appeal to mind explains nothing at all.

In shifting control from autonomous man to the observable environment we do not leave an empty organism. A great deal goes on inside the skin, and physiology will eventually tell us more about it. It will explain why behavior is indeed related to the antecedent events of which it can be shown to be a function. The assignment is not always correctly understood. Many physiologists regard themselves as looking for the "physiological correlates" of mental events. Physiological research is regarded as simply a more scientific version of introspection. But physiological techniques are not, of course, designed to detect or measure personalities, ideas, attitudes, feelings, impulses, thoughts, or purposes. (If they were, we should have to answer a third question in addition to those raised in Chapter I: How can a personality, idea, feeling, or purpose affect the instruments of the physiologist?) At the moment neither introspection nor physiology supplies very adequate information about what is going on inside a man as he behaves, and since they are both directed inward, they have the same effect of diverting attention from the external environment.

Much of the misunderstanding about an inner man comes from the metaphor of storage. Evolutionary and environmental histories change an organism, but they are not stored within it. Thus, we observe that babies suck their mothers' breasts, and we can easily imagine that a strong tendency to do so has survival value, but much more is implied by a "sucking instinct" regarded as something a baby possesses which enables it to suck. The concept of "human nature" or "genetic endowment" is dangerous when taken in that sense. We are closer to human nature in a baby than in an adult, or in a primitive culture than in an advanced, in the sense that environmental contingencies are less likely to have obscured the genetic endowment, and it is tempting to dramatize that endowment by implying that earlier stages have survived in concealed form: man is a naked ape, and "the paleolithic bull which survives in man's inner self still paws the earth whenever a threatening gesture is made on the social scene." But anatomists and physiologists will not find an ape, or a bull, or for that matter instincts. They will find anatomical and physiological features which are the product of an evolutionary history.

The personal history of the individual is also often said to be stored within him. For "instinct" read "habit." The cigarette habit is presumably something more than the behavior said to show that a person possesses it; but the only other information we have concerns the reinforcers and the schedules of reinforcement which make a person smoke a great deal. The contingencies are not stored; they have simply left a changed person.

The environment is often said to be stored in the form of memories: to recall something we search for a copy of it, which can then be seen as the original thing was seen. As far as we know, however, there are no copies of the environment in the individual *at any time,* even when a thing is present and being observed. The products of more complex contingencies are also said to be stored; the repertoire acquired as a person learns to speak French is called a "knowledge of French."

Traits of character, whether derived from contingencies of survival or contingencies of reinforcement, are also said to be stored. A curious example occurs in Follett's *Modern American Usage:* "We say *He faced these adversities bravely,* aware without thought that the bravery is a property of the man, not of the facing; a brave act is poetic shorthand for the act of a person who shows bravery by performing it." But we call a man brave because of his acts, and he behaves bravely when environmental circumstances induce him to do so. The circumstances have changed his behavior; they have not implanted a trait or virtue.

Philosophies are also spoken of as things possessed. A man is said to speak or act in certain ways because he has a particular philosophy—such as idealism, dialectical materialism, or Calvinism. Terms of this kind summarize the effect of environmental conditions which it would now be hard to trace, but the conditions must have existed and should not be ignored. A person who possesses a "philosophy of freedom" is one who has been changed in certain ways by the literature of freedom.

The issue has had a curious place in theology. Does man sin because he is sinful, or is he sinful because he sins? Neither question points to anything very useful. To say that a man is sinful because he sins is to give an operational definition of sin. To say that he sins because he is sinful is to trace his behavior to a supposed inner trait. But whether or not a person engages in the kind of behavior called sinful depends upon circumstances which are not mentioned in either question. The sin assigned as an inner possession (the sin a person "knows") is to be found in a history of reinforcement. (The expression "God-fearing" suggests such a history, but piety, virtue, the immanence of God, a moral sense, or morality does not. As we have seen, man is not a moral animal in the sense of possessing a special trait or virtue; he has built a kind of social environment which induces him to behave in moral ways.)

These distinctions have practical implications. A recent survey of white Americans is said to have shown that "more than half blamed the inferior educational and economic status of blacks on 'something about Negroes themselves.'" The "something" was further identified as "lack of motivation," which was to be distinguished from *both* genetic and environmental factors. Significantly, motivation was said to be associated with "free will." To neglect the role of the environment in this way is to discourage any inquiry into the defective contingencies responsible for a "lack of motivation."

It is in the nature of an experimental analysis of human behavior that it should strip away the functions previously assigned to autonomous man and transfer them one by one to the controlling environment. The analysis leaves less and less for autonomous man to do. But what about man himself? Is there not something about a person which is more than a living body? Unless something called a self survives, how can we speak of self-knowledge or self-control? To whom is the injunction "Know thyself" addressed?

It is an important part of the contingencies to which a young child is exposed that his own body is the only part of his environment which remains the same *(idem)* from moment to moment and day to day. We say that he discovers his *identity* as he learns to distinguish between his body and the rest of the world. He does this long before the community teaches him to call things by name and to distinguish "me" from "it" or "you."

A self is a repertoire of behavior appropriate to a given set of contingencies. A substantial part of the conditions to which a person is exposed may play a dominant role, and under other conditions a person may report, "I'm not myself today," or, "I couldn't have done what you said I did, because that's not like me." The identity conferred upon a self arises from the contingencies responsible for the behavior. Two or more repertoires generated by different sets of contingencies compose two or more selves. A person possesses one repertoire appropriate to his life with his friends and another appropriate to his life with his family, and a friend may find him a very different person if he sees him with his family or his family if they see him with his friends. The problem of identity arises when situations are intermingled, as when a person finds himself with both his family and his friends at the same time.

Self-knowledge and self-control imply two selves in this sense. The self-knower is almost always a product of social contingencies, but the self that is known may come from other sources. The controlling self (the conscience or superego) is of social origin, but the controlled self is more likely to be the product of genetic susceptibilities to reinforcement (the id, or the Old Adam). The controlling self generally represents the interests of others, the controlled self the interests of the individual.

The picture which emerges from a scientific analysis is not of a body with a person inside, but of a body which *is* a person in the sense that it displays a complex repertoire of behavior. The picture is, of course, unfamiliar. The man thus portrayed is a stranger, and from the traditional point of view he may not seem to be a man at all. "For at least one hundred years," said Joseph Wood Krutch, "we have been prejudiced in every theory, including economic determinism, mechanistic behaviorism, and relativism, that reduces the stature of man until he ceases to be man at all in any sense that the humanists of an earlier generation would recognize." Matson has argued that "the empirical behavioral scientist . . . denies, if only by implication, that a unique being, called Man, exists." "What is now under attack," said Maslow, "is the 'being' of man." C. S. Lewis put it quite bluntly: Man is being abolished.

There is clearly some difficulty in identifying the man to whom these expressions refer. Lewis cannot have meant the human species, for not only is it not being abolished, it is filling the earth. (As a result it may eventually abolish itself through disease, famine, pollution, or a nuclear holocaust, but that is not what Lewis meant.) Nor are individual men growing less effective or productive. We are told that what is threatened is "man *qua* man," or "man in his humanity," or "man as Thou not It," or "man as a person not a thing." These are not very helpful expressions, but they supply a clue. What is being abolished is autonomous man—the inner man, the homunculus, the possessing demon, the man defended by the literatures of freedom and dignity.

His abolition has long been overdue. Autonomous man is a device used to explain what we cannot explain in any other way. He has been constructed from our ignorance, and as our understanding increases, the very stuff of which he is composed vanishes. Science does not dehumanize man, it dehomunculizes him, and it must do so if it is to prevent the abolition of the human species. To man *qua* man we readily say good riddance. Only by dispossessing him can we turn to the real causes of human behavior. Only then can we turn from the inferred to the observed, from the miraculous to the natural, from the inaccessible to the manipulable.

It is often said that in doing so we must treat the man who survives as a mere animal. "Animal" is a pejorative term, but only because "man" has been made spuriously honorific. Krutch has argued that whereas the traditional view supports Hamlet's exclamation, "How like a god!," Pavlov, the behavioral scientist, emphasized "How like a dog!" But that was a step forward. A god is the archetypal pattern of an explanatory fiction, of a miracleworking mind, of the metaphysical. Man is much more than a dog, but like a dog he is within range of a scientific analysis.

It is true that much of the experimental analysis of behavior has been concerned with lower organisms. Genetic differences are minimized by using special strains; environmental histories can be controlled, perhaps from birth; strict regimens can be maintained during long experiments; and very little of this is possible with human subjects. Moreover, in working with lower animals the scientist is less likely to put his own responses to the experimental conditions among his data, or to design contingencies with an eye to their effect on him rather than on the experimental organism he is studying. No one is disturbed when physiologists study respiration, reproduction, nutrition, or endocrine systems in animals; they do so to take advantage of very great similarities. Comparable similarities in behavior are being discovered. There is, of course, always the danger that methods designed for the study of lower animals will emphasize only those characteristics which they have in common with men, but we cannot discover what is "essentially" human until we have investigated nonhuman subjects. Traditional theories of autonomous man have exaggerated species differences. Some of the complex contingencies of reinforcement now under investigation generate behavior in lower organisms which, if the subjects were human, would traditionally be said to involve higher mental processes.

Man is not made into a machine by analyzing his behavior in mechanical terms. Early theories of behavior, as we have seen, represented man as a push-pull automaton, close to the nineteenth-century notion of a machine, but progress has been made. Man is a machine in the sense that he is a complex system behaving in lawful ways, but the complexity is extraordinary. His capacity to adjust to contingencies of reinforcement will perhaps be eventually simulated by machines, but this has not yet been done, and the living system thus simulated will remain unique in other ways.

Nor is man made into a machine by inducing him to use machines. Some machines call for behavior which is repetitious and monotonous, and we escape from them when we can, but others enormously extend our effectiveness in dealing with the world around us. A person may respond to very small things with the help of an electron microscope and to very large things with radiotelescopes, and in doing so he may seem quite inhuman to those who use only their unaided senses. A person may act upon the environment with the delicate precision of a micromanipulator or with the range and power of a space rocket, and his behavior may seem inhuman to those who rely only on muscular contractions. (It has been argued that the apparatus used in the operant laboratory misrepresents natural behavior because it introduces an external source of power, but men use external sources when they fly kites, sail boats, or shoot bows and arrows. They would have to abandon all but a small fraction of their achievements if they used only the power of their muscles.) People record their behavior in books and other media, and the use they make of the records may seem quite inhuman to those who can use only what they remember. People describe complex contingencies in the form of rules, and rules for manipulating rules, and they introduce them into electronic systems which "think" with a speed that seems quite inhuman to the unaided thinker. Human beings do all this with machines, and they would be less than human if they did not. What we now regard as machine-like behavior was, in fact, much commoner before the invention of these devices. The slave in the cotton field, the bookkeeper on his high stool, the student being drilled by a teacher—these were the machine-like men.

Machines replace people when they do what people have done, and the social consequences may be serious. As technology advances, machines will take over more and more of the functions of men, but only up to a point. We build machines which reduce some of the aversive features of our environment (grueling labor, for example) and which produce more positive reinforcers. We build them precisely because they do so. We have no reason to build machines to be reinforced by these consequences, and to do so would be to deprive ourselves of reinforcement. If the machines man makes eventually make him wholly expendable, it will be by accident, not design.

An important role of autonomous man has been to give human behavior direction, and it is often said that in dispossessing an inner agent we leave man himself without a purpose. As one writer has put it, "Since a scientific psychology must regard human behavior objectively, as determined by necessary laws, it must represent human behavior as unintentional." But "necessary laws" would have this effect only if they referred exclusively to antecedent conditions. Intention and purpose refer to selective consequences, the effects of which can be formulated in "necessary laws." Has life, in all the forms in which it exists on the surface of the earth, a purpose, and is this evidence of intentional design? The primate hand evolved *in order that* things might be more successfully manipulated, but its purpose is to be found not in a prior design but rather in the process of selection. Similarly, in operant conditioning the purpose of a skilled movement of the hand is to be found in the consequences which follow it. A pianist neither acquires nor executes the behavior of playing a scale smoothly because of a prior intention of doing so. Smoothly played scales are reinforcing for many reasons, and they select skilled movements. In neither the evolution of the human hand nor in the acquired use of the hand is any prior intention or purpose at issue.

The argument for purpose seems to be strengthened by moving back into the darker recesses of mutation. Jacques Barzun has argued that Darwin and Marx both neglected not only human purpose but the creative purpose responsible for the variations upon which natural selection plays. It may prove to be the case, as some geneticists have argued, that mutations are not entirely random, but nonrandomness is not necessarily the proof of a creative mind. Mutations will not be random when geneticists explicitly design them in order that an organism will meet specific conditions of selection more successfully, and geneticists will then seem to be playing the role of the creative mind in pre-evolutionary theory, but the purpose they display will have to be sought in their culture, in the social environment which has induced them to make genetic changes appropriate to contingencies of survival.

There is a difference between biological and individual purpose in that the latter can be felt. No one could have felt the purpose in the development of the human hand, whereas a person can in a sense feel the purpose with which he plays a smooth scale. But he does not play a smooth scale *because* he feels the purpose of doing so; what he feels is a by-product of his behavior in relation to its consequences. The relation of the human hand to the contingencies of survival under which it evolved is, of course, out of reach of personal observation; the relation of the behavior to contingencies of reinforcement which have generated it is not.

A scientific analysis of behavior dispossesses autonomous man and turns the control he has been said to exert over to the environment. The individual may then seem particularly vulnerable. He is henceforth to be controlled by the world around him, and in large part by other men. Is he not then simply a victim? Certainly men have been victims, as they been victimizers, but the word is too strong. It implies despoliation, which is by no means an essential consequence of interpersonal control. But even under benevolent control is the individual not at best a spectator who may watch what happens but is helpless to do anything about it? Is he not "at a dead end in his long struggle to control his own destiny"?

It is only autonomous man who has reached a dead end. Man himself may be controlled by his environment, but it is an environment which is almost wholly of his own making. The physical environment of most people is largely man-made. The surfaces a person walks on, the walls which shelter him, the clothing he wears, many of the foods he eats, the tools he uses, the vehicles he moves about in, most of the things he listens to and looks at are human products. The social environment is obviously man-made—it generates the language a person speaks, the customs he follows, and the behavior he exhibits with respect to the ethical, religious, governmental, economic, educational, and psychotherapeutic institutions which control him. The evolution of a culture is in fact a kind of gigantic exercise in self-control. As the individual controls himself by manipulating the world in which he lives, so the human species has constructed an environment in which its members behave in a highly effective way. Mistakes have been made, and we have no assurance that the environment man has constructed will continue to provide gains which outstrip the losses, but man as we know him, for better or for worse, is what man has made of man.

This will not satisfy those who cry "Victim!" C. S. Lewis protested: ". . . the power of man to make himself what he pleases . . . means . . . the power of some men to make other men what they please." This is inevitable in the nature of cultural evolution. The controlling *self* must be distinguished from the controlled self, even when they are both inside the same skin, and when control is exercised through the design of an external environment, the selves are, with minor exceptions, distinct. The person who unintentionally or intentionally introduces a new cultural practice is only one among possibly billions who will be affected by it. If this does not seem like an act of self-control, it is only because we have misunderstood the nature of self-control in the individual.

When a person changes his physical or social environment "intentionally"—that is, in order to change human behavior, possibly including his own—he plays two roles: one as a controller, as the designer of a controlling culture, and another as the controlled, as the product of a culture. There is nothing inconsistent about this; it follows from the nature of the evolution of a culture, with or without intentional design.

The human species has probably not undergone much genetic change in recorded time. We have only to go back a thousand generations to reach the artists of the caves of Lascaux. Features which bear directly on survival (such as resistance to disease) change substantially in a thousand generations, but the child of one of the Lascaux artists transplanted to the world of today might be almost indistinguishable from a modern child. It is possible that he would learn more slowly than his modern counterpart, that he could maintain only a smaller repertoire without confusion, or that he would forget more quickly; we cannot be sure. But we can be sure that a twentieth-century child transplanted to the civilization of Lascaux would not be very different from the children he met there, for we have seen what happens when a modern child is raised in an impoverished environment.

Man has greatly changed himself as a person in the same period of time by changing the world in which he lives. Something of the order of a hundred generations will cover the development of modern religious practices, and something of the same order of magnitude modern government and law. Perhaps no more than twenty generations will account for modern industrial practices, and possibly no more than four or five for education and psychotherapy. The physical and biological technologies which have increased man's sensitivity to the world around him and his power to change that world have taken no more than four or five generations.

Man has "controlled his own destiny," if that expression means anything at all. The man that man has made is the product of the culture man has devised. He has emerged from two quite different processes of evolution: the biological evolution responsible for the human species and the cultural evolution carried out by that species. Both of these processes of evolution may now accelerate because they are both subject to intentional design. Men have already changed their genetic endowment by breeding selectively and by changing contingencies of survival, and they may now begin to introduce mutations directly related to survival. For a long time men have introduced new practices which serve as cultural mutations, and they have changed the conditions under which practices are selected. They may now begin to do both with a clearer eye to the consequences.

Man will presumably continue to change, but we cannot say in what direction. No one could have predicted the evolution of the human species at any point in its early history, and the direction of intentional genetic design will depend upon the evolution of a culture which is itself unpredictable for similar reasons. "The limits of perfection of the human species," said Étienne Cabet in *Voyage en Icarie,* "are as yet unknown." But, of course, there are no limits. The human species will never reach a final state of perfection before it is exterminated—"some say in fire, some in ice," and some in radiation.

The individual occupies a place in a culture not unlike his place in the species, and in early evolutionary theory that place was hotly debated. Was the species simply a type of individual, and if so, in what sense could it evolve? Darwin himself declared species "to be purely subjective inventions of the taxonomist." A species has no existence except as a collection of individuals, nor has a family, tribe, race, nation, or class. A culture has no existence apart from the behavior of the individuals who maintain its practices. It is always an individual who behaves, who acts upon the environment and is changed by the consequences of his action, and who maintains the social contingencies which *are* a culture. The individual is the carrier of both his species and his culture. Cultural practices, like genetic traits, are transmitted from individual to individual. A new practice, like a new genetic trait, appears first in an individual and tends to be transmitted if it contributes to his survival as an individual.

Yet, the individual is at best a locus in which many lines of development come together in a unique set. His individuality is unquestioned. Every cell in his body is a unique genetic product, as unique as that classic mark of individuality, the fingerprint. And even within the most regimented culture every personal history is unique. No intentional culture can destroy that uniqueness, and, as we have seen, any effort to do so would be bad design. But the individual nevertheless remains merely a stage in a process which began long before he came into existence and will long outlast him. He has no ultimate responsibility for a species trait or a cultural practice, even though it was he who underwent the mutation or introduced the practice which became part of the species or culture. Even if Lamarck had been right in supposing that the individual could change his genetic structure through personal effort, we should have to point to the environmental circumstances responsible for the effort, as we shall have to do when geneticists begin to change the human endowment. And when an individual engages in the intentional design of a culture practice, we must turn to the culture which induces him to do so and supplies the art or science he uses.

One of the great problems of individualism, seldom recognized as such, is death—the inescapable fate of the individual, the final assault on freedom and dignity. Death is one of those remote events which are brought to bear on behavior only with the aid of cultural practices. What we see is the death of others, as in Pascal's famous metaphor: "Imagine a number of men in chains, all under sentence of death, some of whom are each day butchered in the sight of the others; those remaining see their own condition in that of their fellows, and looking at each other with grief and despair await their turn. This is an image of the human condition." Some religions have made death more important by picturing a future existence in heaven or hell, but the individualist has a special reason to fear death, engineered not by a religion but by the literatures of freedom and dignity. It is the prospect of personal annihilation. The individualist can find no solace in reflecting upon any contribution which will survive him. He has refused to act for the good of others and is therefore not reinforced by the fact that others whom he has helped will outlive him. He has refused to be concerned for the survival of his culture and is not reinforced by the fact that the culture will long survive him. In the defense of his own freedom and dignity he has denied the contributions of the past and must therefore relinquish all claim upon the future. Science has probably never demanded a more sweeping change in a traditional way of thinking about a subject, nor has there ever been a more important subject. In the traditional picture a person perceives the world around him, selects features to be perceived, discriminates among them, judges them good or bad, changes them to make them better (or, if he is careless, worse), and may be held responsible for his action and justly rewarded or punished for its consequences. In the scientific picture a person is a member of a species shaped by evolutionary contingencies of survival, displaying behavioral processes which bring him under the control of the environment in which he lives, and largely under the control of a social environment which he and millions of others like him have constructed and maintained during the evolution of a culture. The direction of the controlling relation is reversed: a person does not act upon the world, the world acts upon him.

It is difficult to accept such a change simply on intellectual grounds and nearly impossible to accept its implications. The reaction of the traditionalist is usually described in terms of feelings. One of these, to which the Freudians have appealed in explaining the resistance to psychoanalysis, is wounded vanity. Freud himself expounded, as Ernest Jones has said, "the three heavy blows which narcissism or self-love of mankind had suffered at the hands of science. The first was cosmological and was dealt by Copernicus; the second was biological and was dealt by Darwin; the third was psychological and was dealt by Freud." (The blow was suffered by the belief that something at the center of man knows all that goes on within him and that an instrument called will power exercises command and control over the rest of one's personality.) But what are the signs or symptoms of wounded vanity, and how shall we explain them? What people *do* about such a scientific picture of man is call it wrong, demeaning, and dangerous, argue against it, and attack those who propose or defend it. They do so not out of wounded vanity but because the scientific formulation has destroyed accustomed reinforcers. If a person can no longer take credit or be admired for what he does, then he seems to suffer a loss of dignity or worth, and behavior previously reinforced by credit or admiration will undergo extinction. Extinction often leads to aggressive attack.

Another effect of the scientific picture has been described as a loss of faith or "nerve," as a sense of doubt or powerlessness, or as discouragement, depression, or despondency. A person is said to feel that he can do nothing about his own destiny. But what he feels is a weakening of old responses which are no longer reinforced. People are indeed "powerless" when long-established verbal repertoires prove useless. For example, one historian has complained that if the deeds of men are "to be dismissed as simply the product of material and psychological conditioning," there is nothing to write about; "change must be at least partially the result of conscious mental activity."

Another effect is a kind of nostalgia. Old repertoires break through, as similarities between present and past are seized upon and exaggerated. Old days are called the good old days, when the inherent dignity of man and the importance of spiritual values were recognized. Such fragments of outmoded behavior tend to be "wistful"—that is, they have the character of increasingly unsuccessful behavior.

These reactions to a scientific conception of man are certainly unfortunate. They immobilize men of good will, and anyone concerned with the future of his culture will do what he can to correct them. No theory changes what it is a theory is about. Nothing is changed because we look at it, talk about it, or analyze it in a new way. Keats drank confusion to Newton for analyzing the rainbow, but the rainbow remained as beautiful as ever and became for many even more beautiful. Man has not changed because we look at him, talk about him, and analyze him scientifically. His achievements in science, government, religion, art, and literature remain as they have always been, to be admired as one admires a storm at sea or autumn foliage or a mountain peak, quite apart from their origins and untouched by a scientific analysis. What does change is our chance of doing something about the subject of a theory. Newton's analysis of the light in a rainbow was a step in the direction of the laser.

The traditional conception of man is flattering; it confers reinforcing privileges. It is therefore easily defended and can be changed only with difficulty. It was designed to build up the individual as an instrument of counter-control, and it did so effectively but in such a way as to limit progress. We have seen how the literatures of freedom and dignity, with their concern for autonomous man, have perpetuated the use of punishment and condoned the use of only weak nonpunitive techniques, and it is not difficult to demonstrate a connection between the unlimited right of the individual to pursue happiness and the catastrophes threatened by unchecked breeding, the unrestrained affluence which exhausts resources and pollutes the environment, and the imminence of nuclear war.

Physical and biological technologies have alleviated pestilence and famine and many painful, dangerous, and exhausting features of daily life, and behavioral technology can begin to alleviate other kinds of ills. In the analysis of human behavior it is just possible that we are slightly beyond Newton's position in the analysis of light, for we are beginning to make technological applications. There are wonderful possibilities—and all the more wonderful because traditional approaches have been so ineffective. It is hard to imagine a world in which people live together without quarreling, maintain themselves by producing the food, shelter, and clothing they need, enjoy themselves and contribute to the enjoyment of others in art, music, literature, and games, consume only a reasonable part of the resources of the world and add as little as possible to its pollution, bear no more children than can be raised decently, continue to explore the world around them and discover better ways of dealing with it, and come to know themselves accurately and, therefore, manage themselves efficiently. Yet all this is possible, and even the slightest sign of progress should bring a kind of change which in traditional terms would be said to assuage wounded vanity, offset a sense of hopelessness or nostalgia, correct the impression that "we neither can nor need to do anything for ourselves," and promote a "sense of freedom and dignity" by building "a sense of confidence and worth." In other words, it should abundantly reinforce those who have been induced by their culture to work for its survival.

An experimental analysis shifts the determination of behavior from autonomous man to the environment—an environment responsible both for the evolution of the species and for the repertoire acquired by each member. Early versions of environmentalism were inadequate because they could not explain how the environment worked, and much seemed to be left for autonomous man to do. But environmental contingencies now take over functions once attributed to autonomous man, and certain questions arise. Is man then "abolished"? Certainly not as a species or as an individual achiever. It is the autonomous inner man who is abolished, and that is a step forward. But does man not then become merely a victim or passive observer of what is happening to him? He is indeed controlled by his environment, but we must remember that it is an environment largely of his own making. The evolution of a culture is a gigantic exercise in self-control. It is often said that a scientific view of man leads to wounded vanity, a sense of hopelessness, and nostalgia. But no theory changes what it is a theory about; man remains what he has always been. And a new theory may change what can be done with its subject matter. A scientific view of man offers exciting possibilities. We have not yet seen what man can make of man.

QUESTIONS FOR A CRITICAL REREADING

After you have read the essay through once, while constructing your informal sentence outline, use the following questions to begin rereading the essay more critically. As you reread, use these questions and your sentence outline to formulate an enthymemic thesis for his argument.

1. As we have discussed, the title of Skinner's essay gives us a general impression of what he will address. However, the question "What is man?" is too general to help you identify how a psychologist would approach the subject. To identify the more specific question he is addressing, examine the writer/reader contract implicit in his first sentence: "As a science of behavior adopts the strategy of physics and biology, the autonomous agent to which behavior has traditionally been attributed is replaced by the environment. . . . " What does he mean by "autonomous agent?" Why have we traditionally believed in it? How does Skinner develop his introduction, and what specific question does it pose to compel us to listen to what he has to say? (*Hint:* His answer to the question is posed as a hypothesis in the introduction.)

2. At the end of paragraph 3, Skinner introduces the method he will use to establish the truth of his hypothesis and emphasizes why this issue is important for us to discuss: "We must know how the environment works before we can change it to change behavior." Why does he assume, here and later in his essay, that we might wish to "change behavior?"

3. Skinner strips away human qualities that we normally attribute to our autonomy and explains how these qualities are really only behaviors that have arisen in response to "contingencies of reinforcement." What does this phrase mean? What aspects of our inner self does Skinner discuss, and how does he explain them to be merely responses to contingencies? (Note that this is the most important new information that Skinner has to contribute to the field of psychology, and should be an essential part of the enthymemic thesis you formulate.)

4. After Skinner feels he has proven that we can never act independently but merely react to our environment, he acknowledges that some of his readers might fear that "in dispossessing an inner agent we leave man himself without a purpose" (paragraph 42). In one attempt to reassure these readers, he asserts, "It is only autonomous man who has reached a dead end. Man himself may be controlled by his environment, but it is an environment which is almost wholly of his own making." What does this statement mean?

5. What is Skinner's answer to the question you formulated for question 1? To formulate an enthymemic thesis for the essay, attach to his answer a "because" clause that represents why he believes it is right. (Remember that the "because" clause should contain an evaluation of the new information that dominates the center of his essay.) When you have done this, return to your sentence outline and reshape it around the thesis. (Although your reading will differ a little, you might wish to refer to the following example of how one student interpreted the logical structure of Skinner's essay.)

A Possible Enthymeme for Skinner's Essay

A	V1	B
Our environment	determines	who we are
	because	
A*	V2	C
contingencies of reinforcement	produce	what we normally attribute to man's autonomy.

[*Assumption* (relating unshared terms B–C): Anything that produces what we attribute to man's autonomy determines who we are.]

Logical Outline for Skinner's Essay

Introduction

Question at issue: What is man? Why does he behave as he does?

A–A*: Our environment influences our behavior through contingencies of reinforcement. (Shared terms are related through definition.)

Body

A*–V2: These contingencies produce man's aggression, industry, and cognitive activity.

C: Even man's ability to achieve self-knowledge arises from the presence of a verbal community and is useful merely as a means of helping us adapt to our environment. Thus, even man's thought process (usually attributed to man's autonomous self) can be explained as learned behavior. (Burden of proof: primary new information.)

Conclusion

B–C: And since this aspect of our supposed autonomy determines who we are, then . . .

A–B: Our environment must be the sole determinant of who we are. (Answer to question posed at introduction.)

POSSIBLE ISSUES FOR WRITING

After you have revised your logical outline for Skinner's argument, note which sections of his argument seem weaker than others. As you discuss the following questions with your classmates, see if the questions that become at issue for the class are related to the weak points you have identified. (This can help you discover what to explore in your own essay later on.)

1. Skinner believes the primary new information about our inner selves will address the major objection we might have to his argument. Does it? Is his proof convincing? Are there any human behaviors he does not discuss that you still believe are initiated by the self and not a response to environmental conditioning? What are they?
2. Skinner concludes his essay with a call to action, a statement that suggests what we should do with what he has discovered: "We have not yet seen what man can make of man." What do you think he wants you to do? Assuming that we are powerless to act independently, what present contingencies of reinforcement does Skinner expose to lead us to *improve* humankind? Does his idea of "improvement" agree with yours?
3. How do you feel about Skinner's use of the word "man"? Is it sexist? Does his use of the term to refer to all humans lead him to ignore aspects of female behavior that might contradict his thesis? Give examples.

Silence

Mary Field Belenky, Blythe McVicker Clinchy, Nancy Rule Goldberger, and Jill Mattuck Tarule

This essay is taken from a relatively new contribution to the field of psychology: Women's Ways of Knowing: The Development of Self, Voice, and Mind *(1986). This work reflects the impact the feminist movement has had on the field of psychology. A gauge of the success of the feminist movement in the 1960s is how effectively it has affected academic discussions in several disciplines: linguistics has begun to explore the impact language has on sexist attitudes (see Nilsen's essay in Chapter 2); political science has started developing affirmative action policies that recognize women's right to equal pay for equal work; science is developing new ways for woman to control their lives through advances in contraception and artificial insemination; history, sociology, literature, and economics have all started to examine the role women have played in the development of our culture. Psychology, though, addresses an even more immediate problem revealed by the feminist movement: how a primarily patriarchal society has affected the behavior of women.*

Although the authors' findings are quite revolutionary, their argument conforms to the requirements of the reasoning process used in psychology. As you read, use your reading notebook to construct an informal sentence outline, noting in particular how the question the authors pose is one of consequence and how the new evidence they use to support their answer is justified by old information previously established in the field.

> Where language and naming are power,
> silence is oppression, is violence.
> —*Adrienne Rich, 1977*

A woman we call Ann described being locked into a world of silence throughout her childhood and early adult years: "I could never understand what they were talking about. My schooling was very limited. I didn't learn anything. I would just sit there and let people ramble on about something I didn't understand and would say, You, you. I would be too embarrassed to ask, What do you really mean?" Trying to find meaning in the words that others spoke was painfully difficult for Ann, but talking with others was even more terrifying. Feeling dumb, Ann was certain that no one could understand her, or that if someone did, it would be only to tell her she "had it wrong." "I had trouble talking. If I tried to explain something and someone told me that it was wrong, I'd burst into tears over it. I'd just fall apart."

Responding to the demands and status conferred by motherhood and to the support of a children's health program, Ann had just begun to acknowledge and cultivate her intellectual capacities. Ann's story of herself as a knower—the notions that she had adopted, questioned, and replaced—

weaves in and out of the first chapters of this book. She is a particularly articulate spokesperson for adolescents and adults who have only begun to think about thinking.

In this chapter we begin our description of women's ways of knowing with the simplest way we could discern. While only two or three women viewed the world from this perspective at the time of the interview, others, like Ann, described the outlook in retrospect. These silent women were among the youngest and most socially, economically, and educationally deprived of all those we interviewed. We met them in the social agencies for parents, not on the college campuses. We recognize that the designation of *silence* is not parallel to the terms we have chosen for the other epistemological positions; nevertheless, we selected it because the absence of voice in these women is so salient. This position, though rare, at least in our sample, is an important anchoring point for our epistemological scheme, representing an extreme in denial of self and in dependence on external authority for direction.

FEELING "DEAF AND DUMB"

Figures of speech suggesting gaining a voice were used repeatedly by many of the women we interviewed to describe how they experienced their own growth and development—particularly the growth of mind. Such images, however, were conspicuously absent from the descriptions given by the women of silence.

Even though each of the women had the gifts of intelligence and of all their senses, they were unaware of the potential of such gifts. While no one was actually "deaf and dumb," this metaphor suggests their experience more accurately than does "gaining a voice." They felt "deaf" because they assumed they could not learn from the words of others, "dumb" because they felt so voiceless. As one person said, "Someone has to show me—not tell me—or I can't get it."

In trying to understand the experience of voice for the silent women, we searched their stories for all references that had, by the broadest stretch of the imagination, any association with the idea of voice and found that one theme stood out in bold relief: Words were perceived as weapons. Words were used to separate and diminish people, not to connect and empower them. The silent women worried that they would be punished just for using words—any words. The following examples give the flavor of their experience.

> *I deserved to be hit, because I was always mouthing off.*
> *I don't like talking to my husband. If I were to say no, he might hit me.*
> *I had to get drunk so I could tell people off.*
> *The baby listens to him. Men have deep voices. But me, I can't do anything with him.*

At home people talk about you. People know your business and everything else. . . . Lots of rumors are always going around.

The silent women lived cut off from others in a world full of rumor and innuendo. Words arise out of wrath, and they provoke wrath. One young woman described the war of words that was waged in the aftermath of her father's being sent to jail for their incestuous relationship. "Nobody liked me. Everybody used to make fun of me. This girl came over and beat me up and she said, 'I wouldn't spit on you if your guts were on fire!' Then the landlord yelled at me—not my mother—because the house was such a mess. It was all too much for me to handle, so I ran away." The young woman had only one way to think of herself: "I was a loudmouth. I didn't think nothing of telling someone where to go." She conceived of her voice as aggressive and incriminating.

While we found in these interviews a few descriptions suggesting the barest experience of dialogue with others, there were no indications of dialogue with "the self." There were no words that suggested an awareness of mental acts, consciousness, or introspection. When asked to finish the sentence "My conscience bothers me if . . .," Cindy, a pregnant fifteen-year-old, wrote "someone picks on me." She did not comprehend words that suggest an interior voice that could give herself mental directions and exhortations.[1]

EXPERIENCING DISCONNECTION

Although the silent women develop language, they do not cultivate their capacities for representational thought. They do not explore the power that words have for either expressing or developing thought. Language is a tool for representing experience, and tools contribute to creative endeavors only when used. Language—even literacy—alone does not lead automatically to reflective, abstract thought (Scribner and Cole 1981; Sigel and Cocking 1977). In order for reflection to occur, the oral and written forms of language must pass back and forth between persons who both speak and listen or read and write—sharing, expanding, and reflecting on each other's experiences. Such interchanges lead to ways of knowing that enable individuals to enter into the social and intellectual life of their community. Without them, individuals remain isolated from others; and without tools for representing their experiences, people also remain isolated from the self.

The seminal work of Russian psychologist A. R. Luria (1979, 1981) was one of the first attempts to describe structures of thought held by those who had not developed their capacities for representational thinking. He interviewed illiterate peasants still living a medieval way of life at the time of the Russian Revolution. To distinguish practical from conceptual forms of thought, Luria (1979, pp. 77–80) asked the peasants to solve problems whose

[1]See Jaynes (1977) for a historical account of the development of consciousness and the experience of voice in humankind.

content was presented in the form of words divorced from the peasants' practical experience, such as: "In the far north, where there is snow, all bears are white. Novaya Zemlya is in the far north. What color are the bears there?" By following their answers, Luria determined if they were able to draw conclusions based on logical deductions from linguistic propositions as well as from their actual experience. Unable to work from words for making inferences, the peasants would say such things as, "If you want an answer to that question, you should ask people who have been there and seen them," "We don't talk about what we haven't seen. What I know, I say, and nothing beyond that," "Your words can be answered only by someone who was there, and if a person wasn't there, he can't say anything on the basis of your words."

While Luria's peasants had considerable difficulties working and learning from the verbal accounts of others, these interview fragments suggest that they speak with a high degree of confidence in the knowledge they have gained through their own observations, experiences, and actions. The repeated use of the pronoun *we* in the interviews also intimates collaborative efforts and shared learning. Although the peasants' world may exclude meaningful learning and communication with those beyond their immediate experience, one may assume that they live in the midst of a richly populated community where common experiences are readily shared and understood.

Unlike Luria's peasants, the silent women have no more confidence in their ability to learn from their own experience than they have in learning from the words that others use. Because the women have relatively underdeveloped representational thought, the ways of knowing available to them are limited to the present (not the past or the future); to the actual (not the imaginary and the metaphorical); to the concrete (not the deduced or the induced); to the specific (not the generalized or the contextualized); and to behaviors actually enacted (not values and motives entertained).

Unlike Luria's peasants they have no sense of "we-ness" with others. Their difficulties with establishing the most basic connections with others are dramatically illustrated by Bonnie's inability to find meaning in the cries of her baby, an inability that seems similar to the difficulties she experienced in trying to find meaning in the words used by others. When her baby was first born, Bonnie thought all her daughter's cries sounded alike. Later Bonnie realized that her daughter's cries could be differentiated.

> There are certain cries to a baby. If they want to be held, or if they want a bottle—things like that. I never used to listen to her cries. I used to pick her up and put a bottle in her mouth. I thought that's all babies wanted. You put a bottle in the baby's mouth and she'll be quiet. That was before I kind of realized that there's more than just a bottle. For some reason, I never thought about changing her diapers. I don't know why. I couldn't. It never clicked in my head to change her diaper. There are some things that just wouldn't click in my head that I should have done. Now I think of all those nights that I could have just changed her diaper.

Bonnie's retrospective account leads us to believe that assuming the responsibilities of parenthood had encouraged her to move out of silence, and that with this move she had become more able to find meaning in her daughter's utterances.[2]

OBEYING THE WORDLESS AUTHORITIES

The inability of the silent women to find meaning in the words of others is reflected also in their relations with authorities. While they feel passive, reactive, and dependent, they see authorities as being all-powerful, if not overpowering. These women are aware of power that is accrued to authorities through might but not through expertise. They do not envision authorities communicating their thoughts through words imbued with shared meanings. In their experience authorities seldom tell you what they want you to do; they apparently expect you to know in advance. If authorities do tell you *what* is right, they never tell you *why* it is right. Authorities bellow but do not explain. They are unpredictable.

The women see blind obedience to authorities as being of utmost importance for keeping out of trouble and insuring their own survival, because trying to know "why" is not thought to be either particularly possible or important.

Cindy depended almost completely on authorities for direction. She could not consider abortion because her mother doesn't approve of abortions. When asked why her mother doesn't approve, she said it's because her grandmother doesn't approve. When asked why her grandmother doesn't approve, she said, "I don't really know. She just says she doesn't believe in them."

Cindy then went on to say that she, her mother, and her grandmother belonged to a very strict religion and "we, in our religion, don't believe in abortion." Asked why their religion opposes abortion, she said that no one had ever explained the reasons to her. "They didn't say; they just said we didn't believe in them." The wordless/mindless authorities carry great weight.

Even if the authorities explained their reasoning, there is little evidence that the silent women could imagine themselves actively listening to the authorities' ideas, understanding what they were saying, and then choosing to obey. The commands and the actions are undifferentiated—like puppets moving with the jiggle of a thread. To hear is to obey.

The actions of these women are in the form of unquestioned submission to the immediate commands of authorities, not to the directives of their own inner voices. Because their own inner representations or thoughts do not control their behavior, the women are given such labels as immature, impulsive, having a short attention span, acting-out, hyperactive, delinquent, psychotic, and so on.

---

[2]Several studies suggest that it is not uncommon for immature adolescent mothers to have difficulty communicating with their infants and conceptualizing their infant's psychological states and needs (Epstein 1982; McLaughlin et al. 1979; Osofsky and Osofsky 1971).

Feeling cut off from all internal and external sources of intelligence, the women fail to develop their minds and see themselves as remarkably powerless and dependent on others for survival. Since they cannot trust their ability to understand and to remember what was said, they rely on the continual presence of authorities to guide their actions, if they do not act on impulse. Those adolescents with no confidence in themselves as knowers, when faced with the responsibility of motherhood, cling desperately to their own mothers and other authorities for guidance. Cindy, anticipating the birth of her first child, would not let her mother out of her sight. "I go wherever she goes. She has a hard time getting away from me now. I told her I didn't know that much about babies. If it started to choke or something, I wouldn't know what to do." Another very young mother recalled similar anxieties. "After I had the baby, I had a fear of being by myself. I just felt scared that there would be something that I did not know about. I didn't know what was going on. Right now I know most of it, but—you know, before you thought that you were dumb. Being nervous . . . lost. I thought I was the dumbest one of all." She, like Cindy, was flooded with panic at the thought of losing contact with her mother.

MAINTAINING THE WOMAN'S PLACE

The extreme sex-role stereotypes that the silent women accept reflect the powerlessness they have experienced. Men are active and get things done, while women are passive and incompetent. This view undoubtedly helps the women make sense of their own dependence and deference to authorities. The culture, needless to say, supplies many experiences that maintain and nourish such notions. As Ann recounted, "I was brought up thinking a woman was supposed to be very feminine and sit back and let the man do all the stuff. . . . You just had to have a man."

Unable to understand what others were talking about and having no sense of her own ability to figure things out, Ann relied on her husband to do everything. She believed that if he were to die, "I would be lost." In actuality, it was she who supported the family financially and raised the children. Given her husband's drinking, violence, and thefts of the family's meager resources, Ann might have seen him as life-threatening to both her and her children, rather than as a source of security.

Another woman explained her dependence on a brutal, violent husband in terms similar to Ann's. "The only reason I did not kick him out a long time ago was 'cause I was afraid I just wouldn't live. I didn't know how to do anything. I couldn't—I was just scared to death." Although the silent are by no means the only women in our sample who have experienced sexual and physical abuse, they are notable for their inability to speak out to protest. Thinking for themselves violates their conceptions of what is proper for a woman. Another woman said, "I didn't think I had a right to think. That probably goes back to my folks. When my father yelled, everybody automatically jumped. Every woman I ever saw, then, the man barked and the woman jumped. I just thought that women were no good and had to be told everything to do."

These women are passive, subdued, and subordinate. However power-less their men may feel, it is agreed that the women will be even more powerless. The men to whom they subjugate themselves, while being very loud, are remarkably inarticulate. A seventeen-year-old described such a husband: "Sometimes he loses control. He gets mad at the baby and then he hauls off and swings at me. So I do whatever makes him happy. As long as he is happy, I am happy. I'm afraid to say no, as he might hit me." This woman even aborted her second pregnancy on her husband's orders: "He told me that I should have it done. I was listening to everyone." Some months later, the husband decided that he wanted another child. Responding to the jiggle of the thread, she submitted, although she wanted no more children and was deeply worried about her ability to care for the child they already had.

The silent women see life in terms of polarities. Everything is either big or little, good or bad, win or lose. "Every now and then, he thinks that he's always right in something and I'm not. Or else, I'm always right in something and he's not. That's what it is with us." They believe that if another were to win, they, of necessity, must lose. Because the women see themselves as slated to lose, they focus their efforts on assuring their own continued existence during a losing battle. They wage their struggle for survival without an awareness of the power inherent in their own minds and voices and without expectation of cooperation from others. It is a stacked game waged against men who seem to be bigger and better, men who think they have a right to be the winner, to be right no matter what the circumstances.

A young mother who has begun to orchestrate her own life looked back on a time when she felt totally dependent on others for the most minute and constant directions, because she could not trust her mind either to know or to remember anything. Trying to explain why she stayed with a man who battered her for ten long years, she said, "You know, I used to only hear his words, and his words kept coming out of my mouth. He had me thinking that I didn't know anything. But now, you know, I realize I'm not so dumb. . . . And my own words are coming out of my mouth now." She now connects the voicelessness, the confusion of tongues, and her blind obedience with her belief that she had been mindless—dumb. "How would you describe yourself to yourself?" "Is the way you describe yourself now different from the way you would have described yourself in the past?" "How do you see yourself changing in the future?" We borrowed these questions from Carol Gilligan and her colleagues (Belenky 1978; Gilligan 1977, 1982; Lyons 1983) and posed them, not to ascertain what each person's "real self" was actually like but to understand how women with different ways of knowing might conceptualize the self—to see what kind of picture of the self they were able to hold out for their own viewing. The themes we found in the self-descriptions were intricately related to the themes we found in the ways the women thought about thinking.

Describing the self was a difficult task for all of the women we interviewed, but it was almost impossible for the silent ones. One young woman, deeply puzzled by such questions, said, "I don't know. . . . No one has told me yet what they thought of me." As is common with young children (Rosenberg

1979), these women believe that the source of self-knowledge is lodged in others—not in the self. Because the silent women live in a world with so little conversation, those who might have told them about themselves and helped them begin building a sense of self never said a word.

When the women finally attempted to answer the question, they described themselves in terms of their own movements in and around the geographic space that surrounded them. Again, Cindy presented the clearest example:

> I am a person who likes to stay home. Before I got pregnant, I used to go and come as I wanted. [*Is the way you describe yourself now different from the way you used to describe yourself?*] Yah, 'cause I used to describe myself as not being home. And now I am home all the time. So that's about the only thing that is different.

Another young mother spoke in remarkably similar terms. Although she could not describe herself, she could say how she was changing.

> When I was younger I was constantly running the streets. I was never staying home or anything like that. And now that I've got my kids, I stay at home with my kids more often. As a matter of fact, I very seldom go out. I'm just with my kids more than what I would have been back then.

When these women attempt to describe the self, they remain standing in their own shoes, describing only what they see gazing outward from their own eyes. They find no vantage point outside of the self that enables them to look backward, bringing the whole self into view. They do not even provide a portrait of the physical self. No one says anything like, "I'm tall, fat, blonde." None could describe the changes she anticipates would or should occur in the future. As Cindy said, "I haven't thought about the future."

SEEN BUT NEVER HEARD

Women who live in silence have much in common with each other. While we will explore in chapter 8 the family contexts that give rise to each of the ways of knowing, we will touch on the familial roots of such silence here.

Each of the women grew up in great isolation and, for one reason or another, seldom had friends while growing up. The families themselves were cut off from the broader community. Discussion with family members and anyone else was actively discouraged. "I was never able to ask for help before. I was brought up to think that you kept your troubles to yourself. You didn't talk about them. I never let anyone know what was going on—what was troubling you. You just didn't do it."

In their families at least one parent routinely used violence rather than words for influencing others' behavior. Typically, the other parent remained silent and compliant, often victimized. A woman described the pattern. "My father was a first-class bastard. The only way he believed of doing anything was with a club, a stick, or with the back of his hand. All you had to do was to breathe."

The bleak images that emerge from these stories suggest childhoods with neither much play nor dialogue. Growing up without opportunities for play and for dialogue poses the gravest danger for the growing child. Lev Vygotsky (1962, 1978) and his colleagues suggest that exterior dialogues are a necessary precursor to inner speech and an awareness of one's own thought process. They argue that play itself is a precursor to symbolization and meaning-making. Play provides children with their first experiences in creating metaphors, where an object and the children's actions combine to suggest other objects and events. Thus, when children saddle a stick and ride off on their imaginary horses, the stick becomes a symbol for the horse; and that symbol and the power of their own ideas govern their behavior. The physical stick becomes a tool that helps them dislodge the meaning of horse from its usual embodiment. In play, it is the meaning chosen by children that determines the significance of the stick. Play provides children with their first opportunities for adopting a pretend or a hypothetical stance.

In the ordinary course of development, the use of play metaphors gives way to language—a consensually validated symbol system—allowing for more precise communication of meanings between persons. Outer speech becomes increasingly internalized as it is transformed into inner speech. Impulsive behavior gives way to behavior that is guided by the actor's own symbolic representations of hopes, plans, and meanings. Without playing, conversing, listening to others, and drawing out their own voice, people fail to develop a sense that they can talk and think things through (Vygotsky 1978). (See also Gardner 1982; Luria 1961, 1979, 1981; Piaget 1951.)

A recent review (Belenky 1984) of research on the intellectual and ethical development of the deaf illustrates the importance of face-to-face conversations and the utilization of an effective symbol system. This research suggests that development is greatly facilitated when hearing-impaired children are raised in a sign-rich environment, enabling them to be full participants in any ongoing dialogue. Children with early access to signed language do not have the difficulties with impulsiveness, social immaturity, and academic work that routinely plague hearing-impaired children who have not had such opportunities. When deaf children, adolescents, or adults who have been denied these opportunities move into a stimulating, sign-rich environment, not only do they learn that form of the language very rapidly, they largely overcome the developmental delays that are typical of deaf children (Furth 1973). Such findings lend support to Vygotsky's claims about the importance of outer speech for the development of inner speech and the sense of mind.

The silent women like Ann and Cindy had had little formal schooling or had found school to be a place of chronic failure. Most had been passed along from one grade to the next, as all those words just slipped past. Typically, educators assume that by the time a child enters school he or she will have a well-developed capacity for representational thought (Sigel and Cocking 1977). In most schools, beginning with the earliest grades, the main focus is on the manipulation of symbol systems. However, these symbols and metaphors are likely to be dissociated from the concrete referents, actions, and experiences that the symbols stem from and express (Greenfield 1972; Green-field and Lave 1982; Scribner and Cole 1973, 1981). Furthermore, most schools continue to provide meager opportunities for the give-and-take of dialogue. Verbal interchanges tend to be unilateral and highly constrained as they are predominantly teacher-initiated and -dominated (Sirotnik 1983). As one adolescent said, "In school you get detention for talking to others."

While the lack of dialogue and the dissociation of language from experi-ence is problematic for all children, concentrating on the written forms of the language before children have developed proficiency in wielding the oral forms is likely to be tragic. The silent women had limited experience and confidence in their ability to find meaning in metaphors were lost in the sea of words and numbers that flooded their schools. For them school was an unlikely place to "gain a voice." For them the experience of school only confirmed their fears of being "deaf and dumb."

We believe that individuals grow up to see themselves as "deaf and dumb" when they are raised in profound isolation under the most demeaning circumstances, not because of their genetic intellectual endowment. That anyone emerges from their childhood years with so little confidence in their meaning-making and their meaning-sharing abilities as did Ann and Cindy signals the failure of the community to receive all of those entrusted into its care.

QUESTIONS FOR A CRITICAL REREADING

After you have read the essay through once, while constructing your informal sen-tence outline, use the following questions to begin your critical rereading of the argument. As you reread, use these questions and your sentence outline to formulate an enthymemic thesis that represents the argument being made by Belenky et al.

1. This selection is the first chapter of a book entitled *Women's Ways of Knowing* and serves to establish what the authors call "an important anchoring point" for the rest of the book. In other words, through this first discussion, the writers are attempting to establish a premise from which the rest of the book's argument will develop. (The thesis behind this selection constitutes that premise.) To discover the thesis of this essay, analyze the writer/reader contract: What question does this chapter address and what method do the authors imply they will use to address it? (Note how the subheadings in the essay signal the logical steps the authors take to explore this question, and, hence, can guide you as you construct a sentence outline.)

2. Belenky et al. explore how gaining a voice is essential to developing a sense of self. What do they mean by "voice"? How do they establish that this is a concept important in the field of psychology? (You will want to use this answer to discover the assumed information that their enthymemic thesis depends on.)

3. After establishing that voice is important, the authors begin to discuss the primary new information they have to contribute to the field of psychology. What is this information and how have they acquired it? Comparing their examples to the kind that Skinner used, how does their research method conform to what you know about how psychologists acquire their evidence? (Remember that the way they

evaluate this new information will become the "because" clause of the enthymemic thesis you formulate for this essay.)

4. Focusing on the conclusion, formulate an answer to the question you identified
from their introduction. (Be aware that their final paragraph both asserts their
thesis and makes a judgment about their finding.) Reviewing your sentence outline, construct a "because" clause that reflects the primary new information they
presented. Formulate this two-clause thesis into a valid enthymeme (testing the
logical assumption behind it to make certain it is not the new information they
have presented). Once you have done this, revise your outline to represent the
logical structure behind the thesis and essay.

POSSIBLE ISSUES FOR WRITING

Following are a few of the questions that you might find at issue after you have
constructed a logical outline for "Silence." Again, as you discuss these questions with
your classmates, see if what becomes at issue for the class is related to a particularly
weak step in the authors' logic. This can help you discover where you might turn for
information when you begin writing your own essay in response to the class discussion.

1. Drawing from the work of a Russian psychologist, Lev Vygotsky, the authors
focus their argument on the premise that "exterior dialogues are a necessary
precursor to inner speech and an awareness of one's own thought process." What
does this passage mean? Do you agree that your sense of "self" depends on how
much you are aware of your own thought processes? Would Skinner agree? Why
or why not?

2. The authors end their essay with the claim that these "silent" women have been
victimized by a community that raised them "in profound isolation under the
most demeaning circumstances." Does this mean that the authors agree with
Skinner that we have no self independent of society? Or would they condemn the
implications of Skinner's theories, seeing this as what happens when we see "what
man can make of *woman?*" Justify your answer.

3. The authors pass judgment on their finding by saying it "signals the failure of the
community to receive all of those entrusted into its care." Note how they have
moved from talking about effects or consequences (why something has occurred)
to considering their value (whether this occurrence is good or bad). How have the
authors earned the right to make this judgment? (Remember that psychology
reasons about questions of consequence.)

WRITING YOUR ESSAY

Now that you have listened in on these psychologists and have continued their conversation informally with your classmates, you are prepared to make a more formal
contribution to the discussion. Write an essay that responds to one of the psychological arguments your classmates have offered. Utilize what you know about reasoning
in the field of psychology to discover the real issue you want to address, then formulate
your answer as a logical thesis statement. Before drafting a logical outline around this
enthymemic thesis, you will want to test it by identifying what old information you
are assuming your reader already has (it will probably be some idea that arose in the

readings or class discussion). If you have difficulty doing this, refer to the following discussion for special help.

USING THE ENTHYMEME AND LOGICAL OUTLINE TO WRITE

The sentence outlines you constructed as you read the previous essays should have helped you discover how to formulate each argument into a two-clause thesis statement. Once you discover their thesis statements—and discuss these in class to get an idea what your classmates' stances are—you are ready to formulate your own working thesis. As you prepare to write, use your own enthymeme (which always should be viewed as a hypothesis at this stage) to construct a sentence outline for your essay.

Sometimes you will not be able to know enough about the precise issue you want to address to develop a logical thesis and outline. In this event, draft an exploratory essay first, beginning with a summary of the particular discussion that has interested you. Be careful to pose questions in your introduction rather than attempt to pose answers that may later become impossible to prove. Then explore possible answers to these questions in the body of your draft, testing the stances you have heard until you arrive at one you feel most certain about. After you have finished with this rough draft, structure a sentence outline to see what you have discovered. Then formulate an enthymemic thesis statement for your argument and revise your outline to reveal the logical structure of the argument you want to make. This logical outline can help you revise by revealing which sections of your draft need to be cut (because they either are irrelevant or prove what you can assume your audience knows) and which sections need to be developed further (because they present the new information your audience needs to know).

However you arrive at your thesis and logical outline, be certain the question you address and the information you use to answer it conform to the reasoning process psychologists use. To support your "because" clause, you may utilize evidence from the essays or similar evidence taken from your own experience, and the logical outline you work from will lead you to reason about it as a psychologist would.

———————
———————
———————

Unit Five

CHAPTER NINE

Revising the Structure of Your Essay

*I*n Chapter 1, you learned that the writing process is a learning process. As you write, you explore what others have said, discover what you think about their ideas, and develop a way to communicate your thoughts to others. This writing process was broken down into four stages, each stage defined by a question that focused on a related stage in the critical thinking process:

Invention:	What do others think? (Analysis)
Drafting:	How does that fit with what I think? (Synthesis)
Revising:	What do I *really* think? (Evaluation)
Editing:	How well have I delivered this argument to my readers?

The invention stage focuses on reaching an understanding of the material. When you use enthymemes and logical outlines to analyze the argument of essays you read, you are beginning to invent the ideas you will want to use in your own writing. However, you do not stop inventing when you leave the critical reading stage to begin drafting your response to what you have read. When you formulate a thesis statement and logical outline to help you draft *your* argument, and even when you later use the new ideas that arose when you wrote your draft to revise your thesis, outline, and argument, you invent a more precise argument for your essay. Think of invention as something you do not only *before* you write, but also throughout the writing process as you explore and revise what you want to say and discover new ways to support it.

In Chapters 5 and 7, you learned how to use the enthymeme and logical outline to invent the argument you wish to write. In this chapter, you will learn more about how these logical skills can help you revise your draft. The revision stage focuses on the arrangement of the ideas in your essay. There are two primary aspects of your draft that you need to consider when you revise: (1) the logical structure of your argument, and (2) how well it accommodates what your readers already know. This is essentially a matter of analyzing the premises behind your enthymemic thesis and adjusting your thesis and logical outline (and, ultimately, your essay) to focus on the new information you need to provide your readers.

ARRANGEMENT: THE ORDERING OF YOUR EVIDENCE

Sometimes you may find it fairly easy to invent your enthymeme and logical outline *before* composing the rough draft of your essay. This kind of prewriting activity helps you focus your writing, directing your attention to the ideas your reader will need to have clarified. At other times, you may discover that you cannot formulate a thesis until you know more about the subject. This is when you might need to write your rough draft first, using your writing to discover the question at issue, your stance (thesis), and the new information you can give to support it. To understand how you would write your rough draft differently depending on your familiarity with the subject, let's examine each of these methods separately.

WRITING AN EXPLORATORY DRAFT

No matter how rough, your drafts will always contain the seeds of your argument. Even if a subject is relatively new to you and you only have a general idea of the issue you want to address (and an even more general sense of what your stance on that issue will be), reading critically and listening closely to what others have said about it will give you something to write about. A first draft that helps you invent the issue and stance you want to address is an exploratory draft.

An exploratory draft begins with a summary of what you have heard others saying about the subject, testing the ideas you encountered in your reading and class discussions to identify where they agree and disagree. As you read the following exploratory draft written by Paula, note how she begins with summary to analyze the different issues and discover which of these issues she feels most prepared to take a stand on.

Paula's Exploratory Draft

In the textbook by Bensel-Meyers, we are told that the writing process is more than just writing. Somehow, this process also involves reading and discussing what we read. In our class discussion of this process, some thought reading was not always necessary. They argued that often we already have ideas that we can write about, and that reading and discussion of that reading takes them away from the real business of writing.

Not everyone thought this way. In fact, our discussion led to general agreement that Bensel-Meyers was defining writing as a process of learning, a way to use our writing to learn new ideas, and that writing about what we already know is not "real" writing. I was surprised, though, when most of the class still complained about class discussion.

Even those who felt we should read a lot to become better writers, argued that oral discussion of the readings was a waste of time. One student even said oral discussion was destructive, that she felt many of the comments were not honest. She admitted that she often made remarks to impress the teacher or her friends, and seemed to use this confession to imply that students in a classroom feel too vulnerable to others' criticism to risk new ideas in class discussion.

This position has some truth to it. If students always use class discussion to say what they think others want to hear, then they are not testing new ideas they have discovered. They are really saying what they already have heard, and the essays they eventually write will merely summarize what they already know. But doesn't this reasoning assume that class discussion always ends in agreement?

Although I confess I was afraid to express my discomfort in class, the fact that I felt pressured to accept my classmates' argument against class discussion bothered me. Now that I am forced to defend this position in my own writing, I can think of several objections that lead me to argue against the class. For example, not all students know what the others think. Many times, what a student probably thought would be a safe comment stimulated a heated discussion in our own class. Even though these students had wanted merely to impress their friends, they found themselves having to defend their statement, having to find reasons they thought others would use to support it. Even if the original idea is not their own, students who say merely what they think others want to hear will have to test what they have said. In a sense, oral discussion forces them to make the idea their own.

After Paula wrote her exploratory draft, she constructed the following informal sentence outline to identify the seeds of the argument she had discovered. Note how she discovered that the majority of her argument appeared in the last paragraph:

Para. 1-3:

1. Does class discussion always end in agreement?

Para. 4:

2. Students tend to express what they think others want to hear.

3. However, they do not always know what others want to hear.

4. Students do object when they hear something they disagree with.

5. When their classmates object to what they have said, students are forced to defend their statement even if the idea wasn't their own to begin with.

6. And since having to discover ways to defend an idea forces a student to make the idea his or her own,

7. Class discussion forces students to discover new ideas.

Because the first paragraphs of Paula's exploratory draft were mere summary, Paula began her sentence outline at the point that her draft had exposed the issue. In this way, she made her sentence outline focus on the logical steps in her draft rather than on the paragraphs.

After Paula wrote a sentence outline representing what she had discovered in her exploratory draft, she used the outline to formulate the precise issue she needed to address. Although her draft and sentence outline had posed the question as "Does class discussion always end in agreement?", Paula looked at the last sentences in her outline to discover if what she had concluded really addressed that precise issue. She decided that the real issue she was addressing was "Can students learn new ideas from oral discussion in class?"

Next, Paula used this revised issue to discover her thesis. Referring again to the last sentences in her outline, she began with this answer as the first clause of her logical thesis statement: "Class discussion forces students to discover new ideas." To discover her "because" clause, she examined the middle sentences of her outline to review how she had arrived at this conclusion. She put together sentences 7 and 5 to arrive at this rough thesis:

> Class discussion forces students to discover new ideas because, when their class-mates object to what they have said, students are forced to defend their statement even if the idea wasn't their own to begin with.

To test the logic of this enthymemic thesis, Paula tried to identify the major assumption behind it. She first looked at her sentence outline to see if any statement she had there resembled the assumption. She decided that number 6, "And since having to discover ways to defend an idea forces a student to make the idea his or her own," sounded like the missing premise that she was using as her assumed agreement with her readers.

To test whether this was the primary assumption behind her argument, though, she had to return to her rough thesis and identify the shared terms. She decided that the complete subject of the "because" clause ("when their classmates object to what they have said, students . . .") was a definition for "class discussion." To consider the subjects of the two clauses as shared terms, however, she had to make sure this was a definition her readers would agree with. She again reviewed her sentence outline, this time looking at the statements she had made about class discussion:

2. Students tend to express what they think others want to hear.
3. However, they do not always know what others want to hear.
4. Students do object when they hear something they disagree with.

She realized a major flaw: "If students tend to say only what they think others want to hear, why do they object when they hear something they disagree with?" This led her to consider that she did not really agree with the class's definition of what happens in class discussion. In fact, in her exploratory draft she had mentioned evidence she could use to prove that students do tend to criticize one another's comments. To revise her thesis, Paula decided her "because" clause would have to use this evidence in some way.

First, she would have to revise the definition of class discussion implied in her shared terms. What did she and her readers agree on about class discussions? She decided she still believed students were afraid to offend others, but only when they were the first to speak in a discussion. Once a comment was made, students tended to relax and get involved in the ideas rather than worry about what others thought of them. It certainly is easier to criticize someone else than to present one's own argument, she thought. Here is how she revised her thesis so the "because" clause would reflect a modified definition of class discussion and the evidence she was going to use:

> Class discussion helps students discover new ideas because students who say what they think others want to hear often meet with criticism that forces everyone to defend an argument.

She discovered her assumption only needed minor adjustment: "Criticism that forces everyone to defend an argument helps students discover new ideas." She could now construct a logical outline around her thesis and see how she would develop her exploratory draft around the new information contained in her new "because" clause.

REVISING THE LOGICAL STRUCTURE

As you have just learned, writing an exploratory draft is one way to invent the issue you want to address and the precise argument you want to make in your essay. When you are more familiar with what you want to argue in your essay, you will probably find it more efficient to develop a two-clause thesis statement and logical outline before you draft your argument. However, you will still find you discover new information as you develop an argument around your rough draft. Even if you have written an exploratory draft first, your next draft may uncover information that will lead you to revise your thesis and outline further. This is why, whichever method you use to invent your argument, you will always want to test how well you have used your logical outline to draft your argument. Here are two questions that you should ask:

1. *What logical thesis statement does my draft support?* Does it reflect the thesis I thought I was arguing? If not, should I revise my thesis statement to reflect more accurately what I *have* proven in this draft, or should I revise my draft to follow my original thesis? Does most of my draft discuss the "because" clause of my thesis, or another point that could be more essential to the argument?
2. *Does my rough draft clearly proceed in the logical steps of my sentence outline?* Although you may clarify minor points not reflected in your outline or address how your readers might reject certain claims, your essay should clearly follow the logical steps reflected in your outline.

These questions can help you make the most of your logical outline as a revision tool, highlighting the major steps in the logic you have used to answer the question you are addressing. Even if your rough draft seems "perfect" after you have tested it against your outline, the new perspective it gives you can reveal how you can make that logic clearer to your reader. For this reason, your revisions may be merely *stylistic* (e.g., a matter of adding transitional phrases to signal logical steps in your argument).

REVISING TO ACCOMMODATE YOUR AUDIENCE

As you revise your drafts, most of your ability to make your argument more precise will depend on how well you can anticipate what your readers will say when they read it. As you saw with Paula's revision of her thesis, to invent what you need to prove, you need to recognize where you and your readers disagree. (By recognizing that her readers wouldn't accept her definition of class discussions, Paula discovered how to revise her "because" clause). Ultimately, your essay is only as good as your thesis, and your thesis is "good" only if it earns the right to offer a new perspective on an issue your reader cares about.

If you have difficulty analyzing exactly how to accommodate your audience's perspective, particularly when revising your rough draft, a logical outline can be invaluable. As a way to objectify how you have structured your argument, your outline can reveal where you need to reason from your reader's perspective to justify the worth of your new conclusion.

Following is an example of how a student revised her thesis and logical outline to accommodate her reader's thesis. Andrea's thesis and outline represent the rough argument she had drafted in response to a discussion of the essay "Silence" included in Chapter 8. This is the same discussion Paula addressed in her exploratory draft; unlike Paula, however, Andrea has lost sight of her audience's position. To discover what her audience would think about her position, Andrea gave a fellow classmate, Mark, a chance to read and respond to her draft. He gave her a thesis representing his different position on the issue. Note how Andrea subsequently restructured her outline to accommodate Mark's response and ultimately further her own understanding of the subject.

Andrea's Logical Thesis Statement

A	V1	B
Being forced to explore your ideas orally	develops	your ability to think independently

because

A*	V2	C
this is the only way you	can discover	your thought process.

[*Assumption* (B–C): Your ability to think independently requires that you discover your thought process.]

Andrea's Logical Outline

Introduction of Issue: Should students be forced to test their ideas orally? Does this help their ability to think independently?

A–A* (Definition of key terms): Exploring ideas orally is a way to think aloud, to test and defend ideas before you commit yourself to a particular position.

A*–V2: Thinking aloud helps you discover the words you need to express what you really think.

C: When you write only to yourself, you aren't as concerned about how well you articulate your beliefs. However, if you discuss these beliefs with your classmates, you wil have to defend them, which means discovering the thought process that led you to your beliefs.

B–C: And since your ability to think independently requires that you discover your thought process . . .

A–B: Being forced to explore your ideas orally develops your ability to think independently.

The Thesis Behind Mark's Peer Response

When students are forced to express their ideas orally before they are sure of them, they are prevented from independent thinking because their oral arguments are always affected by what they think their peers want to hear.

Andrea's Revised Thesis and Outline

A	V1	B
Exploring ideas orally before committing them to paper	helps develop	our ability to think independently

because

A*	V2	C
exposing our thoughts to others	forces	us to recognize what we need to defend.

[*Assumption* (B–C): Our ability to think independently requires that we recognize what ideas we need to defend.]

Andrea's Revised Sentence Outline

Introduction of Issue: Should students be forced to test their ideas orally? Does this help their ability to think independently?

A–A*: Exploring ideas orally exposes our ideas to others. It is a difficult process to make ourselves so vulnerable to others' criticisms, and we may be tempted to adopt the ideas that our peers appear to respect.

A*–V2: Although we may be tempted to say what we think our peers want to hear, we are still forced to test those positions orally.

C: When we discover that we cannot justify an idea we thought our peers wanted to hear, we discover what part of their arguments we do not understand or are inclined to disagree with. This ultimately forces us to discover the real argument we want to make and will have to defend.

B–C: And because our ability to think independently requires that we recognize what ideas we need to defend

A–B: Exploring ideas orally before committing them to paper helps develop our ability to think independently.

Note how Andrea has altered her thesis and outline to accommodate Mark's objection to her original thesis. As her revised logical outline shows, Andrea used Mark's thesis to discover where she agrees with her reader. She acknowledges that students tend to feel vulnerable when they are asked to express their ideas in class and that this might lead them to say what they think their peers want to hear. By accommodating Mark's objection that the social environment of the classroom would inhibit independent thought, Andrea finds she must change the logical development of her argument to consider how peer pressure could help students discover what they really think.

Note how the revised logical outline reflects the primary change in her thesis:

Original Thesis

Being forced to explore your ideas orally develops your ability to think independently because this is the only way you can discover your thought processes.

Revised Thesis

Exploring ideas orally before committing them to paper helps develop our ability to think independently because exposing our thoughts to others forces us to recognize what we need to defend.

Accommodating her audience has led Andrea to revise her "because" clause significantly. Instead of the vague generalization "this is *the only* way . . ." Andrea has focused on why class discussion is *a good* way to discover new ideas. The process of accommodating Mark's response through a revision of her "because" clause has helped Andrea recognize that her original thesis was a bit overstated, and probably impossible to prove. Since the "because" clause represents how she will prove her argument, revising the "because" clause results in a major revision of her logical outline. The resulting argument and essay becomes a much more precise reflection of what she believes.

As you read the essays in Chapter 10, notice how the authors have developed their arguments to accommodate the reasoning used by their intended readers. Try to identify the audience for their essays and write in your reading notebook a brief description of the different stances they acknowledge. Because these next readings reflect two different (although related) disciplines—history and economics—keep in mind how the essays might change to accommodate the reasoning of the other discipline.

CHAPTER TEN

Reasoning About History and Economics

No matter what field you are studying, when you use your writing to respond to the arguments of others, your own argument is easier to write. Accommodating other perspectives on the subject helps you reason about it as others have. Beginning your side of the conversation with what you have heard others say about the subject helps you adopt the kind of reasoning they have used. When you acknowledge the assumptions behind these other arguments, you utilize what others view as established information in the field.

To analyze the reasoning process behind the writing done in a particular field, you need to focus on these three areas: (1) the kind of question the field explores; (2) the assumptions you can make about what is already valid knowledge in the field; and (3) the kind of reason the field accepts as valid new information. This is where you can use the enthymeme to analyze the reasoning of a discipline. As you saw in Chapter 8, formulating Skinner's argument as an enthymemic thesis can help you identify all three primary aspects of his reasoning.

Skinner's enthymemic thesis: "Our environment determines who we are because contingencies of reinforcement produce what we normally attribute to man's autonomy.

1. *The Question at Issue:* "Why does man behave as he does?"
2. *The Assumption:* "Anything that produces what we attribute to man's autonomy determines who we are."
3. *The Causal Reason:* "Contingencies of reinforcement produce what we normally attribute to man's autonomy."

As the conclusion to his argument, Skinner's enthymemic thesis represents his answer to the question at issue (1) and the primary reason he uses to prove his causal argument (3). The information his thesis assumes his reader already has is the unstated premise behind his reasoning (2).

You need to consider all three aspects of an author's reasoning process to clearly distinguish one discipline from another. Just recognizing the kind of question the discipline asks is not enough. Although it helps to know the specific type of argument an author is using, often fields may ask similar kinds of questions but rely on different kinds of information to answer them. Skinner asked a question that required an argument of consequence (the cause and effect analysis of "Why does man behave as he does?"). However, other social sciences also ask causal questions.

The two fields you will study in this chapter, history and economics, both might explore the past to determine why something occurred. These two fields are particularly illuminating to study together because specialists in one area often develop knowledge that contributes to the other field. (Sometimes we blur this distinction by using the term "economic historian".) What distinguishes historians and economists, though, is they consider different kinds of information when they address similar causal issues.

SEPARATING THE HISTORIAN FROM THE ECONOMIST

Let's first consider how the historian and economist might reason differently even when they address the same general question ("How did World War II affect America?"). You might be able to guess that the subject matter would change. Historians would be discussing American history; economists would be considering American economic policies. But even if you did not know which discipline the authors belonged to, you could discover what kind of arguments they were making by identifying the kind of information they looked at to derive their answers:

Question: How Did World War II Affect America?

WHAT A HISTORIAN ADDRESSES: How did World War II affect the development of American history?

WHAT AN ECONOMIST ADDRESSES: How did World War II affect the economic condition of America?

INFORMATION THE HISTORIAN WOULD LOOK AT: Compare the social, political, economic and cultural structure of pre- and post-World War II America. Consider how others had analyzed this information.

INFORMATION THE ECONOMIST WOULD LOOK AT: Compare the economic condition of the country in pre- and post-World War II America. Consider the changes in formal economic policy. Consider how others have evaluated these changes.

Note how the historian's interests are broader than the economist's, encompassing even some of the economist's concerns. The historians are interested in all the information they can find before they make any judgment about the course American history took. They look at cultural, political, and economic evidence of how the temperament of the American people changed. An economist, on the other hand, is interested only in the economic condition of America: how easily people could find work before and after the war, whether the cost of food, clothing, and housing rose or fell, or how the value of the American dollar was affected by the change in America's relationship with other countries that traded in American goods. Although both the economist and the historian would be asking a causal question about World War II, we say they reason differently because of the kind of information they use.

You can probably understand why the economist who focuses purely on the interrelationships of economic systems in the past can contribute to the historian's investigation into the climate of the country at a particular time. However, there is another side to economic reasoning that is more clearly removed from the historian's concern: the investigation into the theory of economic systems.

Theories of economic systems like those of capitalism or communism hypothesize what effects different economic policies would have on the productive capability of a nation. When conditions of wartime are a constraint on the system, the economist would utilize information from the past to predict which economic policies the government might adopt to prevent collapse of the economy. Their advice helps the government establish new policies that would ensure the most productivity for the nation (i.e., America's prosperity in spite of or because of war).

NONHISTORICAL ECONOMICS

Economists' concern with the theory of economic systems distinguishes their mode of reasoning most clearly from that of historians. Consider the nonhistorical, practical economist who applies knowledge of economic theory to project how a business might best regulate its profits. For example, an economist might know, based on the findings of the historical economist, that the individuals born soon after World War II (what we refer to as "the baby-boom generation") changed the buying habits of the nation. Because they represented a large segment of the population, as they came of age, their preference for certain products became the nation's preference. The older generation began to emulate the baby-boomers' interest in "natural" products, practical fashions, and youthful image. The economist might utilize this information to develop the following formula: X dictates the buying habits of the nation + X begins to exhibit a preference for Y = the nation will begin to exhibit a preference for Y.

This economic theory could in turn help the practical economist advise an automobile company how it might best invest its profits. For example, the economist might argue, "The baby-boom generation has exhibited a preference for gas-efficient mini-vans over large American Cadillacs; therefore, the nation as a whole will begin to buy more gas-efficient mini-vans." If the economist can show that the baby-boom generation has exhibited this preference, the company would be well-advised to invest less of its profits in the traditional American car, and to begin production of more gas-efficient, family mini-vans.

IMPLICATIONS FOR POLICY

It might appear that the practical economist is primarily concerned with questions of policy (e.g., "How should the automobile company invest its profits?"). However, that isn't the case. Economists, historical or practical, examine only the economic consequences of certain actions. You might think it was economically sound to produce more gas-efficient mini-vans because more people want them, but whether it "should" be done would rely upon other factors: Are the mini-vans unsafe? Do they pollute the atmosphere more than other vehicles? Does the market (the numerous individuals who want the cars) know what is best?

Economists merely determine the economic consequences of actions such as World War II or a business decision; they do not pass judgment on whether these consequences were or are "good" or "bad" in terms of moral value. The economic relationships they uncover have implications for economic policy, but it is the political scientist—the president, the governor, the corporate head—that must determine how the economist's theories will affect what should be done. Sometimes we fail to read critically when we accept an economist's reasoning as a policy argument, for then we are assuming that what "should" be done should be undertaken purely on the basis of economic reward. When economists do propose economic policies, they do so overtly, clearly reasoning about how certain decisions can help produce a more stable economy. Economists who reason in this way are often called "political economists," because they assume that a stable economy will allow us to enact other policies for social and political reform.

READING CONSEQUENCE ARGUMENTS CRITICALLY

Any argument addressing a question of consequence will have implications for what we should do. In the essays that follow, note how the historian Barbara Tuchman and the economist John Maynard Keynes both investigate the past because it has implications for the policy decisions we make today. However, they are primarily interested in the conditions that affect human behavior, a question they address by exploring what has affected human behavior in the past. Although they address similar questions, try the following critical reading procedure to discover how they look at the past differently, and to compare their use of information with that of the practical economist, Leonard Silk, whose essay concludes the chapter.

1. Use your reading notebook to keep a sentence outline that identifies the kind of information each author uses.
2. When you are finished, formulate an enthymemic thesis and identify the primary assumption for each argument. See if you can use this to identify how the established knowledge each author uses further defines the community he or she belongs to.
3. Follow the same procedure for Silk's essay. However, this time, examine the question at issue more closely: is he making an economic argument or a policy argument about how we should use economic reasoning?

The Trojans Take the Wooden Horse Within Their Walls

Barbara W. Tuchman (1912–1989)

Born in New York City in 1912, Barbara W. Tuchman grew to become one of our most popular journalists and historians. Graduated from Radcliffe in 1933, she became a well-known correspondent for The Nation, New Statesman and Nation, *and* The Zimmerman Telegram. *She won the Pulitzer Prize twice, once for* The Guns of August *(a study of the beginnings of World War I published in 1962) and again for* Stilwell and the American Experience in China *(published in 1971).*

The excerpt reprinted here is the opening chapter from one of Barbara Tuchman's later works, The March of Folly: From Troy to Vietnam *(1984). The book itself is a brilliant study of four crucial military periods in history, illuminating our understanding of America's involvement in the Vietnam War by revealing a human tendency toward acts of folly. Although this excerpt begins her book by looking at mythic history, note how Tuchman focuses on the way classical historians explained the Wooden Horse episode of the Trojan War. As a historian, her aim is to expose not what actually happened but how it could be plausible. As you read this essay, note how she is exploring the question of why the Trojans could have acted as they did when they took the Wooden Horse within their walls. Also note how she believes we can learn something more from this analysis than the popular lesson, "Beware of Greeks bearing gifts!"*

The most famous story of the Western world, the prototype of all tales of human conflict, the epic that belongs to all people and all times since—and even before—literacy began, contains the legend, with or without some vestige of historical foundation, of the Wooden Horse.

The Trojan War has supplied themes to all subsequent literature and art from Euripides' heart-rending tragedy of *The Trojan Women* to Eugene O'-Neill, Jean Giraudoux and the still enthralled writers of our time. Through Aeneas in Virgil's sequel, it provided the legendary founder and national epic of Rome. A favorite of medieval romancers, it supplied William Caxton with the subject of the first book printed in English, and Chaucer (and later Shakespeare) with the setting, if not the story, of Troilus and Cressida. Racine and Goethe tried to fathom the miserable sacrifice of Iphigenia. Wandering Ulysses inspired writers as far apart as Tennyson and James Joyce. Cassandra and avenging Electra have been made the protagonists of German drama and opera. Some thirty-five poets and scholars have offered English translations since George Chapman in Elizabethan times first opened the realms of gold. Countless painters have found the Judgment of Paris an irresistible scene, and as many poets fallen under the spell of the beauty of Helen.

All of human experience is in the tale of Troy, or Ilium, first put into epic form by Homer around 850–800 B.C.[1] Although the gods are its motivators, what it tells us about humanity is basic, even though—or perhaps because—the circumstances are ancient and primitive. It has endured deep in our minds and memories for twenty-eight centuries because it speaks to us of ourselves, not least when least rational. It mirrors, in the judgment of another storyteller, John Cowper Powys, "what happened, is happening and will happen to us all, from the very beginning until the end of human life upon this earth."

Troy falls at last after ten years of futile, indecisive, noble, mean, tricky, bitter, jealous and only occasionally heroic battle. As the culminating instrumentality for the fall, the story brings in the Wooden Horse. The episode of the Horse exemplifies policy pursued contrary to self-interest—in the face of urgent warning and a feasible alternative. Occurring in this earliest chronicle of Western man, it suggests that such pursuit is an old and inherent human habit. The story first appears, not in the *Iliad,* which ends before the climax of the war, but in the *Odyssey* through the mouth of the blind bard Demodocus, who, at Odysseus' bidding, recounts the exploit to the group gathered in the palace of Alcinous. Despite Odysseus' high praise of the bard's narrative talents, the story is told rather baldly, as if the main facts were already familiar. Minor details are added elsewhere in the poem by Odysseus himself and in what seems an impossible flight of fancy by two other participants, Helen and Menelaus.

Lifted by Homer out of dim mists and memories, the Wooden Horse instantly caught the imagination of his successors in the next two or three centuries and inspired them to elaborate on the episode, notably and importantly by the addition of Laocoön in one of the most striking incidents of the entire epic. He appears earliest in *The Sack of Ilium* by Arctinus of Miletus, composed probably a century or so after Homer. Personifying the Voice of Warning, Laocoön's dramatic role becomes central to the episode of the Horse in all versions thereafter.

The full story as we know it of the device that finally accomplished the fall of Troy took shape in Virgil's *Aeneid,* completed in 20 B.C. By that time the tale incorporated the accumulated versions of more than a thousand years. Arising from geographically separate districts of the Greek world, the various versions are full of discrepancies and inconsistencies. Greek legend is hopelessly contradictory. Incidents do not conform necessarily to narrative logic; motive and behavior are often irreconcilable. We must take the story of the Wooden Horse as it comes, as Aeneas told it to the enraptured Dido, and as it passed, with further revisions and embellishments by Latin successors, to the Middle Ages and from the medieval romancers to us.

It is the ninth year of inconclusive battle on the plains of Troy, where the Greeks are besieging the city of King Priam. The gods are intimately involved

---

[1]Previously widely disputed, this is the span of time more or less agreed upon by scholars since the decipherment of Linear B in 1952.

with the belligerents as a result of jealousies generated ten years earlier when Paris, Prince of Troy, offended Hera and Athena by giving the golden apple as the award of beauty to Aphrodite, goddess of love. Not playing fair (as the Olympians, molded by men, were not disposed to), she had promised him, if he gave her the prize, the most beautiful woman in the world as his bride. This led, as everyone knows, to Paris' abduction of Helen, wife of Menelaus, King of Sparta, and the forming of a federation under his brother, the Greek overlord Agamemnon, to enforce her return. War followed when Troy refused.

Taking sides and playing favorites, potent but fickle, conjuring deceptive images, altering the fortunes of battle to suit their desires, whispering, tricking, falsifying, even inducing the Greeks through deceit to continue when they are ready to give up and go home, the gods keep the combatants engaged while heroes die and homelands suffer. Poseidon, ruler of the sea, who, with Apollo, was said to have built Troy and its walls, has turned against the Trojans because their first king failed to pay him for his work and further because they have stoned to death a priest of his cult for failure to offer sacrifices necessary to arouse the waves against the Greek invasion. Apollo, on the other hand, still favors Troy as its traditional protector, the more so because Agamemnon has angered him by seizing the daughter of a priest of Apollo for his bed. Athena, busiest and most influential of all, is unforgivingly anti-Trojan and pro-Greek because of Paris' original offense. Zeus, ruler of Olympus, is not a strong partisan, and when appealed to by one or another of his extended family, is capable of exercising his influence on either side.

In rage and despair, Troy mourns the death of Hector, slain by Achilles, who brutally drags his corpse by the heels three times around the walls in the dust of his chariot wheels. The Greeks are no better off. The angry Achilles, their champion fighter, shot in his vulnerable heel by Paris with a poisoned arrow, dies. His armor, to be conferred on the most deserving of the Greeks, is awarded to Odysseus, the wisest, instead of to Ajax, the most valorous, whereupon Ajax, maddened by insulted pride, kills himself. His companions' spirits fail and many of the Greek host counsel departure, but Athena puts a stop to that. On her advice, Odysseus proposes a last effort to take Troy by a stratagem—the building of a wooden horse large enough to hold twenty or fifty (or in some versions, as many as three hundred) armed men concealed inside. His plan is for the rest of the army to pretend to sail for home while in fact hiding their ships offshore behind the island of Tenedos. The Wooden Horse will carry an inscription dedicating it to Athena as the Greeks' offering in the hope of her aid in ensuring their safe return home. The figure is intended to excite the veneration of the Trojans, to whom the horse is a sacred animal and who may well be moved to conduct it to their own temple of Athena within the city. If so, the sacred veil said to surround and protect the city will be torn apart, the concealed Greeks will emerge, open the gates to their fellows, summoned by signal, and seize their final opportunity.

In obedience to Athena, who appears to one Epeius in a dream with orders to build the Horse, the "thing of guile" is completed in three days, aided by the goddess' "divine art." Odysseus persuades the rather reluctant leaders and bravest soldiers to enter by rope ladder during the night and take their places "halfway between victory and death."

At dawn, Trojan scouts discover that the siege is lifted and the enemy gone, leaving only the strange and awesome figure at their gates. Priam and his council come out to examine it and fall into anxious and divided discussion. Taking the inscription at face value, Thymoetes, one of the elders, recommends bringing the Horse to Athena's temple in the citadel. "Knowing better," Capys, another of the elders, objects, saying Athena had for too long favored the Greeks, and Troy would be well advised either to burn the pretended offering at once or break it open with brazen axes to see what the belly contains. Here was the feasible alternative.

Hesitant, yet fearful of desecrating Athena's property, Priam decides in favor of bringing the Horse into the city, although the walls must be breached or, in another version, the lintel of the Scean Gate removed to allow it to enter. This is the first warning omen, for it has been prophesied that if ever the Scean lintel is taken down, Troy will fall.

Excited voices from the gathering crowd cry, "Burn it! Hurl it over the rocks into the sea! Cut it open!" Opponents shout as loudly in favor of preserving what they take to be a sacred image. Then occurs a dramatic intervention. Laocoön, a priest of Apollo's temple, comes rushing down from the citadel crying in alarm, "Are you mad, wretched people? Do you think the foe has gone? Do you think gifts of the Greeks lack treachery? What was Odysseus' reputation?

> *"Either the Greeks are hiding in this monster,*
> *Or it's some trick of war, a spy or engine,*
> *To come down on the city. Tricky business*
> *Is hiding in it. Do not trust it, Trojans;*
> *Do not believe this horse. Whatever it may be,*
> *I fear the Greeks, even when bringing gifts."*

With that warning that has echoed down the ages, he flings his spear with all his strength at the Horse, in whose flank it sticks quivering and setting off a moaning sound from the frightened souls within. The blow almost split the wood and let light into the interior, but fate or the gods blunted it; or else, as Aeneas says later, Troy would still be standing.

Just as Laocoön has convinced the majority, guards drag in Sinon, an ostensibly terrified Greek who pretends he has been left behind through the enmity of Odysseus, but who has actually been planted by Odysseus as part of his plan. Asked by Priam to tell the truth about the Wooden Horse, Sinon swears it is a genuine offering to Athena which the Greeks deliberately made huge so the Trojans would *not* take it into their city because that would signify an ultimate Trojan victory. If the Trojans destroy it they will doom themselves, but if they bring it inside they will ensure their city's safety.

Swung around by Sinon's story, the Trojans are wavering between the warning and the false persuasion when a fearful portent convinces them that

Laocoön is wrong. Just as he cautions that Sinon's tale is another trick put into his mouth by Odysseus, two horrible serpents rise in gigantic black spirals out of the waves and advance across the sands,

> *Their burning eyes suffused with blood and fire,*
> *Their darting tongues licking their hissing mouths.*

As the crowd watches paralyzed in terror, they make straight for Laocoön and his two young sons, "fastening their fangs in those poor bodies," coiling around the father's waist and neck and arms and, as he utters strangled inhuman cries, crush him to death. The appalled watchers are now nearly all moved to believe that the ghastly event is Laocoön's punishment for sacrilege in striking what must indeed be a sacred offering.

Troublesome even to the ancient poets, the serpents have defied explanation; myth has its mysteries too, not always resolved. Some narrators say they were sent by Poseidon at Athena's request to prove that his animus against the Trojans was equal to hers. Others say they were sent by Apollo to warn the Trojans of approaching doom (although, since the effect worked the other way, this seems to have a built-in illogic). Virgil's explanation is that Athena herself was responsible in order to convince the Trojans of Sinon's story, thus sealing their doom, and in confirmation he has the serpents take refuge in her temple after the event. So difficult was the problem of the serpents that some collaborators of the time suggested that Laocoön's fate had nothing to do with the Wooden Horse, but was owed to the quite extraneous sin of profaning Apollo's temple by sleeping with his wife in front of the god's image.

The blind bard of the *Odyssey*, who knows nothing of Laocoön, simply states that the argument in favor of welcoming the Horse had to prevail because Troy was ordained to perish—or, as we might interpret it, that mankind in the form of Troy's citizens is addicted to pursuing policy contrary to self-interest.

The instrumentality of the serpents is not a fact of history to be explained, but a work of imagination, one of the most forceful ever described. It produced, in agonized and twisted marble, so vivid that the victims' cries seem almost to be heard, a major masterpiece of classical sculpture. Seeing it in the palace of the Emperor Titus in Rome, Pliny the Elder thought it a work to be preferred "above all that the arts of painting and sculpture have produced." Yet the statue is dumb as to cause and significance. Sophocles wrote a tragedy on the theme of Laocoön but the text disappeared and his thoughts are lost. The existence of the legend can tell us only one thing: that Laocoön was fatally punished for perceiving the truth and warning of it.

While on Priam's orders ropes and rollers are prepared to pull the Horse into the city, unnamed forces still try to warn Troy. Four times at the Gate's threshold, the Horse comes to a halt and four times from the interior the clang of arms sounds, yet though the halts are an omen, the Trojans press on, "heedless and blind with frenzy." They breach the walls and the Gate, unconcerned at thus tearing the sacred veil because they believe its protection is no longer needed. In post-*Aeneid* versions, other portents follow: smoke rises stained with blood, tears flow from the statues of the gods, towers groan as if in pain, mist covers the stars, wolves and jackals howl, laurel withers in the temple of Apollo, but the Trojans take no alarm. Fate drives fear from their minds "so that they might meet their doom and be destroyed."

That night they celebrate, feasting and drinking with carefree hearts. A last chance and a last warning are offered. Cassandra, Priam's daughter, possesses the gift of prophecy conferred on her by Apollo, who, on falling in love with her, gave it in exchange for her promise to lie with him. When Cassandra, dedicating herself to virginity, went back on her promise, the offended god added to his gift a curse providing that her prophecies would never be believed. Ten years before, when Paris first sailed for Sparta, Cassandra had indeed foretold that his voyage would bring doom upon his house, but Priam had paid no attention. "O miserable people," she now cries, "poor fools, you do not understand at all your evil fate." They are acting senselessly, she tells them, toward the very thing "that has your destruction within it." Laughing and drunken, the Trojans tell her she talks too much "windy nonsense." In the fury of the seer ignored, she seizes an axe and a burning brand and rushes at the Wooden Horse but is restrained before she can reach it.

Heavy with wine, the Trojans sleep. Sinon creeps from the hall and opens the trap door of the Horse to release Odysseus and his companions, some of whom, cooped up in the blackness, have been weeping under the tension and "trembling in their legs." They spread through the city to open the remaining gates while Sinon signals to the ships with a flaming torch. In ferocious triumph when the forces are joined, the Greeks fall upon the sleeping foe, slaughtering right and left, burning houses, looting treasure, raping the women. Greeks die too as the Trojans wield their swords, but the advantage has been gained by the invaders. Everywhere the dark blood flows, hacked corpses cover the ground, the crackle of flames rises over the shrieks and groans of the wounded and the wailing of women.

The tragedy is total; no heroics or pity mitigate the end. Achilles' son Pyrrhus (also called Neoptolemus), "mad with murder," pursues the wounded and fleeing Polites, Priam's youngest son, down a corridor of the palace and, "eager for the last thrust," hacks off his head in the sight of his father. When venerable Priam, slipping in his son's blood, flings a feeble spear, Pyrrhus kills him too. The wives and mothers of the defeated are dragged off in indignity to be allotted to the enemy chiefs along with other booty. Hecuba the Queen falls to Odysseus, Hector's wife, Andromache, to the murderer Pyrrhus. Cassandra, raped by another Ajax in the temple of Athena, is dragged out with hair flying and hands bound to be given to Agamemnon and ultimately to kill herself rather than serve his lust. Worse is the fate of Polyxena, another daughter of Priam once desired by Achilles and now demanded by his shade, who is sacrificed on his tomb by the victors. The crowning pity is reserved for the child Astyanax, son of Hector and Andromache, who on Odysseus' orders that no hero's son shall survive to seek vengeance, is hurled from the battlements to his death. Sacked and burned, Troy is left in ruins. Mount Ida groans; the river Xanthus weeps.

Singing of their victory that has ended the long war at last, the Greeks board their ships, offering prayers to Zeus for a safe return home. Few obtain it, but rather, through a balancing fate, suffer disaster parallel to that of their victims. Athena, enraged by the rapist's profanation of her temple, or because the Greeks, careless in victory, have failed to offer prayers to her, asks Zeus for the right to punish them and, given lightning and thunderbolts, raises the sea to a storm. Ships founder and sink or are smashed on the rocks, island shores are strewn with wrecks and the sea with floating corpses. The second Ajax is among those drowned; Odysseus, blown off course, is storm-tossed, shipwrecked and lost for twenty years; arriving home, Agamemnon is murdered by his faithless wife and her lover. The bloodthirsty Pyrrhus is killed by Orestes at Delphi. Curiously, Helen, the cause of it all, survives untouched in perfect beauty, to be forgiven by the bewitched Menelaus and to regain royal husband, home and prosperity. Aeneas too escapes. Because of his filial devotion in carrying his aged father on his back after the battle, he is allowed by Agamemnon to embark with his followers and follow the destiny that will lead him to Rome. With the circular justice that man likes to impose upon history, a survivor of Troy founds the city-state that will conquer Troy's conquerors.

How much fact lies behind the Trojan epic? Archeologists, as we know, have uncovered nine levels of an ancient settlement on the Asian shore of the Hellespont, or Dardanelles, opposite Gallipoli. Its site at the crossroads of Bronze Age trade routes would invite raids and sack and account for the evidence at different levels of frequent demolition and rebuilding. Level VIIA, containing fragments of gold and other artifacts of a royal city, and exhibiting signs of having been violently destroyed by human hands, has been identified as Priam's Troy and its fall dated near the end of the Bronze Age, around 1200 B.C. It is quite possible that Greek mercantile and maritime ambitions came into conflict with Troy and that the overlord of the several communities of the Greek peninsula could have gathered allies for a concerted attack on the city across the straits. The abduction of Helen, as Robert Graves suggests, might have been real in its retaliation for some prior Greek raid.

These were Mycenaean times in Greece, when Agamemnon, son of Atreus, was King at Mycenae in the citadel with the Lion Gate. Its dark remains still stand on a hill just south of Corinth where poppies spring so deeply red they seem forever stained by the blood of the Atridae. Some violent cause, in roughly the same age as the fall of Troy but probably over a more extended period, ended the primacy of Mycenae and of Knossus in Crete with which it was linked. Mycenaean culture was literate as we now know since the script called Linear B found in the ruins of Knossus has been identified as an early form of Greek.

The period following the Mycenaean collapse is a shadowy void of some two centuries called the Greek Dark Ages, whose only communication to us is through shards and artifacts. For some unexplained reason, written language seems to have vanished completely, although recitals of the exploits of

ancestors of a past heroic age were clearly transmitted orally down the generations. Recovery, stimulated by the arrival of the Dorian people from the
north, began around the 10th century B.C. and from that recovery burst the
immortal celebrator whose epic fashioned from familiar tales and legends of
his people started the stream of Western literature.

   Homer is generally pictured as reciting his narrative poems to accom-
paniment on the lyre, but the 16,000 lines of the *Iliad* and 12,000 of the
Odyssey were certainly also either written down by himself or dictated by him
to a scribe. Texts were undoubtedly available to the several bards of the next
two or three centuries who, in supplementary tales of Troy, introduced material from oral tradition to fill in the gaps left by Homer. The sacrifice of
Iphigenia, Achilles' vulnerable heel, the appearance of Penthesilea, Queen of
the Amazons, as an ally of Troy and many of the most memorable episodes
belong to these poems of the post-Homeric cycle which have come down to
us only through summaries made in the 2nd century A.D. of texts since lost.
The *Cypria,* named for Cyprus, home of its supposed author, is the fullest and
earliest of these, followed by, among others, *The Sack of Ilium* by Arctinus
and the *Little Iliad* by a bard of Lesbos. After them, lyric poets and the three
great tragic dramatists took up the Trojan themes, and Greek historians discussed the evidence. Latin authors elaborated further both before and especially after Virgil, adding jeweled eyes for the Wooden Horse and other
glittering fables. Distinction between history and fable faded when the heroes
of Troy and their adventures splendidly filled the tapestries and chronicles of
the Middle Ages. Hector becomes one of the Nine Worthies on a par with
Julius Caesar and Charlemagne.

   The question of whether a historical underpinning existed for the
Wooden Horse was raised by Pausanias, a Latin traveler and geographer with
a true historian's curiosity, who wrote a *Description of Greece* in the 2nd
century A.D. He decided the Horse must have represented some kind of "war
machine" or siege engine because, he argues, to take the legend at face value
would be to impute "utter folly" to the Trojans. The question still provokes
speculation in the 20th century. If the siege engine was a battering ram, why
did not the Greeks use it as such? If it was the kind of housing that brought
assaulters up to the walls, surely it would have been even greater folly for the
Trojans to take it in without breaking it open first. One can be lured this way
down endless paths of the hypothetical. The fact is that although early As-
syrian monuments depict such a device, there is no evidence that any kind
of siege engine was used in Greek warfare in Mycenaean or Homeric times.
That anachronism would not have worried Pausanias, because it was normal
in his, and indeed in much later, days to view the past dressed and equipped
in the image of the present.

   Ruse was indeed used in the siege of walled or fortified places in biblical
lands in the warfare of the 2nd millenium B.C. (200–1000), which covers the
century generally given for the Trojan War. If unable to penetrate by force,
the attacking army would attempt to enter by cunning, using some trick to
gain the confidence of the defenders, and it has been said by a military

historian that "the very existence of legends concerning the conquest of cities by stratagem testifies to a core of truth."

Although silent on the Wooden Horse, Herodotus in the 5th century B.C. wished to attribute more rational behavior to the Trojans than Homer allowed them. On the basis of what priests of Egypt told him in the course of his investigation, he states that Helen was never in Troy at all during the war, but remained in Egypt, where she had landed with Paris when their ship was blown off course following her abduction from Sparta. The local King, disgusted by Paris' ignoble seduction of a host's wife, ordered him to depart; only a phantom Helen came with him to Troy. Had she been real, Herodotus argues, surely Priam and Hector would have delivered her up to the Greeks rather than suffer so many deaths and calamities. They could not have been "so infatuated" as to sustain all that woe for her sake or for the sake of Paris, who was anything but admired by his family.

There speaks reason. As the Father of History, Herodotus might have known that in the lives of his subjects, common sense is rarely a determinant. He argues further that the Trojans assured the Greek envoys that Helen was not in Troy but were not believed because the gods wished for the war and the destruction of Troy to show that great wrongs bring great punishment. Probing for the meaning of the legend, here perhaps he comes closer to it.

In the search for meaning we must not forget that the gods (or God, for that matter) are a concept of the human mind; they are the creatures of man, not vice versa. They are needed and invented to give meaning and purpose to the puzzle that is life on earth, to explain strange and irregular phenomena of nature, haphazard events and, above all, irrational human conduct. They exist to bear the burden of all things that cannot be comprehended except by supernatural intervention or design.

This is especially true of the Greek pantheon, whose members are daily and intimately entangled with human beings and are susceptible to all the emotions of mortals if not to their limitations. What makes the gods so capricious and unprincipled is that in the Greek conception they are devoid of moral and ethical values—like a man lacking a shadow. Consequently, they have no compunction about maliciously deceiving mortals or causing them to violate oaths and commit other disloyal and disgraceful acts. Aphrodite's magic caused Helen to elope with Paris, Athena tricked Hector into fighting Achilles. What is shameful or foolish in mortals is attributed by them to the influence of the gods. "To the gods I owe this woeful war," laments Priam, forgetting that he could have removed the cause by sending Helen home at any time (presuming that she was there, as she very actively was in the Homeric cycle) or by yielding her when Menelaus and Odysseus came to demand her delivery.

The gods' interference does not acquit man of folly; rather, it is man's device for transferring the responsibility for folly. Homer understood this when he made Zeus complain in the opening section of the *Odyssey* how lamentable it was that men should blame the gods as the source of their troubles, "when it is through blindness of their own hearts" (or specifically their "greed and folly" in another translation) that sufferings "beyond that which is ordained" are brought upon them. This is a notable statement for, if the results are indeed worse than what fate had in store, it means that choice and free will were operating, not some implacable predestination. As an example, Zeus cites the case of Aegisthus, who stole Agamemnon's wife and murdered the King on his homecoming, "though he knew the ruin this would entail since we ourselves sent Hermes to warn him neither to kill the man nor to make love to his wife, for Orestes when he grew up was bound to avenge his father and desire his patrimony." In short, though Aegisthus well knew what evils would result from his conduct, he proceeded nevertheless, and paid the price.

"Infatuation," as Herodotus suggested, is what robs man of reason. The ancients knew it and the Greeks had a goddess for it. Named Atē, she was the daughter—and significantly in some genealogies, the eldest daughter—of Zeus. Her mother was Eris, or Discord, goddess of Strife (who in some versions is another identity of Atē). The daughter is the goddess, separately or together, of Infatuation, Mischief, Delusion and Blind Folly, rendering her victims "incapable of rational choice" and blind to distinctions of morality and expedience.

Given her combined heritage, Atē had potent capacity for harm and was in fact the original cause, prior to the Judgment of Paris, of the Trojan War, the prime struggle of the ancient world. Drawn from the earliest versions—the *Iliad,* the *Theogony* of Hesiod, roughly contemporary with Homer and the major authority on Olympian genealogy, and the *Cypria*—the tale of Atē ascribes her initial act to spite at not being invited by Zeus to the wedding of Peleus and the sea-nymph Thetis, future parents of Achilles. Entering the banquet hall unbidden, she maliciously rolls down the table the Golden Apple of Discord inscribed "For the Fairest," immediately setting off the rival claims of Hera, Athena and Aphrodite. As the husband of one and father of another of the quarreling ladies, Zeus, not wishing to invite trouble for himself by deciding the issue, sends the three disputants to Mount Ida, where a handsome young shepherd, reportedly adroit in matters of love, can make the difficult judgment. This, of course, is Paris, whose rustic phase is owed to circumstances that need not concern us here and from whose choice flows the conflict so much greater than perhaps even Atē intended.[2]

Undeterred from mischief, Atē on another occasion devised a complicated piece of trickery by which the birth of Zeus' son Heracles was delayed and an inferior child brought forth ahead of him, thus depriving Heracles of

---

[2]In other versions, the origins of the war are associated with the Flood legend that circulated throughout Asia Minor, probably emanating from the region of the Euphrates, which frequently overflowed. Determined to eliminate the unsatisfactory human species, or alternatively, according to the *Cypria,* to "thin out" the population, which was overburdening the all-nurturing earth, Zeus decided upon "the great struggle of the Ilian war, that its load of death might empty the world." He therefore contrived or took advantage of the goddesses' quarrel over the Apple to bring the war about. Euripides adopts this version when he makes Helen say in the play named for her that Zeus arranged the war that "he might lighten mother earth of her myriad hosts of men." Evidently, very early, there must have been a deep sense of human unworthiness to produce these legends.

his birthright. Furious at the trick (which does indeed seem capricious even for an immortal), Zeus flung Atē out of Olympus, henceforward to live on earth among mankind. On her account the earth is called the Meadow of Atē—not the Meadow of Aphrodite, or the Garden of Demeter, or the Throne of Athena or some other more pleasing title, but, as the ancients already sadly knew it to be, the realm of folly.

Greek myths take care of every contingency. According to a legend told in the *Iliad*, Zeus, repenting of what he had done, created four daughters called *Litai*, or Prayers for Pardon, who offer mortals the means of escape from their folly, but only if they respond. "Lame, wrinkled things with eyes cast down," the Litai follow Atē, or passionate Folly (sometimes translated Ruin or Sin), as healers.

> *If a man*
> *Reveres the daughters of Zeus when they come near,*
> *He is rewarded and his prayers are heard;*
> *But if he spurns them and dismisses them*
> *They make their way back to Zeus again and ask*
> *That Folly dog that man till suffering*
> *Has taken arrogance out of him.*

Meanwhile, Atē came to live among men and lost no time in causing Achilles' famous quarrel with Agamemnon and his ensuing anger, which became the mainspring of the *Iliad* and has always seemed so disproportionate. When at last the feud which has so damaged the Greek cause and prolonged the war is reconciled, Agamemnon blames Atē, or Delusion, for his original infatuation for the girl he took from Achilles.

> *Delusion, the elder daughter of Zeus; the accursed*
> *Who deludes all and leads them astray. . . .*
> *. . . took my wife away from me.*
> *She has entangled others before me—*

and, we might add, many since, the Litai notwithstanding. She appears once again in Mark Antony's fearful vision when, gazing on the murdered corpse at his feet, he foresees how "Caesar's spirit, ranging for revenge with Atē by his side, shall cry 'Havoc' and let slip the dogs of war."

Anthropologists have subjected myth to infinite classification and some wilder theorizing. As the product of the psyche, it is said to be the means of bringing hidden fears and wish fulfillments into the open or of reconciling us to the human condition or of revealing the contradictions and problems, social and personal, that people face in life. Myths are seen as "charters" or "rituals," or serving any number of other functions. All or some of this may or may not be valid; what we can be sure of is that myths are prototypes of human behavior and that one ritual they serve is that of the goat tied with a scarlet thread and sent off into the wilderness to carry away the mistakes and the sins of mankind.

Legend partakes of myth and of something else, a historical connection, however faint and far away and all but forgotten. The Wooden Horse is not myth in the sense of Cronus swallowing his children or Zeus transforming himself into a swan or a shower of gold for purposes of adultery. It is legend with no supernatural elements except for Athena's aid and the intrusion of the serpents, who were added, no doubt, to give the Trojans a reason for rejecting Laocoön's advice (and who are almost too compelling, for they seem to leave the Trojans with little option but to choose the course that contains their doom).

Yet the feasible alternative—that of destroying the Horse—is always open. Capys the Elder advised it before Laocoön's warning, and Cassandra afterward. Notwithstanding the frequent references in the epic to the fall of Troy being ordained, it was not fate but free choice that took the Horse within the walls. "Fate" as a character in legend represents the fulfillment of man's expectations of himself.

QUESTIONS FOR A CRITICAL REREADING

Read the essay through once, constructing an informal sentence outline. Then use the following questions to reread the argument critically. As you reread, use these questions and your sentence outline to formulate an enthymemic thesis for Tuchman's argument.

1. In partial justification for beginning a book about the Vietnam War with a classical myth, Tuchman explains that this story "has endured deep in our minds and memories for twenty-eight centuries because it speaks to us of ourselves, not least when least rational." She implies that even stories "with or without some vestige of historical foundation" have something to teach us about ourselves, and for that reason they should be the province of historians. What does this tell you about the types of questions historians ask when they study the past? What hypothesis does she introduce about what the Trojan Horse legend can teach us?
2. Throughout her examination of the legends surrounding the question of why the Trojans took the horse into their city, Tuchman concentrates on several variations, especially the tale of the two serpents that strangled Laocoön and his two young sons. What does she believe these serpents teach us about the Trojans?
3. To discover a "because" clause for Tuchman's enthymeme, combine your answer for question 2 with the other examples Tuchman uses to prove her point. How is the lesson contained in the serpent tale also embodied in Homer's version, which ignores the serpents and states that Troy's act was "ordained" because "mankind in the form of Troy's citizens is addicted to pursuing policy contrary to self-interest?" (Consider the line "Fate drives fear from their minds 'so that they might meet their doom and be destroyed.' ")
4. Tuchman appears to agree with Herodotus: "There speaks reason. As the Father of History, Herodotus might have known that in the lives of his subjects, common sense is rarely a determinant." She goes on to explain how the Trojan legend reveals this truth about human nature in the terms popular during the time when the legend was popularly accepted:

   In the search for meaning we must not forget that the gods (or God, for that matter) are a concept of the human mind; they are the creatures of man, not vice versa. They are needed and invented to give meaning and purpose to the puzzle that is life on earth, to explain strange and irregular phenomena of nature, haphazard events and, above all, irrational human conduct. They exist to bear the burden of all things that cannot be comprehended except by supernatural intervention or design.

What does she mean in this passage? What lesson might she be implying this has for us today?

5. Paraphrase your answer to question 4 as the first clause of Tuchman's enthymeme. Once you have done this, review your answers to questions 2 and 3 and formulate her "because" clause. Use this enthymeme to identify the three primary aspects of her reasoning: (1) the question she is addressing, (2) the information she assumes we already agree with, and (3) the primary reason she has used to justify her answer. Try structuring a logical outline for her essay.

POSSIBLE ISSUES FOR WRITING

Following are a few of the questions that you might find at issue after you have constructed a logical outline for Tuchman's essay. As you discuss them with your classmates, keep a record in your notebook of the different kinds of information your classmates use to justify their positions. (This can help you discover what kind of information you will want to use in your own essay.)

1. With the unsympathetic and objective eye of the historian, Tuchman emphasizes how "no heroics or pity mitigate the end" and that "with the circular justice that man likes to impose upon history, a survivor of Troy founds the city-state that will conquer Troy's conquerors." Why do we seek to impose a "circular justice" on the past? Does Tuchman imply this is a good thing for historians to do? Does she also impose a circular justice in this essay? Justify your answer.

2. Tuchman mentions Pausanius' remark that the horse must have been some kind of "war machine" or battering ram since "to take the legend at face value would be to impute 'utter folly' to the Trojans." She rejects his interpretation, saying that there is no evidence that war machines such as those Pausanius suggests existed at the time. However, she excuses Pausanius: "That anachronism would not have worried Pausanias, because it was normal in his, and indeed in much later, days to view the past dressed and equipped in the image of the present." What is an "anachronism"? (Compare your definition to that in your dictionary.) Does Tuchman herself avoid anachronistic interpretation? Can any historian? Why or why not?

3. If the historian's purpose is to interpret the past so that we can avoid repeating our mistakes, we might formulate Tuchman's thesis in this way: "The legend of Troy reveals how we are addicted to pursuing policy contrary to our self-interest because the legend's use of 'Fate' as a character is merely a justification for how human will is guided by blind folly rather than reason." As a historian, Tuchman is merely hypothesizing about human truths embodied in historical events and under no obligation to say what we should—or if we can—do anything about it. What implications do *you* think her argument should have for how we should act today?

Economic Possibilities for Our Grandchildren

John Maynard Keynes (1883–1946)

One of the most respected economic thinkers of the twentieth century, John Maynard Keynes greatly influenced the evolution of our modern theories of capitalism. His critical analysis of international and national economic policies following World War I, during the Great Depression, and throughout World War II had a distinct impact on the century.

Keynes' The Economic Consequences of Peace *(1919) predicted the economic effects of the Treaty of Versailles that followed World War I. He highly criticized the United States and his own government, Great Britain, for seeking economic reparations from Germany, a demand that he foresaw could only lead to economic collapse. His* General Theory of Employment, Interest and Money *(1936), criticized the general belief that governments should restrict spending during times of depression. He proposed, instead, that governments increase economic support of social programs to aid economic recovery. Keynes' advice greatly influenced President Roosevelt's economic policies, playing a major role in the United States's recovery from the devastating impact of the depression.*

The essay reprinted here reflects Keynes' ability to see beyond immediate economic conditions to concentrate on their consequences. It was initially given as a speech at Cambridge University in 1928, but was revised for a wider audience during the early years of the depression (it was published in 1930). As you read it, note how Keynes has adapted his remarks to the concerns of his audience, and keep in mind how astonishing his predictions would appear to individuals confronting an economic depression. As an economist, he is tracing the history of and predicting the future effects of our capitalistic system. As you read, consider whether he remains impartially objective in his analysis. Are the "economic possibilities" he arrives at purely economic or are they compromised by moral assumptions about how we should live?

I

We are suffering just now from a bad attack of economic pessimism. It is common to hear people say that the epoch of enormous economic progress which characterised the nineteenth century is over; that the rapid improvement in the standard of life is now going to slow down—at any rate in Great Britain; that a decline in prosperity is more likely than an improvement in the decade which lies ahead of us.

I believe that this is a wildly mistaken interpretation of what is happening to us. We are suffering, not from the rheumatics of old age, but from the growing-pains of over-rapid changes, from the painfulness of readjustment between one economic period and another. The increase of technical efficiency has been taking place faster than we can deal with the problem of labour absorption; the improvement in the standard of life has been a little too quick; the banking and monetary system of the world has been preventing the rate of interest from falling as fast as equilibrium requires. And even so, the waste and confusion which ensue relate to not more than 7½ per cent of the national income; we are muddling away one and sixpence in the £, and have only 18s. 6d., when we might, if we were more sensible, have £1; yet, nevertheless, the 18s. 6d. mounts up to as much as the £1 would have been five or six years ago. We forget that in 1929 the physical output of the industry of Great Britain was greater than ever before, and that the net surplus of our foreign balance available for new foreign investment, after paying for all our imports, was greater last year than that of any other country, being indeed 50 per cent greater than the corresponding surplus of the United States. Or again—if it is to be a matter of comparisons—suppose that we were to reduce our wages by a half, repudiate four-fifths of the national debt, and hoard our surplus wealth in barren gold instead of lending it at 6 per cent or more, we should resemble the now much-envied France. But would it be an improvement?

The prevailing world depression, the enormous anomaly of unemployment in a world full of wants, the disastrous mistakes we have made, blind us to what is going on under the surface—to the true interpretation of the trend of things. For I predict that both of the two opposed errors of pessimism which now make so much noise in the world will be proved wrong in our own time—the pessimism of the revolutionaries who think that things are so bad that nothing can save us but violent change, and the pessimism of the reactionaries who consider the balance of our economic and social life so precarious that we must risk no experiments.

My purpose in this essay, however, is not to examine the present or the near future, but to disembarrass myself of short views and take wings into the future. What can we reasonably expect the level of our economic life to be a hundred years hence? What are the economic possibilities for our grandchildren?

From the earliest times of which we have record—back, say, to two thousand years before Christ—down to the beginning of the eighteenth century, there was no very great change in the standard of life of the average man living in the civilised centres of the earth. Ups and downs certainly. Visitations of plague, famine, and war. Golden intervals. But no progressive, violent change. Some periods perhaps 50 per cent better than others—at the utmost 100 per cent better—in the four thousand years which ended (say) in A.D. 1700.

This slow rate of progress, or lack of progress, was due to two reasons—to the remarkable absence of important technical improvements and to the failure of capital to accumulate.

The absence of important technical inventions between the prehistoric age and comparatively modern times is truly remarkable. Almost everything which really matters and which the world possessed at the commencement of the modern age was already known to man at the dawn of history. Language, fire, the same domestic animals which we have to-day, wheat, barley, the vine and the olive, the plough, the wheel, the oar, the sail, leather, linen and cloth, bricks and pots, gold and silver, copper, tin, and lead—and iron was added to the list before 1000 B.C.—banking, statecraft, mathematics, astronomy, and religion. There is no record of when we first possessed these things.

At some epoch before the dawn of history—perhaps even in one of the comfortable intervals before the last ice age—there must have been an era of progress and invention comparable to that in which we live to-day. But through the greater part of recorded history there was nothing of the kind.

The modern age opened, I think, with the accumulation of capital which began in the sixteenth century. I believe—for reasons with which I must not encumber the present argument—that this was initially due to the rise of prices, and the profits to which that led, which resulted from the treasure of gold and silver which Spain brought from the New World into the Old. From that time until to-day the power of accumulation by compound interest, which seems to have been sleeping for many generations, was re-born and renewed its strength. And the power of compound interest over two hundred years is such as to stagger the imagination.

Let me give in illustration of this a sum which I have worked out. The value of Great Britain's foreign investments to-day is estimated at about £4,000,000,000. This yields us an income at the rate of about 6½ per cent. Half of this we bring home and enjoy; the other half, namely, 3¼ per cent, we leave to accumulate abroad at compound interest. Something of this sort has now been going on for about 250 years.

For I trace the beginnings of British foreign investment to the treasure which Drake stole from Spain in 1580. In that year he returned to England bringing with him the prodigious spoils of the *Golden Hind.* Queen Elizabeth was a considerable shareholder in the syndicate which had financed the expedition. Out of her share she paid off the whole of England's foreign debt, balanced her Budget, and found herself with about £40,000 in hand. This she invested in the Levant Company—which prospered. Out of the profits of the Levant Company, the East India Company was founded; and the profits of this great enterprise were the foundation of England's subsequent foreign investment. Now it happens that £40,000 accumulating at 3¼ per cent compound interest approximately corresponds to the actual volume of England's foreign investments at various dates, and would actually amount to-day to the total of £4,000,000,000 which I have already quoted as being what our foreign investments now are. Thus, every £1 which Drake brought home in 1580 has now become £100,000. Such is the power of compound interest!

From the sixteenth century, with a cumulative crescendo after the eighteenth, the great age of science and technical inventions began, which since the beginning of the nineteenth century has been in full flood—coal, steam, electricity, petrol, steel, rubber, cotton, the chemical industries, automatic machinery and the methods of mass production, wireless, printing, Newton,

Darwin, and Einstein, and thousands of other things and men too famous and familiar to catalogue.

What is the result? In spite of an enormous growth in the population of the world, which it has been necessary to equip with houses and machines, the average standard of life in Europe and the United States has been raised, I think, about fourfold. The growth of capital has been on a scale which is far beyond a hundred-fold of what any previous age had known. And from now on we need not expect so great an increase of population.

If capital increases, say, 2 per cent per annum, the capital equipment of the world will have increased by a half in twenty years, and seven and a half times in a hundred years. Think of this in terms of material things—houses, transport, and the like.

At the same time technical improvements in manufacture and transport have been proceeding at a greater rate in the last ten years than ever before in history. In the United States factory output per head was 40 per cent greater in 1925 than in 1919. In Europe we are held back by temporary obstacles, but even so it is safe to say that technical efficiency is increasing by more than 1 per cent per annum compound. There is evidence that the revolutionary technical changes, which have so far chiefly affected industry, may soon be attacking agriculture. We may be on the eve of improvements in the efficiency of food production as great as those which have already taken place in mining, manufacture, and transport. In quite a few years—in our own lifetimes I mean—we may be able to perform all the operations of agriculture, mining, and manufacture with a quarter of the human effort to which we have been accustomed.

For the moment the very rapidity of these changes is hurting us and bringing difficult problems to solve. Those countries are suffering relatively which are not in the vanguard of progress. We are being afflicted with a new disease of which some readers may not yet have heard the name, but of which they will hear a great deal in the years to come—namely, *technological unemployment*. This means unemployment due to our discovery of means of economising the use of labour outrunning the pace at which we can find new uses for labour.

But this is only a temporary phase of maladjustment. All this means in the long run *that mankind is solving its economic problem.* I would predict that the standard of life in progressive countries one hundred years hence will be between four and eight times as high as it is to-day. There would be nothing surprising in this even in the light of our present knowledge. It would not be foolish to contemplate the possibility of a far greater progress still.

II

Let us, for the sake of argument, suppose that a hundred years hence we are all of us, on the average, eight times better off in the economic sense than we are to-day. Assuredly there need be nothing here to surprise us.

Now it is true that the needs of human beings may seem to be insatiable.

But they fall into two classes—those needs which are absolute in the sense that we feel them whatever the situation of our fellow human beings may be, and those which are relative in the sense that we feel them only if their satisfaction lifts us above, makes us feel superior to, our fellows. Needs of the second class, those which satisfy the desire for superiority, may indeed be insatiable; for the higher the general level, the higher still are they. But this is not so true of the absolute needs—a point may soon be reached, much sooner perhaps than we are all of us aware of, when these needs are satisfied in the sense that we prefer to devote our further energies to non-economic purposes.

Now for my conclusion, which you will find, I think, to become more and more startling to the imagination the longer you think about it.

I draw the conclusion that, assuming no important wars and no important increase in population, the *economic problem* may be solved, or be at least within sight of solution, within a hundred years. This means that the economic problem is not—if we look into the future—*the permanent problem of the human race.*

Why, you may ask, is this so startling? It is startling because—if, instead of looking into the future, we look into the past—we find that the economic problem, the struggle for subsistence, always has been hitherto the primary, most pressing problem of the human race—not only of the human race, but of the whole of the biological kingdom from the beginnings of life in its most primitive forms.

Thus we have been expressly evolved by nature—with all our impulses and deepest instincts—for the purpose of solving the economic problem. If the economic problem is solved, mankind will be deprived of its traditional purpose.

Will this be a benefit? If one believes at all in the real values of life, the prospect at least opens up the possibility of benefit. Yet I think with dread of the readjustment of the habits and instincts of the ordinary man, bred into him for countless generations, which he may be asked to discard within a few decades.

To use the language of to-day—must we not expect a general "nervous breakdown"? We already have a little experience of what I mean—a nervous breakdown of the sort which is already common enough in England and the United States amongst the wives of the well-to-do classes, unfortunate women, many of them, who have been deprived by their wealth of their traditional tasks and occupations—who cannot find it sufficiently amusing, when deprived of the spur of economic necessity, to cook and clean and mend, yet are quite unable to find anything more amusing.

To those who sweat for their daily bread leisure is a longed-for sweet—until they get it.

There is the traditional epitaph written for herself by the old char-woman:—

Don't mourn for me, friends, don't weep for me never,
For I'm going to do nothing for ever and ever.

This was her heaven. Like others who look forward to leisure, she conceived how nice it would be to spend her time listening-in—for there was another couplet which occurred in her poem:—

With psalms and sweet music the heavens'll be ringing,
But I shall have nothing to do with the singing.

Yet it will only be for those who have to do with the singing that life will be tolerable—and how few of us can sing!

Thus for the first time since his creation man will be faced with his real, his permanent problem—how to use his freedom from pressing economic cares, how to occupy the leisure, which science and compound interest will have won for him, to live wisely and agreeably and well.

The strenuous purposeful money-makers may carry all of us along with them into the lap of economic abundance. But it will be those peoples, who can keep alive, and cultivate into a fuller perfection, the art of life itself and do not sell themselves for the means of life, who will be able to enjoy the abundance when it comes.

Yet there is no country and no people, I think, who can look forward to the age of leisure and of abundance without a dread. For we have been trained too long to strive and not to enjoy. It is a fearful problem for the ordinary person, with no special talents, to occupy himself, especially if he no longer has roots in the soil or in custom or in the beloved conventions of a traditional society. To judge from the behaviour and the achievements of the wealthy classes to-day in any quarter of the world, the outlook is very depressing! For these are, so to speak, our advance guard—those who are spying out the promised land for the rest of us and pitching their camp there. For they have most of them failed disastrously, so it seems to me—those who have an independent income but no associations or duties or ties—to solve the problem which has been set them.

I feel sure that with a little more experience we shall use the new-found bounty of nature quite differently from the way in which the rich use it to-day, and will map out for ourselves a plan of life quite otherwise than theirs.

For many ages to come the old Adam will be so strong in us that everybody will need to do *some* work if he is to be contented. We shall do more things for ourselves than is usual with the rich to-day, only too glad to have small duties and tasks and routines. But beyond this, we shall endeavour to spread the bread thin on the butter—to make what work there is still to be done to be as widely shared as possible. Three-hour shifts or a fifteen-hour week may put off the problem for a great while. For three hours a day is quite enough to satisfy the old Adam in most of us!

There are changes in other spheres too which we must expect to come. When the accumulation of wealth is no longer of high social importance, there will be great changes in the code of morals. We shall be able to rid ourselves of many of the pseudo-moral principles which have hag-ridden us for two hundred years, by which we have exalted some of the most distasteful of human qualities into the position of the highest virtues. We shall be able to afford to dare to assess the money-motive at its true value. The love of money as a possession—as distinguished from the love of money as a means to the enjoyments and realities of life—will be recognised for what it is, a somewhat disgusting morbidity, one of those semi-criminal, semi-pathological propensities which one hands over with a shudder to the specialists in mental disease. All kinds of social customs and economic practices, affecting the distribution of wealth and of economic rewards and penalties, which we now maintain at all costs, however distasteful and unjust they may be in themselves, because they are tremendously useful in promoting the accumulation of capital, we shall then be free, at last, to discard.

Of course there will still be many people with intense, unsatisfied purposiveness who will blindly pursue wealth—unless they can find some plausible substitute. But the rest of us will no longer be under any obligation to applaud and encourage them. For we shall inquire more curiously than is safe to-day into the true character of this "purposiveness" with which in varying degrees Nature has endowed almost all of us. For purposiveness means that we are more concerned with the remote future results of our actions than with their own quality or their immediate effects on our own environment. The "purposive" man is always trying to secure a spurious and delusive immortality for his acts by pushing his interest in them forward into time. He does not love his cat, but his cat's kittens; nor, in truth, the kittens, but only the kittens' kittens, and so on forward for ever to the end of cat-dom. For him jam is not jam unless it is a case of jam to-morrow and never jam to-day. Thus by pushing his jam always forward into the future, he strives to secure for his act of boiling it an immortality.

Let me remind you of the Professor in *Sylvie and Bruno:*—

"Only the tailor, sir, with your little bill," said a meek voice outside the door.

"Ah, well, I can soon settle *his* business," the Professor said to the children, "if you'll just wait a minute. How much is it, this year, my man?" The tailor had come in while he was speaking.

"Well, it's been a-doubling so many years, you see," the tailor replied, a little gruffly, "and I think I'd like the money now. It's two thousand pound, it is!"

"Oh, that's nothing!" the Professor carelessly remarked, feeling in his pocket, as if he always carried at least *that* amount about with him. "But wouldn't you like to wait just another year and make it *four* thousand? Just think how rich you'd be! Why, you might be a *king*, if you liked!"

"I don't know as I'd care about being a king," the man said thoughtfully. "But it *dew* sound a powerful sight o' money! Well, I think I'll wait——"

"Of course you will!" said the Professor. "There's good sense in *you,* I see. Good-day to you, my man!"

"Will you ever have to pay him that four thousand pounds?" Sylvie asked as the door closed on the departing creditor.

"Never, my child!" the Professor replied emphatically. "He'll go on doubling it till he dies. You see, it's *always* worth while waiting another year to get twice as much money!"

Perhaps it is not an accident that the race which did most to bring the promise of immortality into the heart and essence of our religions has also done most for the principle of compound interest and particularly loves this most purposive of human institutions.

I see us free, therefore, to return to some of the most sure and certain principles of religion and traditional virtue—that avarice is a vice, that the exaction of usury is a misdemeanour, and the love of money is detestable, that those walk most truly in the paths of virtue and sane wisdom who take least thought for the morrow. We shall once more value ends above means and prefer the good to the useful. We shall honour those who can teach us how to pluck the hour and the day virtuously and well, the delightful people who are capable of taking direct enjoyment in things, the lilies of the field who toil not, neither do they spin.

But beware! The time for all this is not yet. For at least another hundred years we must pretend to ourselves and to every one that fair is foul and foul is fair; for foul is useful and fair is not. Avarice and usury and precaution must be our gods for a little longer still. For only they can lead us out of the tunnel of economic necessity into daylight.

I look forward, therefore, in days not so very remote, to the greatest change which has ever occurred in the material environment of life for human beings in the aggregate. But, of course, it will all happen gradually, not as a catastrophe. Indeed, it has already begun. The course of affairs will simply be that there will be ever larger and larger classes and groups of people from whom problems of economic necessity have been practically removed. The critical difference will be realised when this condition has become so general that the nature of one's duty to one's neighbour is changed. For it will remain reasonable to be economically purposive for others after it has ceased to be reasonable for oneself.

The *pace* at which we can reach our destination of economic bliss will be governed by four things—our power to control population, our determination to avoid wars and civil dissensions, our willingness to entrust to science the direction of those matters which are properly the concern of science, and the rate of accumulation as fixed by the margin between our production and our consumption; of which the last will easily look after itself, given the first three.

Meanwhile there will be no harm in making mild preparations for our destiny, in encouraging, and experimenting in, the arts of life as well as the activities of purpose.

But, chiefly, do not let us overestimate the importance of the economic problem, or sacrifice to its supposed necessities other matters of greater and more permanent significance. It should be a matter for specialists—like dentistry. If economists could manage to get themselves thought of as humble, competent people, on a level with dentists, that would be splendid!

QUESTIONS FOR A CRITICAL REREADING

Construct an informal sentence outline based on your first reading of Keynes' essay and see if you can formulate a tentative thesis. Then, as you reread the essay, answer these questions in your notebook to help you clarify your understanding of Keynes' argument and how it compares to Tuchman's.

1. Like Tuchman, Keynes relies on an analysis of historical events to arrive at his thesis (Tuchman focuses on an incident during the Trojan War; Keynes examines the history of capitalism from 1580 on). As an economist, however, Keynes's purpose for exploring the past is different from Tuchman's. Identify the introduction to Keynes's argument and how the question he promises to explore differs from Tuchman's.
2. Paragraphs 5–17 constitute Keynes's historical survey. Why does he start his essay with this analysis? What point of agreement does he wish to establish with his audience? Is it essentially "old information" for the economic historian? Why or why not?
3. In paragraph 19, Keynes outlines two classes of human needs that appear to be insatiable: the "absolute" and the "relative." How does he define these terms? Why does he make this distinction in his argument?
4. The remainder of Keynes's argument turns to examine what the past implies for how our economic conditions will change in the future. Utilizing the terms you defined for question 3, formulate a potential "because" clause representing this section of Keynes's argument.
5. Keynes's final thesis is optimistic, attempting to resolve our doubts about the economic future for our grandchildren by saying they will have the unique opportunity to cultivate an "art of life" independent of economic concerns. What does this mean?
6. What is the final answer Keynes's arrives at for the question you identified in his introduction? Although his final paragraphs appear to pose a policy we need to follow for the future, be careful to phrase Keynes's answer as a statement of consequence (e.g., instead of saying what you think Keynes says "should" be done, say what you think Keynes's analysis of economic history "will lead to" in the future). Using the "because" clause you arrived at in question 4, formulate an enthymeme for Keynes's argument and tailor your sentence outline to make it logical.

POSSIBLE ISSUES FOR WRITING

As you discuss the following possible issues with your classmates, as before, try to keep a record in your notebook of the kinds of information your classmates use to justify their responses.

1. At the end of his essay, Keynes cautions us to beware: "Avarice and usury and precaution must be our gods for a little longer still." Do you believe they have been our gods? Are we motivated primarily by economic concerns? Would Tuchman agree?

2. Keynes claims that "if the economic problem is solved, mankind will be deprived of its traditional purpose." Do you think that we are already no longer working for mere sustenance but for "the love of money as a possession?" Is this "pseudo-moral principle" (as Keynes defines it) necessarily bad in your opinion?

3. Keynes's last five paragraphs imply what we need to do *now* to ensure "economic bliss" in the future. What type of economic policies does this section endorse? Do you believe you should be "economically purposive for others after it has ceased to be reasonable" for yourself? Do you feel you are already doing so? Explain your answer.

4. At the end of his essay, Keynes asks us to encourage and experiment in "the arts of life as well as the activities of purpose." How would you suggest we do this? Are your suggestions the concerns of an economist? If not, what field of knowledge have you used to arrive at them?

5. Although both Tuchman and Keynes argue about a question of consequence, the conclusions they draw about how we tend to behave differ. Which view of human behavior is preferable to you—the historian's or the economist's? How do Tuchman's and Keynes's perspectives differ from those of the psychologists discussed in Chapter 8? Can they all be right? Why or why not?

What Economics Can Do for You

Leonard Silk (1918–

As a practical economist, Leonard Silk has contributed greatly to the general public's understanding of economics. His work reflects a remarkable ability to communicate abstract economic theory to a general audience. After receiving his Ph.D. from Duke University, Silk taught at numerous colleges and universities as well as distinguished himself as a visiting lecturer at others. He has also held several appointments as an economic advisor for the government. His ability to communicate, though, is best represented by his experience as a journalist. He was an editor for Business Week *for several years and is currently a columnist for* The New York Times.

Among his several books is Economics in Plain English, *from which this essay was taken. An example of popular, expository writing (that which is written to a less informed, general audience), "What Economics Can Do For You" clearly explains what economic reasoning is. Silk's primary purpose is not to give an economic argument, but this doesn't mean that he hasn't an argument to make. As you read the essay, try to identify the kind of reasoning he uses: What kind of question is he addressing? What kind of information does he use to answer it? Is he reasoning as an economist?*

Most people react emotionally to economic issues—and to the very words in which they are expressed.

For instance, a *New York Times*-CBS public-opinion survey in the summer of 1977 discovered a strange contradiction: Most people were found to be deeply antagonistic to "welfare"—government welfare programs—but were strongly in favor of what welfare programs *do.*

The survey found that the word "welfare" raised a red flag before the public. But once the word was set aside, Americans from all walks of life showed compassion for the destitute and helpless. Of the 1,447 persons polled, 58 percent said that they disapproved of most government-sponsored welfare programs; and 54 percent agreed with the statement that "most people who receive money from welfare could get along without it if they tried."

But when they were asked a series of questions about the substance of welfare programs—questions in which the word "welfare" was omitted—people reacted very differently: 81 percent approved of the government's "providing financial assistance for children raised in low-income homes where one parent is missing." (This was a reference to what is the main component of welfare—Aid to Families with Dependent Children.) Similarly, 81 percent endorsed the government's "helping poor people buy food for their families at cheaper prices" (the essence of the food stamp program). And 82 percent said that they approved of using taxes to "pay for health care for poor people" (a reference to Medicaid). Remarkably enough, the response was much the same among the different types of people surveyed—rich and poor, liberal and conservative, Democrats and Republicans.

There are similar contradictions and confusions in public attitudes toward many other economic issues—government spending and taxation, the national debt, foreign aid, foreign trade, unemployment, job training, inflation, price controls, rent controls, fair trade laws, Federal aid for New York City—or other cities, health and safety laws, raising taxes on oil and gas, imposing price ceilings on natural gas, energy conservation, the minimum wage and its effect on unemployment, job discrimination, equal-opportunity laws, seniority rules, Social Security benefits, compulsory retirement rules, and much more.

People have very strong feelings about such issues but are often uncertain about where their own interests, or the broader social interests, really lie.

Economics can help you reason more clearly about issues. For economics offers a special approach to reasoning about problems, an approach that has six main elements:

1. Define the problem or issue carefully—and assemble the relevant facts.
2. Identify the goals and objectives you hope to achieve.
3. List the alternative means of attaining your goals.
4. Identify the economic concepts needed to understand the problem you are working on and analyze the alternatives in terms of those concepts.
5. Choose the alternative that appears to solve the problem best—and act on it.
6. Verify whether that alternative worked.

Each of these steps in the "problem-solving approach" calls for further explanation.

1. Define the problem or issue carefully—and assemble the relevant facts.
Misconceived problems lead to faulty solutions. A classic example of this occurred during the Second World War when the United States Navy defined its problem in the North Atlantic as reducing the loss of merchant shipping to submarines. With the help of operations research, the Navy discovered that the German kill rate was inversely proportional to the size of convoys—the bigger the convoy, the lower the losses relative to the number of ships in a convoy. Hence, convoys were made bigger and bigger—and took longer and longer to assemble.

This *did* reduce shipping losses. But the main problem was how to win the war by moving matériel and manpower in the largest possible numbers, as fast as possible, to the battlefronts in Europe. While the huge convoys saved shipping, they probably lengthened the war—and may have cost more lives as a result.

In our business and personal lives, it's essential to define our problems correctly. The top management of a supermarket chain was worried about profits and launched a cost-cutting drive. Interest came to focus on cutting the costs of bagging customers' orders. The decision was made to reduce the thickness of the paper and to provide different-sized bags to go with larger or smaller orders.

As a result, the supermarket chain's profits dropped further. Why? Customers were going to other stores where they still could count on getting bigger and stronger bags—which they could use for their trash and garbage. The chain's real problem was not the cost of its bags but the quality of its goods and the pull of its advertising.

Be careful that you don't try to solve the wrong problem.

2. *Identity the goals and objectives you hope to achieve.*

You alone know what you really want—and can determine your priorities or trade-offs among your different objectives. In his book *Working,* the great interviewer Studs Terkel has some marvelous examples of how people define their different goals. For instance, jazz musician Bud Freeman told Terkel:

> I get up about noon. I would only consider myself outside the norm because of the way other people live. . . . I wouldn't work for anybody. I'm working for me. Oddly enough, jazz is a music that came out of the black man's oppression, yet it allows for great freedom of expression, perhaps more than any other art form. The jazz man is expressing freedom in every note he plays. We can only please the audience doing what *we* do. We have to please ourselves first.

> I know a good musician who worked for Lawrence Welk. The man must be terribly in need of money. It's regimented music. It doesn't swing. It doesn't create, it doesn't tell the story of life. It's just the kind of music that people who don't care for music would buy.

> I've had people say to me: "You don't do this for a living, for Heaven's sake?" I was so shocked. I said, "What other way am I going to make a living? You want to send me a check?" [Laughs.] People can't understand that there are artists in the world as well as drones.

Economics can't tell you to be like Bud Freeman. And it can't tell you to be like Lawrence Welk—or the "good musician" who played for Lawrence Welk. It can't tell you to give, or not give, the highest priority to making money or anything else. Admittedly, some critics of conventional economics do believe that it is biased toward materialistic objectives, but this is not an incorrigible fault. Strictly speaking, economics is not a system for prescribing goals for individuals or societies but a way of clarifying goals, discovering any conflicts among them, searching out means of reconciling or compromising different objectives, and of helping people to choose among the alternative routes toward achieving them.

Whatever your goals, you should at least be able to understand them without illusions—such as the "money illusion" that clouded the thinking of the officers of the New York Newspaper Guild in June 1976, when they issued the following bulletin:

> Good news for all Guild members! The official May cost of living figures released last week added to that of the previous eleven months are reported to total six and one-half percent. According to the terms of our new

agreement, Guild employees are to receive a percentage equal to that amount above six percent. Therefore, a raise is due each Guild member based upon one half of one percent of your group top minimum.

Thus, the good news was that money income was going up half of one percent because real income had dropped over six percent.

Money illusion may involve more than a confusion between money income and real income. It may also involve confusing money income with what might be called "psychic income"—the psychological rewards of work and creativity, the knowledge that a job has been worth doing, the respect of the public, and perhaps most important, self-respect.

Yet I must recognize that this may be a subjective view of my own, which others would not accept or even respect. When the muckraking newspaperman Lincoln Steffens exposed how, and by whom, the corporation laws of New Jersey had been written to enable trusts to be formed, and wealth and power to be accumulated, he felt like a hero—but wondered why the lawyer James B. Dill, who had written the laws, had helped Steffens expose them. "Why, Dr. Innocent," Dill told him, "I was advertising my wares and the business of my state. When you and the other reporters and critics wrote as charges against us what financiers could and did actually do in Jersey, when you listed, with examples, what the trust-makers were doing under our laws, you were advertising our business—free.... While I gave you the facts to roast us with, what you wrote as 'bad' struck businessmen all over the United States as good, and they poured in upon us to our profit to do business with us to their profit."

What are your goals in life? Whatever they are, you should have the courage and intelligence to see them as clearly as Dill—or Lincoln Steffens.

3. *List the alternative means of attaining your goals.*

What are the constraints on your freedom of action? What resources do you have that will assist or limit your alternative routes? How much money do you have—or how much can you borrow? Who can help you, and how? What sacrifice will different solutions involve on your part? What risks are involved if you take one course or another? What will be the cost if you fail? What will be the payoff if you succeed?

Each alternative solution must be weighed and evaluated in the light of such questions—bringing to bear upon them as many relevant facts as you can muster.

4. *Identify the economic concepts needed to understand the problem you are working on, and analyze the alternatives in terms of those concepts.*

This is the critical test of how much economics you have learned. Economics is about *systems,* the interrelatedness of economic events. Awareness of the concept of *interdependence* should therefore always cause you to ask, "If I do this, what will X do? And if X does that, what will Y do?"

Walter Salant of the Brookings Institution gives an example of how as an economist he tends to think automatically about *interdependence,* even where the problem is not obviously an economic one. One morning Salant read that the police in Washington, D.C., had captured a large store of heroin. "The question that occurred to me," said Salant, "was whether the capture of a large amount of heroin might not raise the rate of robbery in Washington soon thereafter. I had in mind that if it really reduced the quantity of heroin available in the city, it would raise the price, perhaps considerably. This rise in prices would increase the pressure on users to get money; they would need more money, obviously, to buy the same quantity of heroin as they had been buying before. This might very well cause an increase in the rate of robbery, insofar as that is one of the means that addicts use to finance their purchase of drugs." So the news of the seizure of a hoard of heroin made the economist Salant worry. Driving the price of heroin up might increase the "supply" of crime. What means might drive the price of heroin down? How about a methadone program? How about providing more heroin to addicts under a supervised medical program aimed at rehabilitation? What other means could be tried?

Whatever the problem you are working on, if you have begun to reason like an economist, you ought to be asking yourself: "What will happen then— and then—and then?" Solutions need to fit a whole interdependent system— not just one stage in a process.

Consider another economic concept—*marginalism.* The term sounds tricky, and indeed it is for most people, but it can simply be defined as "What's done is done," or "Let bygones be bygones." Suppose, for instance, that you are moving from a large house into a small apartment, and have to get rid of some of your furniture. You have a dining-room set that cost you $1,500 but have no room for it in the new apartment. How much should you sell it for? What if you are offered only $500? Should you take the "loss" of several hundred dollars—in relation to what you think it is really worth?

Probably the answer is "Sell it for whatever you can get—no matter what you paid for it." The original cost of the dining-room furniture is sunk. Why hold onto it, putting more money into storing it in a warehouse—unless you want to gamble on selling it at a higher price later. You've experienced the pleasure—the "psychic income"—of using it; now get some extra cash.

The same marginal concept applies to an airline (such as Southwest Airlines, as we saw) which is considering whether to run some extra flights to pick up additional revenue, even if the extra flights don't cover the fully allocated costs of equipment, computers, buildings, etc. Again, certain costs are already *sunk*—whether you run the extra flights or not, you can't get these costs back.

As long as the extra flights will return more than their out-of-pocket costs (such as additional gasoline, personnel costs, and landing fees) you will be better off—that is, have higher net earnings—than if you did not run the extra flights.

The marginal-cost, marginal-revenue principles should guide any business to the point where the *excess* of its total revenues over total costs (net profit) is greatest. It doesn't matter whether the problem is that of an airline, publishing house, individual lecturer, hot dog stand, railroad, movie house, or any other business activity, as the following simple example shows.

Here is how a typical business decision, involving the marginal concept, might be set up:

Problem: Shall we undertake Activity X?[1]

The Facts: Fully allocated costs of Activity X $4,500 of which—

Fixed or overhead costs are 2,500
Out-of-pocket or marginal costs are 2,000
Activity X should gross 3,100

Decision: Undertake Activity X. *It will add $1,100 to net profit.* The reason: X will add $3,100 to revenues and add only $2,000 to costs. (The fixed or overhead costs will be incurred whether X is done or not. Hence, fully allocated or average costs of $4,500 are *not* relevant to this business decision.) It is the out-of-pocket or marginal costs that count.

Many business decisions are mistakenly governed by the concept of fully allocated or average costs, instead of marginal costs, with a resulting loss in potential profits.

The right concept for dealing with a problem does not always come ready-made off the economist's shelf. Often one must struggle to fashion the concept that clarifies and solves a problem.

In 1959 I wrote a book called *The Research Revolution.* As it applied to individual companies, the book's main concept was:

The principle and practice of making regular provision for the discovery and development of new ideas, new things, is taking increasing hold in American business. . . . More and more companies have come to regard expenditures for *research* not as a luxury but as a necessity to meet both domestic and foreign competition; many executives have come to refer to research as the lifeblood of successful business operation. . . . That a company has a strong and productive research program has come to be one sure way of judging management's competence and the company's growth prospects.

I then named a group of companies that embodied the research concept and therefore promised stronger than average growth in sales and profits; the list included Haloid Xerox (later Xerox), Eastman Kodak, Polaroid, General Electric, General Telephone & Electronics, IBM, Minnesota Mining, RCA, National Cash Register, Schering, Pfizer, Texas Instruments, Thomas Ramo Wooldridge, Corning Glass, and several others that subsequently proved that the right concept pays off—big.

5. *Choose the alternative that appears to solve the problem best—and act on it.*

[1]Activity X could be a decision whether to run an extra airline flight, publish a new edition of a book, add a speaking engagement on a lecture tour, sell hot dogs at a cheaper price after the seventh inning at a baseball game, offer half-price railroad or movie tickets for wives and children, or any other "marginal" activity.

Of course, there's a good deal of hunch and "feel" about any important decision. But though hunch, feel, instinct, hope, fear, coolness, or other emotions inevitably play their parts in business and personal decisions, one ought to try to reach decisions on the best course to take by a process of reasoning that is systematic, thorough, and objective. That is what I have been trying to lay out here.

Finally, however, one must make up one's mind—and act on it decisively. Not to act is also a decision, and frequently the wrong one.

6. *Verify whether that alternative worked.*

If the plan didn't work, why not? Exactly what went wrong? There are crucial lessons to be learned for next time. Mistakes are part of the learning process—if you can survive them.

And if it *did* work out, the results should be carefully examined, too. You may have succeeded because of your original plan or in spite of it—and for unforeseen reasons. In Sir Francis Bacon's formulation of scientific method, verification is as important as observation, measurement, and explanation. Verification of a forecast or decision is the empirical test on which economic logic stands or falls.

Getting you into the habit of using the problem-solving approach is the main thing economics can do for you. The approach can be applied in any field and to virtually any kind of problem or issue. It's an approach that is liberating, not constricting; it invites you—forces you—to think outside the familiar frame of the problem. It prevents you from thinking off the top of your head and reacting compulsively and routinely. Making you weigh alternative solutions is what economics is all about.

QUESTIONS FOR A CRITICAL REREADING

Construct an informal sentence outline based on your first reading of Silk's essay, focusing on the information he gives you. Then, as you reread his essay, use these questions to discover his underlying argument.

1. Silk's essay introduces a very real problem that he hopes can be resolved by his discussion of economic reasoning. What is this problem as it is set out in the first six paragraphs? Formulate the question at issue in his essay.
2. Silk claims that "economics is not a system for prescribing goals for individuals or societies but a way of clarifying goals, discovering any conflicts among them, searching out means of reconciling or compromising different objectives, and of helping people to choose among the alternative routes toward achieving them" (paragraph 14). Why do you think he feels he needs to assert this? What is he assuming his audience already thinks?
3. What does Silk mean by "money illusion" and "psychic income"? Why does he think it is important for us to be aware of them?
4. Near the end of his essay, Silk cautions that although "hunch, feel, instinct, hope, fear, coolness, or other emotions inevitably play their parts in business and personal decisions, one ought to try to reach decisions on the best course to take by

a process of reasoning that is systematic, thorough, and objective." How does this conclusion answer the question Silk set out in his introduction?

5. Note that the majority of Silk's essay discusses the six steps of his "problem-solving approach." However, as with all arguments, the center of his essay supports a primary reason why his conclusion is true. Referring to your sentence outline, analyze the development of his ideas as he explains each of these steps in turn (paying particular attention to the primary terms discussed in question 3 above). Summarizing this section as a "because" clause, formulate an enthymeme for Silk's argument. (Don't forget to tailor your sentence outline to reflect this logic.)

POSSIBLE ISSUES FOR WRITING

Discuss the following possible issues behind Silk's argument. As before, record in your notebook what types of arguments and information your classmates use to justify their position. This is your last chance to identify the audience for your next essay.

1. Both Keynes and Silk address whether government-supported welfare programs represent sound economic policy. What are their positions? How do they differ? Based on your knowledge of the current welfare program in the United States, do you agree with Keynes and/or Silk? Why or why not? Is your reason based on economic factors or something else?

2. Refer to your notes from the discussion of question 5 under "Possible Issues for Writing" that follows Keynes's essay. What attitude does Silk have towards human behavior? Does it resemble Keynes's? Of the three essays you have read in this chapter, whose attitude do you prefer and why? Does your preference affect your response to these essays?

3. Silk's essay argues that we should approach a problem as objectively as we can. Do you think this is good advice? Is it better advice for the economist than the historian? Of the fields you have studied thus far in this book (or others that you are familiar with), are there any that you feel do not follow this advice? Should they? Why or why not?

WRITING YOUR ESSAY

Now is the time to write your response to the conversation you have been having with your classmates about Tuchman, Keynes, and Silk. Review your reading notebook to identify the issue you most care about. Formulate your answer as an enthymemic thesis statement. Use these three questions to test this thesis before drafting your argument:

1. What kind of question are you addressing—a historian's or an economist's? (Make certain it contains a verb of consequence.)

2. What kind of information does your "because" clause require you to give: historical? theoretical? practical?

3. What assumption are you making about what your audience already believes: is it established old information in the field?

If you are having difficulty identifying whether your thesis requires the reasoning of an historian or economist, refer to the next section for help.

RECOGNIZING YOUR REAL ISSUE

Recognizing the real issue you want to address in your essay can help you decide if your task is to reason primarily as an economist or a historian. After reading and discussing these essays, you probably have a sense of the issue you want to address. Your reading notebook entries can help you identify it even more precisely. Remember you need to identify the stance of your audience: someone in class who expressed an opinion that you feel could benefit from your perspective on the issue. Once you identify your reader's stance and the real question it addresses, you can analyze the assumptions behind his or her reasoning, which would require you to reason in a certain way. The best way to do this is to formulate an enthymeme that represents what you perceive your classmate's argument to be. If you need help, study the following conversation two students had based on Keynes's essay and notice how identifying the logical theses behind their comments can locate the real question at issue:

Dinah: I don't agree with Keynes. Although making a lot of money is important to me, and that is why I want a college degree—to get a higher-paying job—it is not the money that is important, but how well I feel about myself. It's just that people will respect me more—and I will have more self-respect—if I am doing something that society values.

Joe: But doesn't Keynes allow for that? Isn't that what he refers to as a relative need that we will probably never be able to satisfy? I see him saying that we will have to find other outlets for what you seem to be calling social respect. That once our absolute needs—the need we all have to make money for our food and shelter—are satisfied, that we won't have to work as much as we do. I agree with him that when we no longer have work at the center of our lives that we will have to develop some other area from which we can gain a sense of pleasure—self-esteem.

Dinah: But that's just it. How can we get pleasure from something unless we see that society values what we are doing? It seems the only way to express value for something is by placing a price tag on it. If we no longer "worship money," as he seems to imply we do, then we will no longer have a way to worship individual accomplishments.

Joe: Then aren't you really saying we should worship money? You seem to be saying we haven't accomplished anything if we haven't gotten paid for what we've done. But, even today, can we put a price tag on everything? I like to feel I have accomplished something even if I don't have money to show for it. I hate to think I am less valuable as a person—or that my life isn't as good as yours—if I drive an older car than you do. Aren't there other, maybe even more important, things that we can do than make money?

Dinah: I don't think I'm saying that what you have makes you a better person. Just how you get it. For example, I don't admire someone who uses a welfare check to buy a fancy car—they haven't *earned* my admiration. But even people who are totally selfless, like Mother Theresa, get a monetary reward, like the Nobel Prize. I guess what I am saying is I just don't see any quality in a life where everyone pursues pleasure at the expense of self-esteem. How can I enjoy myself if I feel I am only as good as everyone else? This sounds like the sixties era to me, where everyone dropped out of society to indulge themselves, and where did that get them?

Joe: That's just the point!

Obviously, Dinah and Joe have reached an impasse in their discussion. The problem they need to solve is why they cannot agree. Although Keynes's argument implies that at some point money would no longer be at the heart of our concerns, Dinah argues that that can never happen, that we are so protective of our individuality and self-esteem that we will always need money as a way to value individuals. Joe, on the other hand, believes Dinah's position does not refute but actually reinforces what Keynes is talking about, but he doesn't quite know how to communicate this to her. Joe needs to identify the reasoning she is using to substantiate her argument. After reviewing his notes from the discussion, here is the enthymeme he formulated for her position:

Dinah's Thesis

We will never be able to live without money at the center of our lives because money is the only means by which we can evaluate individual worth.

(*Assumption:* We will always need a means of evaluating the worth in individuals.)

Once Joe has articulated the logic of Dinah's argument, he can identify just where he differs. The question at issue behind her argument is whether we can live without money. His last comment about the sixties indicates that he believes one can—and should. However, he is not quite sure why he believes this until he examines the primary reason she uses to support her assertion: that money is the only means we have to evaluate individual worth.

Returning once again to his notes, Joe realizes much of his frustration arose from Dinah's comment about the sixties: "This sounds like the sixties era to me, where everyone dropped out of society to indulge themselves, and where did that get them?" Unlike Dinah, Joe saw the sixties as a time of political action, where the youth did not "drop out to indulge themselves" but to express dissatisfaction with a government that oppressed others. He saw their action as a political act, an expression of dissatisfaction with the war in Vietnam and the discrimination against blacks in the south. Exploring his frustration at what he saw as her flippant comment about the sixties, Joe realizes that he needs to narrow the issue further to clarify his reaction:

Joe's Thesis

The sixties have demonstrated that money is not the only means by which we can evaluate individual worth because they revealed how individuals could find a more fulfilling sense of purposiveness when they deny monetary reward for a common cause.

His assumption that individual worth depends on a fulfilling sense of purposiveness is not entirely different from Dinah's; however, the way he reasons from that assumption to a conclusion is. In writing his essay, Joe will probably discover that he will need to reason as an economist: he will need to define the term "purposiveness" through a historical example where a common cause provided psychic income independent of monetary gain.

Whether you agree with Dinah or with Joe is not important. What *is* important is to note how Joe has learned to argue with Dinah *on her own terms.* The conversation they will have through their written arguments will be based on the economic reasoning Keynes used to initiate the discussion on how systems of valuation affect human behavior. However, if Joe had not isolated the point at which they agree—by analyzing the common issue and assumption behind their arguments—Joe would have had a more difficult time trying to communicate his perspective to his reader.

REVISING TO ADDRESS DIFFERENT AUDIENCES

Let's consider what might happen to Joe's argument if he were attempting to revise his essay to address a historian. Note that his thesis implies that he will analyze history in order to prove the validity of Keynes's economic predictions. However, the primary issue for a historian would not be how individuals are guided by economic concerns, but the more general question of what lessons historical events like the sixties hold for the present: What precipitated the social revolution of the sixties, how influential was it, and what does it teach us about human nature?

To address this audience, Joe might respond to another aspect of Dinah's argument: her comment that implied the sixties were years of self-indulgent unproductivity, whose participants eventually lost a valuable opportunity to make something of their lives. When Dinah assumed Joe agreed the participants of the sixties' protest movements were unproductive (". . . and where did that get them?"), he challenged her assumption with another ("That's just the point!"). Recognizing that Dinah's assumption is the issue behind their conversation, Joe might formulate a possible thesis for the type of historical reasoning Dinah might use to justify her own stance:

> The participants in the sixties protest movements failed to achieve their goals because their attempts to overthrow the capitalist establishment were merely an excuse to avoid growing up, to indulge themselves without accepting responsibility for their actions.

By anticipating the type of argument Dinah might use to justify her comment about the sixties, Joe can clearly identify the type of historical analysis he would have to use to counter her position. Recognizing that the sixties was a complex period in history, he would identify the real issue behind this particular disagreement as not just whether the participants of the sixties really did fail to achieve their goals but exactly what their goals were.

To develop a response to Dinah's argument, Joe might agree with her assumption that self-indulgence is unproductive but attempt to prove that that was not what motivated many individuals who protested during the sixties. His counter-thesis would attempt to analyze what motivated the participants and, thus, whether that motivation actually implies they failed in their attempts. A possible counterargument might be:

> The protesters in the sixties did not fail to achieve their goals because they awakened the country's consciousness to how capitalistic governments need to balance ethical, social, and economic concerns.

Joe's historical analysis would lead Dinah to consider more carefully the effects of the era on human behavior, although, unlike the economic arguments, the effects would be gauged by more than their economic value. For this reason, if he wrote on this thesis rather than the other suggested above, he would be revising his stance to address a different audience: one concerned with a historian's mode of inquiry rather than an economist's.

This discussion of different ways to analyze the rhetorical situation of a class discussion demonstrates that, even though two fields may use the same type of argument (in the case of history and economics, an argument of consequence), the way the issue is phrased and the types of assumptions that control the reasoning process help distinguish between the ways disciplines reason about different subjects.

The next chapter discusses conversations founded on questions of value. Although we always imply that a situation is "good" or "bad," you will discover that when we attempt to argue purely to change such values and attitudes, the emotional dimensions of your argument will tend to dominate the logical. When you examine this area of reasoning overtly, you can begin to understand more clearly the rhetorical dimension of all academic discourse: how the language you use implies a particular stance and ultimately can direct your (and your reader's) reasoning process.

Unit Six

CHAPTER ELEVEN

Communicating Abstract Ideas Clearly

*M*ost conversations you have, whether in your personal or academic life, deal with abstract rather than concrete knowledge. Concrete knowledge comes from first-hand experience with the world, whereas abstract knowledge is that which you acquire indirectly. For example, when you go to the beach with your friends and you are the only one who gets a sunburn, you acquire concrete evidence that you sunburn easily. However, if your parents told you they both tend to sunburn easily, or if you have fair skin and read that fair-skinned individuals are more susceptible to the sun's rays, then you could conclude, in the abstract, that you probably would sunburn easily. Abstract knowledge is that which you acquire indirectly, usually through reading and discussion with others. Most of the academic conversations you have are based on this kind of indirect, abstract reasoning rather than concrete proof.

You work with abstract ideas when you make judgments about the *probable* truth of an argument. If learning were just a matter of memorizing facts, then many fields of study would not even exist. Most of what we know is merely educated conjecture because we make decisions based on interpretations of evidence. Our knowledge that the world was flat came from conjecture based on observation (the world *looks* flat) and discussion (rumors that lost ships had fallen off the edge of the world). It was established knowledge that the world was flat until we discovered how a round world could look flat to the naked eye and heard the stories of sailors who navigated safely to and from distant lands. Today we are still hearing new ideas about just how large—or round—the earth really is, but, as before, these conjectures will become established knowledge only if they prove to an educated majority to be more probably true than the other possible interpretations of the evidence that we already believe.

DEDUCTION AND ABSTRACT REASONING

The development of knowledge about things we cannot observe—answers to questions about who we are, how we should govern, and what happened in the past and might happen in the future—depend on our building upon what we already know, a method we have already defined as deduction. Every time we reason, we base our reasoning on established knowledge, information that is assumed to be probably true. Although this may appear an imprecise method of developing knowledge, this is the only way we have to reason about abstract issues.

The English philosopher, Sir Francis Bacon (1561–1626) described deductive reasoning as spinning a faulty "cobweb of logic." He warned his contemporaries to rely solely on inductive reasoning, to base their conclusions only on empirical (i.e., observable) evidence. However, even Bacon recognized that pure inductive reasoning is impossible: Our past experiences, feelings, and personal preferences always affect how we interpret what we observe. For example, even natural scientists, who rely on their observation of geologic fossils to reason inductively about the origin of human beings, come to different conclusions about what the evidence means. When the fossil evidence they have is incomplete, scientists must establish theories to fill in the gaps, to explain what would *probably* be there if they had the evidence. The multiple theories of creation they have proposed are based on different assumptions, prior beliefs that influence how they organize the evidence into scientific theories. (Note that this is the issue Gould's essay addresses in Chapter 6.)

The more we cannot rely on concrete evidence to draw our conclusions, the more our prior knowledge and beliefs shape our reasoning process, forcing us to weave an abstract cobeweb of deductive reasoning to arrive at conclusions. Comparing deductive reasoning to a cobweb is particularly apt when you consider that the language we use to think and communicate is also abstract. In some disciplines the language can be quite precise because it defines what we can see and touch. It is difficult for an educated person to misinterpret what "fossil," "amoeba," or "lava" mean. In other subjects, though, the available language is less precise, representing interpretations rather than definition; for example, "revolution," "protest movement," or "minor demonstrations" could all refer to the same event in history but change how we perceive it. The more we address ideas rather than objects, the more interpretive our language.

EXERCISE

Analyze the following words or phrases and discuss whether they represent precise definitions or more abstract interpretations. If you see any that could do either, explain why.

1. cold apple
2. head of government
3. weed
4. DNA
5. income
6. man/woman
7. husband/wife
8. market

DENOTATION AND CONNOTATION

You have probably discovered that some of the words and phrases in the exercise above could be identified as either definitions or interpretations depending on the context in which they are used. Since all words are to some extent interpretive and abstract, to control the meaning of the language you use as you write, you need to consider the two primary ways words transmit meaning: denotation and connotation.

Denotation

On the most fundamental level, words attempt to define an object or an idea. We can talk about these things because we have names for them; for example, we can talk about the thing at which we sit to eat our meals because we have the word "table." Because we agree on the definition of "table," we can say that name clearly *denotes* the object. This direct correlation between a name and the thing it represents is the denotation of the word. (Dictionary definitions are denotative.)

This direct correlation between the word and the thing it represents is how we can talk about a table even if it is not presently before us. The name allows us to discuss the object in the abstract. However, even very concrete words like "table" can be slippery. There is always a slight disjunction between the object and the word we use to describe it. For example, we might describe the same scene as either "the boy sat at the table all night" or "the boy sat at his desk all night." Which sentence we choose depends purely on how we *interpret* that scene. Although denotatively, there are times when we can clearly distinguish between the definition of the words "table" and "desk," there are times when the object is not defined so clearly by the words we have available to describe it. Some objects have been designed to serve the function of both a table and desk; some students find it convenient to purchase a table to serve as their desk. When we name an object a "table" we automatically interpret that object as serving a specific function. If we should decide to call it a "desk" instead, we are slightly changing our interpretation of that object's function. Deciding which word most accurately denotes the object, then, depends not just on what it looks like but on how we interpret its function.

When we are confronted with the inadequacy of language, we need to consider how to manipulate the words we have so we can reflect reality as clearly as possible. In the example above, the decision whether to interpret the object as a table or a desk depends on the situation that affects our perception of it. If we perceive a student studying diligently at a table all evening, are we accurately reflecting what has occurred if we say "he sat at the table all night"? Even though we may know how this describes what we saw, we need to consider how we are using language to describe this scene to someone who was not there. How might a mother, particularly one who worries that her son has not been eating well since going to college, interpret that statement? Or, for that matter, a mother who worries her son is spending too much time eating and too little time studying? To prevent her from misinterpreting the situation, we need to consider the connotation of the words we choose.

Connotation

The *connotations* of words are the associations we make between the word and certain activities, experiences, and emotions. No matter how carefully you choose a word for its denotation, you need to be aware of the connotations it might arouse in your reader. Often, the confusion arises from the context the word is used in. A good example is this sentence, written by one student to begin his placement exam: "Unlike students, civilians get lots of exercise mowing their lawns or doing their housework." The words "students" and "civilians" are denotatively correct, but note how they both change meaning in this context. Are students *not* civilians? The contrast could imply to a reader that students are like military personnel or prisoners of war. It could also imply that civilians are never students. The student appears to be assuming that students and civilians live in completely separate worlds.

Although the words "students" and "civilians" appear quite concrete, the connotations that surround them in this context alter their meaning. Other kinds of connotations—what the reader already thinks and feels about "students" or "civilians"—will also affect the meaning of the passage. When I explained to the writer how new students might interpret this passage to mean they are exempt from the responsibilities of civilian life, he responded, "but that's not what I meant!" However, the reader can only interpret what is on the page. What the writer intended to say, what the words imply, and what the reader interprets from them have an effect on the "meaning" of the passage. This writer learned that, to communicate his ideas effectively, he had to be more cautious of the connotations that surrounded the words he chose.

Connotations affect how we interpret not only single words but sentences, paragraphs, and entire works. The connotations that surround the denotative meaning of a word are not easily identified; however, there are three ways you can analyze your writing to help control them. One way is to anticipate how your words inspire certain associations in your audience. Another is to analyze how the other language you have used—the context the word is used in—would prepare your reader to interpret it in a certain way. However, one of the best ways to identify how the connotations of your words affect their meaning is to recognize how your word choice manipulates your *own* thinking. Just as the associations you inspire in your audience affect their interpretation of your writing, the associations your initial sentences inspire in *you* as you write shape your interpretation and reasoning process.

EXERCISE

Read the following sentences and analyze both the denotative meaning and the possible connotations the primary words could arouse. Then choose one of these sentences and, using it as your first sentence, develop the idea into a complete paragraph. When you are finished, begin another paragraph with the same sentence, this time exploring a completely different interpretation. When you are finished, share your paragraphs with others in your class to see if your readers understand what you meant.

1. Black and white and red all over: that's America.
2. When you go out into the streets, you see nothing but derelicts and madmen.
3. He was a student who sought the rich but empty life.

EXAMPLES AND HIDDEN ASSUMPTIONS

Both the denotation and connotation of the words you use can affect what you say as you write: They control how you interpret the subject as well as affect how your readers interpret your writing. Simple choices about whether to refer to a woman as "a working mother" or "a female professional" affect your reader's and your own attitude toward what else you will say about her. The word choice implies a particular evaluation of the person being discussed, an interpretation about where her primary interests lie. In essence, the word choice becomes a decision of how you represent an individual as an example of a particular *idea:* Do you want to emphasize her status as a mother or as a professional? If the latter, then referring to someone as a "working mother" might mislead your reader, because the connotations of "mother" are of one who is nurturing and selfless, loving and forgiving—traits that are not particularly valued in professionals who should be independent, dedicated, and sometimes even ruthless.

Each word you choose is an example. It classifies what you are discussing, comparing a specific object or idea to others that could be represented by the same word. Viewing your words as abstract interpretations of what you are discussing helps you become more conscious of how your word choice reflects and shapes your reasoning process. Just as you use particular examples to illustrate a point you wish to make, you use words as examples of a particular way of looking at the subject you are discussing.

We are not always aware of our own assumptions when we choose certain words to express our ideas. If we choose the phrase "the sixties' revolution" to represent what happened in the 1960s, we assume that our subject belongs to a class of events that succeeded in bringing significant change. On the other hand, if we describe it as "the sixties' protest movement," we interpret it as a rebellion that was not necessarily successful. Even when we think we are describing something precisely and objectively, we are actually arguing for a particular way to interpret the subject.

Words can undermine attempts at careful reasoning. Sometimes the assumptions behind the words we use are not as apparent to us as they should be. For example, if we attempted to respond to Tuchman's essay (in Chapter 10) by describing her subject as "the Trojan horse myth," we could be implying to a reader that what she has to say has little to do with historical reality. As a writer sensitive to the connotations of her language, Tuchman steers her readers away from this misinterpretation, discussing early in her essay how the word "myth" might lead us to faulty assumptions about the worth of her conclusions. If you review Tuchman's essay, you can see how she helps us recognize that the conventional connotations surrounding the word "myth," and the assumptions we might make about myths, can cause us to ignore the element of truth behind them.

Tuchman's discussion of the different versions of the Trojan myth shows how we, even in the distant past, have resorted to telling fictional stories in order to communicate abstract truths. These stories "paint pictures" of our ideas when we investigate an abstract question such as "why did the Trojans act as they did?" Because these early writers did not have the words we now have to describe complex psychological motivations, they resorted to concrete examples (such as the gods and the serpents) to represent abstract forces that precipitated the Trojans' actions: Homer implies these actions were "fated," whereas Tuchman reinterprets them with the modern term "human folly."

E X E R C I S E

Read the following paragraph critically, paying particular attention to how the connotations of the italicized words could mislead a reader. When you have finished, revise any of the italicized words that you feel are inappropriate, replacing them with ones that more clearly fit the passage. When you are finished, see if your revision has changed the meaning of the passage by exchanging it with a classmate's.

Communism has lost its political *muster*. During the Cold War, Eastern Europe was communism's *ambassador* in world politics. Now Russia, the *protective* mother country, has become a *frail*, *old girl* who has lost *command* of her *revolutionary*, *ungrateful* children. Romania and Czechoslovakia *hinted at* the first *quibbles* against communism's *grasp* on power; now Russia's new multiparty system *solidifies* the *complaints*. The *old girl's plague* is democracy's *joy*: The Cold War has *chilled out*.

METAPHORS, ANALOGIES, AND ALLEGORIES

In the preceding exercise, the author has used a picture (Russia as a mother figure) to convey his interpretations of the changes in Eastern European politics. Sometimes you also will need to paint pictures to discuss your ideas more fully, for example, even though we have words to describe feelings—words such as "love," "hate," "despair"—the definitions of these words seldom capture exactly what you will want to say. Abstract words like these name ideas, attitudes, or feelings that your readers can comprehend only when they associate your words with experiences they have had. (Have you ever attempted to describe being in love to someone who has never experienced it?)

Abstract words require you to control the many different connotations they can have for your readers. One way to do this is to illustrate your ideas by comparing them to something that can be described with more concrete words. Metaphors, analogies, and allegories are three ways you can use language to paint pictures of your ideas to make them more comprehensible to your reader.

Metaphor

When you use just a word or a phrase to create a picture of your idea, you are creating a metaphor. "She was in the flower of her youth" paints a picture of a girl that is not only young but fresh, untouched, and full of promise (assuming we associate flowers with the potential to later bear fruit). The metaphor conveys not only what the author sees (a young girl) but what he feels as well. Although he might have described her attributes as I have done, the description could only define what he felt, whereas the metaphor allows us to experience and understand it.

You will want to create metaphors when the denotation of a word is insufficient to capture all of the emotional associations you want to convey. In comparing deductive reasoning to "a cobweb of logic," Bacon impressed upon his readers the strong feelings he felt about it: the cobweb connotes something that is "flimsy, transparent, sticky, full-of-holes, hard to escape from." All of these qualities suggest that Bacon believed deductive reasoning only led us to unreliable conclusions from which we could not free ourselves.

Because of their ability to convey strong feelings toward the subject, you should save metaphors such as those above for the most important points you want to make. Consider the following description: "I flew to my persecution, soon to be my execution, sweating glistening drops of ignorance, my virginal book in arms, pristine as the day I sacrificed my money to win it." Can you guess this is a description of a student going to take an exam? See if you can identify how many metaphors are operating here. It is difficult to decide what is the author's *main* concern. She sounds as if every moment of her life is fraught with emotion.

When you find a metaphor overemphasizes what you want to say, a less powerful form of metaphor that you might use is the simile. Similes (note how the word is related to "similar") make comparisons that are merely suggestive rather than direct by including the words "as" or "like". Instead of saying, "The lion roared at me," you might say "Like a lion, the salesclerk roared at me." Similes are particularly helpful when you cannot guarantee that your reader will know what you are talking about. They clarify both the idea and the thing it is being compared to. Whereas a metaphor uses B to talk about A (i.e., the lion to talk about someone else), a simile talks about both, making the comparison more explicit (e.g., "the salesclerk" is like a "lion").

Language is slippery, though. No matter how carefully you attempt to control the meaning of your words, you need always be aware of the possibility of misinterpretation. As Lakoff and Johnson discussed in Chapter 2, most words we choose to represent our ideas are essentially metaphoric. They represent our thoughts by comparing them to others for which we already have names. For example, a verb like "flew" is a potential metaphor, comparing one to a bird while arousing images of freedom. Do you think that communicates well what the student above felt as he rushed to take his exam?

Analogy

Sometimes a quick glimpse at a picture is all your readers will need so they can understand what you are trying to say. At other times, you will need to lead your readers through all the points of comparison implied by your metaphor. When you extend a metaphor by elaborating on how different aspects of the picture you are painting correlate to specific ideas necessary for your argument, you are creating an analogy. Consider the following metaphor: "Life is an uneaten sandwich." A simile isn't much better: "Life is like an uneaten sandwich." This is an intriguing sentence, and we can probably play with it to guess at what the author means. To communicate effectively, though, the writer should extend the comparison into an analogy: "Life is like an uneaten sandwich because, when we are hungry enough, we will eat it, but we cannot guess how it will taste." The comparison is much clearer now, and we might expect the writer to develop the idea further with examples from his or her own experience. (Note how this would be a nice enthymemic thesis to use to structure an essay.)

E X E R C I S E

Here is a list of abstract words and phrases. Develop each of them into an enthymeme, elaborating their meaning first with a metaphor, then a simile, and finally an analogy.

1. Falling in love
2. Despair
3. Discovering the truth
4. Losing friends
5. The feeling of success

Allegory

Allegories differ from metaphors and analogies in that they communicate an idea through an extended story. Unlike the analogy, which elaborates a simple metaphor to clarify an idea that may or may not become a thesis for the work, an allegory is a longer story that both illustrates and supports the thesis.

Aesop's fables are popular allegories. While stories that present us with a simple thesis or moral, they also present us with memorable characters and actions. For example, in "The Tortoise and the Hare," we cannot understand the author's point until we compare the tortoise to the kind of person who is slow but consistent, and recognize the hare as representing one who is swift but careless and arrogant. Instead of elaborating on one comparison, an allegorical story weaves together different characters, objects, and actions, each of which can be compared to a distinct idea. The interaction of the ideas—the characters and events of the story—leads us to the thesis or moral—that victory comes to those who are humbly persistent.

As you will discover in the next chapter, sometimes you will find the allegory the most effective way to communicate a very abstract idea (for example, a concept like the ideal Good or Beauty). As with the Homeric myths that Tuchman refers to, you will find that allegories are most helpful when you find you do not have a vocabulary to capture your ideas effectively. Myths, allegories, and even literary fictions are similar analogical devices—ways to communicate abstract ideas in terms that can reinforce and strengthen a flimsy cobweb of logic. They all both employ words an audience can more readily comprehend and control the value judgments and associations abstract words inevitably arouse.

EXERCISE

Choose one of the analogies you developed for the exercise on page 270 and rewrite it as an allegorical story. When you are finished, give your allegory to a classmate and ask him or her to summarize your point in literal terms. How has your idea changed in the translation?

CHAPTER TWELVE

Reasoning About Philosophy

*W*hether you are writing about science, psychology, history, economics, or political science, you are reasoning about the world around you. Whether you are questioning natural phenomena, how humans interact as a society, or the consequences of certain behaviors or political policies, your reasoning is based in some way on direct observation, either your own or that of the authors you have read. The field of philosophy, however, asks you to step back from your day-to-day existence and think about the intangible realm of the human mind and spirit. It goes beyond the questions of "What is the earth made of?" or "How do we behave in response to our environment?" to contemplate why those questions are worth asking at all. Philosophical reasoning is an objective inquiry into the human values that give meaning to our lives—an examination into what we mean by the Good, the Bad, the Beautiful, or the Ugly.

Philosophy lurks behind every discipline. When we confront concrete evidence in science that suggests we have evolved from the apes, or psychological studies that imply we have no free will, we find we cannot easily accept those theories without considering the impact they have on how we feel about ourselves and our lives. If B. F. Skinner is right when he says that we have no free will, that everything we think and do is merely a reaction to our environment, then should we care any longer about the decisions we make? It would seem that the environment, not us, would have to accept responsibility for our actions. If Darwin's theory of "survival of the fittest" is true, then wouldn't that make the cockroach more important than we are because it has a superior ability to adapt to environmental changes and survive? These responses reflect ways we assess the value of the knowledge we have. They could lead us to pursue new psychological or scientific theories to refute those we dislike; or, as is most often the case, they could lead us to examine our misgivings philosophically, to find other reasons why our actions and lives are important.

The more you learn about what others think, no matter the subject, the more you need to evaluate the worth of what you have learned. Besides reading and listening to others' arguments critically, you need to step back and evaluate how your new knowledge affects your own philosophy of life. Each of us has a philosophy of life, even if we have not consciously examined what it might be. A philosophy of life is based on questions such as (1) "What is the source of my beliefs?" (2) "What is most important in my life?" and (3) "Why am I here?" Although philosophy attempts to confront these questions objectively, we all ask them to discover what we should value most about our lives, to understand more clearly what makes life "good" or "beautiful."

REASONING ABOUT QUESTIONS OF VALUE

Philosophical reasoning demands that we distance ourselves from our immediate and physical needs to contemplate life as an abstraction. It enables us to address those very fundamental emotional conflicts that arise when what we know through concrete observation gives us insufficient answers as to why we should go on living at all. Unlike questions of fact (e.g., the scientific exploration of the natural world), questions of consequence (e.g., historical investigations into what we have done and how it affects what we are now doing), or questions of policy (e.g., political concerns of how to maintain a just and equitable society), the questions of value that philosophy explores can only be answered through reasoning about the inner world of the human spirit and mind—that is, the abstract realm that determines what is good, useful, or beautiful.

You are probably most familiar with ethical or moral philosophy, the study of what is "good" and how one can achieve it, because it is the subject of much religious doctrine. If you read Thomas Kuhn's essay in Chapter 6, you are also familiar with a kind of pragmatic and utilitarian philosophy, the examination into what is most useful about how we learn, think, and act. A third area of philosophy, which you may have become acquainted with in an art appreciation class, is aesthetics, or the inquiry into the nature of what is beautiful and how it is communicated. No matter what area of philosophy you may be exploring, though, you will discover that to discuss values objectively, you need to distance yourself from the worldly associations words such as "good" or "beautiful" may arouse in order to discover the essential ideals these words represent.

ISSUES AND DEFINITIONS OF VALUE

We all have different standards for what we think is "good" or "beautiful." A work of art, a movie, a new punk fashion, all may seem beautiful to you but ugly to someone else. When standards of evaluation differ, we tend to avoid conflict by concluding, "Well, beauty is in the eye of the beholder." Philosophical arguments, however, cannot be settled in this manner. Instead, they attempt to establish some point of agreement about what we mean by "good" or "beautiful." For this reason, philosophical arguments are primarily extended definitions of value-laden terms.

Questions of value resemble questions of definition, with the primary difference being the presence of a value-laden term that will require extensive definition. For example, in the last reading in this chapter, Susanne K. Langer explores the question "What is Art?" If art were a concrete thing, like a tree, that we could dissect and examine scientifically, then we would be able to construct an answer based on evidence from our observations. The answer would be a definition but proven with empirical evidence. However, art is not as concrete as a tree. Instead of beginning with the object itself, Langer must begin with our varied and sometimes different definitions about what art is and how it makes us feel. Her argument necessarily must focus on identifying the different feelings and associations the word "art" arouses in all of us and carefully construct an elaborate definition that embraces those abstract feelings. Her argument is a definition, but a definition of the kind of value a work of art has that distinguishes it from other things.

Sometimes, the question at issue will not resemble a question of definition, but the presence of a value-laden term will require the writer to develop the argument around an extended definition. For example, in the first reading of this chapter, Plato explores the question, "What kind of ruler has knowledge of divine truth?" If we all agreed about what "divine truth" was, then Plato would only have to discuss how to recognize someone who possessed it. However, we probably have more definitions for "divine truth" than we have religions in the world—is it knowledge acquired from study, experience, intuition, divine inspiration, or all of these? We recognize knowledge of the divine truth as a valuable thing, but we probably don't agree as to what its true value is or where it comes from. For this reason, Plato addresses this issue by attempting to make "divine truth" more concrete, comparing it to the fire of the sun, and developing an extended allegory that defines what that fire represents.

EXERCISE

Following is a list of questions at issue that could lead to philosophical arguments. Identify the value-laden term and explain why it would require extended definition.

1. How can we achieve a happy life?
2. Is it better to know the truth or to remain ignorant?
3. Can one live without faith in a divine being?
4. Can there be beauty in misfortune?
5. How do I know I exist?

Each of the readings in this chapter is a philosophical argument containing extended definitions of value-laden terms. Each is structured around an elaborate, logical definition of an abstract concept—"divine truth," "human happiness," and "art," respectively—terms we all agree represent significant concepts in our lives, but which we each might define differently, depending on our situations and circumstances. As you read the following essays, recognize how the writers attempt to reason objectively, two by creating an alternative world that mirrors what the authors perceive as these essential truths, one by weaving a tight web of logic that carefully defines by manipulating the connotations of value-laden words.

The Allegory of the Cave

Plato (428–347 B.C.)

"The Allegory of the Cave" is from Book 7 of Plato's The Republic, *an extended inquiry into the nature of justice and how the state might best preserve it. In this famous passage, translated from the ancient Greek, Plato investigates the nature of the ideal ruler, specifically the kind of knowledge a ruler should possess. In the course of his argument, Plato introduces other issues as well, including the nature of educators, the human tendency to resist new knowledge, and a concept of divine truth that is equivalent to the appreciation of true beauty.*

Although Plato wrote before the rise of Christianity, many of his ideas have been adopted by Christian philosophers. Plato believed that the knowledge we gain from our lives in this world is flawed, that our perception of truth is blinded by our imperfect senses and human desires. He saw the world as presenting us only indistinct shadows of the real truths and beauty of life. For Plato, the only way to recognize how faulty our perception of reality is, is to ascend to a spiritual realm where the divine truth—the Good—shines whole in all of its beauty. To discuss this divine truth, and how one might attain it, Plato turns to allegory, where concrete objects and details are woven into a story that symbolizes the potential ruler's journey toward wisdom.

In addition to the allegory, Plato dramatizes his argument as a dialogue between Socrates and Glaucon. Plato preferred to write his arguments as Socratic dialogues because he believed that was the best way to prevent a reader from misunderstanding what he had to say. In accordance with his philosophy, Plato was suspicious of rhetoric—the use of words, which he saw as mere shadows of things, to communicate abstract truths. By having Socrates ask a series of simple questions to lead Glaucon through the argument, Plato attempted to control how future readers would respond as well. As you read this excerpt, keep in mind how Plato has structured the questioning in the dialogue. Are there any questions for which Glaucon could have given different answers, responses that might have changed the course of Socrates' reasoning?

"I want you to go on to picture the enlightenment or ignorance of our human conditions somewhat as follows. Imagine an underground chamber, like a cave with an entrance open to the daylight and running a long way underground. In this chamber are men who have been prisoners there since they were children, their legs and necks being so fastened that they can only look straight ahead of them and cannot turn their heads. Behind them and above them a fire is burning, and between the fire and the prisoners runs a road, in front of which a curtain-wall has been built, like the screen at puppet shows between the operators and their audience, above which they show their puppets."

"I see."

"Imagine further that there are men carrying all sorts of gear along behind the curtain-wall, including figures of men and animals made of wood and stone and other materials, and that some of these men, as is natural, are talking and some not."

"An odd picture and an odd sort of prisoner."

"They are drawn from life," I replied. "For, tell me, do you think our prisoners could see anything of themselves or their fellows except the shadows thrown by the fire on the wall of the cave opposite them?"

"How could they see anything else if they were prevented from moving their heads all their lives?"

"And would they see anything more of the objects carried along the road?"

"Of course not."

"Then if they were able to talk to each other, would they not assume that the shadows they saw were real things?"

"Inevitably."

"And if the wall of their prison opposite them reflected sound, don't you think that they would suppose, whenever one of the passers-by on the road spoke, that the voice belonged to the shadow passing before them?"

"They would be bound to think so."

"And so they would believe that the shadows of the objects we mentioned were in all respects real."

"Yes, inevitably."

"Then think what would naturally happen to them if they were released from their bonds and cured of their delusions. Suppose one of them were let loose, and suddenly compelled to stand up and turn his head and look and walk towards the fire; all these actions would be painful and he would be too dazzled to see properly the objects of which he used to see the shadows. So if he was told that what he used to see was more illusion and that he was now nearer reality and seeing more correctly, because he was turned towards objects that were more real, and if on top of that he were compelled to say what each of the passing objects was when it was pointed out to him, don't you think he would be at a loss, and think that what he used to see was more real than the objects now being pointed out to him?"

"Much more real."

"And if he were made to look directly at the light of the fire, it would hurt his eyes and he would turn back and take refuge in the things which he could see, which he would think really far clearer than the things being shown him."

"Yes."

"And if," I went on, "he were forcibly dragged up the steep and rocky ascent and not let go till he had been dragged out into the sunlight, the process would be a painful one, to which he would much object, and when he emerged into the light his eyes would be so overwhelmed by the brightness of it that he wouldn't be able to see a single one of the things he was now told were real."

"Certainly not at first," he agreed.

"Because he would need to grow accustomed to the light before he could see things in the world outside the cave. First he would find it easiest to look at shadows, next at the reflections of men and other objects in water, and later on at the objects themselves. After that he would find it easier to observe the heavenly bodies and the sky at night than by day, and to look at the light of the moon and stars, rather than at the sun and its light."

"Of course."

"The thing he would be able to do last would be to look directly at the sun, and observe its nature without using reflections in water or any other medium, but just as it is."

"That must come last."

"Later on he would come to the conclusion that it is the sun that produces the changing seasons and years and controls everything in the visible world, and is in a sense responsible for everything that he and his fellow-prisoners used to see."

"That is the conclusion which he would obviously reach."

"And when he thought of his first home and what passed for wisdom there, and of his fellow-prisoners, don't you think he would congratulate himself on his good fortune and be sorry for them?"

"Very much so."

"There was probably a certain amount of honour and glory to be won among the prisoners, and prizes for keen-sightedness for anyone who could remember the order of sequence among the passing shadows and so be best able to predict their future appearances. Will our released prisoner hanker after these prizes or envy this power or honour? Won't he be more likely to feel, as Homer says, that he would far rather be 'a serf in the house of some landless man', or indeed anything else in the world, than live and think as they do?"

"Yes," he replied, "he would prefer anything to a life like theirs."

"Then what do you think would happen," I asked, "if he went back to sit in his old seat in the cave? Wouldn't his eyes be blinded by the darkness, because he had come in suddenly out of the daylight?"

"Certainly."

"And if he had to discriminate between the shadows, in competition with the other prisoners, while he was still blinded and before his eyes got used to the darkness—a process that might take some time—wouldn't he be likely to make a fool of himself? And they would say that his visit to the upper world had ruined his sight, and that the ascent was not worth even attempting. And if anyone tried to release them and lead them up, they would kill him if they could lay hands on him."

"They certainly would."

"Now, my dear Glaucon," I went on, "this simile must be connected, throughout, with what preceded it. The visible realm corresponds to the prison, and the light of the fire in the prison to the power of the sun. And you won't go wrong if you connect the ascent into the upper world and the sight of the objects there with the upward progress of the mind into the intelligible realm—that's my guess, which is what you are anxious to hear. The truth of the matter is, after all, known only to God. But in my opinion, for what it is worth, the final thing to be perceived in the intelligible realm, and perceived only with difficulty, is the absolute form of Good; once seen, it is inferred to be responsible for everything right and good, producing in the visible realm light and the source of light, and being, in the intelligible realm itself, controlling source of reality and intelligence. And anyone who is going to act rationally either in public or private must perceive it."

"I agree," he said, "so far as I am able to understand you."

"Then you will perhaps also agree with me that it won't be surprising if those who get so far are unwilling to return to mundane affairs, and if their minds long to remain among higher things. That's what we should expect if our simile is to be trusted."

"Yes, that's to be expected."

"Nor will you think it strange that anyone who descends from contemplation of the divine to the imperfections of human life should blunder and make a fool of himself, if, while still blinded and unaccustomed to the surrounding darkness, he's forcibly put on trial in the law-courts or elsewhere about the images of justice or their shadows, and made to dispute about the conceptions of justice held by men who have never seen absolute justice."

"There's nothing strange in that."

"But anyone with any sense," I said, "will remember that the eyes may be unsighted in two ways, by a transition either from light to darkness or from darkness to light, and that the same distinction applies to the mind. So when he sees a mind confused and unable to see clearly he will not laugh without thinking, but will ask himself whether it has come from a clearer world and is confused by the unaccustomed darkness, or whether it is dazzled by the stronger light of the clearer world to which it has escaped from its previous ignorance. The first state is a reason for congratulation, the second for sympathy, though if one wants to laugh at it one can do so with less absurdity than at the mind that has descended from the daylight of the upper world."

"You put it very reasonably."

"If this is true," I continued, "we must reject the conception of education professed by those who say that they can put into the mind knowledge that was not there before—rather as if they could put sight into blind eyes."

"It is a claim that is certainly made," he said.

"But our argument indicates that this capacity is innate in each man's mind, and that the faculty by which he learns is like an eye which cannot be turned from darkness to light unless the whole body is turned; in the same way the mind as a whole must be turned away from the world of change until it can bear to look straight at reality, and at the brightest of all realities which is what we call the Good. Isn't that so?"

"Yes."

"Then this business of turning the mind round might be made a subject of professional skill, which would effect the conversion as easily and effectively as possible. It would not be concerned to implant sight, but to ensure that someone who had it already was turned in the right direction and looking the right way."

"That may well be so."

"The rest, therefore, of what are commonly called qualities of the mind perhaps resemble those of the body, in that they are not innate, but are implanted by training and practice; but wisdom, it seems, is a quality of some diviner faculty, which never loses its power, but whose effects are good or bad according to the direction in which it is turned. Have you never noticed how shrewd is the glance of the type of men commonly called bad but clever? Their intelligence is limited, but their sight is sharp enough in matters that concern them; it's not that their sight is weak, but that they put it to bad use, so that the keener it is the worse its effects."

"That's true."

"But suppose," I said, "that such natures were cut loose, when they were still children, from the dead weight of worldliness, fastened on them by sensual indulgences like gluttony, which distorts their minds' vision to lower things, and suppose that when so freed they were turned towards the truth, then the same faculty in them would have as keen a vision of truth as it has of the objects on which it is at present turned."

"Very likely."

"And is it not also likely, and indeed a necessary consequence of what we have said, that society will never be properly governed either by the uneducated, who have no knowledge of the truth, or by those who are allowed to spend all their lives in purely intellectual pursuits? The uneducated have no single aim in life to which all their actions, public and private, are directed, the intellectuals will take no practical action of their own accord, fancying themselves to be no longer of this world."

"True."

"Then our job as Lawgivers is to compel the best minds to attain what we have called the highest form of knowledge, and to ascend to the vision of the Good as we have described, and when they have achieved this and seen enough, prevent them behaving as they now do."

"What do you mean by that?"

"Remaining in the upper world, and refusing to return again to the prisoners in the cave below and share their labours and rewards, whether they are worth having or not."

"But surely," he protested, "that will not be fair. We shall be compelling them to live a poorer life than they might live."

"The object of our legislation," I reminded him again, "is not the welfare of any particular class, but of the whole community. It uses persuasion or force to unite all citizens and make them share together the benefits which each individually can confer on the community; and its purpose in fostering this attitude is not to enable everyone to please himself, but to make each man a link in the unity of the whole."

"You are right; I had forgotten," he said.

"You see, then, Glaucon," I went on, "we shan't be unfair to our philosophers, but shall be quite justified in compelling them to have some care and responsibility for others. We shall tell them that philosophers in other states can reasonably refuse to take part in the hard work of politics; for society produces them quite involuntarily and unintentionally, and it is only just that anything that grows up on its own should feel it has nothing to repay for an upbringing which it owes to no one. 'But you,' we shall say, 'have been bred to rule to your own advantage and that of the whole community, like kingbees in a hive; you are better educated than the rest and better qualified to combine the practice of philosophy and politics. You must therefore each descend in turn and live with your fellows in the cave and get used to seeing in the dark; once you get used to it you will see a thousand times better than they do and will recognize the various shadows, and know what they are shadows of, because you have seen the truth about things right and just and good. And so our state and yours will be really awake, and not merely dreaming like most societies to-day, with their shadow battles and their struggles for political power, which they treat as some great prize. The truth is quite different: the state whose rulers come to their duties with least enthusiasm is bound to have the best and most tranquil government, and the state whose rulers are eager to rule the worst.' "

"I quite agree."

"Then will our pupils, when they hear what we say, refuse to take their share of the hard work of government, though spending the greater part of their time together in the pure air of philosophy?"

"They cannot refuse, for we are making a just demand of just men. But of course, unlike present rulers, they will approach the business of government as an unavoidable necessity."

"Yes, of course," I agreed. "The truth is that if you want a well-governed state you must find for your future rulers some career they like better than government; for only then will you have government by the truly rich, those, that is, whose riches consist not of money, but of the happiness of a right and rational life. If you get, in public affairs, men who are so morally impoverished that they have nothing they can contribute themselves, but who hope to snatch some compensation for their own inadequacy from a political career, there can never be good government. They start fighting for power, and the consequent internal and domestic conflicts ruin both them and society."

"True indeed."

"Is there any other life except that of true philosophy which looks down on political power?"

"None that I know of."

"And yet the only men to get power should be men who do not love it, otherwise we shall have rivals' quarrels."

"That is certain."

"Who else, then, are we to compel to undertake the responsibilities of ruling, if it is not to be those who know most about good government and who yet value other things more highly than politics and its rewards?"

"There is no one else."

QUESTIONS FOR A CRITICAL REREADING

After reading Plato's allegory through once, use the following questions to help you reread it more critically. As you note your answers in your notebook, try to reason out the logical outline and thesis statement behind Plato's argument.

1. Because every detail in an allegory contributes to its meaning, a good way to objectify the argument is to draw the picture painted by the allegory. Draw the picture Plato has Socrates paint at the beginning of this essay. What is the subject Plato is inquring about?

2. What part of the essay makes up the introduction? Formulate what appears to be the question at issue at this point in the essay. Why is this an issue for philosophy?

3. As is true for every good argument, this essay attempts to begin on a point of agreement with its audience. However, because the subject Plato is discussing is an abstract, value-laden concept, he must make certain to distance his readers from the faulty associations this subject might arouse. How does he introduce his subject and the question he is asking about it so that we understand what he is talking about but are not encouraged to make value assumptions he would not agree with?

4. We might say that Plato's argument falls into two parts: the exposition of the myth and Socrates' explication about what it means. In your opinion, where does Plato's real argument (the burden of proof) begin? Based on your understanding of this essay, describe what kind of new information philosophy uses to prove an argument.

5. At the end of the essay, Plato reveals his real purpose. Identify where his conclusion begins and test your informal sentence outline against Plato's summary of the deductive process he has used throughout the essay. What appears to be the real issue he is addressing (compare your answer to that of question 2 above)? Formulate an enthymeme that reflects Plato's thesis as summarized in the conclusion.

POSSIBLE ISSUES FOR WRITING

Referring to the logical outline you developed in answer to question 5 above, discuss the following possible issues with your classmates. During class discussion, listen closely for the standards your classmates use to judge the value of life as Plato presents it, and keep a record of these different standards in your notebook to help you with your own essay later on.

1. Now that you recognize the real issue Plato is addressing, in your view does he succeed in reaching those most predisposed to interpret the subject differently? Why or why not?

2. A central point in Plato's argument arises when he criticizes educators for perceiving their task as to "put into the mind knowledge that was not there before." Based on the classes you have taken, do you think modern educators have this attitude? In view of what Plato suggests is the real task of the teacher, can you think of any teachers you have had who might better please Plato? If so, how were their classes different from others you have had? Do you think you learned better as a consequence? (If you have not experienced what Plato describes as the ideal education,

do you think it is because our educational system is faulty or because Plato's ideas are impractical or just plain wrong?)

3. This selection was taken from Plato's *Republic,* a study of what he perceives as the ideal government. Do you agree that the type of ruler he describes in this excerpt would ensure that we lead as ideal a life as possible? How does Plato's republic compare to the American democratic system we live in today? How do they differ in what they uphold as the supreme value of human life? Are there any other values that you believe both systems ignore?

The Myth of Sisyphus

Albert Camus (1913–1960)

Albert Camus is one of France's foremost literary figures. This excerpt is taken from one of his two collections of philosophical essays, The Myth of Sisyphus *(The Rebel was the other). However, Camus is just as well-known for his plays and two novels,* The Stranger *and* The Plague. *The essay included here is probably his most famous, particularly for its succinct expression of the philosophical perspective that Camus dramatizes in his other works.*

Camus' perspective is similar to the school of philosophy we call existentialism. This school, as its name implies, reflects on the nature of human existence to discover answers to the philosophical questions about why we are here and what our purpose in life is. The existentialists broke from the western philosophical tradition that began with Plato and continued with the Christian philosophers. Reflecting the growing cynicism and doubt of the twentieth century, the existentialists question whether absolute ("divine") truth exists, and if it does, whether we could ever comprehend it. Camus, in particular, was influenced by Friedrich Nietzsche (1844–1900), who had boldly proclaimed "God is dead" and " 'Faith' means not wanting to know what is true." Because he did not believe we could find truth by seeking for a transcendent universe or a divine being, Camus focused his inquiry on the nature of our human condition here on earth.

Although Camus came to conclude that life is absurd, he is not what we would call a nihilist (i.e., one who believes in nothing). It has been said that Camus was contemplating suicide when he wrote "The Myth of Sisyphus," but that, through this examination of a Greek myth about a doomed existence, he discovered a new purpose for human existence. As you read his retelling of this myth, note how he shapes your interpretation of Sisyphus's fate and leads you to discover how the "absurd" can lead to "happiness."

The gods had condemned Sisyphus to ceaselessly rolling a rock to the top of a mountain, whence the stone would fall back of its own weight. They had thought with some reason that there is no more dreadful punishment than futile and hopeless labor.

If one believes Homer, Sisyphus was the wisest and most prudent of mortals. According to another tradition, however, he was disposed to practice the profession of highwayman. I see no contradiction in this. Opinions differ as to the reasons why he became the futile laborer of the underworld. To begin with, he is accused of a certain levity in regard to the gods. He stole their secrets. Ægina, the daughter of Æsopus, was carried off by Jupiter. The father was shocked by that disappearance and complained to Sisyphus. He, who knew of the abduction, offered to tell about it on condition that Æsopus would give water to the citadel of Corinth. To the celestial thunderbolts he preferred the benediction of water. He was punished for this in the underworld. Homer tells us also that Sisyphus had put Death in chains. Pluto could not endure the sight of his deserted, silent empire. He dispatched the god of war, who liberated Death from the hands of her conqueror.

It is said also that Sisyphus, being near to death, rashly wanted to test his wife's love. He ordered her to cast his unburied body into the middle of the public square. Sisyphus woke up in the underworld. And there, annoyed by an obedience so contrary to human love, he obtained from Pluto permission to return to earth in order to chastise his wife. But when he had seen again the face of this world, enjoyed water and sun, warm stones and the sea, he no longer wanted to go back to the infernal darkness. Recalls, signs of anger, warnings were of no avail. Many years more he lived facing the curve of the gulf, the sparkling sea, and the smiles of earth. A decree of the gods was necessary. Mercury came and seized the impudent man by the collar and, snatching him from his joys, led him forcibly back to the underworld, where his rock was ready for him.

You have already grasped that Sisyphus is the absurd hero. He *is*, as much through his passions as through his torture. His scorn of the gods, his hatred of death, and his passion for life won him that unspeakable penalty in which the whole being is exerted toward accomplishing nothing. This is the price that must be paid for the passions of this earth. Nothing is told us about Sisyphus in the underworld. Myths are made for the imagination to breathe life into them. As for this myth, one sees merely the whole effort of a body straining to raise the huge stone, to roll it and push it up a slope a hundred times over; one sees the face screwed up, the cheek tight against the stone, the shoulder bracing the clay-covered mass, the foot wedging it, the fresh start with arms outstretched, the wholly human security of two earth-clotted hands. At the very end of his long effort measured by skyless space and time without depth, the purpose is achieved. Then Sisyphus watches the stone rush down in a few moments toward that lower world whence he will have to push it up again toward the summit. He goes back down to the plain.

It is during that return, that pause, that Sisyphus interests me. A face that toils so close to stones is already stone itself! I see that man going back down with a heavy yet measured step toward the torment of which he will never know the end. That hour like a breathing-space which returns as surely as his suffering, that is the hour of consciousness. At each of those moments when he leaves the heights and gradually sinks toward the lairs of the gods, he is superior to his fate. He is stronger than his rock.

If this myth is tragic, that is because its hero is conscious. Where would his torture be, indeed, if at every step the hope of succeeding upheld him? The workman of today works every day in his life at the same tasks, and this fate is no less absurd. But it is tragic only at the rare moments when it becomes conscious. Sisyphus, proletarian of the gods, powerless and rebellious, knows the whole extent of his wretched condition: it is what he thinks of during his descent. The lucidity that was to constitute his torture at the same time crowns his victory. There is no fate that cannot be surmounted by scorn.

If the descent is thus sometimes performed in sorrow, it can also take place in joy. This word is not too much. Again I fancy Sisyphus returning toward his rock, and the sorrow was in the beginning. When the images of earth cling too tightly to memory, when the call of happiness becomes too insistent, it happens that melancholy rises in man's heart: this is the rock's victory, this is the rock itself. The boundless grief is too heavy to bear. These are our nights of Gethsemane. But crushing truths perish from being acknowledged. Thus, Œdipus at the outset obeys fate without knowing it. But from the moment he knows, his tragedy begins. Yet at the same moment, blind and desperate, he realizes that the only bond linking him to the world is the cool hand of a girl. Then a tremendous remark rings out: "Despite so many ordeals, my advanced age and the nobility of my soul make me conclude that all is well." Sophocles' Œdipus, like Dostoevsky's Kirilov, thus gives the recipe for the absurd victory. Ancient wisdom confirms modern heroism.

One does not discover the absurd without being tempted to write a manual of happiness. "What! by such narrow ways—?" There is but one world, however. Happiness and the absurd are two sons of the same earth. They are inseparable. It would be a mistake to say that happiness necessarily springs from the absurd discovery. It happens as well that the feeling of the absurd springs from happiness. "I conclude that all is well," says Œdipus, and that remark is sacred. It echoes in the wild and limited universe of man. It teaches that all is not, has not been, exhausted. It drives out of this world a god who had come into it with dissatisfaction and a preference for futile sufferings. It makes of fate a human matter, which must be settled among men.

All Sisyphus' silent joy is contained therein. His fate belongs to him. His rock is his thing. Likewise, the absurd man, when he contemplates his torment, silences all the idols. In the universe suddenly restored to its silence, the myriad wondering little voices of the earth rise up. Unconscious, secret calls, invitations from all the faces, they are the necessary reverse and price of victory. There is no sun without shadow, and it is essential to know the night. The absurd man says yes and his effort will henceforth be unceasing. If there is a personal fate, there is no higher destiny, or at least there is but one which he concludes is inevitable and despicable. For the rest, he knows himself to be the master of his days. At that subtle moment when man glances backward over his life, Sisyphus returning toward his rock, in that slight pivoting he contemplates that series of unrelated actions which becomes his fate, created by him, combined under his memory's eye and soon sealed by his death. Thus, convinced of the wholly human origin of all that is human, a blind man eager to see who knows that the night has no end, he is still on the go. The rock is still rolling.

I leave Sisyphus at the foot of the mountain! One always finds one's burden again. But Sisyphus teaches the higher fidelity that negates the gods and raises rocks. He too concludes that all is well. This universe henceforth without a master seems to him neither sterile nor futile. Each atom of that stone, each mineral flake of that night-filled mountain, in itself forms a world. The struggle itself toward the heights is enough to fill a man's heart. One must imagine Sisyphus happy.

QUESTIONS FOR A CRITICAL REREADING

Construct an informal sentence outline based on your first reading of Camus' retelling of the myth of Sisyphus. Then, as you reread, use these questions to help you discover the kind of information Camus presents to support his argument.

1. Camus uses a myth to make an abstract subject concrete. What is the subject of his essay? Reread his first paragraph: What point of agreement does he establish at the outset? Be sure to phrase your answers as value statements.

2. Camus concerns himself less with "What is truth?" than with "What should be our attitude toward the reality of life?" A possible phrasing of the question at issue might be: "If our life on earth is all there is, and if our everyday activities are merely 'futile and hopeless labor,' then why should we go on?" How does he use the Sisyphus myth to illustrate this perspective of our efforts here on earth? Draw a picture of Sisyphus's situation as Camus describes it and identify what each detail represents.

3. As Camus explores the myth from the perspective of Sisyphus and not the gods, he discovers a different way to evaluate the worth of Sisyphus's life. Instead of a futile and hopeless victim, Sisyphus becomes an "absurd hero." To define this term, Camus analyzes what happens to Sisyphus as he returns down the hill to repeat his struggle with the stone. What does Camus mean when he says that it is at this time when Sisyphus is "superior to his fate" and "stronger than his rock?"

4. The second half of Camus' essay begins his argument in earnest as the terms he uses to describe life change from "punishment" and "hopeless labor" to "absurd," "surmounted by scorn," and "joy." How does he utilize the connotations of the word "absurd" to change our attitude to one of "joy?" How does the shift in terminology affect the way you value life as he has described it?

5. Formulate an enthymeme for Camus' argument. Be certain it contains the value term that reveals how it can serve as a "manual for happiness."

POSSIBLE ISSUES FOR WRITING

As you discuss the following issues with your classmates, listen for the different standards your classmates use to judge the value of Camus' perspective. Keep a record of these and other issues that arise to help you write your essay later on.

1. How well does the myth Camus has chosen fit his purpose? Is it an accurate representation of how you have viewed your own life at one time or another? Are there other myths, or allegorical fables, that would better describe the human condition as you know it? Why or why not?

2. Camus ends his essay with the statement that "one must imagine Sisyphus happy." How do you interpret this statement? Do you think he has proven that he has discovered the real meaning of life or is he merely manipulating terms to make us feel better—or is there any difference?

3. Camus introduces several value-laden terms as he develops his interpretation of the myth of Sisyphus (note the list contained in question 4 above). What terms would you use to describe your own attitude toward life and the human condition? Would you say your perspective is more like Camus' or Plato's? Why?

4. What are the characteristics of the "absurd hero" as Camus defines the term? Who would most fit that description today (feel free to choose a character from a modern book, a film, or a television show)?

Expressiveness

Susanne K. Langer *(1895–1985)*

Born in New York and educated at Radcliffe College, Susanne K. Langer's greatest contribution was her work in the area of aesthetics: the philosophy of artistic expression and the nature of the beautiful. Her most influential work, Philosophy in a New Key: A Study in the Symbolism of Reason, Rite, and Art *(1942), is a comprehensive examination of symbolic expression. In it she discusses how the language we use, the rituals we participate in, and the fine arts we create all depend on symbols to communicate meaning. The excerpt included here is the second chapter of Langer's* Problems of Art *(1957), a subsequent development of her theory of symbolism and its application to the expression of emotions.*

As the title implies, "Expressiveness" discusses how we communicate our feelings to others. Just as language uses symbols to help us think, remember, and imagine, artistic forms use symbols to help us express our emotions. In this essay, Langer argues that art has value as a unique mode of expression, that the symbolic forms of art communicate feelings that cannot be captured in language. Behind her discussion of what makes something good artistically is the argument that our feelings make up an important part of our lives, that "knowledge" and "understanding" come from our ability to feel as well as think.

As an argument addressing a question of value, Langer's essay explores what we mean when we call something "art." Her analysis begins with a general definition of art and then, to narrow that definition, proceeds to compare art to other forms of communication, almost as a scientist would distinguish different species within a general class of animals. As you read her essay, note the labels she creates to describe different kinds of symbolic form. Does she succeed in giving us an objective description of what art's value is or does she use any value-laden terms that not everyone would agree with?

When we talk about "Art" with a capital "A"—that is, about any or all of the arts: painting, sculpture, architecture, the potter's and goldsmith's and other designers' arts, music, dance, poetry, and prose fiction, drama and film—it is a constant temptation to say things about "Art" in this general sense that are true only in one special domain, or to assume that what holds for one art must hold for another. For instance, the fact that music is made for performance, for presentation to the ear, and is simply not the same thing when it is given only to the tonal imagination of a reader silently perusing the score, has made some aestheticians pass straight to the conclusion that literature, too, must be physically heard to be fully experienced, because words are originally spoken, not written; an obvious parallel, but a careless and, I think, invalid one. It is dangerous to set up principles by analogy, and generalize from a single consideration.

But it is natural, and safe enough, to ask analogous questions: "What is the function of sound in music? What is the function of sound in poetry? What is the function of sound in prose composition? What is the function of sound in drama?" The answers may be quite heterogeneous; and that is itself an important fact, a guide to something more than a simple and sweeping theory. Such findings guide us to exact relations and abstract, variously exemplified basic principles.

At present, however, we are dealing with principles that have proven to be the same in all the arts, when each kind of art—plastic, musical, balletic, poetic, and each major mode, such as literary and dramatic writing, or painting, sculpturing, building plastic shapes—has been studied in its own terms. Such candid study is more rewarding than the usual passionate declaration that all the arts are alike, only their materials differ, their principles are all the same, their techniques all analogous, etc. That is not only unsafe, but untrue. It is in pursuing the differences among them that one arrives, finally, at a point where no more differences appear; then one has found, not postulated, their unity. At that deep level there is only one concept exemplified in all the different arts, and that is the concept of Art.

The principles that obtain wholly and fundamentally in every kind of art are few, but decisive; they determine what is art, and what is not. Expressiveness, in one definite and appropriate sense, is the same in all art works of any kind. What is created is not the same in any two distinct arts—this is, in fact, what makes them distinct—but the principle of creation is the same. And "living form" means the same in all of them.

A work of art is an expressive form created for our perception through sense or imagination, and what it expresses is human feeling. The word "feeling" must be taken here in its broadest sense, meaning *everything that can be felt*, from physical sensation, pain and comfort, excitement and repose, to the most complex emotions, intellectual tensions, or the steady feeling-tones of a conscious human life. In stating what a work of art is, I have just used the words "form," "expressive," and "created"; these are key words. One at a time, they will keep us engaged.

Let us consider first what is meant, in this context, by a *form*. The word has many meanings, all equally legitimate for various purposes; even in connection with art it has several. It may, for instance—and often does—denote the familiar, characteristic structures known as the sonnet form, the sestina, or the ballad form in poetry, the sonata form, the madrigal, or the symphony in music, the contredance or the classical ballet in choreography, and so on. This is not what I mean; or rather, it is only a very small part of what I mean. There is another sense in which artists speak of "form" when they say, for instance, "form follows function," or declare that the one quality shared by all good works of art is "significant form," or entitle a book *The Problem of Form in Painting and Sculpture*, or *The Life of Forms in Art*, or *Search for Form*. They are using "form" in a wider sense, which on the one hand is close to the commonest, popular meaning, namely just the *shape* of a thing, and on the other hand to the quite unpopular meaning it has in science and philosophy, where it designates something more abstract; "form" in its most abstract sense means structure, articulation, a whole resulting from the relation of mutually dependent factors, or more precisely, the way that whole is put together.

The abstract sense, which is sometimes called "logical form," is involved in the notion of expression, at least the kind of expression that characterizes art. That is why artists, when they speak of achieving "form," use the word with something of an abstract connotation, even when they are talking about a visible and tangible art object in which that form is embodied.

The more recondite concept of form is derived, of course, from the naive one, that is, material shape. Perhaps the easiest way to grasp the idea of "logical form" is to trace its derivation.

Let us consider the most obvious sort of form, the shape of an object, say a lampshade. In any department store you will find a wide choice of lampshades, mostly monstrosities, and what is monstrous is usually their shape. You select the least offensive one, maybe even a good one, but realize that the color, say violet, will not fit into your room; so you look about for another shade of the same shape but a different color, perhaps green. In recognizing this same shape in another object, possibly of another material as well as another color, you have quite naturally and easily abstracted the concept of this shape from your actual impression of the first lampshade. Presently it may occur to you that this shade is too big for your lamp; you ask whether they have *this same shade* (meaning another one of this shape) in a smaller size. The clerk understands you.

But what is *the same* in the big violet shade and the little green one? Nothing but the interrelations among their respective various dimensions. They are not "the same" even in their spatial properties, for none of their actual measures are alike; but their shapes are congruent. Their respective spatial factors are put together in the same way, so they exemplify the same form.

It is really astounding what complicated abstractions we make in our ordinary dealing with forms—that is to say, through what twists and transformations we recognize the same logical form. Consider the similarity of your two hands. Put one on the table, palm down, superimpose the other, palm down, as you may have superimposed cut-out geometric shapes in school— they are not alike at all. But their shapes are *exact opposites.* Their respective shapes fit the same description, provided that the description is modified by a principle of application whereby the measures are read one way for one hand and the other way for the other—like a timetable in which the list of stations is marked: "Eastbound, read down; Westbound, read up."

As the two hands exemplify the same form with a principle of reversal understood, so the list of stations describes two ways of moving, indicated by the advice to "read down" for one and "read up" for the other. We can all abstract the common element in these two respective trips, which is called the *route.* With a return ticket we may return only by the same route. The same principle relates a mold to the form of the thing that is cast in it, and establishes their formal correspondence, or common logical form.

So far we have considered only objects—lampshades, hands, or regions of the earth—as having forms. These have fixed shapes; their parts remain in fairly stable relations to each other. But there are also substances that have no definite shapes, such as gases, mist, and water, which take the shape of any bounded space that contains them. The interesting thing about such amorphous fluids is that when they are put into violent motion they do exhibit visible forms, not bounded by any container. Think of the momentary efflorescence of a bursting rocket, the mushroom cloud of an atomic bomb, the funnel of water or dust screwing upward in a whirlwind. The instant the motion stops, or even slows beyond a certain degree, those shapes collapse and the apparent "thing" disappears. They are not shapes of things at all, but forms of motions, or dynamic forms.

Some dynamic forms, however, have more permanent manifestations, because the stuff that moves and makes them visible is constantly replenished. A waterfall seems to hang from the cliff, waving streamers of foam. Actually, of course, nothing stays there in mid-air; the water is always passing; but there is more and more water taking the same paths, so we have a lasting shape made and maintained by its passage—a permanent dynamic form. A quiet river, too, has dynamic form; if it stopped flowing it would either go dry or become a lake. Some twenty-five hundred years ago, Heracleitos was struck by the fact that you cannot step twice into the same river at the same place—at least, if the river means the water, not its dynamic form, the flow.

When a river ceases to flow because the water is deflected or dried up, there remains the river bed, sometimes cut deeply in solid stone. That bed is shaped by the flow, and records as graven lines the currents that have ceased to exist. Its shape is static, but it *expresses* the dynamic form of the river. Again, we have two congruent forms, like a cast and its mold, but this time the congruence is more remarkable because it holds between a dynamic form and a static one. That relation is important; we shall be dealing with it again when we come to consider the meaning of "living form" in art.

The congruence of two given perceptible forms is not always evident upon simple inspection. The common *logical* form they both exhibit may become apparent only when you know the principle whereby to relate them, as you compare the shapes of your hands not by direct correspondence, but by correspondence of opposite parts. Where the two exemplifications of the single logical form are unlike in most other respects one needs a rule for matching up the relevant factors of one with the relevant factors of the other; that is to say, a *rule of translation,* whereby one instance of the logical form is shown to correspond formally to the other.

The logical form itself is not another thing, but an abstract concept, or better an *abstractable* concept. We usually don't abstract it deliberately, but only use it, as we use our vocal cords in speech without first learning all about their operation and then applying our knowledge. Most people perceive intuitively the similarity of their two hands without thinking of them as conversely related; they can guess at the shape of the hollow inside a wooden shoe from the shape of a human foot, without any abstract study of topology. But the first time they see a map in the Mercator projection—with parallel lines of longitude, not meeting at the poles—they find it hard to believe that this corresponds logically to the circular map they used in school, where the meridians bulged apart toward the equator and met at both poles. The visible shapes of the continents are different on the two maps, and it takes abstract thinking to match up the two representations of the same earth. If, however, they have grown up with both maps, they will probably see the geographical relationships either way with equal ease, because these relationships are not *copied* by either map, but *expressed*, and expressed equally well by both; for the two maps are different *projections* of the same logical form, which the spherical earth exhibits in still another—that is, a spherical—projection.

An expressive form is any perceptible or imaginable whole that exhibits relationships of parts, or points, or even qualities or aspects within the whole, so that it may be taken to represent some other whole whose elements have analogous relations. The reason for using such a form as a symbol is usually that the thing it represents is not perceivable or readily imaginable. We cannot see the earth as an object. We let a map or a little globe express the relationships of places on the earth, and think about the earth by means of it. The understanding of one thing through another seems to be a deeply intuitive process in the human brain; it is so natural that we often have difficulty in distinguishing the symbolic expressive form from what it conveys. The symbol seems to be the thing itself, or contain it, or be contained in it. A child interested in a globe will not say: "This means the earth," but: "Look, this is the earth." A similar identification of symbol and meaning underlies the widespread conception of holy names, of the physical efficacy of rites, and many other primitive but culturally persistent phenomena. It has a bearing on our perception of artistic import; that is why I mention it here.

The most astounding and developed symbolic device humanity has evolved is language. By means of language we can conceive the intangible, incorporeal things we call our *ideas,* and the equally inostensible elements of our perceptual world that we call *facts.* It is by virtue of language that we can think, remember, imagine, and finally conceive a universe of facts. We can describe things and represent their relations, express rules of their interactions, speculate and predict and carry on a long symbolizing process known as reasoning. And above all, we can communicate, by producing a serried array of audible or visible words, in a pattern commonly known, and readily understood to reflect our multifarious concepts and percepts and their interconnections. This use of language is *discourse;* and the pattern of discourse is known as *discursive form.* It is a highly versatile, amazingly powerful pattern. It has impressed itself on our tacit thinking, so that we call all systematic reflection "discursive thought." It has made, far more than most people know, the very frame of our sensory experience—the frame of objective facts in which we carry on the practical business of life.

Yet even the discursive pattern has its limits of usefulness. An expressive form can express any complex of conceptions that, via some rule of projection, appears congruent with it, that is, appears to be of that form. Whatever there is in experience that will not take the impress—directly or indirectly—of discursive form, is not discursively communicable or, in the strictest sense, logically thinkable. It is unspeakable, ineffable; according to practically all serious philosophical theories today, it is unknowable.

Yet there is a great deal of experience that is knowable, not only as immediate, formless, meaningless impact, but as one aspect of the intricate web of life yet defies discursive formulation, and therefore verbal expression that is what we sometimes call the *subjective aspect* or experience, the direct feeling of it—what it is like to be waking and moving, to be drowsy, slowing down, or to be sociable, or to feel self-sufficient but alone; what it feels like to pursue an elusive thought or to have a big idea. All such directly felt experiences usually have no names—they are named, if at all, for the outward conditions that normally accompany their occurrence. Only the most striking ones have names like "anger," "hate," "love," "fear," and are collectively called "emotion." But we feel many things that never develop into any designable emotion. The ways we are moved are as various as the lights in a forest; and they may intersect, sometimes without cancelling each other, take shape and dissolve, conflict, explode into passion, or be transfigured. All these inseparable elements of subjective reality compose what we call the "inward life" of human beings. The usual factoring of that life-stream into mental, emotional, and sensory units is an arbitrary scheme of simplification that makes scientific treatment possible to a considerable extent; but we may already be close to the limit of its usefulness, that is, close to the point where its simplicity becomes an obstacle to further questioning and discovery instead of the revealing, ever-suitable logical projection it was expected to be.

Whatever resists projection into the discursive form of language is, indeed, hard to hold in conception, and perhaps impossible to communicate, in the proper and strict sense of the word "communicate." But fortunately our logical intuition, or form-perception, is really much more powerful than we commonly believe, and our knowledge—genuine knowledge, understanding—is considerably wider than our discourse. Even in the use of language, if we want to name something that is too new to have a name (e.g., a newly invented gadget or a newly discovered creature), or want to express a relationship for which there is no verb or other connective word, we resort to metaphor; we mention it or describe it as something else, something analogous. The principle of metaphor is simply the principle of saying one thing and meaning another, and expecting to be understood to mean the other. A metaphor is not language, it is an idea expressed by language, an idea that in its turn functions as a symbol to express something. It is not discursive and therefore does not really make a statement of the idea it conveys; but it formulates a new conception for our direct imaginative grasp.

Sometimes our comprehension of a total experience is mediated by a metaphorical symbol because the experience is new, and language has words and phrases only for familiar notions. Then an extension of language will gradually follow the wordless insight, and discursive expression will supersede the non-discursive pristine symbol. This is, I think, the normal advance of human thought and language in that whole realm of knowledge where discourse is possible at all.

But the symbolic presentation of subjective reality for contemplation is not only tentatively beyond the reach of language—that is, not merely beyond the words we have; it is impossible in the essential frame of language. That is why those semanticists who recognize only discourse as a symbolic form must regard the whole life of feeling as formless, chaotic, capable only of symptomatic expression, typified in exclamations like "Ah!" "Ouch!" "My sainted aunt!" They usually do believe that art is an expression of feeling, but that "expression" in art is of this sort, indicating that the speaker has an emotion, a pain, or other personal experience, perhaps also giving us a clue to the general kind of experience it is—pleasant or unpleasant, violent or mild—but not setting that piece of inward life objectively before us so we may understand its intricacy, its rhythms and shifts of total appearance. The differences in feeling-tones or other elements of subjective experience are regarded as differences in quality, which must be felt to be appreciated. Furthermore, since we have no intellectual access to pure subjectivity, the only way to study it is to study the symptoms of the person who is having subjective experiences. This leads to physiological psychology—a very important and interesting field. But it tells us nothing about the phenomena of subjective life, and sometimes simplifies the problem by saying they don't exist.

Now, I believe the expression of feeling in a work of art—the function that makes the work an expressive form—is not symptomatic at all. An artist working on a tragedy need not be in personal despair or violent upheaval; nobody, indeed, could work in such a state of mind. His mind would be occupied with the causes of his emotional upset. Self-expression does not require composition and lucidity; a screaming baby gives his feeling far more release than any musician, but we don't go into a concert hall to hear a baby scream; in fact, if that baby is brought in we are likely to go out. We don't want self-expression.

A work of art presents feeling (in the broad sense I mentioned before, as everything that can be felt) for our contemplation, making it visible or audible or in some way perceivable through a symbol, not inferable from symptom. Artistic form is congruent with the dynamic forms of our direct sensuous, mental, and emotional life; works of art are projections of "felt life," as Henry James called it, into spatial, temporal, and poetic structures. They are images of feeling, that formulate it for our cognition. What is artistically good is whatever articulates and presents feeling to our understanding.

Artistic forms are more complex than any other symbolic forms we know. They are, indeed, not abstractable from the works that exhibit them. We may abstract a shape from an object that has this shape, by disregarding color, weight and texture, even size; but to the total effect that is an artistic form, the color matters, the thickness of lines matters, and the appearance of texture and weight. A given triangle is the same in any position, but to an artistic form its location, balance, and surroundings are not indifferent. Form, in the sense in which artists speak of "significant form" or "expressive form," is not an abstracted structure, but an apparition; and the vital processes of sense and emotion that a good work of art expresses seem to the beholder to be directly contained in it, not symbolized but really presented. The congruence is so striking that symbol and meaning appear as one reality. Actually, as one psychologist who is also a musician has written, "Music sounds as feelings feel." And likewise, in good painting, sculpture, or building, balanced shapes and colors, lines and masses look as emotions, vital tensions and their resolutions feel.

An artist, then, expresses feeling, but not in the way a politician blows off steam or a baby laughs and cries. He formulates that elusive aspect of reality that is commonly taken to be amorphous and chaotic; that is, he objectifies the subjective realm. What he expresses is, therefore, not his own actual feelings, but what he knows about human feeling. Once he is in possession of a rich symbolism, that knowledge may actually exceed his entire personal experience. A work of art expresses a conception of life, emotion, inward reality. But it is neither a confessional nor a frozen tantrum; it is a developed metaphor, a non-discursive symbol that articulates what is verbally ineffable—the logic of consciousness itself.

QUESTIONS FOR A CRITICAL REREADING

Construct an informal sentence outline based on your first reading of Langer's essay. As you reread, use these questions and your sentence outline to formulate an enthymemic thesis for her argument. Because Langer is discussing quite abstract issues, you might want to underline any value-laden words you use for closer examination later on.

1. Unlike Plato and Camus, Langer chooses to weave her argument not through poetic images but by carefully defining her primary terms (e.g., "form," "expressive," and "created") and establishing several different classifications within each category. Diagram the steps in her argument, referring to your informal sentence outline of Langer's essay to complete the classification tree started below:

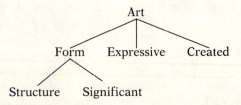

2. Referring to the classification tree, formulate the question Langer is addressing. Now return to Langer's essay and determine where this issue is introduced most

clearly to the reader. (*Hint:* You may discover the question you have formulated needs to be revised to accommodate everything Langer discusses.)

3. Langer uses the method of scientific classification to develop her essay because "art" is a value-laden term for most of us. We often disagree on whether something is or is not true "art" and, as with "beauty," say the definition lies in the eye of the beholder. How does Langer accommodate that perspective? Are any other terms in her essay value-laden? If so, what are they and how well does Langer control how we respond to them?

4. As a philosopher, Langer spends much of her time keeping her readers aware of the analytical method she is using. Note her comment at the end of her discussion of "static shapes" and "dynamic forms" (paragraphs 13–15): "That relation is important; we shall be dealing with it again when we come to consider the meaning of 'living form' in art." Give an example of what Langer means by "dynamic form." How does she later view art as a static shape that expresses a dynamic form of our lives?

5. As Langer nears her conclusion, she distinguishes between art that is mere self-expression and that which "objectifies the subjective realm" for our contemplation. Define the difference, giving an example or two that would help illustrate her point. In light of your answer, construct an enthymeme that represents the real value Langer has assigned to art.

POSSIBLE ISSUES FOR WRITING

Discuss the following questions with your classmates to discover what remains at issue. As you listen to your classmates' arguments, jot down the kinds of value questions they pose and the standards they apply to answer them. This will help you discover how your own value system may differ, and help you explain that difference to your reader when you write your essay for this chapter.

1. Langer defines good art as that which "articulates and presents feeling to our understanding" so that we experience "the logic of consciousness itself." Using this definition, would you describe the "Mona Lisa" as good art? Subway graffiti? A Madonna music video? Defend your answers.

2. At the center of her argument, Langer admits that language itself is an expressive form, although, as a "discursive form," it cannot communicate the "subjective aspect of experience." Where language enables us to think rationally about our lives, art enables us to extend our emotional responses. In essence, she implies that learning to feel is as important as learning to think. Do you agree? Would Plato? Would Camus? Why or why not?

3. Although Langer's essay addresses a very specific issue in the field of aesthetics, we can also view it as a justification for art's value in our lives. Do you think our society values art today? What sorts of art forms are most respected? Because the National Endowment for the Arts is a primary source of funds for starving artists, what should determine which artists deserve financial assistance? Or should the government fund artists at all—if good art is determined by its ability to express emotions within all of us, why not let the value of art be determined by its commercial success?

WRITING YOUR ESSAY

Now is the time to write your response to the conversation you have been having with your classmates about Plato, Camus, and Langer. Review your reading notebook to identify the issue you most care about, formulate your tentative answer as an enthymemic thesis statement, and then use these three questions to test that thesis before drafting your argument:

1. Does the first clause of your thesis statement clearly answer a question of value? Remember that philosophical arguments are extended definitions of abstract concepts carrying value connotations such as "good" or "beautiful." Both the first clause of your thesis and the question it is answering should contain the value-laden term you will need to define in your essay.

Example

Value Question:
   "How does one achieve *happiness?*"

Enthymemic Thesis:
   "Only those who recognize the absurdity
   of life can achieve *happiness*
   because . . ."

2. What kind of information does your "because" clause require you to give? Remember that the "because" clause of your enthymemic thesis reveals what you will have to prove in the body of your argument. In philosophical arguments, your thesis is a value judgment and, to communicate that judgment to your readers, your "because" clause should identify how you plan to define a new value term you will use to make that judgment.

Example

   "Only those who recognize the absurdity
of life can achieve happiness . . .

   • because <u>Camus said</u> so."
   • because <u>history shows</u> that those who don't take life seriously are the most successful."
   • because recognizing the <u>absurdity</u> of life enables one to rise above one's fate."

The underlined portions of each "because" clause stated above reveals the kind of new information needed to prove the claim. The first example would require quotations from Camus, a literary interpretation of what Camus meant rather than a philosophical argument. The second example would require evidence from history, making your essay a historical argument. Only the third example emphasizes a value term ("absurdity") and how you plan to define it ("enables one to rise above one's fate").

3. What assumption are you making about the values your audience believes in? Identify the missing premise behind your enthymeme and test it against your "because" clause to see which value statement you can assume your audience would most likely believe without proof. Be certain your "because" clause contains the value statement that requires the most proof.

Example

"Because" Clause:
    "Recognizing the absurdity of life
enables one to rise above one's fate."

Missing Premise:
    "Happiness is the state of being in
control of one's fate."

Which value statement would your audience most readily accept—the statement about the nature of "absurdity" or the statement about the nature of "happiness?" Note how Camus decided the latter, making the definition of "absurdity" carry the burden of proof in his argument.

Once you have revised your thesis statement to identify the primary value term and how you will define it, you need to consider how you will make your abstract argument accessible to your reader. The readings in this chapter have introduced you to three different ways philosophers present abstract information: (1) by creating a dialogue between two people, (2) by illustrating the value of a concept through an allegory or myth, and/or (3) by scientifically classifying the various components of an objective definition. Whether you decide to adopt just one or all three methods, your decision is basically a stylistic one. For that reason, you may wish to refer to the next section for help.

WHEN THE STYLE IS THE ARGUMENT

When we make a distinction between what is said and how it is said, we are making a distinction between the meaning and the *style* of an argument. However, as we have seen in the readings for this chapter, the two cannot be separated that easily. How something is said will always have an effect on how it is interpreted, and, thus, will always affect the meaning. Plato's dialogue helps distance us from our own value judgments by having us adopt Glaucon's perspective as Socrates leads him through the argument. Plato leads us out of the cave of our own prejudice as we read about it. Through the myth of Sisyphus, Camus forces us to consider our fate objectively, separated from the conditions of modern life. As he interprets the myth while presenting it to us, Camus makes us experience some of the "joy" of Sisyphus himself. When we read Langer, her analytical method forces us to see art independent of our personal response to any particular art work, her new terminology for different expressive forms making us respond intellectually rather than emotionally.

When we write about abstract issues, more often than not our style becomes the argument. The connotations of the words we choose, of the details we select, and of the metaphoric connections we imply will all shape how we and our readers will interpret the subject under consideration. Perhaps the most extreme example of how the style becomes the argument is Plato's allegory—where the picture he paints through his allegory shows us aspects of our lives that we could not see had he merely chosen to describe them in literal terms.

REVISING YOUR STYLE TO DISCOVER YOUR STANCE

As you enter these philosophical conversations, be aware of how the connotations of the words and examples you choose affect your argument. As we discussed in Chapter 11, a careful choice of words and examples can help you reason through your own argument. A careless word choice can arouse associations in your own mind that lead you to make faulty assumptions or overlook other dimensions of the argument. It is easier to stay focused when writing your rough draft if you conscientiously choose words that help you remain as objective as possible. Examine the values your words imply and test whether they are leading you to interpret only one dimension of the subject.

Keep in mind how Langer controls her reasoning by continually classifying and defining her terms as she introduces them. You strengthen your argument when you anticipate the various connotations your words might have for your audience, particularly for one predisposed to disagree. For example, if you were to defend art as something that allows for the expression of "subjective feelings," your reader, one predisposed to see no value in art, would immediately discount your argument because he or she would view "subjectivity" as something that leads us away from objective truth. Without defining the term in a way that makes it a positive rather than a negative quality, your argument would fail to communicate to your reader.

As you revise your essays, examine not only the logic of your argument but the connotations of the words and examples you have used to convey it. Often, it is in revising your words—your style—that you will discover and be able to communicate your real stance. Even if you choose to explore your argument through allegory as a way to distance your readers from undesirable value associations, remember to be careful how you tell your story: the words you choose to describe essential details will necessarily affect the overall picture you are painting and how your readers will respond to it. Remember that, particularly in philosophical arguments, your aim is to change the way your readers value your subject.

———————
———————
———————

Unit Seven

CHAPTER THIRTEEN

Finding a Style with Voice, Tone, and Meaning

"*W*hat's in a name?" asked Shakespeare's Juliet, when she discovered that the boy she loved was Romeo Montague, son of her father's hated enemy. She went on to observe, "That which we call a rose by any other word would smell as sweet." We want to agree with Juliet; it seems unjust to judge Romeo only by name and reputation. But does that mean that we should never take the name into consideration? A rose, when presented to us as "a smelly weed," just might not smell as sweet. And could she love Romeo if his name were "Deceiver Jack"?

Although we might not completely agree with Juliet's philosophy here, the language she uses is important not just for what it means but also for what it tells us about her and Romeo. In the image of the sweet-smelling rose, we see her youth, innocence, and faith in Romeo. Her innocence helps us put her philosophy in perspective, just as her faith lets us know there is something about Romeo that deserves our respect, something his name alone doesn't convey. We would probably see her and Romeo quite differently if she had used different language to express a similar idea. For example, she would not be the Juliet we know had she said, "Fie! The man's a man, and that's all I need know!"

Juliet's style—the words she chooses, and how she puts words together—expresses something unique about her perspective of the world. Her language reflects not only what she is thinking but something about *her* and her attitude toward the boy she is thinking about. Similarly, the language you use, your speaking and writing style, expresses more than your ideas. Even though you may agree with someone on an issue, how you explain that idea differs from how the other person explains it. By expressing an idea in your own words, you change it, and reveal your unique perspective on the subject.

Your unique perspective is revealed through three different stylistic features of your language—your voice, tone, and meaning. Here is a diagram, a modification of the communications triangle, that can help you understand how these terms reflect the different approaches you take when you respond to a rhetorical situation:

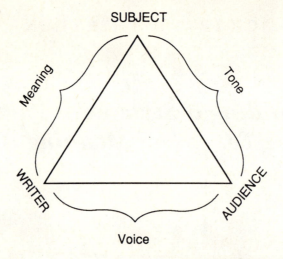

The communications triangle takes into account you (as the speaker), the audience you are addressing, and the subject under discussion. Although the terms "tone" and "voice" are hard to define and sometimes even used to mean the same thing, it is helpful to see them, in conjunction with "meaning," as distinguishing the relationships between the elements of the triangle: The *meaning* is your attitude toward the subject; *voice* is your attitude toward the audience; and *tone* is how you present the subject to the audience. You adopt a "voice" to persuade your reader you are someone worth listening to, and you adopt a "tone" to shape your audience's emotional response to the subject. To help you become aware of these features of your writing style, we will discuss each in turn.

STYLE AND MEANING

Word Choice

In the eighteenth century, a lesser-known poet, the Reverend Samuel Wesley, defined style as "the dress of thought." Perhaps because of the vivid picture that definition paints, the phrase has endured throughout the ages. However, as we have learned more about language and the way it is used (see the readings in Chapter 2), we have come to realize just how much the choice of words doesn't merely "dress thought," but can *change* what is said and how others interpret it. As discussed in Chapter 12, how you express yourself cannot be separated from what you want to say. When you choose a word, formulate a sentence, or tell a story to convey an idea, you interpret your thoughts and create meaning. If language were merely the dress of thought, all of your thinking would be finished before you chose words to communicate your ideas to others. However, writing is a mode of thinking, a way of reasoning about an issue as you discover new meanings behind the words you choose. Writing is more than finding words to communicate what you already know; it is a process by which you let the words on the page direct the path of reasoning your mind will take.

For example, we might say the words "beat," "defeat," "conquer," "overcome," and "vanquish" all convey a similar idea, but there is a great difference in meaning if you chose to say that the army "vanquished" instead of "overcame" the enemy. If you began writing by saying "the army *vanquished* the enemy," the verb would lead you to describe how thoroughly the army had extinguished the enemy's threat. You would probably be prompted to include details of how strong the army was, how thoroughly they dominated the enemy, and how quickly they were able to quench the attack. However, if you began with "the army *overcame* the enemy," the verb could lead you to view the battle from a different perspective. Whereas "vanquished" shifts your attention to the strength of the victor, "overcame" tends to focus on the struggle, prompting you to describe how strong the *enemy* was and to give details of what the army had to do to emerge victorious. The word you chose to introduce the battle would affect how you developed the idea—that is, how you reasoned about why the battle was successful.

EXERCISE

To explore how word choice can affect your interpretation of an idea, re-write each sentence below, replacing the italicized words with synonyms (words that convey similar meanings). Refer to a thesaurus if you get stuck. Then, comparing your new sentences with those of your classmates, discuss how the revised sentences shift your perspective on the subject.

1. "Let other pens *dwell* on guilt and misery." (Jane Austen)
2. "I can *explain* all the poems that ever were invented—and a good many that haven't been invented just yet." (Lewis Carroll)
3. "Success is *counted* sweetest by those who ne'er succeed." (Emily Dickinson)
4. "That man's silence is wonderful to *listen to*." (Thomas Hardy)
5. "As flies to wanton boys, are we to the gods; they kill us for their *sport*." (Shakespeare)

Word Order

A good style not only exhibits careful word choice but also has (to use the words of the eighteenth-century satirist, Jonathan Swift) all the "proper words in proper places." Your style creates meaning—shapes both how you reason as you write and how your readers reason as they read—both through word choice *and* word order. In the English language, our normal word order has the subject precede the verb (e.g., "I saw" not "Saw I") unless we are asking a question (e.g., "I did. Didn't you?"). However, we seldom talk or write in basic sentences such as these. Your unique style arises when you add more information to each of your sentences. What you choose to add and where you place it in your sentence emphasizes some words over others, giving new meaning to your ideas.

Stylistic variations occur when you introduce other information into your sentences. For example, we usually place other information closest to the word it relates to: "The new boy threw the ball to you" has "new" next to "boy" and "the ball to you" next to the verb. A stylistic variation, though, might be: "To you, the new boy threw the ball." Note how this variation changes the meaning somewhat, emphasizing where the boy threw the ball rather than just stating he did it. The basic rule of thumb to use is, whenever the word order deviates from normal usage, the information that is displaced receives greater emphasis.

Knowledge of stylistic variation can help you read more critically, enabling you to get a clearer idea of what the author thinks is important. It also can help you improve your own writing. Recognizing where you have varied your style in a rough draft can help you discover what you are really trying to say. Revising your style for a final draft can help you use a variation in normal word order to emphasize your main points for your readers.

A warning, though: Be certain your stylistic variation makes sense. Words that modify, such as adverbs and adjectives, should remain next to the words they describe. Be careful your modifiers aren't left dangling without the word they refer to; for example, "Coming around the corner, the building appeared" doesn't clearly state who is coming around the corner. Also, be certain the subject is placed next to the modifier, or you risk confusing your reader with a nonsense sentence. Don't say "Coming around the corner, the building I saw" unless you want to claim that buildings can walk. Because it is "I" that is "coming around the corner," your stylistic variations should keep those words together. Here are some possible revisions:

1. "Coming around the corner, I saw the building."
2. "I, coming around the corner, saw the building."
3. "The building I saw *while* coming around the corner."
4. "I saw, *while* coming around the corner, the building."

As the last two examples show, adding clarifying information like "while" can give you more freedom to alter the normal word order.

EXERCISE

Analyze the relationship between style and meaning in one of your past essays by,

- underlining important words that convey your perspective on the subject, and
- underlining any sentences that vary normal word order.

When you have finished, revise any word choices that you feel alter the focus of your argument, and alter the word order of any sentences that you feel give improper emphasis to your ideas. (Remember that the most important information should occur at the beginning and end of your sentences.)

Sentence Rhythm

In addition to word choice and word order, your style is also determined by the rhythm of your prose. Rhythm refers to how your sentences sound. Are they short? Are they long? Are they the same length? Do they sound choppy? Are they like these? Or do they vary in length and word order, slowing down the rhythm with more complex sentences, focusing attention on the most important ideas, then speeding up again, using short sentences, phrases, words, to reinforce what has been said? Short sentences reinforce; long sentences explain. Good writing does both.

When you talk, you emphasize your ideas through rhythm, varying how quickly and how loudly you say your words. When you write, you can vary the length of your sentences and individual words to achieve a similar effect. If you read your writing aloud, drawing a slash at every point where you find yourself pausing, you can discover how rhythmic your style is. If your slash marks occur at regular intervals, your prose is probably too regular to fit your ideas. Because your ideas vary in importance, and your writing should slow down to focus the reader's attention on the most important thoughts, prose that does not vary its rhythm probably doesn't fit the meaning of the passage as well as it might.

To demonstrate how sentence rhythm can affect the meaning of a passage, following are two paragraphs, each discussing the same information. Slash marks indicate where a natural break in the rhythm occurs. Note how, in the second paragraph, even when the sentences all appear to be the same length, the *rhythm* of the passage still varies more than that of the first paragraph.

Example of Stylistic Rhythm

1. "It is a melancholy object. / People walk through this great town. / They travel in the country. / They see streets, / roads, / and cabin-doors. / All are crowded / with beggars of the female sex. / They are followed / by three, / four, / or six children. / All are in rags. / All ask every passenger for money. / These mothers cannot work for their livelihood. / They are forced to employ themselves / begging for their children. / Their children grow up not able to work. / They become thieves, / traitors, / or slaves."

2. "It is a melancholy object/to those who walk through this great town,/or travel in the country,/when they see the streets,/the roads,/and cabin-doors/ crowded with beggars/of the female sex,/followed by three,/four,/or six children,/all in rags,/and importuning every passenger/for an alms./ These mothers,/instead of being able to work/for their honest livelihood,/are forced to employ/all their time/in strolling/to beg sustenance/for their helpless infants:/ who,/as they grow up,/either turn thieves for want of work,/or leave their dear native country/to fight for the Pretender in Spain,/or sell themselves to the Barbadoes." (Jonathan Swift)

The first paragraph has a fairly regular rhythm: each sentence is about the same length, and the slash marks occur primarily at the end of the sentences. If you read the paragraph aloud, it sounds choppy; each sentence begins with subject-verb word order, and it isn't entirely clear how the sentences relate to each other. As a reader, you probably felt yourself drawn more to the regular rhythm of the words than to their meaning. The second paragraph, however, varies the rhythm, subordinating some ideas to others by using words like "who," "as," and "when." Note the spacing of the slash marks; near the middle of the paragraph, they appear closer together, sometimes separated only by one word. The rhythm speeds up as the writer focuses your attention on the meaning of each word. At the end, the slash marks are further apart, separated by longer phrases, slowing down the rhythm to prepare you for the next paragraph and a new idea.

EXERCISE

To practice analyzing the rhythm of your style, return to the paper you were revising for the previous exercise on page 306. Read the introduction and conclusion aloud, and, each time you find yourself pausing, mark off the rhythm in the text by writing a slash mark. When you are finished, compare the length of the spaces between the slash marks. If they are fairly regular, choose a few sentences that are most important to your meaning and alter their rhythm. Some of the techniques you might try are combining short sentences, breaking long sentences into smaller units, adding adjectives or adverbs, or subordinating ideas with words such as "who," "which," "that," "as," or "because."

AUDIENCE AND VOICE

The mechanical aspects of your writing style—word choice, word order, and sentence rhythm—help you make meaning with words. However, to ensure you communicate that meaning to your readers, you need to consider another aspect of your style—your voice. Your writing voice is similar to your public speaking voice. Through both, you establish a working relationship with an audience of people who know little about you. When you speak, your audience interprets what you say in light of what they see: how composed you are, how authoritative you appear, whether you are shy, uncomfortable, or confident. When you write, your audience interprets what you say in light of how you sound: how your words and the way you use them reveal what kind of person you are, and whether that person is someone they want to listen to and respect. If they don't like your voice, even if you are saying something they agree with, they won't want to agree with you. If they like your voice, even if they hold a different view of the subject, they will still respect your opinion. That is why the voice you use is so important—it affects how your reader will respond to what you say.

Your introductory paragraphs play the greatest role in establishing your relationship with your reader. At the beginning of your argument, you are not only introducing the issue but introducing yourself as someone worth listening to. That is one reason why it is important to start on a point of agreement with your readers. Although you may intend to lead your readers to view the subject from a new perspective, they will respect you more if you first show you have listened to what others have said. Those who are predisposed to disagree will be more likely to respect you if you first show you respect their opinions; those readers who still have not decided what they think will see you as a fair and well-informed thinker.

You can tell a lot about a book or essay just from the voice the author uses to introduce the issue to you. Writers who appear to be biased, self-important, or just uninformed at the outset, make us want to close the book; if we do continue to read, we look for ways to disagree with them. Writers who appear to be intelligent and respectable, on the other hand, gain our respect and attention. We cannot always describe why we like a writer's voice because often our response is an emotional one. However, to analyze a writer's voice—or to analyze your own—you might look at the following stylistic features:

1. What kind of relationship has the writer established with the reader? Look at the pronouns the writer has used. Is the focus on "I," "you," "they," or "we"? Why do you think the writer spoke from that point of view?
2. How long are the sentences? How many of the words actually present information? What is the effect of the others? What do they reveal about the writer's personality?
3. Look closely at surprising word choices. Why were they surprising? What do they reveal about the writer's concerns and priorities?

EXERCISE

Read the following introductory paragraphs. For each one, write a short description of the writer's voice: Do you like the writer as a person? Is the writer someone you respect? Would you want to read further? Why or why not? (Use the stylistic features listed above to justify your answer.)

1. I know there are people who would disagree with me, but I think we need to do something about this pollution problem. I can understand why people might need to use styrofoam and disposable diapers. Never having been a mother myself, I can't imagine what it would be like to have to wash dirty diapers everyday. But I also can't imagine what it would be like to live buried in a mound of dirty, disposable diapers that won't decompose. Someone needs to solve this problem.

2. One thing is certain. We need to outlaw the use of disposable diapers. Why? Because they are not biodegradable. They are filling up our landfills, polluting our water, and perpetuating disregard for the environment. Women who choose to use them in light of this evidence are selfish and lazy. The irony is, they claim to be making their children their primary concern, when all they are doing is ruining the world their children will inherit. What happened to the old days, when women didn't slight their duty to the family?

> 3. We are quite lucky today. Modern technology has enabled us, both men and women, to devote our lives to serious pursuits. We no longer worry about making dinner and washing diapers. Styrofoam containers and disposable diapers have made day-to-day living more bearable, and, in some cases, even safer than before. But what are the costs of today's luxuries? Can we afford to ignore what they are doing to our environment? Perhaps we need to reevaluate what should be the "serious pursuits" of our lives.

The rhetorical term for voice is *ethos*. As the term implies, a writer's ethos reveals the ethics—the value system—the writer lives by. When you evaluate the voice of an author, you seek linguistic clues to that writer's moral character. As you may have discovered when you evaluated the paragraphs in the preceding exercise, the relationship a writer adopts with the reader can tell much about a writer's priorities. If the writing sounds apologetic, emphasizing "this is only my opinion," the writer can appear to have only a vague sense of the issue and an even less precise awareness of the standards others use to evaluate it. If the writing sounds dogmatic, as if the writer is lecturing *at* rather than speaking *to* an audience, then the writer appears to have a very fixed—and probably unrealistic—set of moral standards. Often, by sounding as if they are beyond reproach themselves, these writers tempt readers to find fault with the argument. The most effective voice, of course, is *the middle voice.* Rather than "talk up to" your readers by apologizing or "talk down to" your readers by lecturing, you need to "talk with" your readers by recognizing the value of everyone's position.

SUBJECT AND TONE

Using the middle voice described above doesn't mean always sounding the same when you write. You can use your voice in many ways. When you speak to different people, you adjust your voice accordingly. You might yell at your brother, plead with your parents, or appeal for sympathy from a teacher. You adopt a certain tone of voice to appeal to your listener's emotions. Writing is similar: The words you choose and the way you put them together create a tone of voice that will affect your readers emotionally. With voice, you shape how your reader will respond to you as an authority; with tone, you inspire your reader to respond to the subject with feelings similar to your own.

To determine the most effective tone for your purpose, try asking yourself these three questions:

1. What emotional commitments do my readers have invested in their position?
2. How do my feelings differ from theirs?
3. What tone of voice would best lead them to feel about the subject as I do?

Although question number 3 is the most important, you cannot answer it properly without considering the other questions first. The tone of voice you choose will affect how your readers respond to the subject under discussion, whether they find your position emotionally appealing or offensive.

Sincere Emotional Appeals

Whether you choose to present your subject humorously, seriously, indifferently, sarcastically, earnestly, or shockingly, your choice depends on what tone would most effectively persuade your audience to feel as you do. This means you first need to be honest with yourself. Examine why you feel as you do, and test your responses against those of your readers. When you discover your readers are not emotionally committed to the subject under discussion, either because they have not thought much about it or because it does not affect them personally, your mission is to inspire them to care about the subject. In these cases, you will want to choose language that presents your commitment sincerely and emotionally.

Sincere emotional appeals are candid, unpretentious attempts to persuade your readers to adopt your feelings about the subject. Let's consider some of the examples from Stephen J. Gould's "Nonmoral Nature" (see Chapter 6), where the author presents us with how different scientists have described a small parasite. Note how the tone used to discuss the parasite's method of devouring its prey while alive affects how we feel toward it:

> 1. One may see the cricket, bitten to the quick, vainly move its antennae and abdominal styles, open and close its empty jaws, and even move a foot, but the larva is safe and searches its vitals with impunity. What an awful nightmare for the paralyzed cricket!

> 2. Is the caterpillar of a butterfly or moth the appropriate food for her young? You see her alight upon the plants where they are most usually to be met with, run quickly over them, carefully examining every leaf, and, having found the unfortunate object of her search, insert her sting into its flesh, and there deposit an egg. . . . The active Ichneumon braves every danger, and does not desist until her courage and address have insured subsistnce for one of her future progeny.

The first author, makes us look at the parasite from the prey's point of view ("What an awful nightmare for the paralyzed cricket!"), making the parasite appear a terrible creature. The second author, on the other hand, puts us in the parasite's place, seeing "her" as a loving mother who carefully chooses the best food for her "future progeny." The tone of the first is one of outrage at the apparent injustice of nature; the tone of the second is one of awe and respect for one of nature's smallest creatures. The tone is achieved both by the perspective the author takes and by the descriptive language (the cricket "vainly" struggles against its predator; the Ichneumon fly "braves every danger" with "courage").

Although, as Gould points out, a true scientist would adopt a more technical and disinterested tone, we cannot judge these examples as "bad writing" without considering the author's purpose. When choosing the tone of voice you want to use, you need to consider what your readers' emotional response to your position will be. Although there are some subjects, like abortion, flag burning, and censorship, that you expect would inspire strong feelings in your readers, there are others, like the foraging habits of the three-toed sloth, that you might rightly guess would appeal less to your readers. When choosing how to present your subject to your audience, you need to be aware of what your purpose is. Is your purpose to inspire your readers to care in a certain way about something they have not really thought about before? Or is it to get them to consider something a little more objectively, to distance them from emotions that might blind them from seeing your perspective?

The examples above would excite the interest of a reader who has not cared one way or another about the Ichneumon fly. However, if the authors of the two examples were writing to each other, they would probably fail to communicate effectively. Although the authors might sincerely feel what they express, they would not be sincerely and candidly appealing to their *reader's* emotions. When your readers are strongly committed to their position, you need to address them directly. Sometimes this requires you to begin your essay with an acknowledgment of why your readers feel as passionately as they do. You need to show you respect their feelings before you can expect them to respect yours.

EXERCISE

Look back at the two examples discussing the Ichneumon fly, and choose the one you most agree with. Then, in a paragraph or two, rewrite that example introducing it with a tone that would appeal to the author of the other example.

Irony and Satire

When you are faced with readers who are passionately committed to their view, and are predisposed to disagree with yours, a sincere, direct emotional appeal may not be sufficient. Instead, you might consider a tone of irony or satire. An ironic tone reveals the apparent contradictions in your readers' position by extending it to its logical extreme. For example, in the exercise on p. 309, we encountered a writer who was addressing parents who use disposable diapers. These parents had argued that they protect their children from disease by using the most sanitary product. The writer took that logic one step further: "The irony is, they claim to be making their children their primary concern, when all they are doing is ruining the world their children will inherit." Simply defined, irony is the process of proposing the opposite of what you believe. You are probably already familiar with the type of writing that uses irony most often, called satire. Satirists aren't just writers who make fun of others. They use satire to help teach readers or help them see things from a different point of view.

An ironic tone can help you explore your readers' argument thoroughly while you lead them to conclude that your position is more appealing, both rationally and emotionally. By discussing the logical development of their position, you distance your readers from their own emotional bias and enable them to see the issue more objectively. Instead of attacking their position, saying "I am right and you are wrong," you enable them to laugh at themselves.

Because irony achieves a humorous tone by discussing the readers' logic, there are really two thesis statements behind an ironic or satirical argument—an ironic thesis that states the opposite of what the writer believes, and the real thesis that the writer hopes to lead the reader to adopt. To help you understand how to develop an ironic thesis, let's consider the classic example of effective irony, Jonathan Swift's "A Modest Proposal." As you read it, see if you can pull out, first, the thesis that represents the argument he is ironically proposing, and, second, the thesis that represents his real stance.

A Modest Proposal

For Preventing the Children of Poor People in Ireland from Being a Burden to Their Parents or Country, and for Making Them Beneficial to the Public

It is a melancholy object to those who walk through this great town, or travel in the country, when they see the streets, the roads, and cabin-doors crowded with beggars of the female sex, followed by three, four, or six children, all in rags, and importuning every passenger for an alms. These mothers, instead of being able to work for their honest livelihood, are forced to employ all their time in strolling to beg sustenance for their helpless infants, who, as they grow up, either turn thieves for want of work, or leave their dear native country to fight for the Pretender in Spain, or sell themselves to the Barbadoes.

I think it is agreed by all parties, that this prodigious number of children in the arms, or on the backs, or at the heels of their mothers, and frequently of their fathers, is, in the present deplorable state of the kingdom, a very great additional grievance; and, therefore, whoever could find out a fair, cheap, and easy method of making these children sound and useful members of the commonwealth, would deserve so well of the public, as to have his statue set up for a preserver of the nation.

But my intention is very far from being confined to provide only for the children of professed beggars; it is of a much greater extent, and shall take in the whole number of infants at a certain age, who are born of parents in effect as little able to support them as those who demand our charity in the streets.

As to my own part, having turned my thoughts for many years upon this important subject, and maturely weighed the several schemes of other projectors, I have always found them grossly mistaken in their computation. It is true, a child, just dropped from its dam, may be supported by her milk for a solar year with little other nourishment; at most, not above the value of two shillings, which the mother may certainly get, or the value in scraps, by her lawful occupation of begging; and it is exactly at one year old that I propose to provide for them in such a manner, as, instead of being a charge upon their parents or the parish, or wanting food and raiment for the rest of their lives, they shall, on the contrary, contribute to the feeding, and partly to the clothing, of many thousands.

There is likewise another great advantage in my scheme, that it will prevent those voluntary abortions, and that horrid practice of women murdering their bastard children, alas, too frequent among us, sacrificing the poor innocent babes, I doubt more to avoid the expense than the shame, which would move tears and pity in the most savage and inhuman breast.

The number of souls in this kingdom being usually reckoned one million and a half, of these I calculate there may be about two hundred thousand couple whose wives are breeders; from which number I subtract thirty thousand couple, who are able to maintain their own children (although I apprehend there cannot be so many, under the present distresses of the kingdom); but this being granted, there will remain an hundred and seventy thousand breeders. I again subtract fifty thousand for those women who miscarry, or whose children die by accident or disease within the year. There only remain an hundred and twenty thousand children of poor parents annually born. The question therefore is how this number shall be reared and provided for? which, as I have already said, under the present situation of affairs, is utterly impossible by all the methods hitherto proposed. For we can neither employ them in handicraft or agriculture; we neither build houses (I mean in the country) nor cultivate land: they can very seldom pick up a livelihood by stealing until they arrive at six years old, except where they are of towardly parts; although I confess they learn the rudiments much earlier; during which time they can, however, be properly looked upon only as probationers; as I have been informed by a principal gentleman in the county of Cavan, who protested to me, that he never knew above one or two instances under the age of six, even in a part of the kingdom so renowned for the quickest proficiency in that art.

I am assured by our merchants that a boy or a girl before twelve years old is no salable commodity; and even when they come to this age they will not yield above three pounds or three pounds and half-a-crown at most, on the exchange; which cannot turn to account either to the parents or kingdom, the charge of nutriment and rags having been at least four times that value.

I shall now, therefore, humbly propose my own thoughts, which I hope will not be liable to the least objection.

I have been assured by a very knowing American of my acquaintance in London, that a young healthy child, well nursed, is, at a year old, a most delicious, nourishing, and wholesome food, whether stewed, roasted, baked, or boiled; and I make no doubt that it will equally serve in a fricassee or a ragout.

I do therefore humbly offer it to public consideration, that of the hundred and twenty thousand children already computed, twenty thousand may be reserved for breed, whereof only one-fourth part to be males; which is more than we allow to sheep, black cattle, or swine; and my reason is, that these children are seldom the fruits of marriage, a circumstance not much regarded by our savages, therefore one male will be sufficient to serve four females. That the remaining hundred thousand may, at a year old, be offered in sale to the persons of quality and fortune through the kingdom; always advising the mother to let them suck plentifully in the last month, so as to render them plump and fat for a good table. A child will make two dishes at an entertainment for friends; and when the family dines alone, the fore or hind quarter will make a reasonable dish, and, seasoned with a little pepper or salt, will be very good boiled on the fourth day, especially in winter.

I have reckoned, upon a medium, that a child just born will weigh twelve pounds, and in a solar year, if tolerably nursed, increaseth to twenty-eight pounds.

I grant this food will be somewhat dear, and therefore very proper for landlords, who, as they have already devoured most of the parents, seem to have the best title to the children.

Infants' flesh will be in season throughout the year, but more plentifully in March, and a little before and after: for we are told by a grave author, an eminent French physician, that fish being a prolific diet, there are more children born in Roman Catholic countries about nine months after Lent than at any other season; therefore, reckoning a year after Lent, the markets will be more glutted than usual, because the number of popish infants is at least three to one in this kingdom; and therefore it will have one other collateral advantage, by lessening the number of papists among us.

I have already computed the charge of nursing a beggar's child (in which list I reckon all cottagers, labourers, and four-fifths of the farmers) to be about two shillings per annum, rags included; and I believe no gentleman would repine to give ten shillings for the carcass of a good fat child, which, as I have said, will make four dishes of excellent nutritive meat, when he has only some particular friend, or his own family, to dine with him. Thus the squire will learn to be a good landlord, and grow popular among his tenants; the mother will have eight shillings net profit, and be fit for work till she produces another child.

Those who are more thrifty (as I must confess the times require) may flay the carcass; the skin of which, artificially dressed, will make admirable gloves for ladies, and summer-boots for fine gentlemen.

As to our city of Dublin, shambles may be appointed for this purpose in the most convenient parts of it, and butchers we may be assured will not be wanting; although I rather recommend buying the children alive, and dressing them hot from the knife, as we do roasting pigs.

A very worthy person, a true lover of his country, and whose virtues I highly esteem, was lately pleased, in discoursing on this matter, to offer a refinement upon my scheme. He said, that many gentlemen of this kingdom, having of late destroyed their deer, he conceived that the want of venison might be well supplied by the bodies of young lads and maidens, not exceeding fourteen years of age, nor under twelve; so great a number of both sexes in every country being now ready to starve for want of work and service; and these to be disposed of by their parents, if alive, or otherwise by their nearest relations. But, with due deference to so excellent a friend, and so deserving a patriot, I cannot be altogether in his sentiments; for as to the males, my American acquaintance assured me from frequent experience, that their flesh was generally tough and lean, like that of our schoolboys, by continual exercise, and their taste disagreeable; and to fatten them would not answer the charge. Then as to the females, it would, I think, with humble submission, be a loss to the public, because they soon would become breeders themselves: and besides, it is not improbable that some scrupulous people might be apt to censure such a practice (although indeed very unjustly) as a little bordering upon cruelty; which, I confess hath always been with me the strongest objection against any project, how well soever intended.

But in order to justify my friend, he confessed that this expedient was put into his head by the famous Psalmanazar, a native of the island Formosa, who came from thence to London above twenty years ago; and in conversation told my friend, that in his country, when any young person happened to be put to death, the executioner sold the carcass to persons of quality as a prime dainty; and that in his time the body of a plump girl of fifteen, who was crucified for an attempt to poison the emperor, was sold to his Imperial Majesty's prime minister of state, and other great mandarins of the court, in joints from the gibbet, at four hundred crowns. Neither indeed can I deny, that if the same use were made of several plump young girls in this town, who, without one single groat to their fortunes, cannot stir abroad without a chair, and appear at playhouse and assemblies in foreign fineries which they never will pay for, the kingdom would not be the worse.

Some persons of a desponding spirit are in great concern about that vast number of poor people who are aged, diseased, or maimed; and I have been desired to employ my thoughts what course may be taken to ease the nation of so grievous an encumbrance. But I am not in the least pain upon that matter, because it is very well known, that they are every day dying, and rotting, by cold and famine, and filth and vermin, as fast as can be reasonably expected. And as to the younger labourers, they are now in almost as hopeful a condition: they cannot get work, and consequently pine away for want of nourishment, to a degree, that if at any time they are accidentally hired to common labour, they have not strength to perform it; and thus the country and themselves are happily delivered from the evils to come.

I have too long digressed, and therefore shall return to my subject. I think the advantages by the proposal which I have made are obvious and many, as well as of the highest importance.

For first, as I have already observed, it would greatly lessen the number of papists, with whom we are yearly overrun, being the principal breeders of the nation as well as our most dangerous enemies; and who stay at home on purpose with a design to deliver the kingdom to the Pretender, hoping to take their advantage by the absence of so many good Protestants, who have chosen rather to leave their country than stay at home and pay tithes against their conscience to an idolatrous Episcopal curate.

Secondly, the poorer tenants will have something valuable of their own, which by law may be made liable to distress, and help to pay their landlord's rent; their corn and cattle being already seized, and money a thing unknown.

Thirdly, whereas the maintenance of a hundred thousand children, from two years old and upwards, cannot be computed at less than ten shillings a piece per annum, the nation's stock will be thereby increased fifty thousand pounds per annum; besides the profit of a new dish introduced to the tables of all gentlemen of fortune in the kingdom who have any refinement in taste. And the money will circulate among ourselves, the goods being entirely of our own growth and manufacture.

Fourthly, the constant breeders, besides the gain of eight shillings sterling per annum by the sale of their children, will be rid of the charge of maintaining them after the first year.

Fifthly, this food would likewise bring great custom to taverns; where the vintners will certainly be so prudent as to procure the best receipts for dressing it to perfection, and, consequently, have their houses frequented by all the fine gentlemen, who justly value themselves upon their knowledge in good eating: and a skillful cook, who understands how to oblige his guests, will contrive to make it as expensive as they please.

Sixthly, this would be a great inducement to marriage, which all wise nations have either encouraged by rewards, or enforced by laws and penalties. It would increase the care and tenderness of mothers towards their children, when they were sure of a settlement for life to the poor babes, provided in some sort by the public, to their annual profit instead of expense. We should soon see an honest emulation among the married women, which of them could bring the fattest child to the market. Men would become as fond of their wives during the time of their pregnancy, as they are now of their mares in foal, their cows in calf, or sows when they are ready to farrow; nor offer to beat or kick them (as is too frequent a practice) for fear of a miscarriage.

Many other advantages might be enumerated. For instance the addition of some thousand carcasses in our exportation of barrelled beef; the propagation of swine's flesh, and improvement in the art of making good bacon, so much wanted among us by the great destruction of pigs, too frequent at our tables, which are no way comparable in taste or magnificence to a well-grown, fat yearling child, which, roasted whole, will make a considerable figure at a Lord Mayor's feast, or any other public entertainment. But this, and many others, I omit, being studious of brevity.

Supposing that one thousand families in this city would be constant customers for infants' flesh, besides others who might have it at merry meetings, particularly weddings and christenings, I compute that Dublin would take off annually about twenty thousand carcasses; and the rest of the kingdom (where probably they will be sold somewhat cheaper) the remaining eighty thousand.

I can think of no one objection that will possibly be raised against this proposal, unless it should be urged, that the number of people will be thereby much lessened in the kingdom. This I freely own, and it was indeed one principal design in offering it to the world. I desire the reader will observe that I calculate my remedy for this one individual kingdom of Ireland, and for no other that ever was, is, or I think ever can be, upon earth. Therefore let no man talk to me of other expedients: of taxing our absentees at five shillings a pound: of using neither clothes nor household-furniture except what is of our own growth and manufacture: of utterly rejecting the materials and instruments that promote foreign luxury: of curing the expensiveness of pride, vanity, idleness, and gaming in our women: of introducing a vein of parsimony, prudence, and temperance: of learning to love our country, wherein we differ even from Laplanders, and the inhabitants of Topinamboo: of quitting our animosities and factions, nor act any longer like the Jews, who were murdering one another at the very moment their city was taken: of being a little cautious not to sell our country and consciences for nothing: of teaching landlords to have at least one degree of mercy towards their tenants: lastly, of putting a spirit of honesty, industry, and skill into our shopkeepers; who, if a resolution could now be taken to buy only our native goods, would immediately unite to cheat and exact upon us in the price, the measure, and the goodness, nor could ever yet be brought to make one fair proposal of just dealing, though often and earnestly invited to it.

Therefore I repeat, let no man talk to me of these and the like expedients, till he hath at least some glimpse of hope that there will ever be some hearty and sincere attempt to put them in practice.

But, as to myself, having been wearied out for many years with offering vain, idle, visionary thoughts, and at length utterly despairing of success, I fortunately fell upon this proposal; which, as it is wholly new, so it hath something solid and real, of no expense and little trouble, full in our own power, and whereby we can incur no danger in disobliging England. For this kind of commodity will not bear exportation, the flesh being of too tender a consistence to admit a long continuance in salt, although perhaps I could name a country which would be glad to eat up our whole nation without it.

    After all, I am not so violently bent upon my own opinion as to reject any offer proposed by wise men which shall be found equally innocent, cheap, easy, and effectual. But before something of that kind shall be advanced in contradiction to my scheme, and offering a better, I desire the author, or authors, will be pleased maturely to consider two points. First, as things now stand, how they will be able to find food and raiment for a hundred thousand useless mouths and backs? And, secondly, there being a round million of creatures in human figure throughout this kingdom, whose whole subsistence put into a common stock would leave them in debt two million of pounds sterling, adding those who are beggars by profession, to the bulk of farmers, cottagers, and labourers, with the wives and children who are beggars in effect; I desire those politicians who dislike my overture, and may perhaps be so bold as to attempt an answer, that they will first ask the parents of these mortals, whether they would not at this day think it a great happiness to have been sold for food at a year old, in the manner I prescribe, and thereby have avoided such a perpetual scene of misfortunes as they have since gone through, by the oppression of landlords, the impossibility of paying rent without money or trade, the want of common sustenance, with neither house nor clothes to cover them from the inclemencies of weather, and the most inevitable prospect of entailing the like, or greater miseries, upon their breed for ever.

    I profess, in the sincerity of my heart, that I have not the least personal interest in endeavouring to promote this necessary work, having no other motive than the public good of my country, by advancing our trade, providing for infants, relieving the poor, and giving some pleasure to the rich. I have no children by which I can propose to get a single penny; the youngest being nine years old, and my wife past child-bearing.

    Here is a suggested thesis for Swift's ironic argument. Note how it reveals how he has taken his readers' logical arguments one step further to emphasize just why he found them ethically unacceptable:

Swift's Readers' Argument (A)
and Swift's Extension of His Readers' Logic (B):
A. The Irish people should solve their own problems

                        because

they have the means to do so

                        because

B. the children that burden them can be productively marketed as food, clothing, and other commodities.

Note how Swift begins his essay on an emotional and logical point of agreement with his readers about how the problems facing the impoverished Irish are the result of an overpopulation crisis perpetuated by their religious beliefs. The emotional point of agreement is clearest when he expresses how he shares his readers' horror at how the women murder their own children, "sacrificing the poor innocent babes I doubt more to avoid the expense than the shame."

Swift clearly is sincere when he concludes that the murder of bastard children "would move tears and pity in the most savage and inhuman breast." However, he uses this emotional outrage that he shares with his readers to prepare them to arrive at a new conclusion. Where his readers see this horrid practice as evidence of how barbarous and uncivilized the Irish people are, Swift's following argument will lead his readers to see themselves as being just as, if not more, barbarous.

Swift prepares his readers emotionally to help them recognize the hypocrisy of their own position when he takes their logical argument to its practical conclusion: suggesting that the Irish people solve their own problems by killing their surplus children for profit rather than mere expedience. Irony is tricky, though. Imagine what could happen if Swift's readers did not detect the irony in his argument but took it seriously! Even if they did recognize the outrageousness of his proposal, they still might dismiss it as mere sarcasm, without an underlying thesis. To avoid this, Swift carefullly leads his readers through an ironic consideration of the opposition, beginning with the comment, "I can think of no one objection that will possibly be raised against this proposal, unless it should be urged, that the number of people will be thereby much lessened in the kingdom." At this point, Swift makes his readers discover how unattractive, emotionally and ethically, their argument can sound.

Once you recognize Swift's tone, you can revise his apparent thesis to reveal the real point he is making. Here is one way you might do this. Note how the implied thesis reveals Swift's real argument and his emotional commitment to it:

Swift's Ironic Thesis:
The Irish people should solve their own problems

because

the children that burden them can be productively marketed as food, clothing, and other commodities.

Swift's Implied Thesis:
We are more barbaric and uncivilized than the impoverished, illiterate people of Ireland

because

we would rather sacrifice the lives of innocent women and children, the whole people of Ireland, than alter a life of pride, vanity, and idleness.

This revised thesis identifies the real issue behind Swift's argument: "How moral are we?" It also uncovers his real voice, the moral character of Swift the man, through careful word choice: "barbaric," "uncivilized," "pride," "vanity," and "idleness." Note also the tone of the revised thesis, how Swift presents his subject, the Irish people, to us. They are "impoverished," "illiterate," "innocent women and children" who are "sacrificed." Formulating the implied thesis behind the ironic argument can help you both discover Swift's real meaning and clarify your emotional responses to his argument.

Analyzing a thesis statement for tone and voice as well as meaning can help you clarify how you feel and what you really think about something you have read. Similarly, you can also analyze the tone and voice behind your own thesis statement to guide your own writing. If you revise your thesis to make it most appealing to your readers, paying particular attention to its style—the word choice, word order, and rhythm—you can determine the best voice and tone to use when writing out your argument.

EXERCISE

Analyze the voice and tone implied by the style of the following thesis statements. When you have finished, see if you can formulate an ironic thesis that would argue for the same point.

1. Only stupid students skip class because those who skip class think they know all they need to know.
2. Scientific research contributes to the decline of civilization because scientific researchers murder little, innocent animals.
3. Movie rating systems are unconstitutional because they are a form of censorship.
4. True beauty is a joy forever because it allows us to forget our mortal limitations.

As you will discover in the next chapter, you can also develop a thesis that can represent the overall tone and voice behind a literary work. Although writers use fiction to dramatize the interaction among the voices of several different characters, their stories lead us to view the world from their perspective. We may not always agree on what the author is arguing for through his or her dramatizations, but identifying the argument behind the characters' voices and the overall tone of the work can help us recognize, in ways that nonfictional arguments cannot, the value of several different stances.

CHAPTER FOURTEEN

Reasoning About Literature

*T*hroughout this book, we have been discussing how different disciplines use language to make knowledge. An important part of the discussion has been about the reading process and the different ways you can interpret what you read. This kind of reasoning about the rhetoric of others is a fundamental part of reasoning about literature. As you will discover in this chapter, what is at issue when you discuss a story, a poem, or a play is how you read it, how you interpret a literary work as the author's argument for a particular perspective on life itself.

The rhetoric of literature paints an imaginative universe that mirrors your own. When you read a poem, play, or short story, the language invites you to both enter the literary world and to evaluate it, to simultaneously feel with and think about the lives of others. Although the literary world is fictional, it expresses real feelings and attitudes, emotions that can educate your own awareness of what it means to be human. When you reason about a literary work, you explore how the language leads you to empathize with or condemn certain characters or attitudes. No matter what genre (or kind) of literature you read—whether it is poetry, drama, or fiction, comedy or tragedy—the work leads you to reason about questions of value: What is the value of the literature? Why were these human experiences important to the author and what value do they have for today? Which of the characters, actions, or feelings are better than others and why? Asking these questions as you read helps you enter into a conversation with other readers about how the author's imaginative universe can help all of us become better human beings.

A helpful way to reason about the value of a poem, play, or novel is to view the literary work as rhetoric, as the author's contribution to an ongoing conversation about the value of human existence. When you talk with or write to other readers about the work of literature, you interpret what the author's argument might be. More precisely, you reveal how the author's language, description of characters, and/or telling of the story has led you to experience and evaluate life in a very particular way. Your purpose is not altogether different from that of the writing you produce when you wish to clarify Gould's definition of scientific reasoning or Keynes's economic argument for your reader. However, reasoning about a question of definition or consequence differs from reasoning about a question of value. Questions of value, of what is "good" or "bad," "comic" or "tragic," are relative and can result in different answers depending on one's perspective. For example, reading about a suicide in the paper can lead us to despair with the victim, grieve with the family, or better appreciate how lucky we are. To fully appreciate the value of any experience, you need to see your life from different perspectives. A poet, dramatist, or novelist can give you these different perspectives, as they present human experiences through the many kinds of literary "voices" that make up the rhetoric of literature.

LITERARY VOICES

As you remember from Chapter 13, "voice" is that aspect of the writing that reveals the writer's attitude toward the subject under discussion. For example, you detect different voices when one politician discusses a proposal to raise taxes as "a way to *fight our* war on poverty" and another speaker talks about it as "a way to *finance the liberals'* war on poverty." Just changing two or three words makes the difference between a committed, sincere voice and a cynical, disapproving one. Although both speakers are giving the same justification for the tax increase, their perspectives on that justification are diametrically opposed.

Whenever you read, you are affected in one way or another by voice. A stance you find unacceptable may become more appealing because you are attracted to the writer's general attitude toward life; or a stance you thought you supported may become distasteful as you begin to hear how it sounds when presented by someone whose overall attitude you don't respect. The writer's voice helps you see the world from a different perspective, and even when you are not convinced the writer's position is better than your own, testing your perspective against another's helps you commit yourself to a position you can value.

In the nonfiction arguments of political science, history, or psychology, you can usually trust the voice you hear is that of the author. In more "artful" literary essays, such as Jonathan Swift's "A Modest Proposal", you may have to work a little harder to evaluate what the author's voice can tell you. Literary essays, such as Swift's "A Modest Proposal," or philosophical essays, such as Plato's "Allegory of the Cave," use an artificial voice in order to direct our attention to questions of value. By adopting an artificial voice—speaking as one or several different characters or even as the opponent—the author directs the reader's attention to *how* something is being said, to recognize that the real subject is a certain perspective on life, a way of evaluating what is being talked about.

In literary fiction, drama, or poetry, the author speaks to you through several different voices. The more voices you hear, the more you discover different perspectives on the world. On one level, you hear the voice of the speaker of a poem, the voice of a narrator in a novel, or the several different voices of the characters of a play. On another level, you discover an authorial voice as you explore how you value the voice of the speaker or characters, and reason toward answers for why the author created them. And ultimately, you discover the voices of other readers, deliberate about the different ways we can interpret the work, and arrive at new perspectives on the value the story, poem, or play holds for us today.

One way of making sense of these different voices is to consider the three different worlds they represent. The voices of the speaker or characters help you discover what kind of world the author has created. This can help you discover an authorial voice, how the imaginative world is the author's perspective on his or her own life and time. And when you consider the different ways modern readers might evaluate the work, you develop a better perspective on what this authorial voice can tell you about your own life. You might use the following diagram to picture how these different worlds influence each other when you reason about literature:

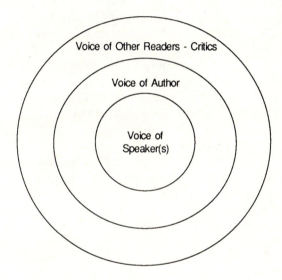

Each of these different spheres represents a kind of literary voice that influences how you reason about literature. Ultimately, other critical readers (not the characters nor the author) are the audience you address when you reason and write about the literature. What you and your audience find at issue in the work, though, will usually focus on one or another of these worlds, whether the question is about how to interpret and evaluate one or another character, about what the author was trying to say, or about the value the literature holds for readers today.

The Voices of Characters, Speakers, and Narrators

To discover the value of the individual voices you hear in literature, you listen for clues about their motivation. What makes the speaker or characters think, speak, or act as they do? How much should you respect, condemn, or pity them? Your answers lead you to consider how much control characters have over their own lives, and how the conditions of their world restrict or determine what they do and say. For example, in Shakespeare's play *Othello*, you hear how Othello feels he has no choice but to murder his beloved wife, Desdemona, because he is almost certain she has committed adultery, and betrayal must be revenged. In his perspective, his act is justified—until after Desdemona dies, and he discovers that Desdemona was not guilty at all. You are left to evaluate Othello's deed in view of his motivation: Was he selfishly deceiving himself, more worried about what a cheating wife would do to his reputation than about her guilt or innocence? Was he a victim of his world, a noble but naive man manipulated and deceived by others who were jealous of his position? Or is he merely human, a victim of circumstances, of an incomprehensible fate, over which no individual has control?

To interpret Othello's motivation, you compare what he says with what he does and with how other characters perceive him. No one perspective is complete, and several are contradictory. To arrive at the most probable answer as to why Othello does what he does, you compare the voices of the different speakers, decide what each values most in life, and determine which voices deserve your respect. Whether the comparison results in an interpretation of Othello as noble, naive, or merely human will determine whether you interpret his fate at the end of the play as unjust, fair, or merely unfortunate. Ultimately, evaluating Othello's fate in view of his motivation leads you to some conclusions about Shakespeare's perspective on the human condition and what it can tell you about your own.

When you read a play, you look behind the voices of the speakers to find the voice of the author. This is also true for how you read a poem. Even when a poem appears to reflect the author's own feelings and thoughts, what you are really hearing is a *persona,* a role a poet adopts to make it easier to explore ways of making sense out of personal experience and feeling. The nineteenth-century poet, William Wordsworth, described poetry as "the spontaneous overflow of feelings recollected in tranquility." What he meant is that, even when a poem conveys heartfelt emotion, it is really a recreation and interpretation of what the poet *once* felt but could not express at the time. Because writing literature requires a disciplined use of words, a poet fashions art out of his or her emotions in order to get a perspective on them, a perspective that can expand our own awareness of what it means to be human.

Let's consider the following poem, an epitaph taken from a gravestone:

Here lies Fred,
Who was alive and is dead:
Had it been his father,
I had much rather;
Had it been his brother,
Still better than another;
Had it been his sister,
No one would have missed her;
Had it been the whole generation,
Still better for the nation:
But since 'tis only Fred,
Who was alive and is dead,—
There's no more to be said.
    —(*Anonymous, repeated by Horace Walpole in* Memoirs of George II, *1847)*

The poem is least about Fred, somewhat more about his family and "the whole generation," even more about the poet's feelings for Fred. Most of all, though, the poem is about how we might make sense out of the death of *any* "Fred." Read the poem aloud, listening to how the short lines and the rhyme affect how you read it. What tone do the words convey (remember that tone is the speaker's attitude toward the subject)? What does that attitude tell you about the speaker's perspective, his or her feelings not just about Fred but about the value of all human life?

The perspective you hear may have been the poet's at one time but it is more the result of a writer using artificial language—short lines, rhyme, the form of an epitaph—to reason about an experience. Note how the poem clearly moves as an argument, beginning with the implied question "What can we say about the death of Fred?" and arriving at the answer "But since 'tis only Fred, / Who was alive and is dead,— / There's no more to be said." The artificial form has organized the poet's emotions into a perspective on life, a perspective where the death of one ordinary human being, while reminding us of our own insignificant lives, leads us away from despair to almost laugh at our need to find meaning in an absurd world. The poet has adopted an artificial "voice" that represents one way the poet could shape mixed emotions toward the value of life and death into significant meaning.

As with any literature, writers of poetry use language to reason, and they can reason about emotions only if they are distanced from them. If you have tried writing poetry when overcome with emotion, you probably have recognized how difficult it is to express your feelings so that they are meaningful to someone else. To make the poetry say something, you have to stop feeling and start thinking about the language you are using and how it would sound to a reader. You adopt a "voice" or persona, one specific perspective that will help organize your thoughts and make them understandable to a reader. Similarly, when you read a poem, you are experiencing a voice that leads you to see the world from a different perspective, if only for a moment.

When you read a short story or novel, you also hear artificial, literary voices. Often, though, you will hear one speaker's voice about the rest—that of the teller of the tale, or the narrator. The narrator, the person who tells you the story, could represent any number of people: one of the characters reminiscing about what happened; an authority figure that tells you how to evaluate what different characters say or do; or a reporter that objectively tells you what happened, even what different characters thought at the time, but doesn't offer any commentary. Only the latter can give you a somewhat impartial view of what happened, but even without commentary, the reporter does shape your perspective of the story. The way any narrator describes the setting—the countryside, the town, the weather, the time of day—creates images that affect your response to and interpretation of the story.

To reason about a fictional work, you explore questions about why the author wrote it and what perspective it can give you on your own life. However, similar to the speaker in the poem, the narrator of a novel is not usually a trustworthy spokesperson for the author. Let's look at how one author uses the narrator's voice to introduce you to what the story is really about. Here is how Mark Twain introduces you to the narrator of *The Adventures of Huckleberry Finn:*

You don't know about me, without you have read a book by the name of "The Adventures of Tom Sawyer," but that ain't no matter. That book was made by Mr. Mark Twain, and he told the truth, mainly. There was things which he stretched, but mainly he told the truth. That is nothing. I never seen anybody but lied, one time or another, . . .

Although Mark Twain is the *author* of the book, the *narrator,* or the teller of the tale, is Huckleberry Finn. As Huck has informed you, his view of the truth is not quite the same as Twain's. The author "stretched" the truth a little before, and you are to rely on Huck as a more credible authority. However, this can become quite confusing when you consider that Twain makes Huck say these things: Is the author really telling you not to trust Huck?

Because Huck is the narrator, you know you will have to rely on his view of what happened to interpret the story; however, you also know you cannot rely on this character's voice alone. Indirectly, the author has told you in those first few sentences that you need to be aware of how Huck's attitudes, prejudices, and fears may color his view of the world. This means you will also have to consider what the other characters say and do, always keeping in mind that they are presented to you through Huck's eyes.

By making a character the narrator, Twain has forced the reader to consider the voices of all of the speakers as keys to evaluating Huck's interpretation of the world. The question at issue for the reader becomes not what happened, or why it did, as much as who is this person Huck and how does he reflect a little of us?

The Voice of the Author

You begin to develop an interpretation of *Huckleberry Finn* as you reason about why Huck and the other characters act and think as they do. To discover what the lives of these characters can tell you about your own life, though, you need to consider what the author's purpose was in creating them, how the fates of the characters reveal something about how humans should or should not lead their lives. To interpret the work is to find an "authorial voice," an authoritative perspective on what is said and what happens. However, keep in mind that this authorial voice is only your interpretation of what the author meant to say.

Mark Twain prefaced *Huckleberry Finn* with this warning: "Persons attempting to find a motive in this narrative will be prosecuted; persons attempting to find a moral in it will be banished; persons attempting to find a plot in it will be shot." Half-serious and half-joking, Twain warns you that reasoning about literature is not finding the author's answer to a literary puzzle. An important part of writing literary criticism is making certain you argue for an interpretation that considers the work as a whole. For example, critics who conclude that Mark Twain's *Huckleberry Finn* is racist cannot just point at the language used by Huck and Jim but also have to consider Twain's purpose in choosing that language. To justify their evaluation, they need to prove that the author's voice is also racist, that the work could clearly be interpreted as presenting a view of life that supports discrimination against blacks. To decide whether their interpretation is authoritative, they need to consider whether it is probable that other readers could interpret the authorial voice in the same way.

There are several ways to discover an authorial voice in a literary work. Most important is viewing the work as an argument, as the author's way of leading the reader to explore a question of value. To understand what the author's own questions were, you can explore what issues were important at the time when the work was written (what we call "historical criticism"), or investigate what concerned the author personally ("biographical criticism"), or analyze how the author revised the work through subsequent drafts ("textual criticism"). Of course, a good reader can always detect evidence of an authorial voice in the work itself.

To discover the author's voice in a work of literature, you need to step back from the fictional world to consider why the author created it. Although the world is fictional, the author wrote it to communicate, to engage in conversation with his or her reader. Although you can never recapture exactly what an author had in mind when he or she wrote (perhaps even the author was not quite sure), you can ask the same questions about the author's intention that you ask of other arguments: What are the questions the author appears to be posing about human nature? What possible answers does he or she explore? What does the author want us to do as a consequence of what he or she has discovered?

The Voice of the Critic

The literary interpretation you develop, the "authorial voice" you hear as you make sense of *Huckleberry Finn,* may or may not fit the intentions of Mark Twain as he wrote in 1885. The interpretation you arrive at is one perspective on the meaning the story holds for you today. However, although there is not one "right" interpretation, there is a difference between a "good" or "bad" one. You can feel pretty sure your interpretation is "good" only if it can be justified to other readers.

To arrive at a good interpretation, you need to read with the voices of other readers in mind. For example, you might read Twain's warning to the readers of *Huckleberry Finn* by imagining the kind of conversation other readers might have about it: "Twain is merely using reverse psychology, challenging us to see if we can find a motive, moral, and plot," says one. "On the contrary, I think Twain is deadly serious. He is probably afraid we will misinterpret his work, that we might say he is advocating racism, for example, rather than merely see that as a part of Huck's character," responds another. "But what if this is not Twain but Huck talking here?" asks another. "Couldn't it be that Huck is merely warning us that the book is about real life, not a mere tale told to teach a lesson?" As you listen to these different voices, you might deliberate further, arriving at the conclusion that Twain is telling you there is not just *one* motive, moral, or plot, but, as in life, many possible ways to explain why the story unfolds as it does. This interpretation of the short passage would be a "better" one than any of them alone because it had accommodated all the possible readings you could imagine.

To anticipate how other readers might interpret a literary work, you must learn to appreciate and interpret literature as other critics do. When you enter into a discussion about the literature with your classmates, you enter into the kind of conversations literary critics have. Academic conversations about literary works are based on a "sugar pill" theory—the belief that literature entertains in order to teach something valuable. Horace, the Roman poet, said the purpose of literature is to delight, teach, and move the reader. Your purpose, as a literary critic, is to expose to your reader how a literary work achieves these ends: How does the story "delight" us? What does it "teach" us about life, fate, or human nature? How does it "move" us to act in our own lives?

The questions literary critics discuss are all based on questions of value, questions about how to evaluate certain characters, events, or feelings as "good" or "bad" in some way. To reason about the question of value in a literary work, you might focus on any one of the literary voices. You might find your information only from the text: how the images, the characters, and/or the story work together to make meaning. Or, to explore how a work moves you, you might analyze the author's purpose and whether you respond as the author intended you to. Or you might discuss how a modern reader might respond to the work, comparing established attitudes towards certain images, ideas, or characters with their representation in the work under discussion. However, because literary worlds are so rich, mirrors of the complexity of life itself, there is no limit to the number of critical approaches you might take. One could approach them from the perspective of any of the other disciplines we have studied in this book.

You will have difficulty appreciating a literary work, however, if you do not let it entertain you first. Let yourself live in the world of the poem, short story, or play before you step back to analyze it. Feel with the characters, try to experience their perspective before passing judgment on them. And remember that literary works survive the test of time because they can be interpreted in many different ways, and can reveal something new to us each time we read and discuss them. The modern readers you will discuss these works with, and ultimately write your essay to, can benefit from the unique perspective your voice can contribute to this ongoing conversation.

To His Coy Mistress

Andrew Marvell (1621–1678)

Andrew Marvell was born five years after Shakespeare's death. After a brief stint at Cambridge, he spent the remainder of his life as a tutor, poet, and political pamphleteer. His life and work reflect many of the difficult changes England went through during this volatile time, beginning with the beheading of King Charles I and the establishment of Parliament in 1640, and continuing through the uneasy reinstatement of monarchy when Charles II returned to take the throne in 1660. Marvell himself shifted his political allegiance during this period, at first supporting the Parliament, only to become an elected member in 1659 and part of the Convention that invited Charles II to return. After the restoration of the monarchy, however, Marvell became increasingly bitter toward England's new government, to the extent that he wrote many powerful verse satires that later gained the admiration of Swift.

Just as Marvell's later work reflects the temperament of the Restoration period, his early work contains elements of the artful playfulness of the English Renaissance. The relatively early poem included here is a good example of how Marvell synthesized the various poetic voices of his time. As you read "To His Coy Mistress," see if you can detect the pastoral tradition, the voice of the passionate shepherd appealing for the love of a young maiden: What images tend to describe making love as an innocent act of nature? Look also for elements of the courtly love tradition: Where is there the voice of a rejected courtier, whose passion springs less from love than from the fact that he is appealing to an unobtainable (perhaps married) lady of the court? See, too, if you can detect traces of a more philosophical and ironic speaker, the voice of the metaphysical tradition. Are there any images that force you to seek connections between two dissimilar images, making you think about the feelings being described? (This technique, called the "conceit," is often credited to John Donne, Marvell's contemporary. A particularly striking example comes from Donne's "The Flea," a poem that compares making love to the mingling of the lovers' blood in the body of a flea.)

Part of the appeal of Marvell's work is how well he could unite these different poetic voices into a perspective on life that could be seen as simultaneously sensual and intellectual, carefree and cynical. As you read the poem, underline any words, lines, or images that seem to be keys to the speaker's real attitude. What do you think is most important to him, winning the lady or something else?

Had we but world enough, and time,
This coyness, lady, were no crime.
We would sit down, and think which way
To walk, and pass our long love's day.
Thou by the Indian Ganges' side   5
Shouldst rubies find: I by the tide
Of Humber would complain. I would
Love you ten years before the Flood:
And you should if you please refuse
Till the conversion of the Jews.   10

My vegetable love should grow
Vaster than empires, and more slow.
An hundred years should go to praise
Thine eyes, and on thy forehead gaze.
Two hundred to adore each breast: 15
But thirty thousand to the rest.
An age at least to every part,
And the last age should show your heart.
For, lady, you deserve this state;
Nor would I love at lower rate.   20
        But at my back I always hear
Time's winged chariot hurrying near:
And yonder all before us lie
Deserts of vast eternity.
Thy beauty shall no more be found,   25
Nor, in thy marble vault, shall sound
My echoing song; then worms shall try
That long preserved virginity:
And your quaint honour turn to dust;
And into ashes all my lust.   30
The grave's a fine and private place,
But none, I think, do there embrace.
        Now therefore, while the youthful hue
Sits on thy skin like morning dew,
And while thy willing soul transpires   35
At every pore with instant fires,
Now let us sport us while we may;
And now, like am'rous birds of prey,
Rather at once our time devour,
Than languish in his slow-chapped pow'r.   40
Let us roll all our strength, and all
Our sweetness, up into one ball:
And tear our pleasures with rough strife,
Through the iron gates of life.
Thus, though we cannot make our sun   45
Stand still, yet we will make him run.

QUESTIONS FOR A CRITICAL REREADING

Once you have read through the poem, underlining the images that made an impression on you, use the following questions to help you reread the poem more critically.

1. Before rereading the poem, analyze what you have underlined. List the images or lines in your notebook in the order in which they appear in the poem. How does the speaker's voice change as the poem progresses? (For example, explain the change from "vegetable love" of line 11 to "am'rous birds of prey" in line 38.) Is his overall attitude reverent, cynical, sincere, or something else?

2. Now that you have a general impression of the speaker's attitude and feelings, you can begin to construct a sentence outline for his logical argument. Read the first stanza (i.e., the first grouping of lines ending at line 20). What appears to be the question at issue? What does he imply is the coy mistress's position on that issue?
3. The middle stanza reveals the new information the speaker presents to change his mistress' mind. Summarize this stanza into one sentence (note that this would be the logical "because" clause of his apparent thesis). When you have finished, summarize the logical conclusion ("Now therefore . . .") presented in the last stanza.
4. How well does the stance expressed in the logical argument fit the voice of the speaker as you defined it for question 1? Do any of the images and metaphors work against the argument? Cite what you see as the three most important images and explain how they affect your response to the poem. How would you define the speaker's attitude toward the coy mistress? Toward life generally?
5. Reread the poem a third time, this time exploring how Marvell has used an artificial voice—regular rhyme, the logical form of three stanzas, perhaps inventing the coy mistress herself—to reason about his feelings. What appears to be the *poet's* major concern? (Note carefully the shifts in perspective indicated by the pronouns "you," "we," and "I." Which perspective comes closest to the author's?) Construct a thesis statement that summarizes what you think Marvell is trying to tell us.

POSSIBLE ISSUES FOR WRITING

Because the major issue behind reasoning about literature is how you interpret the work, some of your answers to the critical rereading questions may be at issue for the class. Keeping that in mind, use the following possible issues to identify just where your interpretation of the poem differs from that of your classmates. Use your notebook to record any interpretations your classmates offer that are new to you, and particular passages or lines they use to support their position. The different perspectives will help you reason out your own interpretation when you write your essay at the end of this chapter.

1. When we talk about the "voice" of the speaker, we are talking about the person's attitude and what it reveals about his character. A good way of discovering what you think about the speaker as a person is to imagine how the coy mistress might respond to his argument. Although you only have his perspective of her to rely on, decide from the poem what kind of person she is. Would she have been persuaded? Why or why not?
2. Knowing what you do about Marvell and the time when he was writing this poem (it was probably written around 1650, after the beheading of Charles I but before the restoration of his son), what attitudes or concerns expressed in the poem are probably conventional for that time? Which do you think reveal something unique about Marvell?
3. As a modern reader, what do you see as the primary value of Marvell's poem? How has it changed your attitude? Consider the view Marvell gives us of women and men, conventional morality, time, and human existence.

A Good Man Is Hard to Find

Flannery O'Connor *(1925–1964)*

*Flannery O'Connor was born and raised in Georgia, and her fiction places her among other important southern writers like William Faulkner, Carson McCullers, and Eudora Welty. During her life, she published two novels—*Wise Blood *(1952) and* The Violent Bear It Away *(1960)—and a collection of short fiction,* A Good Man Is Hard to Find and Other Stories *(1955). Another collection of her short stories,* Everything That Rises Must Converge *(1965), appeared a year after her death from lupus, an autoimmune disease she inherited from her father.*

O'Connor's fiction offers an unusual perspective into the human heart, often proffered through grotesque southern characters—cripples, snake-oil preachers, juvenile delinquents, and self-righteous hypocrites. Her orthodox Roman Catholic upbringing led her to a unique fascination with the demonic and the divine, and the social misfit's struggle for God's grace during life and at death. Although her stories are fraught with disturbing violence and her characters tawdry, tormented souls, O'Connor manages to make her fictional world parallel ours, always making us question why we think we are any better than the pitiful, grotesque creatures she gives us.

Although literature has constantly examined the struggle between the individual will and a destined fate, when O'Connor examines it in "A Good Man is Hard to Find," she confronts us with a disturbing resolution. As you read the story, see if you can reach an answer to the value question implied by the title: Why is a good man hard to find? What makes someone "good"? As you read, try to keep track of the different perspectives O'Connor offers: who are the main characters and is one the "good" we seek? How does the narrator shape our interpretation of the events and characters? And, ultimately, who is O'Connor, and why does she give us this disturbing vision of human existence?

The grandmother didn't want to go to Florida. She wanted to visit some of her connections in east Tennessee and she was seizing at every chance to change Bailey's mind. Bailey was the son she lived with, her only boy. He was sitting on the edge of his chair at the table, bent over the orange sports section of the *Journal*. "Now look here, Bailey," she said, "see here, read this," and she stood with one hand on her thin hip and the other rattling the newspaper at his bald head. "Here this fellow that calls himself The Misfit is aloose from the Federal Pen and headed toward Florida and you read here what it says he did to these people. Just you read it. I wouldn't take my children in any direction with a criminal like that aloose in it. I couldn't answer to my conscience if I did."

Bailey didn't look up from his reading so she wheeled around then and faced the children's mother, a young woman in slacks, whose face was as broad and innocent as a cabbage and was tied around with a gren headkerchief that had two points on the top like rabbit's ears. She was sitting on the sofa, feeding the baby his apricots out of a jar. "The children have been to Florida before," the old lady said. "You all ought to take them somewhere else for a change so they would see different parts of the world and be broad. They never have been to east Tennessee."

The children's mother didn't seem to hear her but the eight-year-old boy, John Wesley, a stocky child with glasses, said, "If you don't want to go to Florida, why dontcha stay at home?" He and the little girl, June Star, were reading the funny papers on the floor.

"She wouldn't stay at home to be queen for a day," June Star said without raising her yellow head.

"Yes and what would you do if this fellow, The Misfit, caught you?" the grandmother asked.

"I'd smack his face," John Wesley said.

"She wouldn't stay at home for a million bucks," June Star said. "Afraid she'd miss something. She has to go everywhere we go."

"All right, Miss," the grandmother said. "Just remember that the next time you want me to curl your hair."

June Star said her hair was naturally curly.

The next morning the grandmother was the first one in the car, ready to go. She had her big black valise that looked like the head of a hippopotamus in one corner, and underneath it she was hiding a basket with Pitty Sing, the cat, in it. She didn't intend for the cat to be left alone in the house for three days because he would miss her too much and she was afraid he might brush against one of the gas burners and accidentally asphyxiate himself. Her son, Bailey, didn't like to arrive at a motel with a cat.

She sat in the middle of the back seat with John Wesley and June Star on either side of her. Bailey and the children's mother and the baby sat in the front and they left Atlanta at eight forty-five with the mileage on the car at 55890. The grandmother wrote this down because she thought it would be interesting to say how many miles they had been when they got back. It took them twenty minutes to reach the outskirts of the city.

The old lady settled herself comfortably, removing her white cotton gloves and putting them up with her purse on the shelf in front of the back window. The children's mother still had on slacks and still had her head tied up in a green kerchief, but the grandmother had on a navy blue straw sailor hat with a bunch of white violets on the brim and a navy blue dress with a small white dot in the print. Her collar and cuffs were white organdy trimmed with lace and at her neckline she had pinned a purple spray of cloth violets containing a sachet. In case of an accident, anyone seeing her dead on the highway would know at once that she was a lady.

She said she thought it was going to be a good day for driving, neither too hot nor too cold, and she cautioned Bailey that the speed limit was fifty-five miles an hour and that the patrolmen hid themselves behind billboards and small clumps of trees and sped out after you before you had a chance to slow down. She pointed out interesting details of the scenery: Stone Mountain; the blue granite that in some places came up to both sides of the highway; the brilliant red clay banks slightly streaked with purple; and the various crops that made rows of green lace-work on the ground. The trees were full of silver-white sunlight and the meanest of them sparkled. The children were reading comic magazines and their mother had gone back to sleep.

"Let's go through Georgia fast so we won't have to look at it much," John Wesley said.

"If I were a little boy," said the grandmother, "I wouldn't talk about my native state that way. Tennessee has the mountains and Georgia has the hills."

"Tennessee is just a hillbilly dumping ground," John Wesley said, "and Georgia is a lousy state too."

"You said it," June Star said.

"In my time," said the grandmother, folding her thin veined fingers, "children were more respectful of their native states and their parents and everything else. People did right then. Oh look at the cute little pickaninny!" she said and pointed to a Negro child standing in the door of a shack. "Wouldn't that make a picture, now?" she asked and they all turned and looked at the little Negro out of the back window. He waved.

"He didn't have any britches on," June Star said.

"He probably didn't have any," the grandmother explained. "Little niggers in the country don't have things like we do. If I could paint, I'd paint that picture," she said.

The children exchanged comic books.

The grandmother offered to hold the baby and the children's mother passed him over the front seat to her. She set him on her knee and bounced him and told him about the things they were passing. She rolled her eyes and screwed up her mouth and stuck her leathery thin face into his smooth bland one. Occasionally he gave her a faraway smile. They passed a large cotton field with five or six graves fenced in the middle of it, like a small island. "Look at the graveyard!" the grandmother said, pointing it out. "That was the old family burying ground. That belonged to the plantation."

"Where's the plantation?" John Wesley asked.

"Gone With the Wind," said the grandmother. "Ha. Ha."

When the children finished all the comic books they had brought, they opened the lunch and ate it. The grandmother ate a peanut butter sandwich and an olive and would not let the children throw the box and the paper napkins out the window. When there was nothing else to do they played a game by choosing a cloud and making the other two guess what shape it suggested. John Wesley took one the shape of a cow and June Star guessed a cow and John Wesley said, no, an automobile, and June Star said he didn't play fair, and they began to slap each other over the grandmother.

The grandmother said she would tell them a story if they would keep quiet. When she told a story, she rolled her eyes and waved her head and was very dramatic. She said once when she was a maiden lady she had been courted by a Mr. Edgar Atkins Teagarden from Jasper, Georgia. She said he was a very good-looking man and a gentleman and that he brought her a watermelon every Saturday afternoon with his initials cut in it, E.A.T. Well, one Saturday, she said, Mr. Teagarden brought the watermelon and there was nobody at home and he left it on the front porch and returned in his buggy to Jasper, but she never got the watermelon, she said, because a nigger boy ate it when he saw the initials, E. A. T.! This story tickled John Wesley's funny bone and he giggled and giggled but June Star didn't think it was any good. She said she wouldn't marry a man that just brought her a watermelon on Saturday. The grandmother said she would have done well to marry Mr. Teagarden because he was a gentleman and had bought Coca-Cola stock when it first came out and that he had died only a few years ago, a very wealthy man.

They stopped at The Tower for barbecued sandwiches. The Tower was a part stucco and part wood filling station and dance hall set in a clearing outside of Timothy. A fat man named Red Sammy Butts ran it and there were signs stuck here and there on the building and for miles up and down the highway saying, TRY RED SAMMY'S FAMOUS BARBECUE. NONE LIKE FAMOUS RED SAMMY'S! RED SAM! THE FAT BOY WITH THE HAPPY LAUGH. A VETERAN! RED SAMMY'S YOUR MAN!

Red Sammy was lying on the bare ground outside The Tower with his head under a truck while a gray monkey about a foot high, chained to a small chinaberry tree, chattered nearby. The monkey sprang back into the tree and got on the highest limb as soon as he saw the children jump out of the car and run toward him.

Inside, The Tower was a long dark room with a counter at one end and tables at the other and dancing space in the middle. They all sat down at a broad table next to the nickelodeon and Red Sam's wife, a tall burnt-brown woman with hair and eyes lighter than her skin, came and took their order. The children's mother put a dime in the machine and played "The Tennessee Waltz," and the grandmother said that tune always made her want to dance. She asked Bailey if he would like to dance but he only glared at her. He didn't have a naturally sunny disposition like she did and trips made him nervous. The grandmother's brown eyes were very bright. She swayed her head from side to side and pretended she was dancing in her chair. June Star said play something she could tap to so the children's mother put in another dime and played a fast number and June Star stepped out onto the dance floor and did her tap routine.

"Ain't she cute?" Red Sam's wife said, leaning over the counter. "Would you like to come be my little girl?"

"No I certainly wouldn't," June Star said. "I wouldn't live in a broken-down place like this for a million bucks!" and she ran back to the table.

"Ain't she cute?" the woman repeated, stretching her mouth politely.

"Aren't you ashamed?" hissed the grandmother.

Red Sam came in and told his wife to quit lounging on the counter and hurry up with these people's order. His khaki trousers reached just to his hip bones and his stomach hung over them like a sack of meal swaying under his shirt. He came over and sat down at a table nearby and let out a combination sigh and yodel. "You can't win," he said. "You can't win," and he wiped his sweating red face off with a gray handkerchief. "These days you don't know who to trust," he said. "Ain't that the truth?"

"People are certainly not nice like they used to be," said the grand-mother.

"Two fellers come in here last week," Red Sammy said, "driving a Chrysler. It was a old beat-up car but it was a good one and these boys looked all right to me. Said they worked at the mill and you know I let them fellers charge the gas they bought? Now why did I do that?"

"Because you're a good man!" the grandmother said at once.

"Yes'm, I suppose so," Red Sam said as if he were struck with this answer.

His wife brought the orders, carrying the five plates all at once without a tray, two in each hand and one balanced on her arm. "It isn't a soul in this green world of God's that you can trust," she said. "And I don't count nobody out of that, not nobody," she repeated, looking at Red Sammy.

"Did you read about that criminal, The Misfit, that's escaped?" asked the grandmother.

"I wouldn't be a bit surprised if he didn't attact this place right here," said the woman. "If he hears about it being here, I wouldn't be none surprised to see him. If he hears it's two cent in the cash register, I wouldn't be a tall surprised if he . . ."

"That'll do," Red Sam said. "Go bring these people their Co'Colas," and the woman went off to get the rest of the order.

"A good man is hard to find," Red Sammy said. "Everything is getting terrible. I remember the day you could go off and leave your screen door unlatched. Not no more."

He and the grandmother discussed better times. The old lady said that in her opinion Europe was entirely to blame for the way things were now. She said the way Europe acted you would think we were made of money and Red Sam said it was no use talking about it, she was exactly right. The children ran outside into the white sunlight and looked at the monkey in the lacy chinaberry tree. He was busy catching fleas on himself and biting each one carefully between his teeth as if it were a delicacy.

They drove off again into the hot afternoon. The grandmother took cat naps and woke up every few minutes with her own snoring. Outside of Toombsboro she woke up and recalled an old plantation that she had visited in this neighborhood once when she was a young lady. She said the house had six white columns across the front and that there was an avenue of oaks leading up to it and two little wooden trellis arbors on either side in front where you sat down with your suitor after a stroll in the garden. She recalled exactly which road to turn off to get to it. She knew that Bailey would not be willing to lose any time looking at an old house, but the more she talked about it, the more she wanted to see it once again and find out if the little twin arbors were still standing. "There was a secret panel in this house," she said craftily, not telling the truth but wishing that she were, "and the story went that all the family silver was hidden in it when Sherman came through but it was never found . . ."

"Hey!" John Wesley said. "Let's go see it! We'll find it! We'll poke all the woodwork and find it! Who lives there? Where do you turn off at? Hey Pop, can't we turn off there?"

"We never have seen a house with a secret panel!" June Star shrieked. "Let's go to the house with the secret panel! Hey, Pop, can't we go see the house with the secret panel!"

"It's not far from here, I know," the grandmother said. "It wouldn't take over twenty minutes."

Bailey was looking straight ahead. His jaw was as rigid as a horseshoe. "No," he said.

The children began to yell and scream that they wanted to see the house with the secret panel. John Wesley kicked the back of the front seat and June Star hung over her mother's shoulder and whined desperately into her ear that they never had any fun even on their vacation, that they could never do what THEY wanted to do. The baby began to scream and John Wesley kicked the back of the seat so hard that his father could feel the blows in his kidney.

"All right!" he shouted and drew the car to a stop at the side of the road. "Will you all shut up? Will you all just shut up for one second? If you don't shut up, we won't go anywhere."

"It would be very educational for them," the grandmother murmured.

"All right," Bailey said, "but get this, this is the only time we're going to stop for anything like this. This is the one and only time."

"The dirt road that you have to turn down is about a mile back," the grandmother directed. "I marked it when we passed."

"A dirt road," Bailey groaned.

After they had turned around and were headed toward the dirt road, the grandmother recalled other points about the house, the beautiful glass over the front doorway and the candle-lamp in the hall. John Wesley said that the secret panel was probably in the fireplace.

"You can't go inside this house," Bailey said. "You don't know who lives there."

"While you all talk to the people in front, I'll run around behind and get in a window," John Wesley suggested.

"We'll all stay in the car," his mother said.

They turned onto the dirt road and the car raced roughly along in a swirl of pink dust. The grandmother recalled the times when there were no paved roads and thirty miles was a day's journey. The dirt road was hilly and there were sudden washes in it and sharp curves on dangerous embankments. All at once they would be on a hill, looking down over the blue tops of trees for miles around, then the next minute, they would be in a red depression with the dust-coated trees looking down on them.

"This place had better turn up in a minute," Bailey said, "or I'm going to turn around."

The road looked as if no one had traveled on it in months.

"It's not much farther," the grandmother said and just as she said it, a horrible thought came to her. The thought was so embarrassing that she turned red in the face and her eyes dilated and her feet jumped up, upsetting her valise in the corner. The instant the valise moved, the newspaper top she had over the basket under it rose with a snarl and Pitty Sing, the cat, sprang onto Bailey's shoulder.

The children were thrown to the floor and their mother, clutching the baby, was thrown out the door onto the ground; the old lady was thrown into the front seat. The car turned over once and landed right-side-up in a gulch on the side of the road. Bailey remained in the driver's seat with the cat—gray-striped with a broad white face and an orange nose—clinging to his neck like a caterpillar.

As soon as the children saw they could move their arms and legs, they scrambled out of the car, shouting, "We've had an ACCIDENT!" The grandmother was curled up under the dashboard, hoping she was injured so that Bailey's wrath would not come down on her all at once. The horrible thought she had had before the accident was that the house she had remembered so vividly was not in Georgia but in Tennessee.

Bailey removed the cat from his neck with both hands and flung it out the window against the side of a pine tree. Then he got out of the car and started looking for the children's mother. She was sitting against the side of the red gutted ditch, holding the screaming baby, but she only had a cut down her face and a broken shoulder. "We've had an ACCIDENT!" the children screamed in a frenzy of delight.

"But nobody's killed," June Star said with disappointment as the grandmother limped out of the car, her hat still pinned to her head but the broken front brim standing up at a jaunty angle and the violet spray hanging off the side. They all sat down in the ditch, except the children, to recover from the shock. They were all shaking.

"Maybe a car will come along," said the children's mother hoarsely.

"I believe I have injured an organ," said the grandmother, pressing her side, but no one answered her. Bailey's teeth were clattering. He had on a yellow sport shirt with bright blue parrots designed in it and his face was as yellow as the shirt. The grandmother decided that she would not mention that the house was in Tennessee.

The road was about ten feet above and they could see only the tops of the trees on the other side of it. Behind the ditch they were sitting in there were more woods, tall and dark and deep. In a few minutes they saw a car some distance away on top of a hill, coming slowly as if the occupants were watching them. The grandmother stood up and waved both arms dramatically to attract their attention. The car continued to come on slowly, disappeared around a bend and appeared again, moving even slower, on top of the hill they had gone over. It was a big black battered hearse-like automobile. There were three men in it.

It came to a stop just over them and for some minutes, the driver looked down with a steady expressionless gaze to where they were sitting, and didn't speak. Then he turned his head and muttered something to the other two and they got out. One was a fat boy in black trousers and a red sweat shirt with a silver stallion embossed on the front of it. He moved around on the right side of them and stood staring, his mouth partly open in a kind of loose grin. The other had on khaki pants and a blue striped coat and a gray hat pulled down very low, hiding most of his face. He came around slowly on the left side. Neither spoke.

The driver got out of the car and stood by the side of it, looking down at them. He was an older man than the other two. His hair was just beginning to gray and he wore silver-rimmed spectacles that gave him a scholarly look. He had a long creased face and didn't have on any shirt or undershirt. He had on blue jeans that were too tight for him and was holding a black hat and a gun. The two boys also had guns.

"We've had an ACCIDENT!" the children screamed.

The grandmother had the peculiar feeling that the bespectacled man was someone she knew. His face was as familiar to her as if she had known him all her life but she could not recall who he was. He moved away from the car and began to come down the embankment, placing his feet carefully so that he wouldn't slip. He had on tan and white shoes and no socks, and his ankles were red and thin. "Good afternoon," he said. "I see you all had you a little spill."

"We turned over twice!" said the grandmother.

"Oncet," he corrected. "We seen it happen. Try their car and see will it run, Hiram," he said quietly to the boy with the gray hat.

"What you got that gun for?" John Wesley asked. "Whatcha gonna do with that gun?"

"Lady," the man said to the children's mother, "would you mind calling them children to sit down by you? Children make me nervous. I want all you all to sit down right together there where you're at."

"What are you telling US what to do for?" June Star asked.

Behind them the line of woods gaped like a dark open mouth. "Come here," said their mother.

"Look here now," Bailey began suddenly, "we're in a predicament! We're in . . ."

The grandmother shrieked. She scrambled to her feet and stood staring. "You're The Misfit!" she said. "I recognized you at once!"

"Yes'm," the man said, smiling slightly as if he were pleased in spite of himself to be known, "but it would have been better for all of you, lady, if you hadn't of reckernized me."

Bailey turned his head sharply and said something to his mother that shocked even the children. The old lady began to cry and The Misfit reddened.

"Lady," he said, "don't you get upset. Sometimes a man says things he don't mean. I don't reckon he meant to talk to you thataway."

"You wouldn't shoot a lady, would you?" the grandmother said and removed a clean handkerchief from her cuff and began to slap at her eyes with it.

The Misfit pointed the toe of his shoe into the ground and made a little hole and then covered it up again. "I would hate to have to," he said.

"Listen," the grandmother almost screamed, "I know you're a good man. You don't look a bit like you have common blood. I know you must come from nice people!"

"Yes mam," he said, "finest people in the world." When he smiled he showed a row of strong white teeth. "God never made a finer woman than my mother and my daddy's heart was pure gold," he said. The boy with the red sweat shirt had come around behind them and was standing with his gun at his hip. The Misfit squatted down on the ground. "Watch them children, Bobby Lee," he said. "You know they make me nervous." He looked at the six of them huddled together in front of him and he seemed to be embarrassed as if he couldn't think of anything to say. "Ain't a cloud in the sky," he remarked, looking up at it. "Don't see no sun but don't see no cloud neither."

"Yes, it's a beautiful day," said the grandmother. "Listen," she said, "you shouldn't call yourself The Misfit because I know you're a good man at heart. I can just look at you and tell."

"Hush!" Bailey yelled. "Hush! Everybody shut up and let me handle this!" He was squatting in the position of a runner about to sprint forward but he didn't move.

"I pre-chate that, lady," The Misfit said and drew a little circle in the ground with the butt of his gun.

"It'll take a half a hour to fix this here car," Hiram called, looking over the raised hood of it.

"Well, first you and Bobby Lee get him and that little boy to step over yonder with you." The Misfit said, pointing to Bailey and John Wesley. "The boys want to ast you something," he said to Bailey. "Would you mind stepping back in them woods there with them?"

"Listen," Bailey began, "we're in a terrible predicament!

Nobody realizes what this is," and his voice cracked. His eyes were as blue and intense as the parrots in his shirt and he remained perfectly still.

The grandmother reached up to adjust her hat brim as if she were going to the woods with him but it came off in her hand. She stood staring at it and after a second she let it fall on the ground. Hiram pulled Bailey up by the arm as if he were assisting an old man. John Wesley caught hold of his father's hand and Bobby Lee followed. They went off toward the woods and just as they reached the dark edge, Bailey turned and supporting himself against a gray naked pine trunk, he shouted, "I'll be back in a minute, Mamma, wait on me!"

"Come back this instant!" his mother shrilled but they all disappeared into the woods.

"Bailey Boy!" the grandmother called in a tragic voice but she found she was looking at The Misfit squatting on the ground in front of her. "I just know you're a good man," she said desperately. "You're not a bit common!"

"Nome, I ain't a good man," The Misfit said after a second as if he had considered her statement carefully, "but I ain't the worst in the world neither.

My daddy said I was different breed of dog from my brothers and sisters. 'You know,' Daddy said, 'it's some that can live their whole life out without asking about it and it's others has to know why it is, and this boy is one of the latters. He's going to be into everything!" He put on his black hat and looked up suddenly and then away deep into the woods as if he were embarrassed again. "I'm sorry I don't have on a shirt before you ladies," he said, hunching his shoulders slightly. "We buried our clothes that we had on when we escaped and we're just making do until we can get better. We borrowed these from some folks we met," he explained.

"That's perfectly all right," the grandmother said. "Maybe Bailey has an extra shirt in his suitcase."

"I'll look and see terrectly," The Misfit said.

"Where are they taking him?" the children's mother screamed.

"Daddy was a card himself," The Misfit said. "You couldn't put anything over on him. He never got in trouble with the Authorities though. Just had the knack of handling them."

"You could be honest too if you'd only try," said the grandmother. "Think how wonderful it would be to settle down and live a comfortable life and not have to think about somebody chasing you all the time."

The Misfit kept scratching in the ground with the butt of his gun as if he were thinking about it. "Yes'm, somebody is always after you," he murmured.

The grandmother noticed how thin his shoulder blades were just behind his hat because she was standing up looking down on him. "Do you ever pray?" she asked.

He shook his head. All she saw was the black hat wiggle between his shoulder blades. "Nome," he said.

There was a pistol shot from the woods, followed closely by another. Then silence. The old lady's head jerked around. She could hear the wind move through the tree tops like a long satisfied insuck of breath. "Bailey Boy!" she called.

"I was a gospel singer for a while," The Misfit said. "I been most everything. Been in the arm service, both land and sea, at home and abroad, been twict married, been an undertaker, been with the railroads, plowed Mother Earth, been in a tornado, seen a man burnt alive oncet," and he looked up at the children's mother and the little girl who were sitting close together, their faces white and their eyes glassy; "I even seen a woman flogged," he said.

"Pray, pray," the grandmother began, "pray, pray . . ."

"I never was a bad boy that I remember of," The Misfit said in an almost dreamy voice, "but somewheres along the line I done something wrong and got sent to the penitentiary. I was buried alive," and he looked up and held her attention to him by a steady stare.

"That's when you should have started to pray," she said. "What did you do to get sent to the penitentiary that first time?"

"Turn to the right, it was a wall," The Misfit said, looking up again at the cloudless sky. "Turn to the left, it was a wall. Look up it was a ceiling, look down it was a floor. I forget what I done, lady. I set there and set there, trying to remember what it was I done and I ain't recalled it to this day. Oncet in a while, I would think it was coming to me, but it never come."

"Maybe they put you in by mistake," the old lady said vaguely.

"Nome," he said. "It wasn't no mistake. They had the papers on me."

"You must have stolen something," she said.

The Misfit sneered slightly. "Nobody had nothing I wanted," he said. "It was a head-doctor at the penitentiary said what I had done was kill my daddy but I known that for a lie. My daddy died in nineteen ought nineteen of the epidemic flu and I never had a thing to do with it. He was buried in the Mount Hopewell Baptist churchyard and you can go there and see for yourself."

"If you would pray," the old lady said, "Jesus would help you."

"That's right," The Misfit said.

"Well then, why don't you pray?" she asked trembling with delight suddenly.

"I don't want no hep," he said. "I'm doing all right by myself."

Bobby Lee and Hiram came ambling back from the woods. Bobby Lee was dragging a yellow shirt with bright blue parrots in it.

"Thow me that shirt, Bobby Lee," The Misfit said. The shirt came flying at him and landed on his shoulder and he put it on. The grandmother couldn't name what the shirt reminded her of. "No, lady," The Misfit said while he was buttoning it up, "I found out the crime don't matter. You can do one thing or you can do another, kill a man or take a tire off his car, because sooner or later you're going to forget what it was you done and just be punished for it."

The children's mother had begun to make heaving noises as if she couldn't get her breath. "Lady," he asked, "would you and that little girl like to step off yonder with Bobby Lee and Hiram and join your husband?"

"Yes, thank you," the mother said faintly. Her left arm dangled helplessly and she was holding the baby, who had gone to sleep, in the other. "Hep that lady up, Hiram," The Misfit said as she struggled to climb out of the ditch, "and Bobby Lee, you hold onto that little girl's hand."

"I don't want to hold hands with him," June Star said. "He reminds me of a pig."

The fat boy blushed and laughed and caught her by the arm and pulled her off into the woods after Hiram and her mother.

Alone with The Misfit, the grandmother found that she had lost her voice. There was not a cloud in the sky nor any sun. There was nothing around her but woods. She wanted to tell him that he must pray. She opened and closed her mouth several times before anything came out. Finally she found herself saying, "Jesus. Jesus," meaning, Jesus will help you, but the way she was saying it, it sounded as if she might be cursing.

"Yes'm," The Misfit said as if he agreed. "Jesus thrown everything off balance. It was the same case with Him as with me except He hadn't committed any crime and they could prove I had committed one because they had the papers on me. Of course," he said, "they never shown me my papers. That's why I sign myself now. I said long ago, you get you a signature and sign everything you do and keep a copy of it. Then you'll know what you done and you can hold up the crime to the punishment and see do they match and in the end you'll have something to prove you ain't been treated right. I call myself The Misfit," he said, "because I can't make what all I done wrong fit what all I gone through in punishment."

There was a piercing scream from the woods, followed closely by a pistol report. "Does is seem right to you, lady, that one is punished a heap and another ain't punished at all?"

"Jesus!" the old lady cried. "You've got good blood! I know you wouldn't shoot a lady! I know you come from nice people! Pray! Jesus, you ought not to shoot a lady. I'll give you all the money I've got!"

"Lady," The Misfit said, looking beyond her far into the woods, "there never was a body that give the undertaker a tip."

There were two more pistol reports and the grandmother raised her head like a parched old turkey hen crying for water and called, "Bailey Boy, Bailey Boy!" as if her heart would break.

"Jesus was the only One that ever raised the dead," The Misfit continued, "and He shouldn't have done it. He thrown everything off balance. If He did what He said, then it's nothing for you to do but throw away everything and follow Him, and if He didn't, then it's nothing for you to do but enjoy the few minutes you got left the best way you can—by killing somebody or burning down his house or doing some other meanness to him. No pleasure but meanness," he said and his voice had become almost a snarl.

"Maybe He didn't raise the dead," the old lady mumbled, not knowing what she was saying and feeling so dizzy that she sank down in the ditch with her legs twisted under her.

"I wasn't there so I can't say He didn't," The Misfit said. "I wisht I had of been there," he said, hitting the ground with his fist. "It ain't right I wasn't there because if I had of been there I would of known. Listen lady," he said in a high voice, "if I had of been there I would of known and I wouldn't be like I am now." His voice seemed about to crack and the grandmother's head cleared for an instant. She saw the man's face twisted close to her own as if he were going to cry and she murmured, "Why you're one of my babies. You're one of my own children!" She reached out and touched him on the shoulder. The Misfit sprang back as if a snake had bitten him and shot her three times through the chest. Then he put his gun down on the ground and took off his glasses and began to clean them.

Hiram and Bobby Lee returned from the woods and stood over the ditch, looking down at the grandmother who half sat and half lay in a puddle of blood with her legs crossed under her like a child's and her face smiling up at the cloudless sky.

Without his glasses, The Misfit's eyes were red-rimmed and pale and defenseless-looking. "Take her off and throw her where you thrown the others," he said, picking up the cat that was rubbing itself against his leg.

"She was a talker, wasn't she?" Bobby Lee said, sliding down the ditch with a yodel.

"She would of been a good woman," The Misfit said, "if it had been somebody there to shoot her every minute of her life."

"Some fun!" Bobby Lee said.

"Shut up, Bobby Lee," The Misfit said. "It's no real pleasure in life."

QUESTIONS FOR A CRITICAL REREADING

After you have read "A Good Man Is Hard to Find," use these questions to help you analyze the story's argument (this is not just the plot, but what you interpret it to mean). As you reread the story with these questions in mind, construct a sentence outline that represents how the argument is structured, how each new episode adds a little more justification for the concluding scene.

1. Analyze the introductory episodes. From whose perspective does the narrator tell the story? How does it affect your reaction to the characters? Is one character more likeable, or at least more appealing, than the others? Who and why?
2. How does the episode at Red Sammy's affect your attitude toward the grandmother? What questions does O'Connor raise through the discussion between the grandmother and Red Sammy? Try to phrase these as questions of value.
3. Do you think the grandmother was responsible for the accident that left them stranded on the dirt road? For them being there in the first place? Does she hold herself responsible? Justify each of your answers by citing evidence from the text.
4. How do you respond to The Misfit? Is he worse or better than the other characters? Why do you think O'Connor didn't give him a name? Compare him to the other characters who are not given names. What point do you think O'Connor is trying to make?
5. At one point near the end, Bobby Lee throws The Misfit "a yellow shirt with bright blue parrots in it." Where did the shirt come from? How does the grandmother's attitude toward The Misfit change after he puts it on? Does your attitude toward him change in anyway at this point in the story? If so, how?
6. At the end of the story, the Misfit gives us a possible clue to how we might make sense out of the apparently senseless violence: "She would of been a good woman, if it had been somebody there to shoot her every minute of her life." Note Bobby's response and The Misfit's final comment. What is the point? See if you can use this passage to formulate an answer to one of the questions you formulated for question 2 above.

POSSIBLE ISSUES FOR WRITING

After you have fashioned a sentence outline from your answers to the questions for a critical rereading, use the following questions to discuss your reading with your classmates. Listen carefully to the different interpretations that are expressed. This is your chance to hear the voices of other readers and develop a fuller response to the story. After the discussion, try to formulate an enthymemic thesis that represents what you have interpreted as the story's *value* argument.

1. Note the references to the sky throughout the story. How does the sky change and who notices? How do different characters respond to it? In what ways can we use

their responses as a clue to their inner feelings and moral condition? As a clue to O'Connor's perspective on life?

2. Is there a central hero or heroine in "A Good Man is Hard to Find"? Who comes closest? Why? Explain how closely any one character comes to your idea of "good." How do you think O'Connor would react to your standard of "goodness"? Why?

3. O'Connor almost never fails to affect the reader emotionally. What is your overall reaction to the story? How has her perspective on life affected your own? Will it change your behavior in any way? If so, for the better or worse? Why?

———————————
———————————
———————————

Riders to the Sea

John Millington Synge *(1871–1909)*

John Millington Synge was born in Dublin, Ireland, and graduated from Trinity College there. His love was language—particularly Gaelic, Hebrew, Latin, and Greek—and he spent his post-graduate days studying abroad in Germany and, later, Paris where he first met and struck up a friendship with William Butler Yeats, the Irish poet. Soon after, Yeats convinced Synge to live for awhile among the primitive people of the Aran Islands. The experience proved valuable: Synge later returned to Dublin and wrote the great plays of Irish peasant life that have given him his reputation.

Synge's Riders to the Sea *is a one-act play that draws on the beauty and power of the language and customs of the Irish peasantry to dramatize a mother confronting the tragedy of a son's death. As you read the play, try to distinguish between the voices of the different characters. How does Synge use the Irish peasant's dialect to capture the state of each character's soul?*

Persons in the Play

First performed at the Molesworth Hall, Dublin, February 25, 1904.

Maurya (an old woman)	Honor Lavelle
Bartley (her son)	W.G. Fay
Cathleen (her daughter)	Sarah Allgood
Nora (a younger daughter)	Emma Vernon
Men and Women	

SCENE. *An Island off the West of Ireland.*

(Cottage kitchen, with nets, oil-skins, spinning wheel, some new boards standing by the wall, etc. Cathleen, a girl of about twenty, finishes kneading cake, and puts it down in the pot-oven by the fire; then wipes her hands, and begins to spin at the wheel. Nora, a young girl, puts her head in at the door.)

NORA *(in a low voice):* Where is she?

CATHLEEN: She's lying down, God help her, and may be sleeping, if she's able.

[Nora comes in softly, and takes a bundle from under her shawl.]

CATHLEEN *(spinning the wheel rapidly):* What is it you have?

NORA: The young priest is after bringing them. It's a shirt and a plain stocking were got off a drowned man in Donegal.

[Cathleen stops her wheel with a sudden movement, and leans out to listen.]

NORA: We're to find out if it's Michael's they are, some time herself will be down looking by the sea.

CATHLEEN: How would they be Michael's, Nora. How would he go the length of that way to the far north?

NORA: The young priest says he's known the like of it. "If it's Michael's they are," says he, "you can tell herself he's got a clean burial by the grace of God, and if they're not his, let no one say a word about them, for she'll be getting her death," says he, "with crying and lamenting."

[The door which Nora half closed is blown open by a gust of wind.]

CATHLEEN *(looking out anxiously):* Did you ask him would he stop Bartley going this day with the horses to the Galway fair?

NORA: "I won't stop him," says he, "but let you not be afraid. Herself does be saying prayers half through the night, and the Almighty God won't leave her destitute," says he, "with no son living."

CATHLEEN: Is the sea bad by the white rocks, Nora?

NORA: Middling bad, God help us. There's a great roaring in the west, and it's worse it'll be getting when the tide's turned to the wind.

[She goes over to the table with the bundle.]

Shall I open it now?

CATHLEEN: Maybe she'd wake up on us, and come in before we'd done. *(Coming to the table.)* It's a long time we'll be, and the two of us crying.

NORA *(goes to the inner door and listens):* She's moving about on the bed. She'll be coming in a minute.

CATHLEEN: Give me the ladder, and I'll put them up in the turf-loft, the way she won't know of them at all, and maybe when the tide turns she'll be going down to see would he be floating from the east.

[They put the ladder against the gable of the chimney; Cathleen goes up a few steps and hides the bundle in the turf-loft. Maurya comes from the inner room.]

MAURYA *(looking up at Cathleen and speaking querulously):* Isn't it turf enough you have for this day and evening?

CATHLEEN: There's a cake baking at the fire for a short space *(throwing down the turf)* and Bartley will want it when the tide turns if he goes to Connemara.

[Nora picks up the turf and puts it round the pot-oven.]

MAURYA *(sitting down on a stool at the fire):* He won't go this day with the wind rising from the south and west. He won't go this day, for the young priest will stop him surely.

NORA: He'll not stop him, mother, and I heard Eamon Simon and Stephen Pheety and Colum Shawn saying he would go.

MAURYA: Where is he itself?

NORA: He went down to see would there be another boat sailing in the week, and I'm thinking it won't be long till he's here now, for the tide's turning at the green head, and the hooker's tacking from the east.

CATHLEEN: I hear some one passing the big stones.

NORA *(looking out):* He's coming now, and he in a hurry.

BARTLEY *(comes in and looks round the room. Speaking sadly and quietly):* Where is the bit of new rope, Cathleen, was bought in Connemara?

CATHLEEN *(coming down):* Give it to him, Nora; it's on a nail by the white boards. I hung it up this morning, for the pig with the black feet was eating it.

NORA *(giving him a rope):* Is that it, Bartley?

MAURYA: You'd do right to leave that rope, Bartley, hanging by the boards. *(Bartley takes the rope.)* It will be wanting in this place, I'm telling you, if Michael is washed up to-morrow morning, or the next morning, or any morning in the week, for it's a deep grave we'll make him by the grace of God.

BARTLEY *(beginning to work with the rope):* I've no halter the way I can ride down on the mare, and I must go now quickly. This is the one boat going for two weeks or beyond it, and the fair will be a good fair for horses I heard them saying below.

MAURYA: It's a hard thing they'll be saying below if the body is washed up and there's no man in it to make the coffin, and I after giving a big price for the finest white boards you'd find in Connemara.

[She looks round at the boards.]

BARTLEY: How would it be washed up, and we after looking each day for nine days, and a strong wind blowing a while back from the west and south?

MAURYA: If it wasn't found itself, that wind is raising the sea, and there was a star up against the moon, and it rising in the night. If it was a hundred horses, or a thousand horses you had itself, what is the price of a thousand horses against a son where there is one son only?

BARTLEY *(working at the halter, to Cathleen):* Let you go down each day, and see the sheep aren't jumping in on the rye, and if the jobber comes you can sell the pig with the black feet if there is a good price going.

MAURYA: How would the like of her get a good price for a pig?

BARTLEY *(to Cathleen):* If the west wind holds with the last bit of the moon let you and Nora get up weed enough for another cock for the kelp. It's hard set we'll be from this day with no one in it but one man to work.

MAURYA: It's hard set we'll be surely the day you're drownd'd with the rest. What way will I live and the girls with me, and I an old woman looking for the grave?

[Bartley lays down the halter, takes off his old coat, and puts on a newer one of the same flannel.]

BARTLEY *(to Nora):* Is she coming to the pier?

NORA *(looking out):* She's passing the green head and letting fall her sails.

BARTLEY (*getting his purse and tobacco*): I'll have half an hour to go down, and you'll see me coming again in two days, or in three days, or maybe in four days if the wind is bad.

MAURYA (*turning round to the fire, and putting her shawl over her head*): Isn't it a hard and cruel man won't hear a word from an old woman, and she holding him from the sea?

CATHLEEN: It's the life of a young man to be going on the sea, and who would listen to an old woman with one thing and she saying it over?

BARTLEY (*taking the halter*): I must go now quickly. I'll ride down on the red mare, and the gray pony'll run behind me. . . . The blessing of God on you.

[*He goes out.*]

MAURYA (*crying out as he is in the door*): He's gone now, God spare us, and we'll not see him again. He's gone now, and when the black night is falling I'll have no son left me in the world.

CATHLEEN: Why wouldn't you give him your blessing and he looking round in the door? Isn't it sorrow enough is on every one in this house without your sending him out with an unlucky word behind him, and a hard word in his ear?

[*Maurya takes up the tongs and begins raking the fire aimlessly without looking round.*]

NORA (*turning towards her*): You're taking away the turf from the cake.

CATHLEEN (*crying out*): The Son of God forgive us, Nora, we're after forgetting his bit of bread.

[*She comes over to the fire.*]

NORA: And it's destroyed he'll be going till dark night, and he after eating nothing since the sun went up.

CATHLEEN (*turning the cake out of the oven*): It's destroyed he'll be, surely. There's no sense left on any person in a house where an old woman will be talking for ever.

[*Maurya sways herself on her stool.*]

CATHLEEN (*cutting off some of the bread and rolling it in a cloth; to Maurya*): Let you go down now to the spring well and give him this and he passing. You'll see him then and the dark word will be broken, and you can say "God speed you," the way he'll be easy in his mind.

MAURYA (*taking the bread*): Will I be in it as soon as himself?

CATHLEEN: If you go now quickly.

MAURYA (*standing up unsteadily*): It's hard set I am to walk.

CATHLEEN (*looking at her anxiously*): Give her the stick, Nora, or maybe she'll slip on the big stones.

NORA: What stick?

CATHLEEN: The stick Michael brought from Connemara.

MAURYA (*taking a stick Nora gives her*): In the big world the old people do be leaving things after them for their sons and children, but in this place it is the young men do be leaving things behind for them that do be old.

[She goes out slowly. Nora goes over to the ladder.]

CATHLEEN: Wait, Nora, maybe she'd turn back quickly. She's that sorry, God help her, you wouldn't know the thing she'd do.

NORA: Is she gone round by the bush?

CATHLEEN *(looking out):* She's gone now. Throw it down quickly, for the Lord knows when she'll be out of it again.

NORA *(getting the bundle from the loft):* The young priest said he'd be passing to-morrow, and we might go down and speak to him below if it's Michael's they are surely.

CATHLEEN *(taking the bundle):* Did he say what way they were found?

NORA *(coming down):* "There were two men," says he, "and they rowing round with poteen before the cocks crowed, and the oar of one of them caught the body, and they passing the black cliffs of the north."

CATHLEEN *(trying to open the bundle):* Give me a knife, Nora, the string's perished with the salt water, and there's a black knot on it you wouldn't loosen in a week.

NORA *(giving her a knife):* I've heard tell it was a long way to Donegal.

CATHLEEN *(cutting the string):* It is surely. There was a man in here a while ago—the man sold us that knife—and he said if you set off walking from the rocks beyond, it would be seven days you'd be in Donegal.

NORA: And what time would a man take, and he floating?

[Cathleen opens the bundle and takes out a bit of a stocking. They look at them eagerly.]

CATHLEEN *(in a low voice):* The Lord spare us, Nora! isn't it a queer hard thing to say if it's his they are surely?

NORA: I'll get his shirt off the hook the way we can put the one flannel on the other. *(She looks through some clothes hanging in the corner.)* It's not with them, Cathleen, and where will it be?

CATHLEEN: I'm thinking Bartley put it on him in the morning, for his own shirt was heavy with the salt in it *(pointing to the corner).* There's a bit of a sleeve was of the same stuff. Give me that and it will do.

[Nora brings it to her and they compare the flannel.]

CATHLEEN: It's the same stuff, Nora; but if it is itself aren't there great rolls of it in the shops of Galway, and isn't it many another man may have a shirt of it as well as Michael himself?

NORA *(who has taken up the stocking and counted the stitches, crying out):* It's Michael, Cathleen, it's Michael; God spare his soul, and what will herself say when she hears this story, and Bartley on the sea?

CATHLEEN *(taking the stocking):* It's a plain stocking.

NORA: It's the second one of the third pair I knitted, and I put up three score stitches, and I dropped four of them.

CATHLEEN *(counts the stitches):* It's that number is in it *(crying out).* Ah, Nora, isn't it a bitter thing to think of him floating that way to the far north, and no one to keen him but the black hags that do be flying on the sea?

NORA *(swinging herself round, and throwing out her arms on the clothes):* And isn't it a pitiful thing when there is nothing left of a man who was a great rower and fisher, but a bit of an old shirt and a plain stocking?

CATHLEEN *(after an instant):* Tell me is herself coming, Nora? I hear a little sound on the path.

NORA *(looking out):* She is, Cathleen. She's coming up to the door.

CATHLEEN: Put these things away before she'll come in. Maybe it's easier she'll be after giving her blessing to Bartley, and we won't let on we've heard anything the time he's on the sea.

NORA *(helping Cathleen to close the bundle):* We'll put them here in the corner.

[They put them into a hole in the chimney corner. Cathleen goes back to the spinning-wheel.]

NORA: Will she see it was crying I was?

CATHLEEN: Keep your back to the door the way the light'll not be on you.

[Nora sits down at the chimney corner, with her back to the door. Maurya comes in very slowly, without looking at the girls, and goes over to her stool at the other side of the fire. The cloth with the bread is still in her hand. The girls look at each other, and Nora points to the bundle of bread.]

CATHLEEN *(after spinning for a moment):* You didn't give him his bit of bread?

[Maurya begins to keen softly, without turning round.]

CATHLEEN: Did you see him riding down?

[Maurya goes on keening.]

CATHLEEN *(a little impatiently):* God forgive you; isn't it a better thing to raise your voice and tell what you seen, than to be making lamentation for a thing that's done? Did you see Bartley, I'm saying to you.

MAURYA *(with a weak voice):* My heart's broken from this day.

CATHLEEN *(as before):* Did you see Bartley?

MAURYA: I seen the fearfulest thing.

CATHLEEN *(leaves her wheel and looks out):* God forgive you; he's riding the mare now over the green head, and the gray pony behind him.

MAURYA *(starts, so that her shawl falls back from her head and shows her white tossed hair. With a frightened voice):* The gray pony behind him.

CATHLEEN *(coming to the fire):* What is it ails you, at all?

MAURYA (*speaking very slowly*): I've seen the fearfulest thing any person has seen, since the day Bride Dara seen the dead man with the child in his arms.

CATHLEEN AND NORA: Uah.

[They crouch down in front of the old woman at the fire.]

NORA: Tell us what it is you seen.

MAURYA: I went down to the spring well, and I stood there saying a prayer to myself. Then Bartley came along, and he riding on the red mare with the gray pony behind him. (*She puts up her hands, as if to hide something from her eyes.*) The Son of God spare us, Nora!

CATHLEEN: What is it you seen.

MAURYA: I seen Michael himself.

CATHLEEN (*speaking softly*): You did not, mother; It wasn't Michael you seen, for his body is after being found in the far north, and he's got a clean burial by the grace of God.

MAURYA (*a little defiantly*): I'm after seeing him this day, and he riding and galloping. Bartley came first on the red mare; and I tried to say "God speed you," but something choked the words in my throat. He went by quickly; and "the blessing of God on you," says he, and I could say nothing. I looked up then, and I crying, at the gray pony, and there was Michael upon it—with fine clothes on him, and new shoes on his feet.

CATHLEEN (*begins to keen*): It's destroyed we are from this day. It's destroyed, surely.

NORA: Didn't the young priest say the Almighty God wouldn't leave her destitute with no son living?

MAURYA (*in a low voice, but clearly*): It's little the like of him knows of the sea. . . . Bartley will be lost now, and let you call in Eamon and make me a good coffin out of the white boards, for I won't live after them. I've had a husband, and a husband's father, and six sons in this house—six fine men, though it was a hard birth I had with every one of them and they coming to the world—and some of them were found and some of them were not found, but they're gone now the lot of them. . . . There were Stephen, and Shawn, were lost in the great wind, and found after in the Bay of Gregory of the Golden Mouth, and carried up the two of them on the one plank, and in by that door.

[She pauses for a moment, the girls start as if they heard something through the door that is half open behind them.]

NORA (*in a whisper*): Did you hear that, Cathleen? Did you hear a noise in the north-east?

CATHLEEN (*in a whisper*): There's some one after crying out by the seashore.

MAURYA (*continues without hearing anything*): There was Sheamus and his father, and his own father again, were lost in a dark night, and not a stick or sign was seen of them when the sun went up. There was Patch after was drowned out of a curagh that turned over. I was sitting here with Bartley, and he a baby, lying on my two knees, and I seen two women, and three women, and four women coming in, and they crossing themselves, and not saying a word. I looked out then, and there were men coming after them, and they holding a thing in the half of a red sail, and water dripping out of it—it was a dry day, Nora—and leaving a track to the door.

[She pauses again with her hand stretched out towards the door. It opens softly and old women begin to come in, crossing themselves on the threshold, and kneeling down in front of the stage with red petticoats over their heads.]

MAURYA *(half in a dream, to Cathleen):* Is it Patch, or Michael, or what is it at all?

CATHLEEN: Michael is after being found in the far north, and when he is found there how could he be here in this place?

MAURYA: There does be a power of young men floating round in the sea, and what way would they know if it was Michael they had, or another man like him, for when a man is nine days in the sea, and the wind blowing, it's hard set his own mother would be to say what man was it.

CATHLEEN: It's Michael, God spare him, for they're after sending us a bit of his clothes from the far north.

[She reaches out and hands Maurya the clothes that belonged to Michael. Maurya stands up slowly and takes them in her hands. Nora looks out.]

NORA: They're carrying a thing among them and there's water dripping out of it and leaving a track by the big stones.

CATHLEEN *(in a whisper to the women who have come in):* Is it Bartley it is?

ONE OF THE WOMEN: It is surely, God rest his soul.

[Two younger women come in and pull out the table. Then men carry in the body of Bartley, laid on a plank, with a bit of a sail over it, and lay it on the table.]

CATHLEEN *(to the women, as they are doing so):* What way was he drowned?

ONE OF THE WOMEN: The gray pony knocked him into the sea, and he was washed out where there is a great surf on the white rocks.

[Maurya has gone over and knelt down at the head of the table. The women are keening softly and swaying themselves with a slow movement. Cathleen and Nora kneel at the other end of the table. The men kneel near the door.]

MAURYA *(raising her head and speaking as if she did not see the people around her):* They're all gone now, and there isn't anything more the sea can do to me. . . . I'll have no call now to be up crying and praying when the wind breaks from the south, and you can hear the surf is in the east, and the surf is in the west, making a great stir with the two noises, and they hitting one on the other. I'll have no call now to be going down and getting Holy Water in the dark nights after Samhain, and I won't care what way the sea is when the other women will be keening. *(To Nora.)* Give me the Holy Water, Nora, there's a small sup still on the dresser.

[Nora gives it to her.]

MAURYA *(drops Michael's clothes across Bartley's feet, and sprinkles the Holy Water over him):* It isn't that I haven't prayed for you, Bartley, to the Almighty God. It isn't that I haven't said prayers in the dark night till you wouldn't know what I'ld be saying; but it's a great rest I'll have now, and it's time surely. It's a great rest I'll have now, and great sleeping in the long nights after Samhain, if it's only a bit of wet flour we do have to eat, and maybe a fish that would be stinking.

[She kneels down again, crossing herself, and saying prayers under her breath.]

CATHLEEN *(to an old man):* Maybe yourself and Eamon would make a coffin when the sun rises. We have fine white boards herself bought, God help her, thinking Michael would be found, and I have a new cake you can eat while you'll be working.

THE OLD MAN *(looking at the boards):* Are there nails with them?

CATHLEEN: There are not, Colum; we didn't think of the nails.

ANOTHER MAN: It's a great wonder she wouldn't think of the nails, and all the coffins she's seen made already.

CATHLEEN: It's getting old she is, and broken.

[Maurya stands up again very slowly and spreads out the pieces of Michael's clothes beside the body, sprinkling them with the last of the Holy Water.]

NORA *(in a whisper to Cathleen):* She's quiet now and easy; but the day Michael was drowned you could hear her crying out from this to the spring well. It's fonder she was of Michael, and would any one have thought that?

CATHLEEN *(slowly and clearly):* An old woman will be soon tired with anything she will do, and isn't it nine days herself is after crying and keening, and making great sorrow in the house?

MAURYA *(puts the empty cup mouth downwards on the table, and lays her hands together on Bartley's feet):* They're all together this time, and the end is come. May the Almighty God have mercy on Bartley's soul, and on Michael's soul, and on the souls of Sheamus and Patch, and Stephen and Shawn *(bending her head);* and may He have mercy on my soul, Nora, and on the soul of every one is left living in the world.

[She pauses, and the keen rises a little more loudly from the women, then sinks away.]

MAURYA *(continuing):* Michael has a clean burial in the far north, by the grace of the Almighty God. Bartley will have a fine coffin out of the white boards, and a deep grave surely. What more can we want than that? No man at all can be living for ever, and we must be satisfied.

[She kneels down again and the curtain falls slowly.]

QUESTIONS FOR A CRITICAL REREADING

After you have read the play through, use the following questions to help you discover how it expresses what we might call a voice of value. As you focus on different speeches in the play, try reading them aloud so you can feel the meaning behind the language. As you draw up a sentence outline that interprets the structure of the play's argument, try to summarize your emotional response to, as well as the meaning of, the characters' speeches.

1. Reread the conversation between Cathleen and Nora before Maurya enters. What do they talk about? How does it prepare you to focus your attention on Maurya when she enters the room? (See if you can articulate the apprehension in these lines as a question that the play will address.)

2. What do Maurya's speeches during Bartley's brief entrance and departure reveal about her state of mind? How does she compare to Cathleen's and Nora's perspective of her? How do you feel about her at this point? (Give examples of the particular speeches or actions that make you feel this way.)

3. After Bartley leaves, what causes the conflict between Cathleen and Maurya? What are each of them upset about? Which one do you respect more? Why?

4. When Maurya returns from seeing Bartley off, how has she changed? What did she see, and how does she interpret it? Has your response to her changed?

5. When word comes that Bartley is dead, does Maurya respond as you would expect her to? Look closely at her last few speeches. How has she resolved the question introduced at the beginning of the play? (To discover a possible thesis behind the play, try to articulate Maurya's attitude at this point and summarize how she arrived at it.)

POSSIBLE ISSUES FOR WRITING

After you have formulated a thesis that represents your interpretation of what the play says, use these questions to help you test it against your classmates' perspectives. Keep a record in your notebook of the different value terms your classmates use to express their responses to the play. This will help you discover how to justify your own interpretive response in the essay you will write after this discussion.

1. As with "A Good Man Is Hard to Find," clothing appears to play a major role in this work. Why does Synge have Bartley change his shirt, and why does he present Maurya's vision of Michael as being dressed in new clothes? What emotional effect does that image have on you? How does it compare to your response to the bright clothing The Misfit puts on at the end of O'Connor's story?

2. An easy generalization we can make is to say that tragedy ends in death, comedy in marriage. All three of the works you have read in this chapter have dealt with death in some way, but do they all present a tragic vision? How might you describe the different attitudes toward death presented in these three works? Is one preferable to the others? Why or why not?

3. We began this chapter by discussing how literature explores the value of being human. Compare the different kinds of value Marvell, O'Connor, and Synge find

in human existence. Are these authors presenting contrasting or complementary visions of life? Justify your answer by citing a passage from each work.

WRITING YOUR ESSAY

Now is the time to write your response to the conversation you have been having with your classmates about the value of the literature you have read. Because you will have to justify your interpretation of the work or works you discuss, remember to phrase your question as an issue of value—for example, "Does O'Connor say life is godless?" "Does Marvell say our lives are merely trivial?" As you reason out your answer to an issue of interpretation and value, keep in mind the different ways your classmates have responded to the works. As you develop your enthymemic thesis, make sure you include the value term you will need to define. And, most important, as you develop your "because" clause, remember that the proof you will use to support it (the "new information") will have to come in the form of evidence from the works themselves.

Acknowledgments

JOHN LEO. Excerpted from "Journalese: A Ground-Breaking Study." Reprinted by permission from *Time,* September 1, 1986. Copyright © 1986 by Time, Inc.

WILLIAM PERRY. "Examsmanship and the Liberal Arts: A Study in Educational Epistemology." Reprinted by permission of the publishers from *Examining in Harvard College: A Collection of Essays by Members of the Harvard Faculty,* Cambridge, Mass.: Harvard University Press, 1963.

GEORGE LAKOFF AND MARK JOHNSON. "Concepts We Live By." Reprinted by permission of the publishers and authors from *Metaphors We Live By,* Chicago, Ill.: The University of Chicago Press, 1980.

ALLEEN PACE NILSEN. "Sexism in English: A 1990s Update." A revised version of "Sexism in English: A Feminist View," which originally appeared in *Female Studies VI: Closer to the Ground Women's Classes, Criticism, Programs—1972,* eds., Nancy Hoffman, Cynthia Secor, and Adrian Tinsley, New York: The Feminist Press, 1972.

NICCOLO MACHIAVELLI. "On Things for Which Princes Are Praised or Blamed." Edited and translated by Thomas Bergin. From *The Prince,* New York: Appleton-Century-Crofts. Copyright © 1947 by F.S. Crofts and Co. Reprinted by permission of J. M. Dent & Sons.

MARTIN LUTHER KING, JR. Excerpt "Letter from Birmingham Jail." Reprinted by permission of the publishers from *Why We Can't Wait,* New York: Harper & Row. Copyright © 1963/1964 by Martin Luther King, Jr.

SHERBURNE F. COOK. "A Study in Human Ecology: The Conflict Between the California Indian and White Civilization." Reprinted and retitled by permission of the publishers from *The Conflict Between the California Indian and White Civilization,* Berkeley, Calif.: University of California Press, 1976.

STEPHEN JAY GOULD. "Nonmoral Nature." Reprinted by permission of the publishers from *Natural History,* Vol. 91, No. 2. Copyright © 1982 by the American Museum of Natural History.

THOMAS S. KUHN. "The Essential Tension: Tradition and Innovation in Scientific Research." Reprinted by permission from *The Essential Tension: Selected Studies in Scientific Tradition and Change,* Chicago, Ill.: University of Chicago Press, 1977. First printing in *The Third (1959) University of Utah Research Conference on the Identification of Scientific Talent,* ed. C. W. Taylor, Salt Lake City: University of Utah Press, 1959, pp. 162–174. Copyright © 1959 by the University of Utah.

B. F. SKINNER. "What Is Man?" From *Beyond Freedom and Dignity.* Copyright © 1971 by B. F. Skinner. Reprinted by permission of Alfred A. Knopf, Inc.

MARY FIELD BELENKY, BLYTHE McVICKER CLINCHY, NANCY RULE GOLDBERGER, AND JILL MATTUCK TARULE. "Silence." From *Women's Ways of Knowing: The Development of Self, Voice, and Mind.* Copyright © 1986 by Basic Books, Inc. Reprinted by permission.

BARBARA TUCHMAN. "The Trojans Take the Wooden Horse Within Their Walls." From *The March of Folly: From Troy to Vietnam* by Barbara W. Tuchman. Copyright © 1984 by Barbara W. Tuchman. Reprinted by permission of Alfred A. Knopf, Inc.

JOHN MAYNARD KEYNES. "Economic Possibilities for Our Grandchildren." Reprinted by permission from *Collected Writings: Volume Nine—Essays in Persuasion,* by John Maynard Keynes, London: Macmillan and Co., Ltd., 1931.

LEONARD SILK. "What Economics Can Do For You." Reprinted with permission from *Economics in Plain English,* New York: Simon & Schuster, Inc., 1978, pp. 159–170.

PLATO. "The Allegory of the Cave." Retitled from "The Simile of the Cave" (excluding notes), from *The Republic.* Translated by Desmond Lee. London: Penguin. Second edition. Copyright © 1955, 1974 by H. D. P. Lee.

ALBERT CAMUS. "The Myth of Sisyphus." From *The Myth of Sisyphus and Other Essays,* translated by Justin O'Brien. Copyright © 1955 by Alfred A. Knopf, Inc. Reprinted by permission of the publishers.

SUSANNE K. LANGER. "Expressiveness." Reprinted by permission of Charles Scribner's Sons, an imprint of Macmillan Publishing Company from *The Problems of Art,* New York: Charles Scribner's Sons. Copyright © 1957 by Susanne K. Langer; renewed 1985 by Leonard Langer.

FLANNERY O'CONNOR. "A Good Man Is Hard to Find." From *A Good Man Is Hard to Find and Other Stories,* copyright © 1953 by Flannery O'Connor and renewed 1981 by Regina O'Connor, reprinted by permission of Harcourt Brace Jovanovich, Inc.

Index